Cannibal Old Me

Cannibal

Old

Me

Spoken Sources in

Melville's Early

Works

Mary K. Bercaw Edwards

Kent State University Press
Kent, Ohio

© 2009 by The Kent State University Press, Kent, Ohio 44242
All rights reserved
Library of Congress Catalog Card Number 2008035880

ISBN 978-0-87338-978-5

Manufactured in the United States of America

Library of Congress Cataloging-in-Publication Data

Edwards, Mary K. Bercaw.
  Cannibal old me : spoken sources in Melville's early works / Mary K. Bercaw Edwards.
    p.   cm.
  Includes bibliographical references and index.
  ISBN 978-0-87338-978-5 (hardcover : alk. paper)   1. Melville, Herman, 1819–1891—
Technique.   2. Melville, Herman, 1819–1891—Travel—South Pacific Ocean.   3. Melville,
Herman, 1819–1891—Knowledge—Language and languages.   4. Narration (Rhetoric)—
History—19th century.   I. Title.
  PS2388.T4E49   2009
  813'.3—dc22
                        2008035880

British Library Cataloging-in-Publication data are available.

13 12 11 10 09   5 4 3 2 1

For my children,
Jesse and Annie

Contents

∽ Acknowledgments

SINCE Herman Melville was first a sailor and then a writer, I will begin by thanking the sailors who most influenced me. The near-legendary Irving Johnson, whose career was dedicated to preserving the traditions of square-rig sail, was a towering and definitive figure in my family's life. My father, Jay Bercaw, who served as Johnson's first mate during the fifth and sixth world voyages aboard the Brigantine *Yankee*, together with my mother, Gretchen S. Bercaw, instilled in me their deep love of the sea and sailing during our family's three-and-a-half-year circumnavigation when I was in my teens. Once I entered academia, Harrison Hayford inspired me with his exacting scholarship throughout my undergraduate and graduate years. I will be forever grateful that he was my teacher. Hershel Parker was the reader on my first book, and his encouragement of and faith in me continue to this day. Thomas Farel Heffernan, my coeditor for *Herman Melville's Whaling Years*, whose confidence in me as a scholar and collaborator strengthened my own, played an important role in setting me on the path that led to this book.

The first chapter of *Cannibal Old Me* grew out of a paper I presented at the fourth international Melville conference in Maui in 2003, and I wish to thank the cochairs of that conference, Charlene Avallone and Carolyn Karcher, for their faith in what seemed then a wild and speculative idea. Samuel Otter suggested that I send the paper to Henry Hughes, who was editing a volume on Melville and the Marquesas; without Sam's encouragement, the paper would never have been anything more than ephemeral. Henry Hughes was kind enough to believe in the

ix

paper from the beginning and tough enough to force me to rework and rethink it again and again: I thank him for both.

I owe much to other Melvilleans for their support of my scholarship through the years, especially past and present members of the Melville Society Cultural Project and Melville Society Executive Committee, including Jennifer Baker, the late Jill Barnum, Dennis Berthold, Gail Coffler, Wyn Kelley, Sanford Marovitz, Timothy Marr, John Matteson, Douglas Robillard, Elizabeth Schultz, Christopher Sten, and Robert K. Wallace. John Bryant, with whom I have butted heads on more than one occasion, challenged my arguments in important ways that served greatly to strengthen this book. I remain in awe of his dedication and passion to Melville and Melville scholarship. Without Dan Brayton and Antonia Losano, this book would have never happened; I wish to thank them deeply for their guidance and advice in the early stages. Dan Brayton, Henry Hughes, Wyn Kelley, Robert D. Madison, Michelle Moon, Peter Sorensen, and Robert C. Suggs all took time from their busy lives to read one or more chapters, and their careful, sometimes critical, and always insightful suggestions enriched the book. Don Sineti, friend, extraordinary sea musician, artist, and incidentally my daughter's godfather, contributed to the evocative and deeply felt artwork for the front cover. Daniel Lanier, Steve Mentz, Priscilla Wells, and Elysa Engelman sent relevant articles and cartoons to me; I wish to thank them as well as all my family, friends, colleagues, and coworkers, especially Christopher Gauld, who listened to me discourse at length on cannibalism and Melville.

My University of Connecticut–funded research assistant, Nathan Adams, stuck with the book through thick and thin. My editors Joanna H. Craig and Mary D. Young have given me enthusiasm and support throughout the long process of publication. I thank them and the designer of the book cover Darryl ml Crosby. My mother, Gretchen S. Bercaw, took my sister, Katrina Bercaw, and me to the South Pacific shortly before I began writing so I could see for the first time what the Marquesas Islands look like. That firsthand view greatly informs my discussion of those islands. My brother, Sean Bercaw, who lived with us at the time, took over household chores and expenses so I could concentrate on the book. My father-in-law, Carl Edwards, first told me about Pliny the Younger; my mother-in-law, Janet Ray Edwards, told me about coterie speech; and my sister-in-law, Gabrielle Hecht, translated French for me.

But most of all I wish to thank my family. My children, Annie and Jesse, 10 and 13 when the project began, listened patiently for countless hours as their parents discussed endless forms of talk. My daughter did ask plaintively one evening, "Mommy, Daddy, could we not talk about cannibalism at dinner tonight?" Beyond all else, I wish to thank my husband, Craig Edwards, who immersed himself in the book and whose love of language makes the book sing.

~ Introduction

By the way[,] Melville reads old Books. He has borrowed Sir Thomas Browne of me and says finely of the speculations of the Religio Medici *that Browne is a kind of "crack'd Archangel." Was ever any thing of this sort said before by a sailor?*
    —*Evert Duyckinck, Letter to George Duyckinck*

BACKGROUND

IF sheer bulk is any measure, one could assert that scholars know all there is to know about Herman Melville's use of sources. Melville now holds an iconic place in American literature, but his sixth book and masterpiece *Moby-Dick* failed to sell out its first printing in his lifetime, and his career and reputation languished in unexamined obscurity for decades after his death. Source study immediately followed the initial biographical analysis of Melville in the Melville Revival of the 1920s, showing that Melville made extensive unacknowledged use of material incorporated from the works of other authors in his own writing.[1] The early studies are significant, for they first reported such important discoveries as Melville's almost transcriptional dependence on Henry Trumbull's *Life and Remarkable Adventures of Israel R. Potter* (1824) for *Israel Potter* (1854–55) and on chapter 18 of Amasa Delano's *A Narrative of Voyages and Travels* (1817) for *Benito Cereno* (1855).[2] These early studies identifying sources and Melville's use of them were succeeded by the more sophisticated and nuanced work of such towering scholars as Harrison Hayford and Merton M. Sealts Jr. Even the most successful of these studies, however, are preliminary. They don't, for example, examine deeply enough why and in what ways Melville altered the original texts. They don't aggressively question Melville's affirmations of the truth of his own experience. They don't look closely enough at the interplay between Melville's engagement with his written sources and certain other influences on his development as a writer. Specifically, they don't include oral cultures and the spoken elements of broader discourses as sources.

Earlier studies failed to consider oral sources because of the ephemeral nature of talk. Scholars were concerned with finding indisputable written evidence. Partly due to the process through which Melville incorporated written sources into his own work, an immense amount of this evidence has been compiled. However, Melville was deeply engaged in a variety of discourses for which the primary means of communication was the spoken rather than the written word. I will develop the idea of talk as a general and pervasive social mechanism and examine the variations in the nineteenth-century discourse of and about sailors and the discourses of cannibalism and missionary enterprise as talk. I will analyze the complex interconnections between Melville's fiction, his experiences in the South Pacific, and the ubiquitous talk that surrounded him. By examining a variety of vernacular and nonliterary sources such as letters, logbooks, newspaper accounts, songs, and sermons and the oral qualities inherent in Melville's written language, I will excavate insofar as possible the oral context of Melville's creative process.

Melville transformed both his contemporary print and oral sources into art. My argument about Melville's use of sources is both an aesthetic and an implicitly political one. In an age of digital information, where a reader has access to vast resources to establish the source and authenticity of a work, ethics requires that readers consider where texts come from, what they owe to sources, what the boundaries of texts are, and the complicated connections between shared cultural heritage, public domain, individual creativity, and the history and current state of intellectual property law. This is in part a study, then, of the aesthetic, linguistic, ethical, and cultural implications of Melville's borrowing.

Melville signed aboard his first ship at the age of nineteen and was thrust into a world completely new to him. The merchant vessel on which he sailed had its own hierarchies, divisions of time, demands of the natural environment, skills, and knowledge—most significantly, the language used to order the seafaring world was a thing apart. Less than two years later when Melville signed on a whaleship and left for the South Pacific, his newly acquired sailor language was again inadequate. He had to learn the language of whaling, everything from the cry "Town ho!" upon sighting a whale, which comes from the Wampanoag *townor*,[3] to understanding the significant difference between the subtly different words "boatheader" and "boatsteerer."

Entering the South Pacific, he encountered beachcombers, deserting seamen who crossed the liminal space of the beach to live with the islanders, sometimes permanently but more often for a much shorter time. When these beachcombers reentered the shipboard world, they brought other experiences and worldviews with them, which required new vocabularies and concepts: those of the islanders and of European missionaries. Melville became immersed in the discourses of seafaring, cannibalism, and missionary enterprise. This book will analyze how these discourses—what I call sailor talk, cannibal talk, and missionary talk— shaped the action, understanding, and language of Melville's first six books: *Typee, Omoo, Mardi, Redburn, White-Jacket,* and *Moby-Dick.*

BIOGRAPHY

As a young woman of sixteen, I began a three-and-a-half-year circumnavigation of the world aboard a thirty-eight-foot sailing vessel captained by my father. Gunkholing, or sailing from port to port, through the South Pacific left me with a passion for those islands and their people. When we returned home to California, I left for Northwestern University on a full scholarship. I knew much about sailing and many of the world's most obscure places, but I was an absolute innocent about American culture. The first movie I saw at college was the Who's *Tommy,* and I was overwhelmed. I felt much like Queequeg—"a creature in the transition state" (*Moby-Dick* 27)—but with none of his cool composure. I had never seen snow falling from the sky before, much less a fraternity party.

In the midst of culture shock, however, I discovered Herman Melville. I had come to the university expecting to concentrate on Henry James, but my major professor, Harrison Hayford, told me, "With your background, you should study Melville." That simple advice irrevocably changed my life.

I spent my undergraduate and graduate years working as a contributing scholar on four volumes of the Northwestern-Newberry edition of *The Writings of Herman Melville* (*Israel Potter, The Confidence-Man, Moby-Dick,* and *The Piazza Tales*). This work led to my interest in source study, resulting in *Melville's Sources,* published by Northwestern University Press in 1987. That scholarship in turn provided a firm foundation to tackle *Herman Melville's Whaling Years,* published by Vanderbilt University Press in 2004. The original research for the volume was done by Wilson Heflin for his 1952 dissertation, but he died in 1985 before the material could be published in book form. My coeditor, Thomas Farel Heffernan, and I spent sixteen and thirteen years respectively reworking the entire dissertation text with the goals of keeping Heflin's voice, incorporating the intervening sixty years of scholarship, and bringing the text to the standards of a published work rather than a dissertation. I searched out every document that Heflin consulted: every original letter, logbook, newspaper, pamphlet, and book on whaling, as well as the consular documents, letters, census records, and logbooks housed in the National Archives. I verified every fact and quotation. This search was exhaustive and exhausting. It was great fun but often frustrating. In the years since Heflin began his work, much had changed, including the cataloging system at the National Archives, which has been completely restructured. Logbooks had traveled from owner to owner. Thankfully many had landed in institutions. I often felt like one of Richard D. Altick's "scholar adventurers"[4] as I attempted to crack the cataloging systems of the various institutions I visited to track down that one particular needed record.

Most of the documents I consulted were maritime, and this led me to a consideration of the language particular to whaleships and to other vessels at sea. My understanding of both nautical terminology and the coded language that sailors speak among themselves is partially founded on my own background of 58,000 miles at sea under sail. I have also spent much of the last twenty-eight years rowing and sailing traditional whaleboats and working aloft in the rigging of the *Charles W. Morgan,* the only remaining wooden whaleship in the world, built six months after and in the same town as Melville's *Acushnet.* For this traditional work at Mystic Seaport Museum, I must have a thorough understanding of historic whaling in order to translate the language of whaling and the skills needed to work a whaleship to trainees, who must then perform the work, *and* to visitors, who must understand the work being performed. Because of his own experience, Melville's understanding of whaling was not only intellectual, aesthetic, and moral but also kinesthetic, and I have had unique opportunities to undertake the more arcane aspects of the physical context of whaling 150 years later.

I have also gotten to know living whalemen who continue traditional ways and seamen who sailed before the mast on square-rigged ships. New England whaleships went to the islands in the Caribbean to recruit men to serve on whaling voyages. There was no indigenous whaling on these islands; instead, the islanders learned whaling aboard Yankee ships and brought the skills and knowledge home to their own communities. Thus, whaling on these Caribbean islands mimics nineteenth-century New England whaling. The hull shape of the island whaleboats, the design of their harpoons and lances, the exchange of boatsteerer and boatheader after the harpooning of the whale all parallel New England whaling design and technique. The whalemen of Barouallie in St. Vincent and the Grenadines came to Mystic Seaport in 2002 and used the museum's whaleboats to reenact for us the hunt and kill of the whale.[5] I also met Makah Indians, who continue to whale on the Northwest Coast, when they too came to Mystic Seaport. Additionally, I have come to know men who earned their living sailing square-rigged ships. My father served as first mate under Captain Irving Johnson, one of the founders of the American sail-training movement, for two world voyages, and I grew close to Captain Johnson and his family. I also spent time with Stan Hugill, considered the last of the chanteymen, who served aboard working commercial sailing vessels in his youth and then spent his later life recording the work songs he had used. Interacting with these men has deeply enriched my understanding of Melville's seafaring world.

Insights deriving from these experiences and relationships, coupled with my immersion in contemporary documents for my work on *Herman Melville's Whaling Years,* led me to question many assumptions, both biographical and textual, made by earlier scholars about Melville and his works. I realized that Melville was no tabula rasa when he deserted the whaleship *Acushnet* at Nuku Hiva in the Marquesas Islands. Much of his response to the island and its inhabitants had already been molded by his expectations, which were in turn formed by prevailing nineteenth-century discourses on shipboard life, cannibalism, missionary enterprise, and the Polynesian "Other." These discourses as much as his own experiences shaped his first five books, *Typee* (1846), *Omoo* (1847), *Mardi* (1849), *Redburn* (1849), and *White-Jacket* (1850), and are incorporated into *Moby-Dick* (1851) in more complex and sophisticated ways.

Melville heard stories of Polynesia and the fierce cannibals of Fiji and the Marquesas from his fellow sailors. On a typical whaleship, such as the *Acushnet,* on which Melville sailed, sixteen to twenty-four men crowded together in the fo'c's'le, or forecastle, at the forward end of the vessel. Harsh conditions, inadequate food, overbearing officers, and voyages that seemed unending led to rampant desertion. Runaways spent their time as beachcombers on the shores of South America and the Pacific islands until they became restless and joined newly arrived ships. These deserters brought tales of the indigenous inhabitants and their cultures to their fellow sailors. After his time on Nuku Hiva, Melville, too, would become a *Tusitala,* a teller of tales.[6]

Melville's engagement with the discourse of the South Pacific only deepened when he came to write his first two books. Melville's methodology was to move from inspiration to library. I argue, however, that his initial inspiration was not solely biographical, as has always been assumed, but also oral. In both his extensive telling and retelling of his experiences and his hearing of other sailors telling their own tales, his account was shaped for dramatic impact and edited for significance. By the time he returned home, the told rendition of his tale had taken on a life of its own.

In composing his earliest works, Melville used the same process he would subsequently employ in *Moby-Dick* and his later books: he "swam through libraries" (*Moby-Dick* 136) and "dived . . . deep" (*Moby-Dick* 148). He borrowed extensively from written sources, including narratives of voyages of exploration, naval expeditions, and missionary settlements. His appropriations are so extensive and unhidden that the scholar can often determine not only what text he used but what *edition* of that text.

Reading works contemporary to Melville, I realized that his use of these written materials was even more extensive than previously thought. I also began to realize that it was not only his direct borrowing that was important but also his engagement with both oral and written accounts of such topics as cannibalism and missionary enterprise. And I began cautiously to entertain other questions: Was Herman Melville ever really in the Taipi valley? How did he first recount his experiences? Did his account of his time in the South Pacific change with his audience and change yet again when it became a written rather than a told story? Why was Melville so harsh in his descriptions of all things Fijian? Is the lack of interaction between Queequeg and Ishmael aboard the *Pequod* related not only to questions of Ishmael's role, the different stages at which *Moby-Dick* was written, and Queequeg's insubstantiality but also to shipboard politics, something so internalized by Melville that he was not even conscious of it?

I was a sailor first and a scholar later. I too have been steeped in the sea and sailing. For both Melville and myself, our libraries were *not* "dukedom large enough,"[7] and it is that synergistic blend of the experiential, oral, and written worlds of seafaring and the South Pacific that I will explore in the following chapters.

SCHOLARSHIP

Like Isaac Newton, I stand humbly on the shoulders of giants. The seminal work of early scholars such as Charles Roberts Anderson, Harrison Hayford, and Wilson Heflin laid the foundation for future research on Melville's time in the Pacific. Important studies followed, and the work of recent scholars, especially Geoffrey Sanborn, has deeply enriched the field. This book, then, is part of a long-running discussion of Melville, cannibalism, and the South Pacific.

Charles Roberts Anderson was one of the first and most thorough of those to search government records, newspapers, logbooks, and South Pacific travelogues for authoritative information on Melville's wanderings, which he published in *Melville in the South Seas* (1939). Anderson also identified almost all the major written sources for *Typee* and *Omoo*. Anderson's work may seem old-fashioned to modern scholars, but the value of his discoveries cannot be overestimated. The amount of work he undertook can be glimpsed in his discussion of finding the true tale of Willie the carpenter, mentioned in chapter 76 of *Omoo*, in Edward T. Perkins's *Na Motu* (1854): "This plain tale furnishes a rich reward for the student of Melville who has made his way through several hundred volumes of South Sea travels—all too frequently with negative results—constantly on the alert for any tidbit of information that might throw light on the Polynesian wanderings of an embryonic author, whether it be a confirmation of his actual adventures or merely a source for his published narratives."[8] Anderson found almost every document of significance for *Typee* and *Omoo* except the British consular records of the mutiny aboard the Australian whaleship *Lucy Ann;* the mutiny aboard the *Julia* in *Omoo* is based on the events on the *Lucy Ann.* The British consular records were uncovered by Ida Leeson, a librarian at the Mitchell Library in Sydney, Australia, who announced her find in the *Philological Quarterly* in 1940, one year after the publication of Anderson's book.[9] Anderson, however, had discovered a reference to the mutiny in the September 23, 1842, entry of the logbook of the French naval frigate *La Reine Blanche* and therefore verified that the mutiny had in fact occurred. The facts and information unearthed by Anderson provide the documented basis for all later discussions of Melville's time in the South Pacific.

Working on Melville's South Sea years at the same time as Anderson was Robert S. Forsythe of the Newberry Library in Chicago. Like Anderson, Forsythe sought out records of Melville's years in the Pacific, and he preceded Anderson with "Herman Melville in Honolulu" (1935), "Herman Melville in the Marquesas" (1936), "Herman Melville in Tahiti" (1937), and "More upon Herman Melville in Tahiti" (1938). In these articles Forsythe questioned the literal truth of Melville's ostensibly factual statements in his early books—for example, those relating to the length of his stay in the Taipi valley—and he used both internal and external evidence to date Melville's stays in the Marquesas and Tahiti. In his review of Anderson's book, however, Forsythe sadly relinquished his own long-time plans for a volume because Anderson had reported so much of what he himself had independently discovered.[10]

Until he left to fight in World War II, Wilson Heflin spent much of the late 1930s and 1940s researching primary documents such as whaling logbooks, French colonial records, consular certificates, and contemporary narratives to recover information about Melville's seafaring. Heflin differed from Anderson in his deep interest in Melville's time at sea. As a seaman himself, Heflin laid out the connections between Melville's seafaring life and his works. It was my immersion in these same documents for the posthumous publication of Heflin's *Herman Melville's Whaling Years* that first led me to question the standard understanding of Melville's time in the Pacific.[11]

Like the work of his predecessors, the work of Harrison Hayford on successive editions of *Typee* and *Omoo* is indispensable. The page proofs for the Hendricks House edition of *Omoo* were completed in 1957, but the book was not published until 1969. Hayford then produced the Signet Classic edition of *Typee* in 1964. As general editor of the Northwestern-Newberry edition of *The Writings of Herman Melville,* Hayford oversaw the critical editions of *Typee* and *Omoo,* both of which appeared in 1968. Besides ensuring that the texts of all these editions were as accurate as possible, Hayford also wrote the afterword and explanatory notes for the Hendricks House and Signet Classic editions. The Hendricks House *Omoo* documents Melville's reliance on written sources, especially the second edition of William Ellis's *Polynesian Researches* (1833), passage by passage. The edition also includes the only complete transcription of the "Revolt Documents" for the mutiny aboard the *Lucy Ann*.[12]

For my work on *Typee* and *Omoo*, I turned not only to Melville scholarship but also to nonliterary disciplines. My study of the Marquesas Islands is especially indebted to the ethnohistorian Greg Dening and the anthropologist Robert C. Suggs. Dening's *Islands and Beaches: Discourse on a Silent Land: Marquesas 1774–1880* (1980) is the primary work on European contact in the Marquesas.[13] For Dening, the beach is not only literal but also a metaphor of encounter, an idea he further developed in *Beach Crossings: Voyaging across Times, Cultures, and Self* (2004).[14] Suggs's *The Hidden Worlds of Polynesia* (1962) records his early anthropological expedition to Nuku Hiva.[15] He has continued his anthropological studies of the Marquesas to the present day. Suggs's interpretation of Melville's time on Nuku Hiva, based on oral history and his knowledge of the Marquesan language, has been strongly questioned by Melvillean John Bryant;[16] nonetheless, his anthropological work is important to any discussion of the islanders Melville encountered when he went ashore in July 1842.

T. Walter Herbert's *Marquesan Encounters: Melville and the Meaning of Civilization* (1980) is a work that looks at both nonfiction and fiction in an attempt to come to an understanding of the term "civilization." "Instead of a chronological presentation showing 'development,'" Herbert writes, "what lies before you is a trilogy: three episodes related to one another according to a protocol that compels their mutual relevance to show itself, three circles of light upon the darkness of a vast social experience."[17] He places the circles against the background of American intellectual history, invoking evangelical Calvinism, Enlightenment thought, and Romanticism. Herbert looks first at the private and public accounts of the mission established by William Alexander and a group of American missionary families in Taioha'e Bay on Nuku Hiva in the Marquesas in 1833.[18] He then discusses David Porter's *Journal of a Cruise*.[19] Porter claimed the Marquesas as an American possession in 1813, during the War of 1812, twenty years before the American mission. The third part of Herbert's discussion concentrates on *Typee*. Although Herbert entitles his first Melville chapter "What It Means to Be a Cannibal," there is little discussion of cannibalism in his book. *Marquesan Encounters* is most relevant to my work when Herbert writes about the missionaries' attempt to put their experiences among the Marquesans into words. The missionaries were terrified by the otherness of the Nuku Hivans and expressed that terror both publicly and privately.

Caleb Crain pairs cannibalism and homosexuality in "Lovers of Human Flesh: Homosexuality and Cannibalism in Melville's Novels" (1994): "In the nineteenth century, cannibalism and homosexuality shared a rhetorical form. Both were represented as 'the unspeakable.'"[20] He continues: "To learn about the homosexual activity of the Marquesans, Melville had to decode veiled allusions and suggestions. What was certain was their cannibalism. In twentieth-century anthropology, the status has been reversed. The homosexuality of the Marquesans is frankly and thoroughly documented. But as reports of cannibalism are challenged to meet modern standards of evidence, they recede into rumor and myth."[21] Crain paired the taboo subjects of cannibalism and homosexuality in his article. I pair cannibalism and missionary enterprise in this book, looking not at the taboo quality of the subjects but at their shared discourse. Crain's discussion of decoding provides important background for my project.

No recent dialogue on cannibalism can ignore William Arens's *The Man-Eating Myth* (1979). The ruckus caused by this slim volume (only 185 pages, exclusive of notes) continues to reverberate. Arens's thesis, neatly summed up in his title, and the virulent responses to it will be discussed in the second chapter. The University of Essex in Great Britain hosted a conference on cannibalism in 1995, out of which grew a collection of essays published as *Cannibalism and the Colonial World* (1998), including a retrospective by Arens entitled "Rethinking Anthropophagy." The collection also includes an essay by Gananath Obeyesekere on Fijian cannibalism, "Cannibal Feasts in Nineteenth-Century Fiji: Seamen's Yarns and the Ethnographic Imagination." That essay led me to Obeyesekere's three hundred–page *Cannibal Talk: The Man-Eating Myth and Human Sacrifice in the South Seas* (2005).[22]

Cannibal Talk does not explicitly discuss Marquesan cannibalism, but it has provoked my thinking about cannibalism in the works of Melville. Obeyesekere argues that cannibalism is mostly "cannibal talk," a discourse on the Other engaged in by both indigenous peoples and colonial intruders. Although some of Obeyesekere's conclusions have been questioned by the anthropologists Marshall Sahlins and Joan-Pau Rubiés,[23] his deconstruction of cannibal talk led me to reconsider sailor discourse, cannibal discourse, and missionary discourse in terms of talk, and I have adopted this phrase specifically to emphasize the role of the spoken word implicit in these discourses.

No study of Melville and cannibalism would be complete without reference to Geoffrey Sanborn's excellent *The Sign of the Cannibal: Melville and the Making of a Postcolonial Reader* (1998). Sanborn researches the history of the discourse on cannibalism between the first Captain James Cook expedition of 1770 and the publication of Melville's *Benito Cereno* in 1855. Why, he asks, were Europeans so obsessed with cannibalism? Sanborn ascribes to Melville "a very specific postcolonial *function:* the articulation of the dynamics of anxiety and menace in the colonial encounter," a function now associated with the work of Homi Bhabha.[24] He argues that cannibalism "represented a masculinity without limits" for Melville, and that "the dreamed-of encounter with this figure of masculinity was always missed." He continues, "In both its content and its form, it was a distinctly postcolonial vision, oriented toward the renovation of a complexly colonized world."[25] Sanborn concentrates on representations of cannibalism in *Typee,* *Moby-Dick,* and *Benito Cereno.* The argument of *The Sign of the Cannibal* is distinct from the argument of his dissertation, which he "was sure" six months after its completion "was wrong."[26] Although I use several of the same sources as Sanborn, my interest in cannibalism is in language and is therefore theoretically different from his. Sanborn's ideas will be referred to at length in the third chapter.

ARGUMENT

This book is a study of the aesthetic, ethical, linguistic, and cultural implications of Melville's borrowing from spoken and written sources. Melville ingested sailor talk, cannibal talk, and missionary talk consciously, subconsciously, and subliminally, and the following chapters will analyze his use of these borrowings.

Chapter 1, "'Where the Wild Things Are': Questioning *Typee*" considers the geographical, historical, and textual evidence and raises the question of whether Herman Melville actually spent time in the Taipi valley. There is at least a suggestion that he spent the month he was ashore on Nuku Hiva, July 9 through August 9, 1842, with the Tai'oa people of Haka'ui Bay rather than with the Taipi. This chapter looks at the French colonial records as well as at such known Melville sources as the narratives of David Porter, Charles S. Stewart, and Georg H. von Langsdorff. The inquiry into where Melville spent that month is intriguing but less important than the questions it raises. If Melville's first reading public wrongly believed that he was the "man who lived among the cannibals,"[27] how would such a false perception shape Melville's view of himself and the development of his writing?

Chapter 2, "'Six Months at Sea! Yes, Reader, as I Live': Sailor Talk," investigates the formative experience that Melville underwent as a working sailor and his immersion in the highly specialized language essential to this occupation. For the rest of his life he maintained a sense of identity as a mariner. Conditions aboard a working ship—the strict discipline necessary to maintain a functioning crew, the demands placed on the crew by wind and weather, the shared hardships, the absolute reliance on one's shipmates and on the competence of the officers, the arcane skills and knowledge acquired, and the sense of being a member of a group set apart—figure strongly in much of Melville's writing. Melville became immersed in the complex spoken discourse permeating the sailor's world. The occupational lingo, folklore, and popular image of the sailor shape his first six books in fundamental ways, and his use of this experience and language in his writing is unparalleled.

Chapter 3, "'They Say They Don't Like Sailor's Flesh, It's Too Salt': Cannibal Talk," establishes the context in which Melville confronts the image of the cannibal, an image that recurs repeatedly in his early works and is a focal metaphor in *Moby-Dick*. It expounds on the early accounts of cannibals from ancient Greece through the age of exploration and the discourse of cannibalism contemporary to Melville's sojourn in the South Pacific. It looks closely at Melville's known written sources concerning cannibalism used in the writing of *Typee* and examines extant sources that suggest the nature of the oral component of the cannibal discourse as it existed in Melville's time. It discusses the current controversy concerning cannibalism in the field of anthropology as it relates to Melville's use of the cannibal and connects cannibal talk in Melville's era to the timeless and pervasive menace and fascination inherent in this image.

Chapter 4, "'Their Gestures Shame the Very Brutes': Missionary Talk," explores the talk of and about missionaries in the South Pacific, a group that often defined itself in opposition to both cannibals and sailors. It posits the definitive role of talk in the world of the missionary and looks at the complicated functions of theology, translation, faith, and cultural imperialism and dislocation. It reflects on the fraught relationships between sailors, natives, and missionaries.

Chapter 5, "'Cannibal Old Me': The Development of Melville's Narrative Voice," argues that the synthesis of the material laid out in the earlier chapters and of Melville's documented prowess as a storyteller, conversationalist, and profound student of language is the key to understanding the development of Melville's narrative voice. Through close readings of *Typee, Omoo, Mardi, Redburn, White-Jacket,* and especially *Moby-Dick,* this chapter shows the evolution of this unique, complex, and influential voice. It discusses the literary predecessors and progeny of this voice and the historic and cultural context in which Melville created his masterpiece. Finally, it analyzes the extraordinary ways in which Melville juxtaposes and combines sailor talk, cannibal talk, and missionary talk in the deep structures of *Moby-Dick*.

The overlapping sailor talk, cannibal talk, and missionary talk that Melville first encountered in the South Pacific exerted formative influence on his development as a writer. Sailor talk provides the concrete, detailed awareness of human interactions with the natural world and the laboratory that reveals the workings of society in miniature. Missionary talk connects Melville's metaphysical ponderings to the sermonic framework through which he delivers his profound questions and insights. Ultimately, the image of the cannibal surfaces as the focal metaphor from the shifting currents that flow between these discourses because of its depth, richness, and extreme nature; the way it tests the boundaries of humanity; and its ultimate elusiveness. With Melville we come to understand that the cannibal is not only the Other but also the shadow of ourselves. Without facing and even embracing the darkest and most horrific depths of ourselves, we cannot realize the fullness of our own humanity. As Queequeg tells us, "It's a mutual, joint-stock world, in all meridians. We cannibals must help these Christians" (*Moby-Dick* 62).

CHAPTER 1

∼ "Where the Wild Things Are"

Questioning *Typee*

Literature was born not the day when a boy crying wolf, wolf came running out
of the Neanderthal valley with a big gray wolf at his heels: literature was born on
the day when a boy came crying wolf, wolf and there was no wolf behind him.
That the poor little fellow because he lied too often was finally eaten up by a real
beast is quite incidental. But here is what is important. Between the wolf in the
tall grass and the wolf in the tall story there is a shimmering go-between. That
go-between, that prism, is the art of literature.
  —Vladimir Nabokov

But the wild things cried, "Oh please don't go—we'll eat you up—we love
you so!"
  —Maurice Sendak

THAT Herman Melville spent at least four weeks living among the inhabitants of the Taipi valley on Nuku Hiva in the Marquesas Islands has never
been questioned. Although scholars have long dismissed Melville's elaborations
and fictional extension of time in the valley, no biographer—not even Andrew
Delbanco, Hershel Parker, or Laurie Robertson-Lorant—has doubted the veracity of the mere fact.[1] Melville presented his time in the valley of the Taipi as the
factual basis for his first work, *Typee: A Peep at Polynesian Life* (1846). That portrayal has long been accepted as truth. Nonetheless, an examination of biographical, geographical, historical, and textual evidence suggests *at least the possibility*
that Melville may never have strayed any farther from the beach than necessary to
avoid capture and that his description of himself as the "man who lived among
the cannibals" is a fiction.[2] I will argue that such a consideration sheds light on
our understanding of Melville as a writer.

Questions concerning Melville's route to the Taipi valley have come to the
forefront with paired essays by anthropologist Robert C. Suggs and Melville
scholar John Bryant in the 2005 issue of *ESQ,* to be discussed below. Bryant contends, "Melville may have been a thief, but he was no liar."[3] The relevant question
is not whether Melville was either a thief or a liar, but whether he commenced his

writing career as a creative artist or a journalist. His concern was always first and foremost his art. That he compromised to the extent of presenting *Typee* as a travelogue in order to have the book accepted by a publisher of such material in a time when he was first attempting to make a living from his writing says nothing about the reliability of any element of the text as an account of his own personal experience.

There are a few incontrovertible facts and some clearly demonstrable evidence-based conclusions concerning Melville's sojourn on Nuku Hiva. It is a happy coincidence that Max Radiguet, Secretary to Rear Admiral Abel Aubert Dupetit-Thouars, was on Nuku Hiva during the same period as Melville. His *Les derniers sauvages: Souvenirs de l'occupation française aux îles Marquises, 1842–1859,* published after *Typee,* demonstrably confirms, for example, Melville's presence in Haka'ui Bay as a witness to incidents Radiguet reports due to the similarities in his and Melville's accounts. And it is likely but not provable that Melville and Richard Tobias Greene did indeed head toward the interior of the island immediately after they deserted the whaleship *Acushnet* knowing that it would increase their chances of evading capture. Other assertions, however, remain conjecture.

The discourse of cannibalism that Melville encountered aboard ship and throughout the islands of the South Pacific profoundly shaped his first book. European dread of the cannibal Other was omnipresent. As with many things, this dread was mixed with desire. Sailors both feared and longed to encounter flesh-eaters. When Melville slipped away from his shipmates during shore leave on Nuku Hiva, he too may have experienced such mixed feelings. At the very least he understood them. Four years later, when he came to write *Typee,* this tension lingered in his mind.

As he did throughout his life, Melville turned to written sources when he began writing *Typee.* The language as well as some of the action is borrowed from David Porter's *Journal of a Cruise Made to the Pacific Ocean* (1815, 1822), which records Porter's encounter with Nuku Hiva thirty years before Melville arrived.[4] Melville's method of composition in *Typee* and the subsequent acceptance of the book as truth are significant not only as a study of the importance and influence of discourse but also because they cast light on the genesis of Melville's literary genius.

Typee was Herman Melville's single biggest commercial success, a widely read first book by a twenty-six-year-old writer.[5] When Gansevoort, Melville's brother, submitted the manuscript of *Typee* to English publisher John Murray, Murray wrote that it read like the work of a "practised writer" who may not have experienced the adventures he described.[6]

The "practised" element that Murray sensed in *Typee* may have come from Melville's years of repeating the story orally, first to his shipmates and then to his family. In his transition from told tale, spoken text, to written text, Melville is much like his contemporary Frederick Douglass. By the time Douglass published his autobiography, *Narrative of the Life of Frederick Douglass, an American Slave, Written by Himself* (1845), he had been telling the story of his life orally to audiences for four years. The *Narrative* is a carefully crafted piece. See, for example, how Mr. Auld reprimands his wife for teaching young Frederick to read: "If you give a [slave] an inch, he will take an ell."[7] When Douglass learns to write at Durgin and Bailey's shipyard, it is the *L* that is his first letter.[8] Analogously, the pain in Tommo's leg in *Typee* appears and disappears according to Tommo's feelings about his confinement by the Typees. When he ceases to brood on his captivity, as he does in much of the middle of the book, the pain in his leg goes away, only to reappear later. Douglass's speaking career began on Nantucket in 1841, four years before the publication of his own *Narrative* in 1845. Melville began telling his story when he left Nuku Hiva aboard the *Lucy Ann* in 1842, four years before the publication of his *Narrative*—*Typee* was published in Great Britain under the title *Narrative of a Four Months' Residence among the Natives of a Valley of the Marquesas Islands*—in 1846. During those four years of oral transmission, the stories were shaped and crafted in response to their audiences.

Gansevoort responded to Murray's concern: "The Author will doubtless be flattered to hear that his production seems to so competent a judge as yourself that of 'a practised writer'—the more so as he is a mere novice in the art, having had no experience."[9] He went on to assure Murray of the truth of the story, presumably on the basis of intra-family storytelling.

Despite Gansevoort's assurances, the problem of authenticity came to a head when British papers began reviewing the book after its February 1846 London publication. Reviewers were skeptical that *Typee* was the work of a common sailor, and skeptical about Melville's adventures. The controversy continued with the March 1846 publication of the American edition. The review that most incensed Melville was printed in the *Morning Courier and New-York Enquirer* of April 17, 1846. The reviewer, possibly Charles F. Daniels, strongly stated:

In all essential respects, it is a *fiction*,—a piece of Munchausenism,—from beginning to end. It may be that the author visited, and spent some time in the Marquesas Islands.... But we have not the slightest confidence in any of the details, while many of the incidents narrated are utterly incredible. We might cite numberless instances of this monstrous exaggeration; but no one can read a dozen pages of the book without detecting them.

This would be a matter to be excused, if the book were not put forth as a simple record of actual experience. It professes to give nothing but what the author actually saw and heard. It must therefore be judged, not as

a romance or a poem, but as a book of travels,—as a statement of facts;—
and in this light it has, in our judgment, no merit whatever.[10]

Melville wrote indignantly: "So many numskulls on this side of the water should
heroically avow their determination not to be 'gulled' by [*Typee*]. The fact is, those
who do not beleive [*sic*] it are the greatest 'gulls'.—full fledged ones too."[11] (Is it
telling that the word misspelled is "beleive"?)

The question of authenticity appeared settled with the dramatic appearance of
Richard Tobias Greene, the "Toby" of *Typee,* whom Melville had feared dead.[12]
Greene wrote the *Buffalo Commercial Advertiser* on July 1, 1846: "I am the true and
veritable 'Toby,' yet living, and I am happy to testify to the entire accuracy of the
work so long as I was with Melville."[13] Greene wrote letters to the *Buffalo Commercial Advertiser* on July 1 and 11, 1846, which were then forwarded to Melville.
Melville and Toby met between July 15 and 22, and Melville subsequently published "The Story of Toby" in late July of 1846. With the publication of Toby's
story, the case for authenticity seemed proved and the questions died away.[14]

Since then, *Typee* has been accepted as an elaborated version of Melville's own
experiences. The nineteenth-century reading public was intrigued that a common man, a sailor, had become an accomplished and popular writer. Melville's
early celebrity was based as much on the sensational aspects of his story—the
narrative is driven by the mounting fear of cannibalism—as on his skill as a
writer, and he became known as the "man who lived among the cannibals."[15] Part
of Melville's success, therefore, was based on the assertion that he really *did* live
among the cannibals. But what if this never occurred? What if, in fact, Melville
never entered the valley of the Taipi? What if Melville's experiences were little different from those of many other deserting whalemen? What if his early success as
a writer was based as much on creative reconstructions from other writing as on
his own experience? Having his fictional creation accepted as reality would have a
profound effect on Melville's sense of himself as a writer.

Melville's status as a common sailor was cause for early skepticism about
Typee. After that skepticism was laid to rest, it continued to be cause for wonder
and interest among his acquaintances, as seen in Evert Duyckinck's letter to his
brother George when he reports: "By the way[,] Melville reads old Books. He has
borrowed Sir Thomas Browne of me and says finely of the speculations of the *Religio Medici* that Browne is a kind of 'crack'd Archangel.' Was ever any thing of
this sort said before by a sailor?"[16]

Duyckinck expected sailor talk from Melville. *Typee,* published two years
before Duyckinck's letter to his brother, is Melville's book closest in time to his
own involvement with sailor talk. He wrote *Typee* before reading "old Books" and
before being caught up in New York literary circles, such as those connected with

Duyckinck, Melville's editor for the American publication of *Typee*. As noted above, by the time Melville began work on *Typee*, he had already been telling his stories of Nuku Hiva and elaborating them for four years. Melville's delight in his prowess as a storyteller gave him confidence that he could be a writer. Even at its most sophisticated, Melville's first book *does* sound like a told tale.

BIOGRAPHICAL BACKGROUND

Herman Melville signed ship's articles for a whaling voyage on Christmas Day 1840. Nine days later, he departed New Bedford, Massachusetts, aboard the whale-ship *Acushnet*, bound around Cape Horn into the Pacific to hunt for sperm whales. Only the fact of Melville's presence made that particular voyage unusual. As Charles Roberts Anderson writes in *Melville in the South Seas:* "With this crew, normal in all respects save that in addition to mortal harpoons it carried an immortal pen, the *Acushnet* set sail on its maiden voyage, January 3, 1841."[17]

Despite his amorous-sounding name and lineage, Melville's captain, Valentine Pease Jr., the son of Valentine Pease Sr. and Love Daggett Pease, is often perceived as a nasty, brutal captain, the individual who single-handedly forced young Melville to desert and hide in the valley of the cannibals. Maritime historian Glenn Grasso has argued persuasively that Captain Pease was no more nor less brutal than any other whaling captain.[18] The fact of Melville's desertion is not proof enough of Captain Pease's brutality, for the whaling industry in the mid-nineteenth century was rife with desertion. Men deserted for many reasons, including insufficient or inedible food, poor living and working conditions, discouragement over the number of whales caught, and boredom.[19] Additionally, desertion was often considered a rite of passage. One captain in 1859 commented in frustration that "if a ship were bound for heaven and should stop at Hell for wood and water[,] some of the crew would run away."[20] While there certainly were brutal captains and reasons for desertion such as harsh treatment, inadequate food, and unsound ships, Grasso's argument that Melville's treatment was in no way atypical is sound and supported by other studies of desertion. Fayette Ringgold, the United States consul at Paita, Peru, wrote to the assistant secretary of state, J. Appleton, on September 1, 1858, that he "deplored what he saw as the loss to his country of thousands of young Americans who each year deserted from whaleships."[21]

Melville's desertion at Nuku Hiva in the Marquesas Islands is unremarkable. It is also indisputable. On June 2, 1843, Captain Pease filed with John B. Stetson, the vice-commercial agent at Lahaina, a comprehensive affidavit noting, among other desertions, that of Herman Melville and Richard T. Greene at Nuku Hiva on July 9, 1842.[22]

In addition to the proof of Melville's desertion provided by the affidavit, there is also confirmation in the logbooks of the whaleships *Potomac* and *Charles*. On Monday, July 4, 1842, William H. Macy, logkeeper of the *Potomac* of Nantucket, Isaac B. Hussey, master, noted, "At anchor ship Acushnet Pease of Fairhaven 18 m[onth]s out 950 Bbls [barrels]." Three days later, he recorded, "Anchored here ship London Packet Howland FA [Fairhaven] 31 m[onth]s 1750 sp[erm] put in leaky having been run through by a Billfish." Then, on Monday, July 11, the *Potomac*'s logbook reads: "Fine day sailed ship Acushnet of [Fairhaven] intending to lay off for a day or two + send boat in for her men who have deserted." The *Acushnet* had lost five men to desertion and by this ruse hoped to recover at least some of them. Pease's stratagem worked: on Wednesday, July 13, the logkeeper recorded, "Touched ship Acushnet + succeeded in getting 3 of her runaways."[23] The two successful deserters were Herman Melville and Richard Tobias Greene. The logkeeper's notice of the *London Packet* is pertinent because Greene eventually left Nuku Hiva aboard that vessel.[24] The logkeeper of the *Charles* also noted the recovery by the *Acushnet* of some of her deserting seamen on July 13.[25]

The next bit of documentary evidence regarding Melville's whereabouts is found in the documents of the Sydney, Australia, whaleship *Lucy Ann*, now preserved in the Mitchell Library, State Library of New South Wales, in Sydney. On August 9, 1842, Melville joined the *Lucy Ann*, as noted in consular records listing additions to the crew: "H. Melville at Do. [ditto—i.e., Nuku Hiva] [August] 9th."[26] The location is listed only as Nuku Hiva; the bay is not specified. That Melville deserted the *Acushnet* on July 9, 1842, and signed onboard the *Lucy Ann* on August 9 are the only facts verified by written documents. No other confirmed facts have been found by any scholar. Where, then, was Melville during the month between those dates?

The late Wilson Heflin, in his 1952 dissertation "Herman Melville's Whaling Years," revised as a book and published posthumously by Vanderbilt University Press in 2004, cautioned: "Beyond the fact of desertion, however, everything that Melville tells his readers in *Typee* about his adventures on Nukahiva must be read with considerable reservation, for it actually contains a complex blend of fiction and reality. . . . The novel is the almost exclusive source of information about Melville's days on the island."[27] I will take Heflin's point a step further and suggest that Melville may never have strayed any farther from the beach at Nuku Hiva than necessary to avoid capture, that he may have stayed with the Tai'oa, as many other deserters did, and that his experience in the Taipi valley is based on published written sources and the cannibal talk rife among sailors.[28]

Even the assertions of Richard Tobias Greene cannot be used as proof of Melville's presence in the Taipi valley. Greene's second letter to the *Buffalo Commercial Advertiser* (July 11, 1846) contains a long account of his and Melville's adventures. The letter was written *before* Greene met with Melville, yet the account is already fictionalized.[29] Greene gives the name of the whaleship as *Dolly*, Melville's fictional appellation in *Typee*, rather than as *Acushnet*, the vessel's true name. Greene's account of his experience on Nuku Hiva was strongly influenced by his reading of the *Typee* passages quoted by the *New York Evangelist*, mentioned in his first letter to the Buffalo *Commercial Advertiser* (July 1, 1846), if not by a reading of the book itself. Since leaving the sea, Greene had lived a humdrum life in upstate New York, until suddenly he appeared as a dashing romantic figure in a widely selling book. Greene leapt from obscurity to celebrity through his association with the author of *Typee* and raised no questions about the book's veracity—and it was not in his interest to do so. Greene relished his connection with Melville and *Typee* throughout his life, even naming his son Herman Melville Greene. In his obituary in the *Chicago News Record* of August 25, 1892, entitled "Death of R. T. Greene. Hero of the Story, The Typee," his ties to Melville and *Typee* are mentioned in the first line.[30]

Geographical Evidence

There are several bays on the south coast of Nuku Hiva. Each bay has deep valleys stretching inland from its shores, and each valley was the home of a distinct group. Westernmost is Haka'ui Bay, home of the Tai'oa people. Moving east, Taioha'e Bay (called "Nukuheva Bay" by Melville), where Porter anchored in 1813 and built his camp, is the home of the Teii people (Melville's "Taeeh"). It was in this bay that the *Acushnet* anchored in 1842. Farthest east is the much larger Comptroller's Bay with its four inlets. The two western inlets of Comptroller's Bay lead to Ha'apa'a (Melville's "Happar") while the central and deepest of the inlets leads to Taipivai, home of the Taipi (Melville's "Typee").

Heflin notes that overland the distance to the Haka'ui valley, southwestward from Taioha'e Bay, where the *Acushnet* was anchored, is about the same as that to Taipivai in the opposite direction, and the way is equally rugged.[31] Furthermore, a person crossing the rugged inland route to the Haka'ui valley would find a magnificent waterfall, very similar to the one depicted in *Typee*. That waterfall is described in a nineteenth-century French geographical dictionary. Translated, it reads: "To the South-west the Taioha reaches the lower valleys as well by the Taiva waterfall, the most beautiful on the island, [with a] height of 315 meters."[32] The cascade described in *Typee* bounds a "full 300 feet" in its final leap into the valley (64).

There are waterfalls, however, in almost every valley in the Marquesas. Melville's descent into the valley of the Taipi comes into more question with the next bit of evidence.

The Reverend Titus Coan visited Nuku Hiva in 1867, twenty-five years after Melville, and he notes that there was then a road leading from Taiohaʻe Bay to Taipivai. Coan writes, "Melville lost his reckoning of distances as well as his track. The enchanted valley of Taipi, Melville's 'Typee,' is only four hours' climb by the trail from Taiohai; and from ancient times there has been a well-known trail from the head of one valley to the other. This of course the young fugitive did not find. The distance is not over five miles, and the Marquesans walk it, or rather climb it, in three or four hours. The valley of Hapa, (Mr. Melville's Happar) lies between Taipi and Taiohae, and is only two or three hours' walk from the latter. . . . During all his four months of romantic captivity, the gifted author of 'Typee' and 'Omoo' was only four or five miles distant from the harbor whence he fled."[33]

Robert C. Suggs spent years on Nuku Hiva and speaks Marquesan. Using information from his archeological and ethnological research, he proposes that Melville and Greene were led by a *tapu* individual into the Taipi valley on the standard path described by Coan. John Bryant demolishes Suggs's article; he contends that Melville and Greene headed into the interior, basing his argument on Melville's description of the terrain. Bryant argues, "Melville's stated and reiterated strategy, which Suggs ignores, is not to go to Taipivai but simply to 'seclude' himself and his companion in the mountains until the *Acushnet* leaves" (*Typee* 33, 48, 51).[34] Bryant's argument makes sense, yet it does not necessarily follow that Melville and Greene went from the interior to Taipivai. Bryant uses Radiguet's *Les Derniers Sauvages* to fortify his position: "Radiguet walked the very beaches that Melville walked and reports sights that Melville also mentions during the same two weeks Melville inhabited Nuku Hiva Bay before his escape. Radiguet was not a source for Melville, but he is an important source for us in discerning fact and fiction in *Typee*." What Bryant says of Radiguet is true. Yet turning to Radiguet does not solve the vexed question of how, or if, Melville went to the Taipi valley. Bryant's three examples of items concurrent to both *Les Derniers Sauvages* and *Typee* are the Chilean horse brought to the island by the French, the trip to Hakaʻui Bay, and the shed containing war canoes. None of these similarities prove or disprove that Melville and Greene journeyed to the Taipi valley; they are not "crucial evidence" for that argument.[35]

HISTORICAL EVIDENCE

During the first two years of the French occupation of Nuku Hiva, 1842–43, the official reports devote considerable attention and space to the various native groups residing on the island and their leaders. Although the reports name several leaders of the Taipi tribe, the name Mehevi, whom Melville calls the king of the Typee, is not among them. In *Typee*, Mehevi is introduced in chapter 11. He is "a superb-looking warrior," of whom the narrator says, "I saw at once that he was some distinguished personage. . . . His aspect was imposing" (77). By chapter 26, Melville has titled him king: "King Mehevi!—A goodly sounding title!—and why should I not bestow it upon the foremost man in the valley of Typee?" (188). When Heflin was researching his dissertation, he searched the French reports in vain for Mehevi or for the less consequential rulers mentioned in *Typee*.[36] *None* of the names that Melville gives appears in the French reports.

The most important of the reports covers the period from April to July 1843. A table at the end of the report entitled "Relevé de la population de Noukahiva" contains a list of the "Noms Des Chefs Et Prêtres."[37] In this list, Hokiahé, not Mehevi, is the ruler of Taipi. None of the Taipi names has even a phonetic resemblance to the name Mehevi. Heflin had to look to the list of notables of the Tai'oa to find a name that is phonetically similar: that of Mataheva, a "grand-prêtresse."[38] Another name that is phonetically similar is that of Maheatité, distinguished by Radiguet, who visited Haka'ui Bay in 1842, as the "vieux chef" of the Tai'oa.[39]

Even more surprising to Heflin was his discovery of the names of two of the four male leaders of Tai'oa, as recorded by the French: Mohi and Mohi-a-Taipis.[40] Mohi, or Braid-Beard, appears in Melville's third book, *Mardi* (1849), as "one of the Keepers of the Chronicles of the Kings of Mardi" (197). As Heflin notes, "Thus it is that the name of Mohi, an actual tribal chief of Nukahiva, appears in a book that is frankly fictional, whereas Mehevi, unidentifiable as a real person, is prominent in a book that is avowedly a true narrative."[41] The fictionality of Mehevi's character is strengthened when one realizes, as shown below, that Melville's depiction of the chief is borrowed from Charles S. Stewart's description of two warriors, *not* Taipis, whom Stewart met in 1829.[42]

That the name Mehevi is missing from the French records is not conclusive evidence. The French records are incomplete. The French preferred to interact with a single chief as "king" rather than with all the chiefs of the various subtribes. Melville himself notes: "On some flimsy pretext or other Mowanna [Moana], the king of Nukuheva, whom the invaders by extravagant presents have cajoled over to their interests, and move about like a mere puppet, has been set up as the rightful sovereign of the entire island,—the alleged ruler by prescription of various clans who for ages perhaps have treated with each other as separate nations" (18). The situation was even more complex than Melville perceived it to be, for there were not only "clans," or tribes, but also subtribes, each with a chief, often related to the other chiefs. The name Mehevi could come from "Mei he Vaiʻiʻi," or "the chief from out of Vaiʻiʻi." Mohi, too, is not an uncommon name.[43] While the absence of a name resembling "Mehevi" as an important figure among the Taipi does not disprove Melville's presence in the valley, it still raises questions. If this figure is as important as Melville portrays him, why wasn't he listed by the French? Indeed, why do the names of *none* of the prominent leaders given by Melville appear in the French records of Taipi? Melville's later use of the name "Mohi" is intriguing within the following context.

One of the real Mohis of Hakaʻui Bay was a chief whose sympathies lay with deserting whalemen rather than with their captains. In February 1843, seven months after Melville deserted at Nuku Hiva, six whalemen from the *George and Susan* of New Bedford stole a whaleboat, jumped ship, and headed for Hakaʻui Bay.[44] Captain Howland reported the incident to the French commandant. Moana (Melville's "Mowanna"), chief of the Teii, then allied with the French, learned that the boat was at Hakaʻui and set out to recover it. He met with determined resistance. In a scene reminiscent of *Typee*, the Taiʻoa chiefs spurned Moana's offer of guns and powder in exchange for the runaway sailors. Then, fearful that the French might attack Hakaʻui Bay, chief Mohi went to Captain Jan Benoit-Amédée Collet, the French commandant of the northwestern group of the Marquesas Islands, and explained that he had done no greater wrong than to harbor runaway seamen. Mohi eventually agreed to restore the whaleboat and deserters to the *George and Susan*.[45] This incident entered the historic record when Mohi conferred with Collet, and it is true that the deserters were returned. But what is striking is Mohi's initial refusal to return the men despite the offer of the highly valued guns and powder. Only the threat of attack caused him to change his mind.

Melville likely visited Hakaʻui Bay by boat on July 6. That was the only day on which Rear Admiral Dupetit-Thouars, French commandant of the Pacific station, visited the Taiʻoa during the stay of the *Acushnet* at Nuku Hiva, according to the logbook of the *La Reine Blanche*, Dupetit-Thouars's flagship.[46] In *Typee*, the captain and a group of foremast hands go by whaleboat to trade with the Taiʻoa natives of Hakaʻui. Melville writes, "It so happened that the very day I was in Tior [Taiʻoa] the French admiral, attended by all the boats of his squadron, came down in state from Nukuheva" (28–29). Radiguet records the visit of Dupetit-Thouars to Hakaʻui in *Les Derniers Sauvages*.[47] Bryant states, "What is important here is that Radiguet confirms that Melville was, in fact, eyewitness to an event he says he witnessed"[48]; what is important to my argument is that it occurred in Hakaʻui. Melville's encounter with the seemingly friendly Taiʻoa may have inspired him to consider heading to Hakaʻui Bay after he deserted three days later at Taiohaʻe Bay.

In *Typee,* Melville claims that this "very day" was his only visit to Haka'ui Bay. However, there is a telling slip in *Omoo,* which Melville told his publisher was a sequel to *Typee* and is ostensibly based on Melville's wanderings on the island of Eimeo (Moorea) subsequent to his stay on Nuku Hiva. At the beginning of chapter 81 of *Omoo,* the narrator recounts meeting Marbonna, a Marquesan from Haka'ui Bay, a member of the Tai'oa tribe. "The first time my eyes lighted upon the Marquesan, I knew his country in a moment; and hailing him in his own language, he turned round, surprised that a person so speaking should be a stranger. He proved to be a native of Tior [Tai'oa], a glen of Nukuheva. I had visited the place *more than once;* and so, on the island of Imeeo [Eimeo], we met like old friends" (307–8; emphasis added). The underlying emotion of this passage is clear. The narrator is meeting someone from a place with which he is very familiar. Melville overlooks in *Omoo* what this little incident says about where he supposedly was on Nuku Hiva. In conjunction with the funeral scene discussed below, it suggests the possibility that Melville spent his time on Nuku Hiva in Haka'ui Bay. Such slips as Melville telling us, "I had visited the place [Haka'ui Bay] more than once," resemble later slips in *Moby-Dick.* For example, in *Moby-Dick* the *Pequod* first has a tiller (70; also 423 and 513) but later a wheel (283, 500). The whalemen sleep mostly in hammocks (128 and frequently elsewhere), but occasionally in bunks (119, 293). Melville several times mentions that there are thirty men onboard (515, 526, 557), but there are actually roughly forty-five individually designated. That such slips are typical of Melville's writing and rewriting reinforces the likely truth of the Marbonna scene.

Did Melville, then, spend his month as a deserter on Nuku Hiva among the Tai'oa, who were amicably disposed toward absconding seamen, rather than in Taipivai? Was his closest acquaintance with the Taipi not even a Taipi but a Tai'oa chief whose name was Mohi-a-Taipis?

Textual Evidence

The element that will be considered at most length in my questioning of *Typee*'s veracity is textual. As early as the 1930s, scholars researching Melville's life and works found, as Harrison Hayford writes, that Melville "greatly understated his indebtedness to other writers."[49] It has long been known, for example, that many of the incidents in *Omoo* (1847), the work closest in time and type to *Typee,* are fictional, or at least not strictly literal. Melville confessed to his English publisher, John Murray, that the description of the dance in *Omoo* is salvaged from a discarded chapter of *Typee.*[50] The early chapters of *Omoo* are based on Melville's time on the *Lucy Ann,* including the bloodless mutiny that occurred aboard that ship.[51] However, since his wanderings on the island of Eimeo, supposedly chronicled in the second half of *Omoo*, consumed only about two weeks in late October and early November 1842,[52] Melville had to delve into other books to enrich his narrative, most notably the second edition of William Ellis's *Polynesian Researches, during a Residence of Nearly Eight Years in the Society and Sandwich Islands* (1833). Hayford notes of Melville's use of Ellis:

> Melville fastened upon the pages of Ellis, and Ellis proved to be a bounteous guide, if not philosopher and friend. Not once did Melville cite Ellis as his authority: he simply set down Ellis's information without credit, or claimed it as his own observation, or credited it to a native informant— to "Captain Bob," or "Tonoi," for example. Little reverence as Melville paid him, Ellis was his historian, geographer, botanist, anthropologist, dictionary of native words common and proper, and even his eyes and ears. Although Melville claimed that in the Calabooza (Ch. 33) he had "a fine opportunity of making observations" on the condition of the natives, it was Ellis who observed for him their diseases, physique, size, color, and preference of dark skin to sickly European white. Melville inserted such details in a lump as his own "observations"; but similar information in the pages of Ellis soon suggested whole chapters of *Omoo* with only a slight infusion of memories.[53]

In a similar way, Melville found much of the information for the middle chapters of *Moby-Dick* (1851), often called the "cetological chapters," in the second edition of Thomas Beale's *The Natural History of the Sperm Whale* (1839). He also borrowed extensively from William Scoresby Jr.'s *An Account of the Arctic Regions, with a History and Description of the Northern Whale Fishery* (1820). Even as he borrowed from Scoresby, he poked fun at him, calling him one of the "most famous" of the Esquimaux doctors, Zogranda (*Moby-Dick* 298); an expert on smells named Fogo Von Slack (*Moby-Dick* 409); and Dr. Snodhead, a "professor of Low Dutch and High German in the college of Santa Claus and St. Pott's" (*Moby-Dick* 445).

Melville continued to write in this fashion. His short story *Benito Cereno* (1855) is rewritten from chapter 18 of Amasa Delano's *A Narrative of Voyages and Travels, in the Northern and Southern Hemispheres* (1817)—so closely rewritten that it can be followed line by line. *Israel Potter* (1854–55), the only one of Melville's full-length works to be serialized, is rewritten from Henry Trumbull's *Life and Remarkable Adventures of Israel R. Potter* (1824).[54]

"I have swam through libraries," Melville writes in *Moby-Dick* (136). He consumed books and was consumed by them. As he read, he argued with them, laughed and cried over them, and became fiercely angry with them. The books he owned are filled with notes and jottings done with slashing pen marks and furious periods. Melville's reading, both literary and factual, inspired his writing. An alchemist of words, Melville transmuted his often mundane sources through his art. As Melville infused dry information with his own humor and philosophical ponderings, he transformed it into literature of the highest order.

Even if Melville did in fact end up in the Taipi valley, so many of the experiences that drive the narrative tension derive either from earlier written sources or from the vast differences between Melville's own cultural background and Marquesan culture that a close reading of the text renders the question of whether it is a portrait of the Taipi as opposed to the Tai'oa more and not less opaque. There is documentary evidence that Melville was treated for an injured leg. If we accept both that he was in the valley of the Taipi and that his leg was injured early on, the scant four weeks' residence with limited mobility would have afforded him small opportunity for the sorts of interactions and observations he describes in *Typee*. All the particularity of Taipi individuals, incidents, and customs becomes more questionable on closer examination.

Much of the physical description of Nuku Hiva in *Typee* is taken from three sources: David Porter's *Journal of a Cruise Made to the Pacific Ocean* (1815, 1822), Charles S. Stewart's *A Visit to the South Seas, in the United States' Ship* Vincennes, *during the Years 1829 and 1830* (1831), and Georg H. von Langsdorff's *Voyages and Travels in Various Parts of the World, during the Years 1803, 1804, 1805, 1806, and 1807* (1813).[55] Melville's borrowings from Porter's *Journal* go beyond physical description and language, however; *Typee* also parallels the *Journal* in action. The following paragraphs will first discuss Melville's borrowings from Stewart and Langsdorff and then concentrate on his use of Porter, the breadth and extent of which, I will argue, has been significantly underestimated by scholars.[56]

In Charles S. Stewart's *A Visit to the South Seas*, Melville found not only a physical description of Nuku Hiva and of the beauty of the Marquesan women, standard to all early nineteenth-century Pacific narratives, but also specific elements that he used in *Typee*. For example, Stewart "crossed the mountain torrent several times, on the back of my kind and attentive guide,"[57] just as Kory-Kory carries Tommo on his back (89, 109).

Melville's "superb-looking warrior," Mehevi, closely resembles "two warriors, in full battle-dress," encountered by Stewart near the *Vincennes*.[58] (As noted above, these warriors are not Taipi.) In the following passage, and in the quoted passages throughout the rest of this discussion, words found in both Melville's original source and *Typee* are italicized. Mehevi's headdress is described thus: "The splendid *long drooping tail-feathers* of the tropical bird, thickly interspersed with the gaudy *plumage* of the cock, were disposed in an immense upright semicircle upon his head, their lower extremities being *fixed* in *a crescent* of guinea-beads which spanned *the forehead*" (77). This is a shortened version of the description of the headdress worn by Stewart's warriors:

> It consisted of *a crescent,* three or four inches broad at its greatest breadth, *fixed* uprightly in front, the lower edge following the line of the hair on *the forehead.* . . . The middle was entirely filled with the small, scarlet berries of the *abrus precatorius,* fastened upon the material of which it was constructed, by a gum which exudes from the bread-fruit tree. The *crescent* formed the front of a cap fitting closely to the head behind, and the foundation in which the heavy *plumage* surmounting it is fixed. This *plumage* consisted of the *long,* black, and burnished *tail-feathers* of the cock—the finest I ever saw; those in the centre being more than two feet in length. They were arranged behind the front-piece as closely as possible, and in such a manner, as to form the shape of a deeply pointed chapeau, placed crosswise on the head—the feathers in the centre standing perpendicularly, and becoming more and more vertical, till the lowest at the edges *drooped* deeply over the shoulders.[59]

On Stewart's warriors, "frizzled bunches of *human hair* were tied around their wrists and ancles; their *loins,* also, being *girt* with thick tufts of the same, over large maros of white *tapa.*" Mehevi's "*loins . . .* were *girt* about with heavy folds of a dark-colored *tappa,* hanging before and behind in clusters of braided tassels, while anklets and bracelets of curling *human hair* completed his unique costume."[60] All carry long spears. Both Mehevi and Stewart's warriors are "imposing"; the warriors are "of the *noblest* stature—every limb, in its muscular *proportions,* presenting a model for the skill of a statuary," while Mehevi, "from the excellence of his physical *proportions,* might certainly have been regarded as one of Nature's *noblemen.*"[61]

In Georg H. von Langsdorff's *Voyages and Travels* again appear the standard descriptions of the geography of Nuku Hiva and the beauty of Marquesan women. Common, too, to Melville, Stewart, and Langsdorff is the description of the dwelling places of the islanders. Other details in *Typee,* however, seem to have a more specific source in Langsdorff. At the Feast of the Calabashes, Tommo is "amused at the appearance of four or five old women who, in a state of utter nudity, with their arms extended flatly down their sides, and holding themselves perfectly erect, were leaping stiffly into the air, like so many sticks bobbing to the surface, after being pressed perpendicularly into the water" (166). He learns from Kory-Kory that they are bereaved widows. Their nudity, dancing, and bereavement likely had their source in *Voyages and Travels.* Langsdorff describes the dancing—"The performers in the dances make many springs and pantomimic gestures, with quick movements of the hands and arms, without moving much from one spot"—and then notes "only those girls, wives, and widows danced, whose husbands or lovers had been taken prisoners or conquered in combat. . . . When we consider that they are obliged to appear naked, contrary to the usual custom, and that they are made objects of sport and mockery to the people, it does indeed appear very probable that the dancing is imposed upon them as a sort of penance."[62] Langsdorff's description of a child's plaything made from a stick may have inspired Tommo's creation of a popgun for a child, "a little spirited urchin," that is quickly coveted by all.[63]

Melville turned primarily to David Porter's *Journal of a Cruise Made to the Pacific Ocean* as he was writing *Typee*, and it is in Porter that Melville found the portrayal of the Taipi as the fiercest and most feared of the tribes on Nuku Hiva. The fearsome Taipi would make a better story than the Tai'oa, who lived along the beach and had long been exposed to whalemen. Porter's depiction of the Taipi is driven by his own experience, for the Taipi were the only indigenous tribe who bested the American in battle.

Porter arrived at Nuku Hiva in October of 1813 aboard the American warship *Essex*, accompanied by three British prizes captured during the War of 1812. Porter meant to careen and provision his ships in Taioha'e Bay. With over three hundred men and four ships to provision, however, the resources of the bay soon proved insufficient. In his attempts to gather food from other parts of the island, Porter became embroiled in the hostilities between the Teii, Ha'apa'a, and Taipi tribes.

When Porter first anchored at Nuku Hiva, as he records in his *Journal,* the Ha'apa'a tribes unfavorably received him. They stood firm against Porter until his men rushed their fortress and shot five men dead. As Porter laconically states: "As soon as this place was taken, all further resistance was at an end."[64] The Ha'apa'a tribes, then, became as eager to please Porter as the other tribes and, as Porter notes, "desired nothing more ardently than peace."[65]

At this point all the tribes of the Marquesas wanted peace with Porter and eagerly supplied him with pork and fruit—all, that is, except one. The Taipi refused to bring food to Porter. In fact, the Taipi told Porter that he and his men "had beat the Happahs because the Happahs were cowards"; they "were white lizards, mere dirt." "The most contemptible epithet which they could apply" was that Porter and his men "were the posteriors and the privates of the Taeehs [Teii]."[66]

From his first mention of the Taipi, Porter describes them as great warriors. He worried that the Taipi resistance would undermine his subjugation of the other tribes. "My aim," he writes, "was to render all the tribes subservient to my views."[67] So he determined to fight the Taipi. Porter's men were routed on the first day of the fight: this solitary defeat by an aboriginal tribe caused Porter to stress the ferocity of the Taipi in his account of the battle.

Incensed by his loss, the next day Porter gathered two hundred of his men and laid waste to the Taipi valley, burning ten villages, destroying breadfruit trees, and killing and wounding great numbers of the Taipi.[68] Ultimately even Porter feels sorrow for what he did, and his description of the war is painful to read. Before the destruction of the valley began, Porter writes: "We halted to take breath, and view, for a few minutes, this delightful valley, which was soon to become a scene of desolation.... Never in my life did I witness a more delightful scene, or experience more repugnancy than I now felt, for the necessity which compelled me to make war against this happy and heroic people."[69] That night, he again viewed the valley: "I stopped to contemplate that valley which, in the morning, we had viewed in all its beauty, the scene of abundance and happiness. A long line of smoking ruins now marked our traces from one end to the other; the opposite hills were covered with the unhappy fugitives, and the whole presented a scene of desolation and horror."[70] Porter writes: "Many may censure my conduct as wanton and unjust."[71] He then attempts to justify his actions: "Wars are not always just, and are rarely free from excesses. However I may regret the harshness with which motives of self-preservation, that operate every where, compelled me to treat these high-spirited and incorrigible people, my conscience acquits me of any injustice; and no excesses were committed, but what the Typees had it in their power to stop by ceasing hostilities. The evils they experienced they brought upon themselves, and the blood of their relations and friends must be on their own heads. Had no opposition been made, none would have been killed."[72]

With the large number of killed and wounded, Porter's was a different kind of warfare. Native warfare resulted in the ritualistic defeat of the enemy rather than in the destruction of a people. Porter's earlier "Happah War" had resulted in just five dead, and to the Marquesans this seemed a vast number: "the number of dead which [the Teii] had borne off as trophies, had far exceeded that of any former battle within [their leader's] recollection; as they fight for weeks, nay, for months sometimes, without killing any on either side, though many are, in all their engagements, severely wounded."[73]

For Melville, as for any reader of Porter's *Journal*, the Taipi were the fiercest of the Nuku Hivan tribes. Ethnohistorian Greg Dening, the most respected of the historians of European contact in the Marquesas, notes in *Islands and Beaches: Discourse on a Silent Land: Marquesas 1774–1880:* "By being Porter's enemy the Taipi became a savage, treacherous, sullen group of warriors whose ferocity was a compliment to those who defeated them."[74] Melville himself says that the Taipi are "reputed the most ferocious in the South Seas" (*Typee* 170). Is it any wonder, then, that he chose to place his protagonist in the Taipi valley, whether Melville was there in reality or not?

If one reads Porter's *Journal* and follows that immediately with a reading of *Typee*, one finds that the similarities are striking. Melville's descriptions of the Taipi are much closer to Porter's descriptions of the Marquesans he encountered during his visit of 1813 than they are to descriptions of the islanders contemporary to Melville's visit in July 1842.[75] Greg Dening, in *Beach Crossings: Voyaging across Times, Cultures, and Self*, notes that Melville landed at "no pristine beach. The sands were a jumble of footsteps. The beach was a much negotiated space. It would be Melville's fiction to make it 'native.'"[76] For Dening, the beach is not only literal but also a metaphor of encounter. Dening adds: "The beach was divided over what the intrusion of so many strangers meant and what it did to native life, and how it was to be managed, if not controlled."[77] Radiguet, following his 1842 visit to Nuku Hiva, questioned: "Nous nous demandions si ce radieux paysage que remplissaient d'un côté la bruyante allégresse d'une population en fête, le frais parfum de la feuillée humide et des fleurs, qu'assombrissaient de l'autre cette case pleine de morts et d'agonisants, cette odeur d'huile rance et de cadavres, ne nous offrait pas, dans son bizarre assemblage de gaieté, de douleur et d'insouciance, une véritable et complète expression de la vie polynésienne" (We wondered whether this radiant landscape, filled on one side by the loud joy of a celebratory people and the fresh scent of flowers and damp foliage, and clouded on the other side by this hut full of dead and suffering bodies and the stench of corpses and rancid oil, might not offer us, in its strange mixture of joy, pain, and unconcern, a true and full expression of Polynesian life).[78] Radiguet's vision is darker than Melville's. All Marquesans including the Taipis had been much visited by 1842; they were not an isolated people with little knowledge of Europeans.

Parallels between Porter's *Journal* and *Typee* can be seen early in the narrative. The local pilot in *Typee*, who helped navigate ships in and out of Taioha'e Bay, "a genuine South-Sea vagabond" (12), an Englishman who deserted ship in the Marquesas, is based on the Englishman James Fitz,[79] who served as a pilot for ships visiting Nuku Hiva—but Porter also describes a naked, tattooed interpreter, Wilson, another Englishman,[80] who may have enriched Melville's portrait.

Melville's description of the Taipi valley, Taipivai, is very close to Porter's, as has been noted by Charles Roberts Anderson, Ruth Blair, and others.[81] Looking down on the valley, Melville's narrator is "transfixed with surprise and delight," while Porter writes, "From the hill we had a distant view of every part [of the valley], and all appeared equally delightful."[82] Yet it is not only Porter's view of the valley that is paralleled in *Typee*: it is also his journey across the mountains to get there. Nuku Hivan valleys were usually entered from the sea.[83] Porter, however, chose to enter the valley from the mountains in order to attack the Taipi from a more tactically advantageous direction. Although Bryant denies that Melville used any written sources in describing the protagonists' five-day journey to the Typee valley, telling us "the chapters dealing with Melville's escape (chaps. 6–9) are, to my knowledge, devoid of source borrowings,"[84] Porter's description of his passage through the mountains is strikingly like Tommo's and Toby's.

Porter and his men walked "in silence up and down the steep sides of rocks and mountains, through rivulets, thickets, and reed brakes, and by the sides of precipices which sometimes caused us to *shudder*."[85] They spent a night on the mountain, because the natives told them that it would be "impossible to *descend* it without daylight; that the mountain was *almost perpendicular*, and that in many places [they] should be under the necessity of lowering [them]selves down with great caution."[86] Their night on the mountain was miserable because of the "violence of the *rain*," which was pouring down in "*torrents*." "Never, *in the course of my life*," Porter writes, "did I spend a more anxious or disagreeable *night*. . . . A *cold* and piercing wind accompanied the deluge . . . and chilled us to the heart."[87]

Compare this description to Melville's: "During this wretched *night* there seemed nothing wanting to complete the perfect misery of our condition. The *rain* descended in . . . *torrents*. . . . I have had many a ducking *in the course of my life*, and in general cared little about it; but the accumulated horrors of that night, the deathlike *cold*ness of the place, the appalling darkness, and the dismal sense of our forlorn condition, almost unmanned me" (46). After their miserable night, Tommo and Toby enter the valley: "Accordingly we now commenced [our journey] by *descending* the *almost perpendicular* side of a steep and narrow gorge" (52). "With an insensibility to danger which I cannot call to mind without *shuddering*," they lower themselves down the steep side of the ravine, "reckless whether the slight roots and twigs we clutched at sustained us for the while, or treacherously yielded to our grasp" (53). Melville tells us, "I have no doubt that we were the first white men who ever penetrated thus far back into [the Taipi] territories" (74)—that is, except for Porter and his men. Did Melville ever make his way through the mountains to Taipivai, or did he only transform Porter's night of misery to five nights and make it part of *Typee*?

The parallels between *Journal of a Cruise* and *Typee* continue. The scaly appearance of the "five hideous old wretches" in *Typee* (92) reflects that of Gattanewa, the leader of the Teii in Porter. When Porter first met Gattanewa, he was astonished by his appearance: "an infirm old man of seventy years of age . . . his face and body were as black as a negro's, from the quantity of tattooing, which entirely covered them, and his skin was rough, and appeared to be peeling off in scales."[88] For Melville's old men, "all the figures sketched upon their limbs in youth have been blended together" and "their skin had a frightful scaly appearance" (92). The appearance of blackness caused by heavy tattooing depicted by

Porter is also described in Stewart and Langsdorff,[89] but it is the mention of scales in Porter that is significant here. "Scales" and "scaly" are unusual words, not generally used in reference to human beings. Melville's "old wretches" are imagined as even more frightful than Gattanewa, but Gattanewa may have been their inspiration.

Porter gives a short dissertation on the word *motakee,* which means "every degree of good."[90] In *Typee,* "'Mortarkee' [is] . . . equivalent to the word 'good'" (69). The *a* of *motakee* has become *ar* in Melville's rendering, just as Ha'apa'a becomes "Happar" and Tai'oa "Tior" (and as idea becomes "ideer," and Donna "Donner" throughout much of New England). "*Kie-kie* signifies *to eat*" in Porter, just as it does in *Typee:* "'Ki-Ki, nuee nuee, ah! moee moee mortarkee' (eat plenty, ah! sleep very good)."[91]

Melville's initial disgust at Fayaway's eating of a raw fish—"Raw fish! Shall I ever forget my sensations when I first saw my island beauty devour one? Oh, heavens! Fayaway, how could you ever have contracted so vile a habit?"—is similar to Porter's on first seeing Gattanewa eat a raw fish.[92] Melville, however, overcomes his repugnance and joins in, finding "the undertaking was not so *disagreeable* in the main," but Porter has his interpreter, Wilson, tell Gattanewa "the practice of eating raw fish was *disagreeable* to me."[93] Note the duplication of the word "disagreeable" despite the difference in meaning.

Melville's description of the monumental stone platforms, which he, like Porter, calls "morais," bears many signs of having been lifted from Porter. In Porter, "some of them are *one hundred yards in length,* and forty yards *in width*"; in Melville, they "cannot be less than *one hundred yards in length* and twenty *in width.*"[94] Porter reflects on "the means used in hewing them into such perfect forms, with tools perhaps little harder, than the materials worked on." Melville describes the sides of the blocks, which "are quite smooth, but though square, and of pretty regular formation, they bear no mark of the chisel."[95] Porter notes that "the appearance of many of these places strongly mark their *antiquity.*" Melville writes, "These structures bear every indication of a very high *antiquity.*"[96] They both discuss the massiveness of the blocks used in building the platforms and the amount of labor involved.

These verbal parallels prove little by themselves. Porter has long been known as a source for *Typee,* despite Melville's disingenuous statement that Porter's *Journal* "is a work, however, which I have never happened to meet with."[97] More important are the parallels of action. The most striking of these is the descent into the valley from the mountains discussed above, but also haunting is Melville's discovery of human remains, with its suggestion of cannibalism. Porter finds the bodies of two Taipi killed during the "Typee War" in a canoe "and many other human carcasses, with the flesh still on them, lying about the canoe."[98] Late in

Typee, Tommo finds a similar canoe—"a curiously carved vessel of wood"—and steals a look inside: "the slight glimpse sufficed; my eyes fell upon the disordered members of a human skeleton, the bones still fresh with moisture, and with particles of flesh clinging to them here and there!" (238).

Porter's attitude toward the bodies could best be described as nonchalant, but Melville instills dread and the fear of cannibalism into his discovery. The fears of Melville's narrator create the narrative tension that leads to the end of *Typee* and the protagonist's dramatic escape from the one-eyed Mow-Mow—fears that could easily be founded on the visuality of Porter's description of the victims of the Typee War or Langsdorff's discourse on anthropophagy rather than on Melville's own visual evidence of cannibalism. Melville's purpose, as Dening notes, is "not history or autobiography but significant narrative."[99]

Not everything in *Typee* is borrowed. Melville describes the death of a young man on the beach at Nuku Hiva, *not* in the Taipi valley. This is a scene, he writes, that he "chanced to witness at Nukuheva" (193). This scene ought to have taken place in Taipivai, where Melville, according to *Typee*, spent his time ashore. Melville hurriedly covers the confusion of the scene's location by adding, "None of its inmates were so accommodating as to die and be buried in order to gratify my curiosity" (193). Since his description is not found in Porter, perhaps this is a scene he *did* witness, and on the beach. Another event not borrowed from written sources is the protagonist's hurt leg. Melville, like Tommo, did injure his leg. In 1848, Lieutenant Henry A. Wise studied Dr. Johnstone's dose book, where he found a record of the prescriptions made by the physician for Melville.[100] Yet perhaps Melville did not hurt his leg descending a precipice slippery with rain, but in a more mundane manner. All we know for certain is that Melville's leg was injured, yet that injury may have been the inspiration for Melville once again to take the ordinary and make it dramatic.

Melville continued to mine Porter's *Journal* as a source in later works. All *The Encantadas* are indebted to Porter, but four of the ten sketches—sketches 5, 6, 9, and 10—especially so. The story of the renegade Irishman Patrick Watkins was well known among Pacific voyagers. Watkins was said to have been marooned for nearly a year in 1808 on Charles Island.[101] But when Melville transformed Watkins's story into sketch 9, "Hood's Isle and the Hermit Oberlus," his source was Porter. Most of the details and even the name Oberlus come from Porter. Verbal echoes of Porter's *Journal* appear elsewhere in Melville's works. Porter's "I found it necessary to get to sea as soon as possible" in his letter of July 3, 1814, to the secretary of the navy is a more prosaic version of Ishmael's "I account it high time to get to sea as soon as I can."[102]

From Porter, then, I would argue that Melville borrowed two of the pivotal events of *Typee:* the descent into the valley and the discovery of the cannibalized bodies. The latter is especially important because the *Typee* narrative is driven by the fear of cannibalism. Cannibalism was the element of Marquesan life on which early narratives—those of Edward Robarts, Jean Cabri, Georg H. von Langsdorff, Charles Stewart, Max Radiguet[103]—concentrated: it was the inescapable factor. For Melville, the fear of cannibalism provides narrative tension; he, therefore, took the stories he had heard from shipmates and details from Porter, Stewart, and Langsdorff and centered cannibalism in *Typee*.

THE WRITING OF *TYPEE*

Melville writes of cannibalism so vividly in *Typee* that he despaired, as he wrote to Nathaniel Hawthorne, that he would "go down to posterity . . . as a 'man who lived among the cannibals'!"[104] The public acceptance of the truth of his account established one of the essential elements of Melville's writing. Melville had found that he could take actual events and imagination and blend them together so powerfully that the combination took on a reality of its own. As he continued to write, the transformative qualities of literary reality became increasingly important to him. Throughout the rest of his writing career, especially in *Moby-Dick*, Melville explored how many individuals can share the same encounter and yet perceive it differently. The experience of creating a new literary reality thrust Melville toward a higher level of literary consciousness.

In *Typee*, Melville calls his protagonist Tommo. Toby has a real name, but the character based on Melville himself does not. Perhaps he initially planned for the work to be a fiction. But upon its acceptance for publication by an English firm dedicated to releasing nonfiction travel accounts and then upon being questioned by his English publisher, John Murray, and the reviewers, Melville more and more affirmed the veracity of the book. The consideration of *Typee* as a work founded on the factual basis of a four-month stay in the valley of the Taipi subsequently became a given. It is a measure of Melville's genius that with this perception of *Typee* as truth he leapt to greatness. He used the creation of literary reality as a base from which to explore the grand philosophical questions of truth, knowledge, and justice.

Paradoxically, the acceptance of *Typee* as truth fired Melville's literary ambitions rather than making him a maritime chronicler like Frank T. Bullen, in *The Cruise of the Cachalot* (1898), or Richard Henry Dana Jr., in *Two Years before the Mast* (1840). With his first attempt at literary construction, Melville was able to attain, in Nabokov's words, "that go-between, that prism, [that] is the art of literature."[105] Melville may well in fact have been describing himself in the following passage from *Typee*, hiding his admission of the fiction he has created in plain sight, much as the blackmailer uncovered by C. Auguste Dupin hides the stolen missive in Edgar Allan Poe's "The Purloined Letter" (1845). By the time he wrote *Typee,* Melville had joined the company of

> retired old South-Sea rovers, who have domesticated themselves among the barbarous tribes of the Pacific. Jack [read Melville], who has long been accustomed to the long-bow, and to spin tough yarns on a ship's forecastle, invariably officiates as showman of the island on which he has settled, and having mastered a few dozen words of the language, is supposed to know all about the people who speak it. A natural desire to make himself of conse- quence in the eyes of strangers, prompts him to lay claim to a much greater knowledge of such matters than he actually possesses. In reply to incessant queries, he communicates not only all he knows but a good deal more, and if there be any information deficient still he is at no loss to supply it. The avidity with which his anecdotes are noted down tickles his vanity, and his powers of invention increase with the credulity of his auditors. He knows just the sort of information wanted, and furnishes it to any extent.
>
> This is not a supposed case [indeed!]; I have met with several individu- als like the one described, and I have been present at two or three of their interviews with strangers. (*Typee* 170)

Jack was the generic name given to all sailors. Like the anonymous Jack of whom he writes, Melville was prompted "to lay claim to a much greater knowledge" and experience than he possessed as he crafted a narrative enabling him to elaborate his four-week sojourn into a compelling full-length book.

Where Melville spent the weeks between July 9 and August 9, 1842, is still un- known. There is, though, at least a question of whether he spent it in the valley of the Taipi. Instead, he may have spent those weeks living with the Tai'oa, just as deserters from the whaleship *George and Susan* did seven months later. The Tai'oa lived in a valley marked by a thunderous and beautiful waterfall and were governed by chiefs and priests whose names appear in later Melville texts: Mohi, Mohi-a-Taipis, even Mataheva, the closest name to "Mehevi" listed in the French records. Melville borrowed his description of the Taipi valley and perhaps the perilous overland route to that valley, even the miserable night of torrential rain, from David Porter's *Journal of a Cruise.*

Typee is Melville's first book, but it is not juvenilia. He is already using the technique he used the rest of his life, that of taking dull—or, as with Porter, some- times not so dull—written sources and kindling them into incandescence. While the fact that Melville borrowed much of his information from other writers has long been known, the extent to which he boldly claimed this material as his own experience in his first book sheds a new and vivid light on his development as a writer. As T. S. Eliot asserts in *The Sacred Wood*, "One of the surest of tests is the way in which a poet borrows. Immature poets imitate; mature poets steal."[106] The idea of Melville lustily lifting large chunks of his work from Porter, Stewart, and Langsdorff and then brazenly claiming them as his own in the face of doubt by publishers and reviewers offers an intriguing look at the early heights of ambition and imagination that he achieved. As John Dryden wrote of Ben Jonson, "He invades Authours [*sic*] like a Monarch, and what would be theft in other Poets, is onely [*sic*] victory in him."[107]

CHAPTER 2

~ "Six Months at Sea! Yes, Reader, as I Live"
Sailor Talk

People who have never gone to sea for the first time as sailors, can not imagine how puzzling and confounding it is. It must be like going into a barbarous country, where they speak a strange dialect, and dress in strange clothes, and live in strange houses. For sailors have their own names, even for things that are familiar ashore; and if you call a thing by its shore name, you are laughed at for an ignoramus and a land-lubber.
   —Redburn *(65)*

MELVILLE based the above statement on his own experiences aboard the merchant vessel *St. Lawrence* in 1839. Following the untimely death of his father and the subsequent lapse of the family's fortunes, Melville joined this vessel as a greenhand and embarked on his first direct experience of the maritime world. This was his initial immersion in sailor talk. The four years he spent at sea from 1841 through 1844 on three whaleships and a naval frigate deepened this immersion and established his self-identification as a mariner and wanderer. The insights, perspectives, and language he acquired during this time exerted a formative, encompassing influence on his early creative development as he transcended the role of yarn-spinner to become an increasingly ambitious literary artist.

In this work, I use the term "sailor talk" to refer to the technical terminology used by sailors, to the occupational lore and coterie speech, or coded language, that arises out of the shared experience of particular crews, to the more broadly shared folkloric forms of music, argument, and yarning, and to the discourse, or generalized language, that is used by and to describe seamen. All sailors share the more formalized occupational lingo, but on any voyage the crew develops speech particular to that specific group of people, when the already arcane set of terms that is nautical terminology, the occupational dialect, shades into the more personal rubric of coterie speech. Much folklore is engendered by particularly striking individual expression that is therefore repeated and spread beyond the coterie group and absorbed into the oral tradition of the larger folk group, in this case the occupational folk group of sailors. The broader discourse of sailor talk includes both the complex mosaic of self-image expressed by sailors and the similarly complex views of sailors expressed by society in general. Throughout his early works, the subtle, shifting voices of Melville's narrators cast their nets broadly to fish up a tremendous variety of sailor talk upon which his readers can feast. Melville employs sailor talk at all its levels in a more sophisticated, comprehensive, and profound way than any other maritime author.

Work Talk

At sea, sailors need technical language the way a body needs breath—or a ship needs wind. Consider the richness and depth of the sailor's relationship to language and to wind. The unambiguous terms of the shipboard language of command translate into highly specific actions that, properly performed, forge a crew and ship into a single machine that harnesses the world's wind to the navigator's will. Spoken language is transported from speaker to listener by breath, the forcing of wind from one's lungs through one's mouth. Breath, which conveys the signifiers of meaning in the form of speech, was perceived by sailors as a controlled form of wind to the point that they had various superstitions concerning this identification.

Prior to 1805, when the Englishman Sir Francis Beaufort created the Beaufort Wind Scale, and even to some extent afterward, sailors used terms directly relating to the amount of sail that could be spread in winds of a particular force. Before the quantified scientific measurement of air currents, sailors' understanding of wind had an inextricable relationship with the working of the ship. A "t'gallant breeze," for instance, referred to the speed of wind in which the topgallant sail, the third sail up from the deck on the mast of an eighteenth- or early nineteenth-century full-rigged ship, could remain set. Once the wind exceeds that speed, the sail must be furled, or tied into a tight bundle lashed to the spar from which it hangs. When a sailor used a term such as "t'gallant breeze," he encompassed his personally acquired knowledge of the physical experience involved in climbing eighty or ninety feet up a mast in twenty-five to thirty knots of wind in company with half a dozen other men in order to wrestle seven hundred square feet or more of flapping, sometimes sodden or frozen, canvas under control.

Wind provides the power that drives a sailing vessel, yet it also causes constant "chafe," or wear. Such chafe must be continuously attended to. A piece of rigging worn down by chafe could break under the press of wind, causing the whole rig, which is held up under tension, to plummet to the deck, injuring or killing crewmen or, in the worst of circumstances, causing the vessel to founder and thus destroying the lives of all aboard. However, the lack of wind renders the ship motionless and helpless. Such strong feelings attached to the presence or absence of wind that sailors personified it. The Greek god of wind, Aeolus, pursues a fickle vendetta against Odysseus throughout *The Odyssey*. Nineteenth-century deep-water sailors with a fresh breeze behind their vessel on the homeward leg of a voyage employed such sayings as "The Boston girls have a hold of the towrope." The sounds produced by wind gave rise to two superstitious beliefs regarding whistling. The first was that whistling a melody was considered tremendously bad luck. It was feared the wind would punish the vessel on which a human had the hubris to control wind in such a way, and that such whistling would bring on a destructive gale. However, on a ship becalmed, one might witness sailors and even officers making low tuneless whistling sounds in the direction from which they wanted wind to spring up in hopes that the wind would say, "I can do better than that"—a form of sympathetic magic known as whistling for a wind.

Various meanings of wind and breath are evident in William Shakespeare's *The Tempest* (1611), the title of which evokes the awesome power of wind. In the first scene of the first act, the nobles outcry the storm. The boatswain calls out, "A plague upon this howling! They are louder than the weather or our office," the necessary commands given by the boatswain to the sailors.[1] The language of command cannot be heard, and the nobles "do assist the storm."[2] Breath is not controlled. In the epilogue, however, breath and wind are now gentle. Prospero tells the audience: "Gentle breath of yours my sails / Must fill."[3]

The practice of chanteying, or singing work songs to coordinate the intense physical effort necessary to accomplish many of the tasks required of the crew, furnishes another example of breath as controlled wind. The inspiration of shared song knits together the efforts of a number of men. Here breath partakes of spirit (inspiration) that serves to unify, imparting a synergistic power to the group that adds up to more than the sum of its parts. "A chantey is worth ten men on the line" is an old truism of sailor talk. Without the chantey, the work of the men remains diffuse, but shared breath serves to unify and empower the men in their task.

Melville writes of the power of work songs in *Redburn*:

I soon got used to this singing; for the sailors never touched a rope without it. Sometimes, when no one happened to strike up, and the pulling, whatever it might be, did not seem to be getting forward very well, the mate would always say, "*Come, men, can't any of you sing? Sing now, and raise the dead.*" And then some one of them would begin, and if every man's arms were as much relieved as mine by the song, and he could pull as much better as I did, with such a cheering accompaniment, I am sure the song was well worth the breath expended on it. (46; emphasis in original)

In this passage, the officer uses two definitions of the word "inspiration"— the common, literal one of motivation and the archaic one of infusing life by breathing—when he calls to the men, "Sing now, and raise the dead." He wants the men to breathe life into the inanimate. Here the inanimate is the repetitive, stultifying work of pulling and the dead weight of the gear being raised. That the extra breath required to sing choruses should cause the work to become *easier* seems counterintuitive, but it is nonetheless true. Breath and wind are intertwined with sailor language, metaphorically and literally.

Melville was exceptionally qualified to use sailor language in his books. Before he even went to sea, he had heard stories of maritime life from his relations. His uncle John D'Wolf II was a merchant mariner in the Russian-American trade and had sailed to such places as the sea of Okhotsk; Kodiak and Oonalaska in what is now Alaska; and Archangel, Russia. He visited Melville's family in New York in 1828 when Melville was nine. Melville's paternal cousin Thomas Melvill served as a midshipman aboard the United States frigate *Brandywine* (mentioned in *White-Jacket*), then aboard several vessels, including the United States sloop of war *Vincennes*, on which Melville's maternal cousin, Hunn Gansevoort, would later serve. In 1829 the *Vincennes* called at Nuku Hiva, Tahiti, and Oahu, all of which Melville himself would later visit. The crew of the *Vincennes* even spent a day in the Taipi valley. Thomas's life ended sadly. He was court-martialed, broke off communication with his father, served on whalers, was wasted by scurvy, died at sea, and was buried at Lahaina, Maui.

Four of Melville's maternal Gansevoort cousins also went to sea. As Wilson Heflin notes in *Herman Melville's Whaling Years,* "At first hand—and at second hand—Herman had heard during his youth and early manhood stimulating tales of the nautical experiences of his cousins, the brothers Guert, Peter, and Leonard Gansevoort and Hunn Gansevoort."[4] In 1842 Guert Gansevoort was first lieutenant of the United States brig *Somers,* commanded by Alexander Slidell Mackenzie, when three men, including the son of the secretary of war, were hung for mutiny, an event often regarded as a basis for Melville's posthumously published *Billy Budd* (1924). Peter Gansevoort served first as a merchant sailor and then as a midshipman before being lost at sea. Leonard Gansevoort worked as a sailor aboard whaling and merchant vessels. Hunn Gansevoort's career is most closely tied to Melville's. He served aboard the U.S. sloop of war *Vincennes* on her 1835–36 voyage. The crew of the *Vincennes* spent nineteen days at Nuku Hiva, during which they unsuccessfully attempted to capture a Marquesan chief, Paregla, who had murdered an American. Later they sailed to Tahiti, where the ship was visited by Queen Pomare IV, then crossed to the island of Eimeo. The crew of the *Vincennes* also rescued survivors of the shipwrecked New Bedford whaleship *Mentor* from islanders.

Melville's early career did not follow that of his cousins. He was raised by a New York merchant and came relatively late to the maritime life. His first working voyage occurred at age nineteen when he shipped as a greenhand, the lowest rank of sailor, aboard the merchant vessel *St. Lawrence* during a transatlantic crossing from New York to Liverpool, England, and back. Melville later captured some of the feelings of being the son of a gentleman suddenly transformed into a lowly sailor in his fourth book, *Redburn: His First Voyage,* subtitled *Being the Sailor-boy Confessions and Reminiscences of the Son-of-a-Gentleman, in the Merchant Service.* Melville had heard sailor talk from his cousins and his Uncle D'Wolf, but using the language was a different matter.

Melville was forced to learn concrete terminology quickly aboard the *St. Lawrence.* He explains in *Redburn:* "There is such an infinite number of totally new names of new things to learn, that at first it seemed impossible for me to master them all. If you have ever seen a ship, you must have remarked what a thicket of ropes there are; and how they all seemed mixed and entangled together like a great skein of yarn. Now the very smallest of these ropes has its own proper name, and many of them are very lengthy, like the names of young royal princes, such as the *starboard-main-top-gallant-bow-line,* or the *larboard-fore-top-sail-clue-line*" (65; emphasis in original). Although Melville's examples seem over the top, they are in fact the true names of lines found onboard a square-rigged sailing ship. Melville as always throws in humor with his reference to the "names of young royal princes." Unlike a prince's name, however, all parts of the rope's name are necessarily always used. Consider Melville's example: the "larboard-fore-top-sail-clue-line." Many sails have clewlines, so this particular line is distinguished by the fact that it is a *topsail* clewline. However, a full-rigged ship such as the *St. Lawrence* or the fictional *Highlander* has three topsails—one on each of the three masts—so this particular clewline is the clewline for the *fore* topsail. Even then, the fore topsail has two clewlines, so the line being referred to is the *larboard* (or port) clewline.

A full-rigged ship such as the *St. Lawrence* would have close to two hundred separate lines. By definition a line is a rope put to work. Once a rope is rigged into its place, it is, with very few exceptions—such as the footrope on which the sailors stand when working aloft, the boltrope sewn into the edges of the sails, and the bell rope used to ring the ship's bell—always called a line. The term "line" therefore refers to the function and its place within the context of the overall system of rigging. The material of which it is made is rope. Melville is correct that "People who have never gone to sea for the first time as sailors, can not imagine how puzzling and confounding it is" (*Redburn* 65). The lines are rigged in a pattern, however, that is mirrored from side to side, mast to mast, and ship to ship. Even a greenhand can usually master the names of all the lines within a week, as testified by the speed with which present-day students on sailing school vessels and trainees aboard the square-rigged ships at Mystic Seaport Museum learn the names and locations of all the lines. Line drills and constant repetition were— and are—used to reinforce knowledge of the lines. Being able to identify lines by name is far more than an esoteric pleasure; it is an absolute necessity. For example, braces are the lines fastened to the ends of the yards used to swivel those yards and the sails stretched between them from side to side to catch the wind from different angles. This means a ship can sail straight forward with wind coming from directly off the side. Sailors stand on footropes attached to the yards when setting and furling sails. If a sailor were to release a brace while his shipmates were working aloft, his action would cause the yard to swing wildly, and his shipmates could be thrown from the yard and flung to their deaths.

In Rudyard Kipling's *Captains Courageous* (1897), young Harvey Cheyne must learn the lines on a fishing vessel, admittedly a much simpler rig than that of the *St. Lawrence.* "For an hour [the experienced sailor] Long Jack walked his prey up and down, teaching, as he said, 'things at the sea that ivry [*sic*] man must know, blind, dhrunk [*sic*], or asleep.' There is not much gear to a seventy-ton schooner with a stump-foremast, but Long Jack had a gift of expression. When he wished to draw Harvey's attention to the peak-halyards, he dug his knuckles into the back of the boy's neck and kept him at gaze for half a minute."[5] Long Jack tells Harvey: "There's a good and just reason for ivry rope aboard, or else 't would be overboard."[6] Kipling repeats a scene found in countless sea narratives: that of a neophyte learning the equipment and workings of a ship. Of course, one purpose of such a scene is for the author to teach the reader the vocabulary and workings of an alien environment. For this reason, a high percentage of sea narratives are told from the point of view of a newcomer to the seafaring world. Patrick O'Brian stretches this device rather thin in the twenty books of his Aubrey-Maturin series, when he has Stephen Maturin, an otherwise highly intelligent and observant naturalist, linguist, and political spy, unable to learn the names of lines and the workings of a ship even after many years at sea with Captain Jack Aubrey. Wellingborough Redburn, Harvey Cheyne, and the students aboard sail-training ships acquire the same knowledge in a week.

When a writer uses sailor terminology correctly, the specificity of the language focuses the power of the writing in the same way that it focuses the actions of the crew. During the storm encountered by the warship *Neversink* off Cape Horn in *White-Jacket,* Captain Claret bursts from his cabin in his nightdress, shouting, "Hard *up* the helm!" (106; emphasis in original). This is the worst possible command under the circumstances, for it would make the shortening of the overstrained sails even more difficult. Putting the helm hard up would cause the vessel to turn away from the wind and therefore would create even more wind pressure on the sails from behind. Mad Jack, the lieutenant, countermands Captain Claret's order, crying: "Damn you! . . . Hard *down*—hard *down,* I say, and be damned to you!" (106; emphasis in original). Mad Jack's command is instantly obeyed. With less wind filling the sails, the men are able to reduce the amount of canvas, and the *Neversink* is rescued from foundering off Cape Horn. White-Jacket tells us, "I owe this right hand, that is this moment flying over my sheet, and all my present being to Mad Jack" (106).

Mad Jack's transcendent awareness of every element of the moment of crisis—the power and direction of wind and wave, the ship's position in relation to them, the resulting strain on line, spar, and sail, and the location and capability of the men at his command—exemplifies "present being." The absolute conviction with which he utters the countermanding order overrides the formal lines of authority. The crew's instantaneous and unthinking response encapsulates the ultimate identity of signifier, signified, and referent—and White-Jacket and all the crew live to tell the tale. Present being, indeed.

Mad Jack illustrates the importance of what Margaret Cohen, in a piece published in *New Literary History,* calls "know-how," which she defines as

> a particular intelligence, a kind of practical, results-oriented acumen making use of both theoretical and practical knowledge, including the most specific technical detail. This is a kind of knowledge I would call *know-how,* thinking of the term's associations with practice, skills, and technological savoir faire as well as Gilbert Ryle's distinction between "knowing how" and "knowing that." . . . The place of know-how is on the deck, not the desk; it reveals itself in particular conjunctures, at once random and specific to the location where they occur. Know-how requires an understanding of technology, which is demonstrated in the ability to use it (what is called in manuals of practical seamanship "performance"), rather than to explain it, which is always taken as a gauge of knowing that. But the full power of know-how is revealed only when a technology reaches its limit, whether because it breaks down or because it does not suffice on its own. Know-how is opposed to domination or sheer force. As much an art as a science, know-how is needed in future-oriented situations whose outcomes are uncertain, particularly in boundary zones which push existing technologies and knowledge to their limits. The extreme nature of boundary zones aggravates the kind of provisional and shifting conditions that know-how navigates with flexibility, cunning, prudence, foresight, and audacity.[7]

Mad Jack certainly responds to the critical situation in which the *Neversink* finds herself with "flexibility, cunning, prudence, foresight, and audacity." Cohen's conceptualization of know-how is illustrated in sailor language, especially in the correct use of nautical terminology.

Writers who use the language of sailors have occasionally been criticized for the obscurity of that language or for cliquishness. Samuel Johnson declares in *Prefaces Biographical and Critical* (1779), now known as *The Lives of the English Poets,* that such use was not acceptable: "It is a general rule in poetry that all appropriated terms of art should be sunk in general expressions because poetry is to speak an universal language. This rule is still stronger with regard to arts not liberal or confined to few, and therefore far removed from common knowledge; and of this kind certainly is technical knowledge." Quoting a passage from John Dryden's *Annus Mirabilis* (1667) with such forbidden words as "calking-iron," "marling," and "shrouds," Johnson writes: "I suppose here is not one term which every reader does not wish away."[8]

Sailor terminology is often rendered humorously. Greg Dening notes in *Mr. Bligh's Bad Language:* "The precise, terse, unequivocal language by which seamen controlled their 'wooden world' was thought to be incongruous and laughable on land. Otherness . . . is often controlled by a joke."[9] For this reason, a sailor on land was frequently portrayed as a buffoon. Yet sailors do not use nautical terminology at whim. When ashore, they do not say, "Ahoy, mateys. Let's tack to starboard," instead of "Let's turn right." Such use of sailor talk separates them from all landsmen by turning them into caricatures—caricatures that dehumanize sailors, depicting them as childish and carefree but fundamentally unintelligent, only capable when installed in their particular shipboard environment. Dening writes that "Georgian England invented the jolly, simple, incongruous tar."[10] Cartoon characters such as Popeye the Sailor Man exemplify and perpetuate this stereotypical view of seamen. Sailors were perceived as free and independent, able to fly across the waves, leaving the sordidness and politics of the land astern. This freedom frightened those left behind, and the image of the sailor as awkward and simple on land, unable to speak the common vernacular, less than fully human, controlled that fear.

At sea, the specificity of sailor language is an absolute necessity for the safety of the ship and crew. The cry "Let fly fore t'gallant sheets. Haul clews!" results in one direct action that may be crucial to keep the vessel from destruction. In obedience to this cry, the sailors release the lines attached to the corners of the fore topgallant sail, the third-highest sail on the mast in the front of the ship, and bundle it up, thus releasing the wind from the sail and allowing the vessel's bow to lift up. Without such an action, the wind filling even a lowered fore topgallant sail could drive the vessel underwater.

Another example of specificity is the use of the term "avast" for "stop." "Stop" is employed in everyday life and will cause an action to terminate, but the power of "avast" is that it cuts through common vernacular and results in instantaneous cessation. Unambiguous language dictates definite and specific actions.

The necessity for this highly specific language derives from the complex technology of sailing ships and the tremendous power of the forces they engage. A sailing vessel is in essence a machine that enables a navigator to translate the power of wind into directed motion. An able navigator with a well-found vessel and sufficient sea room can eventually move a vessel to points straight upwind from the point of origin. The body of knowledge and set of skills required to effect this must sometimes be exercised almost instantaneously in the face of tremendous natural forces.

Used correctly, and sparingly, nautical terminology enhances literary text. But used incorrectly, what, in Melville's words, will compare with it (*Moby-Dick* 6)? One has only to read Sena Jeter Naslund's *Ahab's Wife* to see how egregious the disconnect between signifier and signified can become.[11] In 1849, James Fenimore Cooper published a new preface to *The Pilot* (1824), in which he explains that he wrote *The Pilot* out of frustration at Walter Scott's poor knowledge and portrayal of seamanship in *The Pirate* (1821). Cooper responds to a friend's comment on Scott's knowledge of the sea as evidenced in *The Pirate:*

> It would have been hypercritical to object to the Pirate, that it was not strictly nautical, or true in its details; but, when the reverse was urged as a proof of what, considering the character of other portions of the work, would have been most extraordinary attainments, it was a sort of provocation to dispute the seamanship of the Pirate, a quality to which the book has certainly very little just pretension. The result of this conversation was a sudden determination to produce a work which, if it had no other merit, might present truer pictures of the ocean and ships than any that are to be found in the Pirate.[12]

The result of this provocation, *The Pilot,* is generally considered the first true sea novel. Cooper believed that a writer needs direct acquaintance with maritime life in order to write authentic maritime fiction.

The misuse of sailor terminology can be seen in the fo'c's'le song "Paddy West." A fo'c's'le song was not a chantey or work song, but one sung for enjoyment by sailors while off duty. In "Paddy West," the title character is a Liverpool boardinghouse keeper who could "school" a greenhand into an able-bodied sailor in one week rather than the usual four years. While he persuaded the greenhands that this schooling was to their benefit so they could earn a higher wage immediately, he was in fact being purely rapacious, as he collected a higher fee for shipping an able-bodied seaman than for shipping a greenhand. Once the sailor was at sea, the subterfuge would immediately become apparent, and the sailor's rating and pay rate would be reduced to that of a greenhand, although Paddy West's whole fee would still be deducted from the sailor's now-reduced wage. Paddy West gives the greenhands a surface brushing of sailor terminology and also uses mnemonic devices such as walking around a horn.

> Now [Paddy West] axed me if I had ever bin to sea,
> I told him not till that morn;
> "Well, be Jasus," sez he, "a sailor ye'll be,
> From the hour that yiz wuz born;
> Just go into the parlour, walk round the ol' cow-horn,
> An tell the mate that ye have bin, oh, three times round the Horn!"[13]

The "Horn" referred to is Cape Horn; to sail around Cape Horn was the ultimate test of a sailor. As Melville states in *White-Jacket:*

> Who has not heard of it? Cape Horn, Cape Horn—a *horn* indeed, that has tossed many a good ship. Was the descent of Orpheus, Ulysses, or Dante into Hell, one whit more hardy and sublime than the first navigator's weathering of that terrible Cape? . . . You may approach it from this direction or that—in any way you please—from the East, or from the West; with the wind astern, or abeam, or on the quarter; and still Cape Horn is Cape Horn. Cape Horn it is that takes the conceit out of fresh-water sailors, and steeps in a still salter brine the saltest. (96–97)

Melville writes as someone who has seen the full power of Cape Horn, which he rounded twice, first en route to the Pacific aboard the whaleship *Acushnet* and then homeward bound from the Pacific aboard the naval frigate *United States.* Paddy West willfully, wrongly, undermines the true skill required to sail around Cape Horn when he has a greenhand walk around a cow's horn and then ship as an able-bodied sailor. Experienced sailors deeply resented such subterfuge, because it meant that the ship left port without a full complement of able-bodied sailors, and so those with experience and knowledge had to work that much harder.

Paddy West played a similar trick with a line, having a greenhand step back and forth across a line stretched on the floor, so he could say he had crossed "the line," the sailor's term for the equator. Melville and the crew of the *Acushnet* engaged in similar wordplay. Melville's shipmate, Richard Tobias Greene, wrote to the *Sandusky Register* in 1855:

> We had a shipmate once, whom we named "Jack Nastyface," from the fact that his face was as rough as a MacAdemized road. The first time that we

crossed the equator in the Pacific, "Jack" was at the mast head looking out for whales. As soon as "eight bells" were struck, and "Jack" was relieved, he was informed that we had crossed the line. "Jack" never would be behind anybody in intelligence. "The devil we did!" says "Jack." "Can't ye tell us some news? didn't I see it as well as you did, and better too? wasn't I aloft? I saw the line before any man aboard."[14]

Greene tells this story for its humor. The song "Paddy West" is much more equivocal. The song itself is funny and clever, but it covers a deep resentment and anger on the part of all sailors toward charlatans like Paddy West.

Melville learned basic sailor terminology aboard the merchant vessel *St. Lawrence,* but the language he acquired from his first voyage was not sufficient when he signed onboard the whaleship *Acushnet.* There he had to acquire the additional idiom of whaling. Peleg tells Ishmael when he applies to sail on the *Pequod,* "Merchant service be damned. Talk not that lingo to me" (*Moby-Dick* 71).

The incompatibility between the two languages is seen in *White-Jacket.* Peleg has raised whaling above the merchant service, but Jack Chase reverses the order and more conventionally places whaling at the bottom of the hierarchy, with the merchant service above it, and naval service as the pinnacle. Tubbs, a whaleman newly recruited into the navy, "a long, lank Vineyarder, eternally talking of line-tubs, Nantucket, sperm oil, stove boats, and Japan" (15), is invited to the maintop. Flattered, he quickly climbs aloft to join the other sailors and begins to laud his former occupation. Outraged, Jack Chase bursts out:

Why, you limb of Nantucket! you train-oil man! you sea-tallow strainer! you bobber after carrion! . . . And what did you know, you bumpkin! before you came on board this *Andrew Miller?* What knew you of gun-deck, or orlop, mustering round the capstan, beating to quarters, and piping to dinner? Did you ever roll to *grog* on board your greasy bally-hoo of blazes? Did you ever winter at Mahon? Did you ever "*lash and carry*?" . . . Bah! You are full of the fore-peak and the forecastle; you are only familiar with Burtons and Billy-tackles; your ambition never mounted above pig-killing! which, in my poor opinion, is the proper phrase for whaling! Top-mates! has not this Tubbs here been but a misuser of good oak planks, and a vile desecrator of the thrice holy sea? . . . Begone! you graceless, godless knave! (16)

Jack Chase condemns Tubbs's language—although, interestingly, he is able to use it correctly when he himself speaks of "train-oil," "burtons," and "billy-tackles"—and praises his own. Knowledge of the specificity of "orlop," "mustering," and "beating to quarters" is necessary for survival on a man-of-war, both within the ship and against one's enemies.

Perhaps Melville was on the receiving end of speeches similar to the above withering blast when he first joined the naval vessel *United States* and attempted to establish his status in a way similar to Tubbs. One would conjecture that he learned quickly from such faux pas and, incipient master of language that he was, put the full force of his intelligence to learning this new dialect. Like Jack Chase, Melville could use the language of several different maritime trades. By the time he began writing, he had spent almost four years at sea. He was immersed in the language of sailors. Such language was essential to his early works—not, now, to blow a ship on its course, but to speed his narrative along.

Social Talk

Sailor talk has a social importance as well as a physical importance. Nautical terminology is important for keeping the sailors alive—the breath in their bodies, the wind in their sails—but occupational lore and coterie speech keep their social groups working. These forms of sailor talk illustrate how sailors make friends, keep their social bonds tight, and combat isolation.

Jack Chase crosses from technical terminology into generalized occupational lore in the quotation above. Occupational lore is the lore that is known and understood throughout an occupational group, such as sailors, or more specifically throughout an occupational subgroup such as whalemen, man-of-war's men, or coastermen. Jack's question "Did you ever winter at Mahon?" is an example of occupational lore. Port Mahon on the Spanish island of Minorca served as a winter base for the American naval fleet between 1815 and 1826, and many American midshipmen received their naval training there. Port Mahon also connects the American navy and Chase, a British sailor serving in the American fleet, with the British navy, because the British held Port Mahon off and on throughout the Napoleonic wars. These varied references were understood by Chase's shipmates aboard the man-of-war.

Tubbs cannot use the language of the man-of-war and therefore is godless—"Begone! you graceless, godless knave!" (*White-Jacket* 16)—without access to the holy; he is not a blasphemer like Ahab, but simply godless. The correct use of language evokes divinity: "In the beginning was the Word, and the Word was with God, and the Word was God" (John 1:1). Likewise one of the signal attributes of Adam, the first human, is that he names all things.

Wellingborough Redburn bumps into occupational lore when he ignorantly tries to make conversation with an experienced sailor: "To my great surprise and mortification, he in the rudest kind of manner laughed aloud in my face, and called me a 'Jimmy Dux,' though that was not my real name, and he must have known it; and also the 'son of a farmer,' though as I have previously related, my father was a great merchant and French importer in Broad-street in New York" (*Redburn* 49). Jimmy Dux is the man onboard ship who takes care of the poultry. Sailors consider such a man contemptible because of his connection with land animals and thus with the land. Seamen revile landsmen, especially farmers and soldiers, for their lack of seafaring knowledge. In fact, "sojering," the sailor's term for avoiding work—"*sogering,* as they called it; that is, any thing that savored of a desire to get rid of downright hard work" (*Redburn* 59)—derives from the word "soldier." A soldier is perceived as the ultimate landsman, and landsmen are thought to be incapable of the real work demanded of sailors. The short verse "We'll all shave under the chin," from the bunting chantey "Paddy Doyle's Boots," reinforces sailors' perception of themselves as real men. Only real men can grow beards; therefore, only real men shave under the chin. Interestingly, the average age of whalemen was nineteen: many whalemen sailed at the age of sixteen, seventeen, or eighteen. How many of them, one wonders, actually *needed* to shave under the chin?

Sometimes the occupational lore of sailors was simply an understood allusion, often difficult to recover a century and a half later. When the sailors sang about "the girls in Booble Alley" (*Moby-Dick* 103) as they raised the anchor, they knew it was a reference to Liverpool prostitutes, even if we do not. "Booble Alley" is recorded in a variant of the tack-and-sheet chantey "Haul Away, Joe."[15] Similarly, the "Sally Brown" who inhabits so many of the sailors' work songs is a prostitute. Sailors understood the "line" to be the equator and the "Horn" to be Cape Horn. "Jack Nastyface" was such a common term for a sailor whose face was pitted by smallpox that it was used by William Robinson as the title of his 1805 novel.

The socialization of sailors in the context of a particular trade is implicit in occupational lore and coterie speech. Coterie speech is the speech used within a community. It is coded so that the listener only has to hear part of the reference to understand the whole. It is different from idiolect (the speech pattern of one individual at a particular period of his or her life) because of its community base, and from dialect, defined here as the variety of a language used by members of an occupational group, because it refers to a subset within an occupational group. Coterie speech is spoken by a group of individuals who have been around each other long enough to establish a coded language more specific than the particular language of their occupation.

The term "coterie speech" as I use it here comes from the scholarship surrounding Thomas and especially Jane Carlyle. Thomas Carlyle writes of the coterie speech that appears in his wife's letters: "*Coterie-sprache,* as the Germans call it, 'family circle dialect,' occurs every line or two; nobody ever so rich in that as she; ready to pick up every diamond-spark, out of the common floor-dust, and keep it brightly available; so that hardly, I think, in any house, was there more of *coterie-sprache*, shining innocently, with a perpetual expressiveness and twinkle generally of quiz and real humour about it, than ours."[16] Sailors lived in such close quarters for such a great length of time that they, too, developed *coterie-sprache*, the type of coded speech usually found only within families.

An example of coterie speech appears in *Moby-Dick* in the "Clam or Cod?" scene at the Try Pots. When Ishmael and Queequeg arrive at the tavern, the tavern keeper's wife, Mrs. Hussey, ushers them to a table and asks, "Clam or Cod?" Ishmael has great fun with this question:

> "What's that about Cods, ma'am?" said I, with much politeness.
> "Clam or Cod?" she repeated.
> "A clam for supper? a cold clam; is *that* what you mean, Mrs. Hussey?" says I; "but that's a rather cold and clammy reception in the winter time, ain't it, Mrs. Hussey?" (66).

Mrs. Hussey's elliptical question is coterie speech. She expects all whalemen resident in her tavern to understand her question despite its brevity. And anyone resident even one day would understand, for "Fishiest of all fishy places was the Try Pots, which well deserved its name; for the pots there were always boiling chowders. Chowders for breakfast, and chowder for dinner, and chowder for supper, till you began to look for fish-bones coming through your clothes" (67). Ishmael and Queequeg have just arrived, however, and so do not yet understand the coterie speech. Melville's sophisticated use of such coterie speech shows in the humorousness of Ishmael's misunderstanding and the exuberance with which Melville plays with the word "clam."

The coterie speech of sailors often appears in the sea music they created. Helen Creighton collected "The Eight Famous Fishermen," composed and sung by Edward Deal of Seabright, Nova Scotia. Verses 5 and 6 in particular contain coterie speech:

> 5. Now there is George Hubley, the splitting machine,
> The tub and the table which he stands between,
> With his bald head a-shining and his chizzy-cat grin
> He looks like the moon rising over Benny's old hill.
> 6. There is Byron McDonald in an old pair of brogues
> With a baseball team of whiskers smeared over his jaws,
> With a baseball team of whiskers and his long eagle claws
> He pulls the gills out from their tails to their jaws.[17]

George Hubley's placement between the tub and the splitting board ("the table") and Byron McDonald's way of pulling the gills from the fish, presumably codfish, are simply occupational knowledge, but "Benny's old hill" and "a baseball team" of whiskers are coterie speech. The other fishermen would know the location of Benny's old hill and why the moon rising above it is noteworthy. The baseball team of whiskers is intriguing. Does that mean that Byron McDonald has only nine whiskers on his jaws, but that those nine whiskers are long and therefore get smeared over his jaws by fish slime? Or is there another allusion lost to those of us not in his coterie group?

"The Eight Famous Fishermen" was written for the coterie mentioned in the song and had great significance for them. The song would be fully fleshed out by their shared memory. The baseball team of whiskers is something everybody knows: the fishermen see that face all their working days. The song has much less significance for us.

Another sailor's song that contains coterie speech is "Shearing Day," written aboard the whaleship *Maria* by first mate Charles Murphy in 1832 and collected by Gale Huntington in *Songs the Whalemen Sang*. Murphy was homesick for this annual event on Nantucket, which Melville mentions in the "The Quarter-Deck," chapter 36 of *Moby-Dick:* "Aye, Daggoo, his spout is a big one, like a whole shock of wheat, and white as a pile of our Nantucket wool after the great annual sheep-shearing" (162). Verse 10 of Murphy's song reads:

> Now all the Siasconsett folks
> Drive into town like thunder
> And rattling o'er the pavement they
> Make gawkies stare and wonder.[18]

Murphy's coterie group of Nantucket whalemen would know the term "gawkies," where Siasconsett is, how far it is from the main town, and the fact that the main town is paved with cobblestones, whereas most of the roads on Nantucket are dirt and therefore a wagon rattling over the cobblestones would sound like thunder.[19]

Coterie speech among sailors is found in the nicknames they bestow on each other. Many of these occur in Melville. Doctor Long Ghost, Dough-Boy, and old Mogul for Ahab (*Moby-Dick* 174) are just a few. In *Omoo,* one of his new ship-mates cries to the narrator: "Halloa, who's that croaking? . . . Ay, Typee, my king of the cannibals, is it you! But I say, my lad, how's that spar of your'n? the mate says it's in a devil of a way; and last night set the steward to sharpening the handsaw: hope he won't have the carving of ye" (8). The narrator is indeed traveling under the name of a tribe reputed to be fearsome cannibals, and this joking remark accords him royal status. The Taipi were second only to Fijians in their reputation as savage cannibals. Since this is coded speech, details of the Taipi reputation need not be given; it is enough to use the term "king of the cannibals." Spars are masts, yards, gaffs, and booms—the wooden parts of the rig to which sails and lines are attached. The narrator's injured leg does indeed resemble a spar, and his shipmate suggests that it will need to be amputated, sawn off as one would saw off a broken boom, in order to prevent gangrenous infection from spreading throughout the injured sailor's body. The same tool, a handsaw, is used in both cases. Rather than simply asking, "How are you?" the shipmate employs coterie speech, and his short communication with the narrator becomes simultaneously terrifying and darkly humorous.

In Joseph Conrad's *The Nigger of the* Narcissus (1897), the *Narcissus* has been knocked down in a storm. The men lash themselves to the rail in bitter cold to keep from being swept over the side. Mr. Baker, the chief mate, tells Podmore, the cook, that the men are perishing from the cold and asks him to get them a little water. Podmore makes his way on the vertical deck forward to the galley, crying, "As long as she swims I will cook! I will get you coffee."[20] After the cook *does* reappear, incredibly, a long time later with coffee so hot that it blisters the men's mouths, his statement becomes coterie speech. The narrator tells us: "Later, whenever one of us was puzzled by a task and advised to relinquish it, he would express his determination to persevere and to succeed by the words:—'As long as she swims I will cook!'"[21]

A similar scene occurs in Richard Henry Dana Jr.'s *Two Years Before the Mast,* written almost fifty years before *The Nigger of the* Narcissus. The mate relishes the speed with which the *Alert* flies across the waves, although all the vessel's spars are snapping and creaking under the spread of too much canvas. He cries out, in words that prefigure Podmore's, "There she goes!—There she goes,—handsomely!—As long as she cracks she holds!"[22] The ship continues to fly northward, and the seamen make a ritual exchange at the change of watch in words that are coterie speech grounded in occupational speech and folklore: "At each change of the watch, those coming on deck asked those going below—'How does she go along?' and got for answer, the rate [the vessel's speed], and the customary addition—'Aye! and the Boston girls have had hold of the tow-rope all the watch, and can't haul half the slack in!'"[23] The image of girls hauling on the tow-rope to pull the sailors back home to them as fast as possible becomes a standard trope in sea music soon after this, but Dana plays with this image by suggesting that the *Alert* moves so quickly that the vessel overruns the tow-rope and the girls cannot keep up with the slack.

In *Moby-Dick*, the cook Fleece's statement at the end of "Stubb's Supper" (chapter 64) has every chance of becoming part of the coterie speech of the whalemen. Fleece mutters, "I'm bressed if [Stubb] ain't more of shark dan Massa

Shark hisself" (297). Similarly, Queequeg's statement after he is bitten by a dead shark—"Queequeg no care what god made him shark . . . wedder Fejee god or Nantucket god; but de god wat made shark must be one dam Ingin" (*Moby-Dick* 302)—also has the markings of becoming part of coterie speech. Melville's placement of both statements at the end of their respective chapters reinforces this perspective on them. Imagine if the crew had heard Fleece's statement, which was muttered alone and in the dark, or if more than presumably Ishmael alone had heard Queequeg. Then, these statements, like Podmore's, would have become coterie speech for the whalemen—just as they have for Melville scholars and other readers of *Moby-Dick,* for such readers quote these lines frequently.

In the above examples, coterie speech, or coded language, occurs between shipmates. In *Typee,* however, the narrator, Tommo, directly addresses the reader in code: "The 'Dolly' was fairly captured; and never I will say was vessel carried before by such a dashing and irresistible party of boarders! The ship taken, we could not do otherwise than yield ourselves prisoners" (15). By using metaphors of naval battle, Melville can avoid saying directly what occurs when the beautiful, young Marquesan girls swarm over the gunwales of the *Dolly* and greet the sex-deprived sailors. Yet he knows that the reader knows how to break the linguistic metaphoric code. The multilayering of these two sentences involves the knowledge of the erotic nature of what is occurring, the enjoyment of breaking the code, the knowingness of Tommo's direct address to the reader, the fun of the military allusions, and the pleasure of all these sensations combined.

Sailor talk was uniquely shaped by the length of time mariners spent in isolation from the rest of the world, the closeness engendered between men who depended on each other for their lives, and the wonders they encountered. Mariners beheld nature at its most sublime, but they were also forced to live in appalling conditions, with little fresh air, less light, and absolutely no privacy for years on end. The average whaling voyage lasted two to five years, a weary length of time.

Being continuously at sea, completely cut off from the land, led to a profound seclusion that in turn engendered sailor talk. This seclusion is difficult for non-sailors to comprehend. In pre-radio days, the crew of a ship at sea was far more isolated than any astronaut and in an environment that could be more hostile. Space itself can kill a human, but it is not actively trying to invade and kill you or wear down your ship, as the sea is.

Such isolation, with its settled routine, lack of distractions, and sense of camaraderie, can lead to happiness. Conrad writes in *The Nigger of the* Narcissus: "The men working about the deck were healthy and contented—as most seamen are, when once well out to sea. The true peace of God begins at any spot a thousand miles from the nearest land."[24] Melville asks in *Moby-Dick:* "Why upon your first voyage as a passenger, did you yourself feel such a mystical vibration, when first told that you and your ship were now out of sight of land?" (5). "What most amazed me," Redburn tells us, "was the sight of the great ocean itself, for we were out of sight of land. . . . Never did I realize till now what the ocean was: how grand and majestic, how solitary, and boundless, and beautiful and blue" (*Redburn* 64). The alliteration of the last passage emphasizes Redburn's poetic vision of the ocean.

The thought of being out of sight of land can be alluring, but Melville sees the tyranny that can come with such isolation, for which the nineteenth-century sailor had little or no legal recourse. The captain and officers held sway aboard ship, and consuls and courts on land favored those same officers if a case actually did make it to court. Melville asks in *Typee:* "To whom could we apply for redress? We had left both law and equity on the other side of the Cape" (21). Dana's *Two Years before the Mast* powerfully presents an example of such lawlessness. After flogging a sailor without just cause, Captain Frank Thompson states: "If you want to know what I flog you for, I'll tell you. It's because I like to do it!—because I like to do it!—It suits me! That's what I do it for!" The sailor cries out in pain, "Oh, Jesus Christ! Oh, Jesus Christ!" The captain responds, "Don't call on Jesus Christ . . . *he can't help you. Call on Captain T———. He's the man! He can help you! Jesus Christ can't help you now!"[25]

Melville drew on the social language of sailors in multiple ways. At times such language makes the reader a part of the inner circle; the reader is not the newly arrived Wellingborough Redburn aboard the *Highlander,* but an experienced sailor who understands the social boundaries. At other times Melville uses the social language of sailors to draw the lines more forcefully around his narrative. We are emphatically not in the coterie group. We must remain on the outside looking in. Most of us will never truly understand the utter isolation of being at sea for months on end. And such a story as *Moby-Dick* can only happen in the midst of such isolation.

Play Talk

Although often illiterate, sailors nonetheless created a rich oral repository of information and stories during their separation from the shore. These oral repositories are seen in sailors' songs, arguments, and yarning. A study of sailors' work songs is revealing. There certainly were bawdy work songs, but far more chanteys exploiting such verbal dexterity as double entendre and word substitution survive and are ultimately more satisfying. The variant verse line from the pumps chantey "The Ebenezer"—"Our bread wuz tough as any brass,/ An' the meat wuz as salt as Lot's wife's feet"—is far more humorous than the insertion of a less dignified word to rhyme with "brass."[26] The richness of this verse line is also found in its reference to Genesis 19:26—"But Lot's wife behind him looked back, and she became a pillar of salt"—and the irreverence with which it plays with that reference.

The lengthy voyages commencing in the age of exploration gave rise to the development of a broad vernacular sea music literature. The highly expressive Portuguese music known as fado, for instance, is sometimes said to have its roots in the laments written by fifteenth-century Portuguese sailors. The increasing conflict between European maritime powers spawned a wealth of balladry concerning naval actions and piracy. These ballads, love songs and laments rooted in the medieval song traditions of the troubadours and trouvères, topical songs, and event songs formed the basis for much of what existed as sea music into the late eighteenth century. The rapid expansion of wind-powered commercial shipping and the dwindling of naval warfare and piracy under sail created the shipboard traditions that led to the rise of the work songs that came to be known as chanteys. It is important to note that the word "chantey" itself does not appear in print before the mid-nineteenth century. Indeed, Melville himself never uses it. The expanded rigging plans and reduced crew numbers of cargo ships in the 1820s and 1830s created an increased need for the rhythmic coordination of work provided by song. The origins of chanteying are obscure, but certainly the cotton ports of Mobile, Alabama, and New Orleans were seminal locations. The jumble of cultures and the commercial hothouse in these busy ports led to a rich musical exchange between Irish and African American cotton stowers and dock workers, American frontiersmen bringing cargo to market on rafts and later steamboats, West Indians, and the international crews of commercial shipping. The driving call-and-response work songs deriving from African traditions gave form to a whole new catalog of songs fitted to the varying physical motions. Within these repetitive forms, sets of conventional "floating verses" mixed with more spontaneous improvisations and occasional composed texts to create a shared occupational musical literature that by the 1850s was widespread to the point of ubiquity aboard deepwater commercial shipping.

The song "Spanish Ladies" begins "Midnight, Forecastle," chapter 40 of *Moby-Dick*. Melville uses this particular song to begin the chapter in which the men react collectively to the overwhelming tension created by Ahab's declaration that they have shipped to hunt the white whale. "Spanish Ladies," then, begins a chapter of intensely shared experience. The song itself partakes of the more broadly shared experience of a much wider group: in this case, British naval sailors in the Napoleonic era. That shared experience is precisely the point of the song, for the song contains no drama, no real narrative, and no characters; rather, it embodies a state of mind created by a particular experience shared by members of this group. The impact of the song lies in the details of technical knowledge that carry on from verse to verse and that are also found in the chorus:

We'll rant an' we'll roar, like true British sailors,
We'll rant an' we'll rave across the salt seas.
'Till we strike soundings in the Channel of Old England.
From Ushant to Scilly is thirty-four leagues.[27]

"Ushant," spelled "Ouessant" by the French, is the British rendering of the name of the westernmost island in Brittany at the mouth of the English Channel. The Scilly Islands lie north-northwest on the British side of the channel—as the song says, thirty-four leagues, or roughly one hundred miles, away. A vessel making the passage from the Bay of Biscay to London would cross that stretch of water and pass the series of headlands in the exact order named in the song: Deadman, Ramshead off Plymouth, Start, Portland, Wight, Beachie, Fairlee, Dungeyness, and the South Foreland Light. For the listener who had shared this experience, the song would call up the emotions of the approach of home, liberty, and safety. The rest of the song continues to use technical and navigational details to reinforce the sense of camaraderie that motivates the song. Even for listeners thoroughly unversed in the nautical, the detailed references build a clear picture that is enhanced by a melody strong enough that it was parodied in numerous other nautical songs, such as "Talcahuano Girls." "Spanish Ladies" remains current in popular culture, as evidenced by the film *Jaws* (1975)—it is the song that Quint sings constantly as he trudges the deck of his fishing boat. "Spanish Ladies" is also sung by the crew of HMS *Surprise* in the film *Master and Commander* (2003). Interestingly, "Spanish Ladies" is one of only three songs for which Melville gives lyrics in *Moby-Dick*. It is fitting that the song itself is included in the film *Jaws*, for Peter Benchley consciously wrote the novel *Jaws* (1974) as an updating of *Moby-Dick*.

The range of the rich oral repository of information and stories that sailors created in their songs can be seen in the use of technical terms in the capstan chantey "The Old Moke Pickin' on the Banjo,"[28] in the depiction of a beachcomber falling in love with a Fayaway-like maiden in the ballad "The Lass of Mowee," recorded aboard the whaleship *Cortes* in 1847 and extant in many versions,[29] and in the visceral tale of double murder in the capstan chantey "Aboard the Henry Clay."[30]

Songs were not the only oral repository of information. Sailors often transmitted knowledge through argument, which at times became a form of verbal art. The seal hunters in Jack London's *The Sea Wolf* (1904) argue about whether a seal pup is born knowing how to swim or not:

[Kerfoot, one of the hunters, was] vociferating, bellowing, waving his arms, and cursing like a fiend, and all because of a disagreement with another hunter as to whether a seal pup knew instinctively how to swim. He held that it did, that it could swim the moment it was born. The other hunter, Latimer . . . held otherwise, held that the seal pup was born on the land for no other reason than that it could not swim, that its mother was compelled to teach it to swim as birds were compelled to teach their nestlings how to fly.

For the most part, the remaining four hunters leaned on the table or lay in their bunks and left the discussion to the two antagonists. But they were supremely interested, for every little while they ardently took sides, and sometimes all were talking at once, till their voices surged back and forth in waves of sound like mimic thunder-rolls in the confined space.[31]

Frederick Pease Harlow has a similar scene in *The Making of a Sailor* (1928), his narrative of sailing as a young man in the 1870s aboard the full-rigged ship *Akbar*. Two sailors argue about which of two lighthouses, Cape Cod Light or Navesink Light, is brighter. To stop the argument, the young Harlow consults the *Light List* published by the Department of Commerce. Both men are disappointed: the argument itself, not the answer to the argument, is the purpose of the conversation and the source of the sailors' enjoyment. O'Rourke cries, "'An phat th' bloody hell do th' book know about candlepower? Any——could print thet in a book." Harlow continues: "Dave and O'Rourke went on with their argument until [Cape Cod] light disappeared in the distance astern."[32]

In *Redburn*, two sailors dispute over who has been seafaring the longest. Their shipmate Jackson, a true Jack Nastyface, by Melville's description of him, ends the dispute, to the disappointment of the arguers and the discomfort of the other sailors, by looking in their mouths, "for, said he, I can tell a sailor's age just like a horse's—by his teeth." Jackson probes in one sailor's mouth with a jackknife, and Redburn trembles for the man, for Jackson looks as if he longs to kill him. At last Jackson declares that "the first man was the oldest sailor, for the ends of his teeth were the evenest and most worn down; which, he said, arose from eating so much hard sea-biscuit" (60). The crew uncomfortably laughs a little too loudly. Harlow ends a sailors' argument, a verbal play in which, in Jack London's words, the sailors are "supremely interested," out of innocence. Jackson is not innocent; he ends a sailors' argument as an act of dominance. The violence of his act is seen in his drawing of his knife and in his eye, which Redburn, alluding to Satan, describes as "snapping, and a sort of going in and out, very quick, as if it were something like a forked tongue" (60). Jackson's statement that the older sailor's teeth are more worn down from eating sea biscuit partakes of the verbal exaggeration that is so integral to the humor of sailor talk. And his shipmates do laugh—but they laugh out of fear and discomfort, not out of enjoyment.

The verbal richness of sailor talk can be seen in work songs and arguments, but it is most obvious in sailors' yarns. Such yarns often follow a similar pattern. First, the teller of the yarn lays the groundwork for the yarn with not only believable but mundane and picayune detail that seems unquestionable. This is followed by a believable crisis. The yarn concludes with a preposterous ending, any particular detail of which is predicated on the earlier material, leading the listener to credulity until the ultimate moment (and, for the unwary innocent, beyond).

An example of such a yarn occurs toward the beginning of *Typee*. Melville discourses on the length of South Sea whaling voyages. He tells us of the quantity of provisions put onboard a whaleship in "successive tiers of casks and barrels" (22). This believable, mundane detail appears unquestionable—and indeed it is completely factual. The crisis that follows is the length of the voyage that these tiers upon tiers of provisions signify. For a ship's company to consume so many provisions literally took years. As already noted, the average whaling voyage lasted between two and five years. Melville's yarn concludes with the preposterous story of the whaleship *Perseverance*:

> Spoken somewhere in the vicinity of the ends of the earth, cruizing along as leisurely as ever, her sails all bepatched and bequilted with rope-yarns, her spars fished with old pipe staves, and her rigging knotted and spliced in every possible direction. Her crew was composed of some twenty venerable Greenwich-pensioner-looking old salts, who just managed to hobble about the deck. . . . Her hull was incrusted with barnacles, which completely encased her. Three pet sharks followed in her wake, and every day came alongside to regale themselves from the contents of the cook's bucket, which were pitched over to them. A vast shoal of bonetas and albicores always kept her company. . . . She never reached home, and I suppose she is still regularly tacking twice in the twenty-four hours somewhere off Buggerry Island, or the Devil's-Tail Peak. (22–23)

The details of this story are realistic. Sails could be patched with rope yarns, the spun fibers that are twisted counterclockwise to form the strands of a rope. The hull of a vessel that long at sea would certainly be encrusted with barnacles, and both sharks and shoals of fish are known to follow vessels far offshore. But the preposterousness of the vessel's length of time at sea is made explicit with her twice-daily tacking off the fantastical—and homoerotic—Buggerry Island and Devil's-Tail Peak.

Typee itself follows the standard pattern for a sailor's yarn. Indeed, Melville tells us in the preface to *Typee:* "The incidents recorded in the following pages have often served, when 'spun as a yarn,' not only to relieve the weariness of many a night-watch at sea, but to excite the warmest sympathies of the author's ship-mates" (xiii). Melville lays the groundwork for the yarn with credible details of Tommo's life at sea, which lead to his decision to desert his ship, and then with detailed descriptions of the inhabitants of the Typee valley. This groundwork is followed by a believable crisis, that of Tommo's belief that the Typees are holding him in captivity until such time as they are ready to devour him, and concludes with a preposterous ending: Tommo's escape from the Typee valley, including the sailors' mauling of the wrists of a pursuing Typee with their knives and Tommo's savage attack on Mow-Mow. Any particular detail of this ending is predicated on the earlier material and leads the listener—and eventually the reader—to credulity until the ultimate moment—and for some, beyond.

Melville was very conscious, even if we are not, of the close ties between his narrative and sailor's yarns. In *Typee* Melville first establishes the oral quality that characterizes much of his writing and most of his maritime work. Even with the addition of information from written sources such as David Porter's *Journal of a Cruise*, most of *Typee* still reads like a told tale.

Jackson's yarns in *Redburn* evoke different emotions. Jackson's yarning is foul, besmirched; his yarns reflect his disagreeable personality. Redburn tells us:

> His whole talk was of this kind; full of piracies, plagues and poisonings. And often he narrated many passages in his own individual career, which were almost incredible, from the consideration that few men could have plunged into such infamous vices, and clung to them so long, without paying the death-penalty.
>
> But in truth, he carried about with him the traces of these things, and the mark of a fearful end nigh at hand. . . . Nothing was left of this Jackson but the foul lees and dregs of a man. (58)

Here Melville's alliteration on the letter *p* invokes not beauty but disagreeableness. Jackson's yarns are exaggerated, but it is not the lighthearted exaggeration so characteristic of sailor yarns; rather, it is sordid and sad. The finality of Melville's last sentence is unsettling: "Nothing was left of this Jackson but the foul lees and dregs of a man."

An important section of *Moby-Dick* is presented as a yarn: chapter 54, entitled "The Town-Ho's Story (As told at the Golden Inn)." The subtitle reinforces the frame of the story: it is a tale told later by an older Ishmael on a future voyage to Lima. "For my humor's sake," Ishmael tells us, "I shall preserve the style in which I once narrated it at Lima, to a lounging circle of my Spanish friends, one saint's eve, smoking upon the thick-gilt tiled piazza of the Golden Inn" (243). If there was ever a setup for a yarn, that is one. The telling of the tale in the white-hot heat of Lima enhances its intensity and overwrought emotions. Ishmael's swearing upon the Evangelists, a section of the New Testament, at the end of the yarn suggests its blasphemy—and by extension, the blasphemy of the tale of *Moby-Dick* itself.

Yarning refers in general to the telling of sailor's stories, not just the telling of stories that follow the standard pattern. Melville was a brilliant and compelling storyteller. His tales of the Marquesas were often repeated to his shipmates in the two years he remained at sea after joining the whaleship *Lucy Ann* at Nuku Hiva on August 9, 1842. Richard Tobias Greene, who deserted the *Acushnet* with Melville at Nuku Hiva, recalled such yarning when he wrote Melville years later: "I would be delighted to see you and 'freshen the nip' while you would be spinning a yarn as long as the Main top bowline."[33]

Melville's tales of adventure had become polished by the time he returned to New England. Julian Hawthorne, son of Sophia and Nathaniel Hawthorne, gives a vivid account of Melville's storytelling ability in *Nathaniel Hawthorne and His Wife* (1884). Melville visited with the Hawthornes in the summer of 1851 and told "the story of a fight which he had seen on an island in the Pacific, between some savages, and of the prodigies of valor one of them performed with a heavy club." After Melville left, Sophia asked her husband, "'Where is that club with which Mr. Melville was laying about him so?' Mr. Hawthorne thought he must have taken it with him; Mrs. Hawthorne thought he had put it in the corner; but it was not to be found. The next time Melville came, they asked him about it; whereupon it appeared that the club was still in the Pacific island, if it were anywhere."[34]

For someone whose work is so largely based on written sources, Melville is a remarkably oral writer. The transformative experience of hearing *Moby-Dick* read aloud reinforces its orality. Hearing *Moby-Dick* read aloud in moonlight aboard the only remaining wooden whaleship in the world, the *Charles W. Morgan,* during the annual twenty-four-hour marathon at Mystic Seaport is magical, as is hearing the annual marathon reading of the book at the New Bedford Whaling Museum. In *Moby-Dick,* Melville converts his written sources into text that rings in the ear when read aloud. This can be heard in a comparison of the "Whales" entry in volume 27 of *The Penny Cyclopædia* (1843) to "Cetology," chapter 32 of *Moby-Dick. The Penny Cyclopædia* pedantically states: "Linnaeus then declares that he has separated these cetaceans from the fishes, and associated them with the mammals, on account of their warm bilocular heart, their lungs, their moveable eyelids, their hollow ears, *penem intrantem feminam mammis lactantem,* and this, to use his own expressive words, *ex lege naturae jure meritoque.*"[35] Melville lifts the quotation directly into *Moby-Dick,* but his addition of humor signals to the reader that the quotation should be read dryly, quizzically.

In just one passage, Melville leads the reader to question scientific endeavor, sailor talk, and Christianity as well as all attempts at classification:

> The grounds upon which Linnaeus would fain have banished the whales from the waters, he states as follows: "On account of their warm bilocular heart, their lungs, their movable eyelids, their hollow ears, penem intrantem feminam mammis lactantem," and finally, "ex lege naturae jure meritoque." I submitted all this to my friends Simeon Macey and Charley Coffin, of Nantucket, both messmates of mine in a certain voyage, and they united in the opinion that the reasons set forth were altogether insufficient. Charley profanely hinted they were humbug.
>
> Be it known that, waiving all argument, I take the good old fashioned ground that the whale is a fish, and call upon holy Jonah to back me. (136)

Melville pokes fun at Linnaeus and by extension all scientists for the stiffness of their language and their retreat into Latin, but he also pokes fun at sailors for their conservative attitude and ignorance. Macey and Coffin are old Nantucket names; Simeon and Charley, therefore, are Nantucket whalemen, known, as Nathaniel Philbrick points out, for their conservativeness in everything connected with the whale fishery.[36] Finally, Melville pokes fun at biblical fundamentalists, who even in the mid-nineteenth century still held that the whale is a fish. To poke fun is also to question. The power of the humor and questioning in this passage is emphasized and reinforced by its orality.

MYTH TALK

The forms of sailor talk discussed above are all forms of talk *by* sailors. Sailor talk also includes talk *about* sailors. In the nineteenth century, mythology and lore surrounded mariners. Sailors were represented as corrupt and innocent, depraved and heroic. Men who went to sea were far more central to the consciousness of the general public than they are today. All transoceanic travel and much intercity travel were conducted on ships. Even inland travel occurred on boats, either by steamboat on rivers and lakes or by canal boat on the vast system of canals that then crisscrossed the country. Therefore, the public saw sailors, formed opinions of them, and talked about them. Melville was aware of this culture-speak and used it in his writing, often in subversive ways.

Nineteenth-century newspapers most often portrayed sailors as drunken and debauched, prone to the vilest of impulses. Startlingly vivid images of contamination and putrefaction surround these portrayals. An 1823 column in the *Boston Recorder* is typical:

It is a fact which every careful observer must have noticed, and deplored, that the morals of seamen, influence to a great extent, the morals of society at large. Their profaneness, debauchery, drunkenness, and contempt of the Sabbath, vices to which they are much addicted, have a most ruinous effect on the morals of our cities and principal towns. Children can with difficulty enter the streets at all, without hearing the very dialect of hell, before they know its horrid import: they see the Sabbath profaned, hear the songs of the drunkard, and the obscene ditties of the brothel, and "know that the dead are there," and that these paths lead down to the very gates of hell. . . . The sailor feeds, with his hard earned wages, the brothels, and polluted boarding houses, those sinks of pollution from which issue streams of vice to run in every direction.[37]

The writer of the article ultimately argues that seamen can be reformed. First, however, he portrays the sailor as depraved, debauched, almost putrid in his pollution, and speaking "the very dialect of hell." The writer expects his newspaper readers to be familiar with this portrayal—and indeed they must be, judging by its repetition in newspapers during the next twenty years. An 1827 piece on India entitled "Anecdotes of the Hindoos" notes that "the perjury and corruption of the Bengalees . . . are as notorious as the drunkenness and debauchery of our English sailors."[38] The New-York Mirror argued in 1828 that sailors are "lost in the torrent of dissipation which is ready to carry them away to the brink of ruin."[39] In 1836 the New-York Evangelist warned: "We must go ahead in benevolence, as [sailors] go ahead in labors of unparalleled enterprise, or they will get beyond our reach, and come back upon our country, laden with vices of such a gigantic cast as will swallow up all that is good, and desirable, and holy in the land."[40] Captain Sleeper reports in the 1842 Christian Reflector that when he arrived in Savannah twenty-five years earlier, he had been unable to find a decent boardinghouse in which to stay:

We were thus compelled, against our will, to take up residence at the sign of the General Armstrong; a house which was overrun with old privateersmen and man-of-war's-men: where every excess was not only allowed, but encouraged; and where, at almost every hour of the day or night, scenes of drunkenness, of gaming, of quarrelling, of fighting, of dissipation and debauchery in all its most odious shapes, were witnessed, and spread afar their contaminating influence.[41]

An 1846 piece in the New York Observer and Chronicle ringingly denounces the contamination caused by the boatmen working New York's canals:

When the canal boats of our own State were once manned by irreligious and licentious youth, without a teacher or a Sabbath, they left a line of moral blight along the course of their travel. Like a magnetic telegraph in the hands of robbers and murderers, they sent wrong and wo [sic], to and fro, as on the wings of the lightning, along the rout [sic] they traversed and desolated. Constantly travelling, the sin they left behind was a contamination but too permanent, whilst the sinner outran punishment and evaded shame by his constant itinerancy from place to place.[42]

Sin races like lightning along a magnetic telegraph, leaving desolation and blight in its wake.

These images are over the top. The sailor is not only drunk but utterly debauched. He causes contamination and dissipation "in all its most odious shapes." The writers fear that sailors are "laden with vices of such a gigantic cast as will swallow up all that is good." Melville partakes of this same quality of exaggeration in *Redburn* in the "infamous vices" in which the character of Jackson had indulged. "In truth, he carried with him the traces of these things, and the mark of a fearful end nigh at hand; like that of King Antiochus of Syria, who died a worse death, history says, than if he had been stung out of the world by wasps and hornets" (58). In II Maccabees 9, King Antiochus's body rots and is consumed by worms even before he is dead. The stench is so great that none will attend him in his last days. With the comparison of Jackson to King Antiochus, Melville employs the same type of hyperbole as the *New-York Mirror* when the latter states that sailors are "lost in the torrent of dissipation which is ready to carry them away to the brink of ruin." Melville's following line—"Nothing was left of this Jackson but the foul lees and dregs of a man" (58)—has the same tone as newspaper articles on the degradation of sailors. In fact, if Melville's line were put into one of the newspaper commentaries, it would not sound incongruous.

Most of the newspaper articles quoted above ultimately argue for some form of reform for sailors. Above all they advocate either the distribution of Bibles among men aboard ships or the establishment of sailors' homes, where seamen can stay without fear of losing their earnings to corrupt landlords or prostitutes. To reinforce the necessity for reform, the newspaper writers need to show the absolute corruption that would result if sailors were not rescued by the charity of others. Therefore, they use exaggeration to force their argument.

Melville created Jackson out of a different impulse. He was intrigued with the location of evil in human form. Why does such depravity exist? What causes it? Is there anything ordinary humans can do to combat it? In Jackson, Melville deconstructs depravity. This deconstruction, begun with Jackson, culminates in the character of Claggart in *Billy Budd*. In his deconstruction Melville exploits the imagery and language employed by newspaper writers to portray the corruption and vice associated with sailors.

The subtitle of the 1823 *Boston Recorder* piece argues "The Salvation of Seamen Important."[43] Newspaper writers supported this contention with several different arguments. One was that sailors are men, not animals, and need to be treated as such. The *New-York Evangelist* argued in 1836: "Ah, Sir, doth God care for oxen and horses, and shall we not care for men? Sailors, Sir, are men, and they prove it, and have proved it, that they have souls, and are as much men as any on the face of the earth, and should be cared for as such."[44] "The sailor is a man, and a whole man," the *Christian Reflector* added in 1843. "If we would improve the condition of the sailor, it must be by treating him not only as a moral being, but as gifted with social affections."[45] The fugitive slave Frederick Douglass was lecturing the same year for the antislavery cause. One strong argument for the abolition of slavery was that slaves are men and women, *not* cattle. Part of what convinced the audience was the force of Douglass's presence on stage. After hearing Douglass speak, how could anyone contend that he was not a man—and by extension that slaves are not human beings capable of reasoned thought? Lacking such a presence as Douglass's, the *New-York Evangelist* and the *Christian Reflector* have only words to make their case, but their repetition of the terms "men" and "man" reinforce their line of reasoning.

A second major strand of the argument that the salvation of seamen is important is that sailors carry goods around the world and represent their home governments as they interact with foreigners on a continuous basis. "They are the carriers of the world's commerce," the *New York Observer and Chronicle* noted in 1846, "the out-posts of its governments, and the channels of its travel, its colonization and its evangelization."[46] Ten years earlier, in 1836, the *New-York Evangelist* vociferated even more strongly: "The obligations of this nation to her sailors are incalculable. Our commercial prosperity, our comforts and luxuries, the embellishments [*sic*] that adorn our houses, the care and skill that transmits our christian charity to the most distant land, all depends on the sailor."[47] Sailors carry on this trade heroically, staunchly facing all that such living upon the waves entails. Foreshadowing Melville's paean to Nantucketers in *Moby-Dick*, the editor of the *Christian Reflector* asks in 1843: "Has the sailor any home but the forecastle, amidst cables and chains? Can he sleep except in a wet jacket, and on his lonely hammock? . . . Is there anything in the mind of the sailor that can find music in anything else than the howling of the storm, or the whistling of the wind through the rigging of his ship?"[48] The editor of the *Christian Reflector* praises the seaman for being unable to live anywhere except at sea, but Melville transcends such praise and exalts the Nantucket whaleman to biblical proportions:

The Nantucketer, he alone resides and rests on the sea; he alone, in bible language, goes down to it in ships; to and fro ploughing it as his own special plantation. *There* is his home; *there* lies his business, which a Noah's flood would not interrupt, though it overwhelmed all the millions in China. He lives on the sea, as prairie cocks in the prairie; he hides among the waves, he climbs them as chamois hunters climb Alps. For years he knows not the land; so that when he comes to it at last, it smells like another world, more strangely than the moon would to an Earthsman. With the landless gull, that at sunset folds her wings and is rocked to sleep between billows; so at nightfall, the Nantucketer, out of sight of land, furls his sails, and lays him to his rest, while under his very pillow rush herds of walruses and whales. (64)

Even though he far transcends the newspaper piece, Melville grounds his passage in the same view of sailors. For the editor of the *Christian Reflector,* the seaman cannot sleep "except in a wet jacket, and on his lonely hammock"; for Melville, the seaman "with the landless gull, that at sunset folds her wings and is rocked to sleep between billows; so at nightfall . . . out of sight of land, furls his sails, and lays him to his rest."

Paradoxically, newspaper writers often portrayed sailors as innocents, seemingly the virtual opposite of sailors as drunken, debauched dregs. But such writers saw sailors as not innocent of vice but innocent in the ways of the world. Unsophisticated, sailors often succumbed to temptation because they did not recognize its danger and so avoid it. Part of what led the crew of the *Bounty* to mutiny, Dening argues in *Mr. Bligh's Bad Language,* was William Bligh's perception of sailors as children. Even Joseph Conrad, who himself spent twenty years at sea as a sailor, first gave the title *Children of the Sea* to the book he later renamed *The Nigger of the* Narcissus.

Humor occasionally threads the newspaper articles about sailors, but it is more often found in aphorisms about them. The saying that the masthead is the closest the sailor will ever get to heaven is found in many places, including the *New-York Evangelist:* "when poor Jack gets at mast head as his ship rides the top of the mountain wave, he is nearer heaven than he ever will be again."[49] Melville plays with this idea when Stubb jocularly asks the black cook Fleece where he will go when he dies.

"Up dere," said Fleece, holding his tongs straight over his head, and keeping it there very solemnly.

"So, then, you expect to go up into our main-top, do you, cook, when you are dead? . . . Main-top eh?"

"Didn't say dat t'all," said Fleece, again in the sulks. (*Moby-Dick* 297)

Stating that the closest a sailor will ever get to heaven is the masthead is humorous, but it is also demeaning, as Fleece understands and makes plain in the sulkiness of his response to Stubb's repartee. The *New-York Evangelist* understands the demeaning quality of this aphorism as well; it introduces the saying with the statement: "The wits (for there are such beings) thought they were saying a clever thing."[50]

The sailors' own view of going to heaven can be seen in the following wonderful poem, transmitted orally from sailor to sailor:

> A sailor stood at the pearly gates;
> His face was lined and old.
> He'd come to see the man of fate
> For admission to the fold.
> "And what have you done," St. Peter said,
> "To gain admission here?"
> "I've been a sailor, sir," said he,
> "For many and many a year."
> The pearly gates swung open wide;
> St. Peter rang the bell.
> "Come in," says he, "and choose your harp.
> You've had your share of hell."[51]

Stan Hugill, the last of the working chanteymen, heard this poem as a young man on his first voyage around Cape Horn. As the youngest sailor, he was assigned the worst bunk: the upper bunk in the peak of the forecastle, with sprung planking above it that sent water shooting into the bunk with every wave that washed the deck. Off Cape Horn he went below after a grueling forty hours on deck, planning to turn in "all-standing," wearing all his clothes, including his foul-weather jacket. His bunk, soaked and crawling with bedbugs, looked to him at the moment as close to heaven as he would ever need to get. Just as he was about to crawl into his bunk, an older sailor put his hand on Hugill's shoulder and recited the poem.

It is hard to recover the sailors' own response to their representation among the public. Sailors generally did not portray themselves as debauched, but rather as tough and hard working—and at times heroic. Their lot was hard but ennobling. To work a sailing vessel across the ocean was deeply exhausting and took a great deal of skill, but it made men of the sailors. After the publication of Richard Henry Dana Jr.'s *Two Years before the Mast* in 1840, other first-person sailor narratives were published with such titles as *Ten Years before the Mast*, *Twenty Years before the Mast*, *Thirty Years before the Mast*, and *Forty Years before the Mast*. If Dana could sail two years as a common seaman before the mast, others could sail for far longer periods. Samuel Samuels, the most famous of the packet-ship masters, portrays the notorious mariners of Liverpool, England, commonly known as the "Liverpool packet rats," as violent and unyielding. But then he writes: "I never rejected a crew . . . on account of their bad character. I generally found among these men the toughest and best sailors."[52]

As a young man, the playwright Eugene O'Neill worked aboard steamships as well as on a Norwegian square-rigger, experiences that he later mined for many of his plays. In *The Hairy Ape* (1922), the stoker, Yank, the acknowledged leader of the men, tells his fellow workers: "Hell in de stokehole? Sure! It takes a man to work in hell. Hell, sure, dat's my fav'rite climate. I eat it up! I git fat on it! It's me makes it hot! It's me makes it roar! It's me makes it move!"[53] Yank turns the hell of the stokehole into something powerful and positive. He inverts the popular view of sailors, as presented in the *Boston Recorder,* where sailors are portrayed as following "these paths [that] lead down to the very gates of hell."[54] Sure, Yank says, these paths do lead to Hell, and only a sailor is manly enough to go there.

Within the range of first-person accounts written by mariners, one finds reflected the whole array of the general public's perception of sailors. Different authors have different motives. Samuel Samuels, driven by the desire for self-aggrandizement, has nonetheless written a rollicking tale in *From Forecastle to Cabin* (1887). Richard Henry Dana uses *Two Years before the Mast* for the propagation of useful knowledge, but he combines that with a deep hatred of flogging. As one of the nation's preeminent maritime lawyers, Dana was later instrumental in having flogging outlawed. In *The Making of a Sailor,* Frederick Pease Harlow spins an intriguing but largely accurate yarn. Harlow's description of sailor work and the relation of work and music unites extreme accuracy with extraordinarily clear language. He likewise indulges in at least mildly exaggerated stereotypes, such as that of the Flying Dutchman. A comparison of Harlow's shipboard journal to *The Making of a Sailor,* based on the journal but written over fifty years later, shows that the major difference between the two is the addition of dialogue.

In his writing, Melville subverts the tone of most of the newspaper pieces. He uses the exaggeration but not the earnestness of the newspaper writers. What I would argue most strongly, however, is that Melville incorporates sailor talk—the tone and verbal qualities of the talk itself—into his maritime novels. Looking at newspapers is an attempt to recover the sense of the talk itself, rather than to recover specific articles from which Melville may have drawn.

Newspaper articles can be read as transcribing the general popular view of sailors, but such articles are frequently agenda driven, presenting some form of argument. This is especially true of articles in religious newspapers. Literary works, however, often do not present popular views, but they are still shaped by the culture in which they are produced. In the eighteenth century, as best seen in the works of Tobias Smollett, sailors in literature were presented satirically, as hard-living, hard-loving tars who survive in a sea of hard knocks. In the nineteenth century, sailors in literature were often presented heroically, especially in works written by authors who themselves had been to sea.[55] Long Tom Coffin in James Fenimore Cooper's *The Pilot* is a man ennobled by his long contact with nature at its most sublime. At six feet six inches, he is heroic in stature as well as in deed. In the midst of a Revolutionary War sea battle between the British and the Americans, Long Tom Coffin rises from the sea with "his grizzled locks drenched with the briny element, from which he had risen, looking like Neptune with his trident. Without speaking, he poised his harpoon, and with a powerful effort, pinned the unfortunate [British commander] to the mast of his own vessel." This ends the battle: "A few of the Englishmen stood, chained to the spot in silent horror at the sight, but most of them fled to their lower deck, or hastened to conceal themselves in the secret parts of the vessel, leaving to the Americans the undisputed possession of the Alacrity," the British vessel.[56] Even at his death, Long Tom Coffin remains noble. He refuses to leave the *Ariel* when she is wrecked upon the British coast. "God's will be done with me," he cries. "I saw the first timber of the Ariel laid, and shall live just long enough to see it torn out of her bottom; after which I wish to live no longer." He tells Dillon, his fellow sufferer, "These waves, to me, are what the land is to you; I was born on them, and I have always meant that they should be my grave."[57]

Joseph Conrad, who worked at sea for almost twenty years, mostly in the British merchant marine, also saw sailors as heroic, especially those who spent their lives at sea. In *The Nigger of the* Narcissus, the aged Singleton steers the *Narcissus* for endless hours after a knockdown. Conrad concludes the chapter on the knockdown with a passage describing Singleton at the wheel that ends simply, evocatively, "He steered with care."[58] In the next chapter, Singleton ponders his significance: "For many years he had heard himself called 'Old Singleton,' and had serenely accepted the qualification, taking it as a tribute of respect due to a man who through half a century had measured his strength against the favours and the rages of the sea. He had never given a thought to his mortal self. He lived unscathed, as though he had been indestructible, surrendering to all the temptations, weathering many gales. He had panted in sunshine, shivered in the cold; suffered hunger, thirst, debauch; passed through many trials—known all the furies."[59] Unlike Cooper, Conrad acknowledges the unthinking quality of Singleton's life and the debauchery in which he has indulged. Ashore to collect his pay, he becomes a disgusting old man: "Singleton came up, venerable—and uncertain as to daylight; brown drops of tobacco juice hung in his white beard; his hands, that never hesitated in the great light of the open sea, could hardly find the small pile of gold in the profound darkness of the shore."[60] Nonetheless, at sea Singleton *is* heroic.

Cooper's heroization of the sailor is not universal. Even before Mark Twain's fierce criticism of Cooper in his "Fenimore Cooper's Literary Offenses" (1895), James Russell Lowell compared Long Tom Coffin to Natty Bumppo of Cooper's *Leatherstocking Tales* in "A Fable for Critics" (1848): "And [Cooper's] very Long Toms are the same useful Nat, / Rigged up in duck pants and a sou'-wester hat, / (Though, once in a Coffin, a good chance was found / To have slipt the old fellow away underground.)"[61]

Melville certainly has heroic sailors. Jack Chase in *White-Jacket* is one. Even the officers aboard the *Neversink* acknowledge his superior qualities. Billy Budd, except for his unfortunate defect, is another. Captain Vere calls him "an Angel of God!" (*Billy Budd* 101). Unlike Jack Chase, Billy Budd has the unthinking quality of Singleton.

Writing at a different time and with different purposes, Melville's and Conrad's sailors are more complex and more questioned than Cooper's. Both Melville and Conrad knew firsthand the prevailing attitude toward sailors as ignorant, mostly illiterate, questionable beings. The unconsciousness of this attitude is seen in Evert Duyckinck's 1848 letter to his brother when he writes of Melville's reading of Sir Thomas Browne: "By the way[,] Melville reads old Books. He has borrowed Sir Thomas Browne of me and says finely of the speculations of the *Religio Medici* that Browne is a kind of 'crack'd Archangel.' Was ever any thing of this sort said before by a sailor?"[62]

When Melville began to write his first book, he was immersed in sailor talk. He used the terminology he had so painstakingly learned aboard the merchant vessel *St. Lawrence*, the whaleship *Acushnet*, and the naval frigate *United States*; the occupational lore and coterie speech in which he had indulged with other sailors; folkloric discourse; and the more general attitude that was created by myths and misunderstandings about sailors to shape *Typee* and his subsequent books. But beyond that, his artist's ear and deft pen selected and ordered the variety of sailor talk so as to express the increasingly profound vision that develops throughout his maritime works. The society of a ship is structured to serve a single simple objective: harnessing the wind to move the ship from one place to another on its particular business as efficiently as possible. All other concerns are subjected to this one overriding purpose. Melville's immersion in this sequestered self-referential world was his first step in conceiving the Other through his own experience. Questions of alienation, individual identity within a group, identification with a group, and the ability to don the different masks worn as the son of a gentleman, a young man selling his labor, a merchant sailor, a whaleman, a naval sailor, and a beachcomber inform the complex questions of identity and consciousness Melville explores throughout his maritime works. To society the sailor had become the Other, almost as much as the people the sailors themselves encountered around the world. Recognizing this Otherness in sailors and in himself, Melville describes the *Pequod*'s crew and, by extension, all seamen as "mongrel renegades, and castaways, and cannibals" (*Moby-Dick* 186). Reentering the mundane bourgeois world of his conventional mid-nineteenth-century American family, Melville began to create an identity based on his natural abilities as an observer, a storyteller, and then a writer. Throughout this transformation, he relied on the Otherness he had experienced in those formative years and the specialized language he had acquired at sea to breathe life into his writing.

CHAPTER 3

∾ "They Say They Don't Like Sailor's Flesh, It's Too Salt"

Cannibal Talk

New Bedford beats all Water street and Wapping. In these last-mentioned haunts you see only sailors; but in New Bedford, actual cannibals stand chatting at street corners; savages outright; many of whom yet carry on their bones unholy flesh. . . . As we were going along the people stared; not at Queequeg so much—for they were used to seeing cannibals like him in their streets,—but at seeing him and me upon such confidential terms.

—Moby-Dick *(31, 58)*

WHEN Herman Melville deserted the whaleship *Acushnet* at Nuku Hiva in the Marquesas Islands on July 9, 1842, he crossed the beach, both literally and metaphorically, with a set of preconceptions about the identification and nature of cannibals. His sojourn among the inhabitants of a reputed "cannibal isle," whatever he actually did there, proved to be a defining event in Melville's life, a catalyst for the profound reflections on the human condition that provide the driving artistic force in his work. The prevailing discourse of cannibalism that characterized early contact between Europeans and South Pacific islanders from the age of exploration onward was pervasive and ubiquitous. Gananath Obeyesekere deconstructs this discourse in his cultural anthropology study *Cannibal Talk: The Man-Eating Myth and Human Sacrifice in the South Seas*. Although Obeyesekere never writes explicitly about the Marquesas, I have adopted his term "cannibal talk" throughout this chapter in order to emphasize the role of the spoken word implicit in the discourse surrounding Melville.

I do not intend to attempt to settle here the fraught question of whether the practice of ritual cannibalism has ever been proved beyond doubt. The occurrence of human sacrifice, in which human lives are offered to the deities in a ritual manner as payment for their intervention, to prevent unfavorable events, or to purchase disclosures about the physical world, is generally accepted. Yet even where human sacrifice is incontrovertible, the existence of ritual cannibalism remains questionable or unwitnessed. My interest lies in the complex elusiveness of cannibalism and the immense amount of elliptical and self-referential talk the idea has generated. As will be shown, a healthy skepticism of any particular account of ritual cannibalism is essential to an examination of the subject, whatever the final verdict on the evidence of the existence of the practice in general.

INVENTION OF THE CANNIBAL

The term "cannibal" only came into being in the fifteenth century. Until then, eaters of human flesh were called anthropophagi, a term derived from ancient Greek. The anthropophagi are exotic Others, beyond the boundaries of the known world. Knowledge of them is brought back by explorers, who also tell tales of people with faces in the middle of their stomachs, men with dogs' heads, and Amazons.

Charges of anthropophagy have most often been directed at non-Europeans, but this was not always so. One of the earliest written accounts of cannibalism occurs in *The History of Herodotus,* written by Herodotus in 440 B.C.E. Herodotus located the flesh-eating Androphagi (in Greek, *Andro* = human; *phagi* = eater of) in northern Europe on the edge of known civilization. In book 4 of the *History,* Herodotus tells us that the Scythian soldier drinks the blood of the first man he overthrows and carries the head to the king. Beyond the land of the Scythians is a vast tract that is uninhabited. Above this desolate region dwell the Androphagi, "who are a people apart."[1] The Androphagi are northern Europeans, but they live beyond the "desolate region." They inhabit the liminal space at the edge of the lands known to civilized men.

The *Natural History* (*Naturalis Historiae*) of Pliny the Elder, first partially published in 77 C.E. , includes in book 6 a description of the Scythian cannibals. "Here are the abodes of the Scythian Anthropophagi," Pliny tells us, "who feed on human flesh. Hence it is that all around them consists of vast desserts, inhabited by multitudes of wild beasts, which are continually lying in wait, ready to fall upon human beings as savage as themselves."[2] The savagery of the Scythians is made explicit in their cannibalism, an act that equates them with wild beasts. Like most of the Europeans who wrote about the Scythians, Pliny assembled his encyclopedia from other reports; his knowledge of the Scythians is not personal but bibliographic.

Charges of anthropophagy continue. From Pliny's nephew and heir, Pliny the Younger, we learn of the Romans' charge that Christians partook of human flesh in their banquets.[3] During the Middle Ages, Jews were accused of eating Christian babies. As the borders of the world known to Europeans were pushed back, the identification of the anthropophagi changed. What remains consistent is that those labeled cannibals are on the fringes of the world known to those doing the labeling and that they are enumerated among other monstrosities and oddities.

William Shakespeare's *Othello* (1603–4) illustrates this extension of the borders of civilization. Othello, the black Moor, is not the one labeled a cannibal. Instead, he has been to the fringes of the known world, and he is the one doing the labeling. When he explains to the duke why Desdemona has fallen in love with him, he recalls having told her tales of the anthropophagi.

> It was my hint to speak—such was the process;
> And of the Cannibals that each other eat,
> The Anthropophagi, and men whose heads
> Do grow beneath their shoulders. This to hear
> Would Desdemona seriously incline;
> But still the house affairs would draw her thence;
> Which ever as she could with haste dispatch,
> She'd come again, and with a greedy ear
> Devour up my discourse.[4]

According to Othello, Desdemona, like Europeans before and after her, *devoured* his discourse. It's crucial to note here that we do not witness Othello's encounters with cannibals, nor do we behold his telling of such encounters to Desdemona. We only see his recollection of the telling of such encounters, which puts the reality of the encounters at one more remove and makes this oft-cited reference to cannibalism one more example of cannibal talk.

Othello uses both terms: "anthropophagi" and "cannibal." The word "cannibal" derives from the Spanish pronunciation of "Carib," the Indians encountered by Christopher Columbus on his first voyage in 1492. By the time Columbus sailed, the rediscovered ancient Roman and Greek texts that helped to fuel and shape the Renaissance had been invested with an aura of unquestionable authority. The natural histories that mention such human oddities led Columbus and other explorers to expect such encounters in the unexplored spaces to which they traveled. Columbus first encountered the Arawak, whom he deemed gentle and peaceful. From them he heard of the Carib: "Far from there were men with one eye, and others with dogs' noses who ate men, and that when they took a man, they cut off his head and drank his blood and castrated him."[5] Such monstrosities match those found in classical texts.

In a parallel case to Columbus's description mentioned above, the Amazon River was not named for a local people but for a mythical people that were assumed to exist based on the texts of the ancient natural historians. The Tupinamba of Brazil, themselves alleged to be cannibals, allegedly told European explorers of a tribe of Amazon women farther into the interior—yet who today would argue that a nation of warrior women ever existed along the banks of the river that bears the name of this mythical group? Europeans at the time of Columbus steeped in the classical texts expected to find cannibals on the edges and also expected to find other creatures. The details allegedly given by the Tupinamba of this all-female society coincide perfectly with descriptions of the Amazons from the ancient texts, including the rule that no men were permitted to reside with the Amazons. Once a year, men visited in order to keep the race from dying out. Male children born from these visits were either killed outright or sent back to their fathers; female children were raised by their mothers. These parallels raise an interesting question: how can one assert that the extensive detail in descriptions of Tupinamba cannibalistic practices confirms the existence of Tupinamba cannibalism when there is similarly extensive detail about Amazon women in which no one now believes? Europeans expected to find cannibals and Amazons—and therefore they found them.

The Carib were the enemy of the Arawak and were portrayed by the Arawak as savage and inhuman. Had Columbus encountered the Carib first, perhaps his view of the Arawak might have been different. With remarkable tenacity, Columbus's portrayal of the Carib as fierce and heartless flesh-eaters has lasted for over five hundred years. In fact, the 2006 film *Pirates of the Caribbean: Dead Man's Chest* has been strongly protested by Carib groups for its portrayal of their ancestors as cannibals.[6]

The term "cannibal" has been applied to almost all groups of people at one time or another. Humans generally consider the eating of another human an anathema. Cannibalism, like incest or necrophilia, is the boundary beyond which we cannot stray and remain fully human. Those who do eat people are monstrous—animals, savages, witches, nonhumans. To label a group of people cannibals is a way to gain power over them and to control them. It has also served as the justification for often horrific acts of violence.

Melville subverts the use of cannibalism as a form of othering when he asks in *Moby-Dick:* "Cannibals? who is not a cannibal?" (300). He forces us to contemplate what he earlier calls "the universal cannibalism" (*Moby-Dick* 274). In *Typee,* Melville begins to consider the savagery inherent in all of us, especially with Tommo's violence against Mow-Mow at the end of the book. By *Moby-Dick,* this consideration has become an understanding that the cannibal is not only the Other but also the shadow of ourselves. Queequeg is a cannibal, Ahab calls himself a cannibal, the *Pequod* is a "cannibal of a craft" (70)—all, all are cannibals. Melville forces us to accept that we must face and even embrace the darkest and most horrific depths of ourselves to realize the fullness of our own humanity.

Melville's comprehension, however, is not the common one. In the popular European understanding, cannibalism was first associated with Africa, then with the Caribs of the Caribbean, then with the Aztecs of Mexico, then with the Tupinamba of Brazil, then with the Maoris of New Zealand, then with the islanders of the South Pacific, especially the Fijians and Marquesans, and finally with the inhabitants of the highlands of Papua–New Guinea.

The association of cannibalism with Papua–New Guinea became explicit when D. Carleton Gajdusek shared the 1976 Nobel Prize in Physiology or Medicine for his work on Kuru among the Fore people who live in the New Guinea highlands. Kuru is a TSE, or transmissible spongiform encephalopathy, a slow, wasting disease related to Creutzfeldt-Jakob disease and mad cow disease. Gajdusek, who studied the Fore in the 1950s, argued that Kuru was transmitted via cannibalism. Strong evidence has now been cited that the spread of the disease resulted from contact with the infected tissue of Kuru victims through cuts in the skin, for example, rather than from the eating of the flesh of those who died. Arens, who has written at length about this controversy, both in *The Man-Eating Myth* and in "Rethinking Anthropophagy," quotes Gajdusek himself as stating: "Infection was most probably through the cuts and abrasions of the skin or through nose picking, eye rubbing, or mucosal injury."[7] Lyle Steadman, an Arizona State University anthropologist, cast doubt on Gajdusek's field work in a 1982 paper published in *American Anthropologist*. Steadman asked why Gajdusek assumed that cannibalism was the only means of coming into contact with infected human tissue when it could be shown that Fore women regularly touched infected tissue, including brain tissue, during mortuary rituals without eating it.[8] Kuru only emerged as a disease in New Guinea around the turn of the century, and Steadman suggested the possibility of a European origin. Shirley Lindenbaum, an anthropologist at the CUNY Graduate Center, exploded in response: "That's just nonsense," she told *Lingua Franca* journalist Lawrence Osborne. "Frankly, I'm sick and tired of this Arens stuff about how it's all misrepresented.... I've taped people who've witnessed it. And as for the epidemiology of *kuru*, it fits the cannibalism hypothesis perfectly. We studied who ate whom, we have their *names*, we followed the biohistory of each case through to the end." As Osborne points out, however, "taping people who have witnessed cannibalism isn't the same as witnessing it firsthand."[9] No new cases of Kuru have appeared, and Gajdusek and Lindenbaum argue that Kuru has disappeared since the Australian ban on cannibalism. But more questions arise. What was actually banned? Were the mortuary practices banned, or just cannibalism? How does one ban cannibalism? How was the ban worded? How was it enforced? Despite serious questions over the connection between Kuru and cannibalism, Web sites still blithely claim that "the rapid spread of kuru was linked to the Fore's funeral rituals: the Fore cooked and ate their dead relatives.... The Fore quickly stopped eating their dead, and the spread of the disease stopped"and "Prevention worked in New Guinea. The epidemic has tapered off, and no child born since cannibalism ceased has caught kuru."[10]

Discussion of Kuru has spread through Western discourse. The alleged connection between the disease and cannibalism is the modern form of cannibal talk. Inhabitants of Papua–New Guinea are widely considered to be cannibals. With their dark skin and fierce-looking bone ornaments, they fit the European construction of the cannibal Other.[11] When Gajdusek won the Nobel Prize, such cannibal talk was given a legitimacy far beyond that given to most.

The legitimacy of modern-day cannibal talk in reference to New Guinea natives was again asserted with the publication of Paul Raffaele's article "Sleeping with Cannibals" in the September 2006 issue of the *Smithsonian*. Raffaele does not witness cannibalism, nor does he have any incontrovertible proof of it. Nonetheless, he tells us that when cold, wet, and unable to sleep, he was hugged by the Korowai tribesman Boas for warmth and had "the strangest thought: this is the first time I've ever slept with a cannibal."[12] Raffaele's statement shows the enduring power of Melville's use of cannibal talk in *Moby-Dick,* for his thought—consciously or not—echoes Ishmael's "Better sleep with a sober cannibal than a drunken Christian" (24).

Raffaele tells us that the Korowai kill and eat those thought to be *khakhua,* witches who take on the form of men, disguise themselves as a relative or friend, and cause mysterious deaths. After such deaths, clan members seize, kill, and eat the *khakhua,* who is usually a relative or friend of the deceased. Korowai tribesmen Bailom and his brother Kilikili describe for Raffaele the killing and eating of a *khakhua* in graphic detail. Aware that this description may be taken as fantasy rather than solid truth, Raffaele tells us: "Some readers may believe that these two are having me on—that they are just telling a visitor what he wants to hear. . . . But I believe that they were telling the truth. I spent eight days with Bailom, and everything else he told me proved factual."[13] Nonetheless, Raffaele's article, even with the prestige of the Smithsonian Institution behind it, is cannibal talk. The headnote to the article, evidently written by an editor, reinforces the element of talk: "Our intrepid reporter gets up close and personal with remote New Guinea natives *who say* they still eat their fellow tribesmen."[14] Yet the *Smithsonian* uses the word "cannibal" in the title of the article—"Sleeping with Cannibals"—to hook its audience, just as Melville hooked his readers with his title *Typee* (a tribe with a reputation as fierce and savage cannibals) and just as Mary Wallis in 1851 chose to publish her journal under the title *Life in Feejee: Five Years among the Cannibals.*

Tribesmen living in remote villages in the New Guinea highlands in the second half of the twentieth century were caught in a historical moment similar to that experienced by the Marquesan islanders in the 1840s. Melville stepped ashore on

Nuku Hiva at the precise moment when the Marquesas were passing from an unknown liminal space into the glare of documented history. Part of the popularity of *Typee* centers on its purported account of a way of life unchanged since ancient times on the cusp of the moment "civilization" arrives, and Melville consciously represents the Taipi valley as the edge of the known world—the arena in which cannibalism is expected to be found.

One of Melville's most important written sources for cannibal talk about the Marquesas was Georg H. von Langsdorff's *Voyages and Travels in Various Parts of the World*. Langsdorff's book informs a considerable amount of *Typee*. It also references the early history of cannibalism. Langsdorff mentions the third book of Herodotus, in which Cambyses, king of Persia, leads a desert expedition against the king of Ethiopia. Distressed for food, "they were at last constrained to kill every tenth man for the nourishment of the rest."[15] Langsdorff then notes that Pliny relates that the Scythian and Tartar tribes in Asia were cannibals.[16] Although Melville does not refer specifically to Herodotus or Pliny in *Typee,* he was later to remember Cambyses in "The Affidavit," chapter 45 of *Moby-Dick.*

Another source for Melville's knowledge of cannibalism is Montaigne's essay "Of Cannibals." In Rouen, France, in 1562, the French essayist Michel de Montaigne met and evidently spoke through a translator with Tupinamba Indians from Brazil who had been brought to France by the French explorer Nicolas Durand de Villegaignon. His subsequent essay, "Of Cannibals," was published in 1580 and first translated into English in 1603. It is an important early essay on cannibalism. Echoing Pliny, Montaigne notes that the ancient Scythians ate human flesh for nourishment. The Brazilian Indians, in contrast, eat their prisoners "as a representation of extreme revenge."[17] A prisoner is treated well until he is dispatched, after which the Tupinamba "roast him, eat him among them, and send some chops to their absent friends."[18] Living in an age of immense institutional cruelty practiced both by governments and organized religion, Montaigne takes the opportunity to question not the barbarity of the Tupinamba, but the barbarity of Europeans:

> I am not sorry that we should here take notice of the barbarous horror of so cruel an action, but that, seeing so clearly into their faults, we should be so blind to our own. I conceive there is more barbarity in eating a man alive, than when he is dead; in tearing a body limb from limb by racks and torments, that is yet in perfect sense; in roasting it by degrees; in causing it to be bitten and worried by dogs and swine (as we have not only read, but lately seen, not among inveterate and mortal enemies, but among neighbors and fellow-citizens, and, which is worse, under color of piety and religion), than to roast and eat him after he is dead.[19]

Melville read Montaigne's essays in either the 1842 or more likely the 1845 impression of William Hazlitt's edition that he bought January 18, 1848. His use of Montaigne, especially for *Mardi, Moby-Dick,* and *Billy Budd,* is well established by Sister Mary Dominic Stevens in her 1967 dissertation and by other scholars.[20] Since Melville did not buy his own copy of Montaigne until 1848, that particular copy could not have been a source for *Typee* or *Omoo,* but he may have read "Of Cannibals" in another edition.

Montaigne's castigation of his own culture can be read subtextually in the works of Melville. For example, one of the signifiers of Queequeg's status as a cannibal is his peddling of embalmed New Zealand heads through the streets of New Bedford in the early chapters of *Moby-Dick.* In an interesting discussion of this trade, Geoffrey Sanborn notes in *The Sign of the Cannibal* that the sale of embalmed heads "was a *white man's* business."[21] The trade had been in existence since the 1770s, at first supplying an occasional curiosity to museums or private collectors, but after 1820 the European desire for such curiosities greatly increased. The demand for human heads transformed Maori warfare. Before the turn of the nineteenth century, the Maori had preserved the heads of their friends and relatives to honor and memorialize them. But with the increasing European demand for shrunken heads, the Maori no longer preserved the heads of their friends and relatives because they now feared those heads would become objects of commerce. Instead, wars were fought to obtain enemy heads. The persistence of shrunken heads as an element of cannibal talk within popular culture can be seen in the availability and popularity of plastic and rubber versions of shrunken heads in novelty shops and in booths at fairs to this very day.

Despite their strong desire to obtain embalmed heads, Europeans viewed the native killing of one's enemies to obtain their heads as brutal and unnatural. Yet these were often the same Europeans who looked with equanimity upon the owning of slaves. Both the slave trade and the trade in shrunken heads were trades founded on European demand. The work done by African enslaved peoples brought to parts of the Caribbean and Brazil was so deadly that the slave trade continued long after it was made illegal by most European countries because the birth rate could not keep up with the death rate. Montaigne's denunciation of his own culture for inhumanity and brutality can be applied to both the trade in shrunken heads and the slave trade. Both trades were motivated by economics and made psychologically possible by the othering of non-Europeans.

Adopting a similar stance to that of Montaigne, Melville will not permit the monolithic othering of non-whites. He subverts the distinction between cannibals and those fully human in many ways in *Moby-Dick.* At times he invests the label "cannibal" with deep humanity rather than with its opposite: inhumanity or savagery. The "little cannibal urchins" playing marbles with the tiny tail bones of the whale's skeleton in the Arsacides create a gentle and very human image (454). Queequeg is far more human and humane in his treatment of Ishmael than Ishmael—at least in the beginning—is in his treatment of Queequeg. After Quee-queg saves the bumpkin who has mocked him aboard the Nantucket packet schooner *Moss,* he mildly eyes the other passengers and "seemed to be saying to himself—'It's a mutual, joint-stock world, in all meridians. We cannibals must help these Christians'" (62).

WRITTEN SOURCES OF *TYPEE*

The Marquesas lie under the same tropical sun as the rest of the South Pacific, but both the islands themselves and their inhabitants were perceived differently by early European visitors. Most of the islands of the South Pacific are calderas, large volcanic craters formed by the collapse or subsidence of the central part of a volcano. Caldera walls are steep, almost perpendicular at times, and jagged at the top. On many if not most of the South Pacific islands, these calderas are surrounded by fringing coral reefs that create the bone-white sand beaches and sapphire-blue water with which the South Pacific is associated.

But the Marquesas are different. They have no fringing reef and thus no white-sand beaches. The Marquesas are tall, grim, dark sided. Rain clouds catch on the mountains, causing great waterfalls that rush into the surrounding ocean laden with mud. The water around the Marquesas is murky and turgid. Perhaps the differences in terrain and environment caused by the lack of a fringing reef pro-duced a different European response to the Marquesas.

By the time of Melville's arrival in 1842, Marquesan islanders had a reputa-tion as fearsome cannibals, second only to the reputation held by Fijians. On dark, rain-shrouded islands, the possibility of inhabitants practicing blood sacri-fice and eating human flesh seemed to lurk in the tangled undergrowth. In *Typee,* Melville states that "the natives of [the Marquesas] are irreclaimable canni-bals" (24). Melville's statement is based on the cannibal talk he heard from fellow sailors before arriving at the Marquesas. Such a sailor is Ned in *Typee.* As they sail along the coast of Nuku Hiva, Ned tells the narrator, "There—there's Typee. Oh, the bloody cannibals, what a meal they'd make of us" (25). But Melville's statement is also based on references to cannibals and cannibalism found in his three major written sources for *Typee:* Langsdorff, Stewart, and Porter. All three narratives discuss cannibalism at length, yet in very different ways and with highly divergent conclusions. Although he borrowed heavily from all three, Melville ultimately did not follow the anthropophagic thesis of any.

Georg H. von Langsdorff visited the Marquesas in 1804 on a Russian expedi-tion around the world under the command of Captain Adam Johann von Krusenstern. Langsdorff served as physician and naturalist. In his narrative, *Voyages and Travels in Various Parts of the World, during the Years 1803, 1804, 1805, 1806, and 1807,* the section devoted to the northern Marquesas, then called the Washington Islands, is filled with the cannibal talk that Melville would encounter throughout the literature of the South Pacific.

Langsdorff delights in the "lovely creatures" and the "fair sex" that the crew encountered when the vessels of the Russian expedition anchored off Nuku Hiva. He tells a story conveyed to him by the captain of the missionary ship *Duff* of that vessel's goats eating the greenery with which the native girls covered their nakedness: "'The knavish goats,' he says, 'were guilty of a very great offence, with regard to the poor young maidens, for they would not leave them even the little clothing they had: they flocked round them to get at the green leaves, till most of them were left entirely in their native beauty.'"[22] Langsdorff clearly relishes this story as much as Melville delights in the story of the native Marquesan queen displaying her tattooed backside to the "aghast Frenchmen" at the end of chapter 1 of *Typee* (8).

Langsdorff brings the same enthusiasm to his discussion of cannibalism that he brings to his talk of sex and of the maidens covering with their hands the "Medicean Venus."[23] Inhabitants of cannibal nations, he tells us, "not only eat the prisoners they take in war, but their own wives and children; they even buy and sell human flesh publicly. To them are we indebted for the information that white men are finer flavoured than negroes, and that Englishmen are preferable to Frenchmen. Farther, the flesh of young girls and women, particularly of new-born children, far exceeds in delicacy that of the finest youths, or grown men. Finally, they tell us that the inside of the hand and sole of the foot are the nicest parts of the human body."[24] Langsdorff's discussion of cannibalism is not drenched in horror but in macabre jocularity that veers into the absurd—especially with the statement that cannibals eat "their own wives and children"! Melville achieves the same tone when he has the sailor Ned tell the narrator of *Typee* that the Typees "don't like sailor's flesh, it's too salt" (26). Concentrating on the preference for Englishmen over Frenchmen and for landsmen over sailors does not humanize the islanders, but it at least lightens their representation by the introduction of absurdity.

Does Melville's jocular tone originate in Ned, or in Langsdorff, or in Melville himself? Certainly Melville expands and uses this tone throughout much of his work, developing it more fully in his next book, *Omoo.* Melville will exploit this jocular tone in the cool, ironic voice of the narrator of *Omoo.* However, in *Omoo,* this tone most often serves to highlight the hypocrisy or foibles of missionaries, partly acculturated natives, beachcombers, and the general jumble of humanity the narrator encounters in his wanderings. In *Typee,* this ironic humor has a role that cuts much closer to the bone. Here the tone serves to relieve the unbearable tension produced by the horror of cannibalism. Sensations of jocularity and horror are closely related. The comedian Richard Pryor achieved this close relation in his stand-up comic routine reenacting his 1978 heart attack as a dialogue between himself and his heart.[25] As Pryor delivers both sides of the dialogue, his hand clutches his chest. As the heart attack progresses, a twist of the hand hurls Pryor to the floor, where he pleads and whimpers as his heart berates him for the bad habits that led to the heart attack. An extraordinary emotional effect is produced on the audience, demonstrating unforgettably how closely laughter, fear, and horror are related at their deepest roots. Horror films also take advantage of this closely related complex of emotional reactions. Such films often present the murderer as a faceless or masked Other whose psyche cannot be penetrated by any human. These movies commonly relieve tension with macabre humor. Frequently, horror blends into humor and back across and becomes self-parody.

Mow-Mow in *Typee* is like a horror film character. Tommo first feels his presence before he sees him, which adds to the dread of the situation. Tommo is being pressed backward by Kory-Kory "when I felt a heavy hand laid upon my shoulder, and turning round, encountered the bulky form of Mow-Mow, a one-eyed chief, who had just detached himself from the crowd below" (236). Not until chapter 32, the third chapter from the end, does Tommo first encounter this character, who will be so important at the conclusion of the book. He appears like a specter, a felt presence, before Tommo is presented with the horror of his corporeal being. Mow-Mow's cheek, Melville tells us, "had been pierced by the point of a spear, and the wound imparted a still more frightful expression to his hideously tattooed face, already deformed by the loss of an eye" (236). Mow-Mow's face is as dreadful to contemplate as Freddy Kreuger's burned face in the horror film *A Nightmare on Elm Street* (1984), an iconic film of the slasher genre. Neither Mow-Mow nor Freddy wears a mask, but the wounds to their faces have caused the faces themselves to become masks, impenetrable to others, effectively separating Mow-Mow and Freddy from all humanity. His perception of Mow-Mow's lack of humanity allows Tommo to commit such violence against him at the end of *Typee*. But there is also a dark humor in the horror associated with Mow-Mow's face. Mow-Mow is just too dreadful. Not only does he have only one eye, but his face is also "hideously tattooed," and to top it off, his cheek has been pierced by a spear.

Melville's era was steeped in an earnest, humorless gothic horror, much of which the modern reader finds hilarious. At its best, this humorless gothic horror produces a real sense of dread. How many readers have felt a shiver in their spine while reading Edgar Allan Poe's "The Tell-Tale Heart" (1843) or Mary Shelley's *Frankenstein* (1818)? American writers just a generation later, such as Mark

Twain and the Southwest humorists, reacted to the excessively somber earnestness of gothic horror with parody and satire. Twain's "Cannibalism in the Car"
(1868) follows the trajectory of cannibal talk after *Typee.*

Melville's achievement in *Typee,* however, is more complex than simple
parody. He masterfully uses the tropes of gothic horror: the veiled allusion, the
grotesque, the brief glimpse of the unspeakable, the increasingly unbelievable
patina of hospitable warmth masking the inhuman desire to devour the narrator's flesh, the mask-like countenance of the Typee chief Mehevi as he orders
Tommo away from the Ti to keep him from the suspected cannibal feast. At the
same time, he artfully interposes humorous sketches and encounters at precisely
the moments when relief is most needed.

In contrast to Melville, Langsdorff becomes more earnest when he directly
discusses the reality of cannibalism. "Many persons of speculative and philosophic minds doubt," he tells us, "the truth of anthrophagism. It is, however,
incontrovertible."[26] Langsdorff does not prove its incontrovertibility; instead, he
lists four reasons for cannibalism and gives examples of each from ancient texts.
The first reason is extreme scarcity of food. The second is inordinate desire—
in other words, a taste for human flesh. The third Langsdorff calls "the most extraordinary of all, since it appears the most contrary to nature and sound reason. . . . Under the pretence of humanity, man becomes inhuman."[27] This is a
form of funerary cannibalism, in which older relations are killed and their flesh
ingested in order that they be interred within the entrails of their loved ones. The
fourth reason is hatred and revenge. Langsdorff does not investigate these divisions of cannibalism but simply lists them. His incontrovertible proof is not
proof at all but simply the assertion of the universal existence of cannibalism.

In a second major source for *Typee,* Charles S. Stewart does not dispute the
existence of cannibalism, but unlike Langsdorff, he views the supposed cannibalism of the Marquesans with utter seriousness. Stewart spent two weeks in the
Washington Islands in July and August 1839. His *A Visit to the South Seas in the
U.S. Ship Vincennes* includes eleven letters written from the Marquesas. Human
sacrifice is mentioned explicitly in the fifth letter from the Marquesas (letter 6),
but only at the end of that letter is there even the faintest hint of cannibalism:
"The priests alone have the privilege of eating of any thing offered in sacrifice to
the gods."[28] Finally, in the eighth letter from the Marquesas (letter 9), cannibalism
is specifically discussed. The Taipis are asked if they are cannibals. "In answer to
the direct question, whether it was true, that they did eat the bodies of their enemies, and of prisoners taken in battle, they without a moment's hesitation declared positively and repeatedly that they did. On expressing our horror at such
an abomination, they said they would do so no more."[29] Stewart writes here as
a good missionary should. Once the islanders have been shown the light, they

abdicate cannibalism. But what is surprising here is the speed with which that abdication occurs. The Taipis say they will "do so no more"—they will no longer eat human flesh—simply because the Europeans have expressed their "horror at such an abomination." William Arens in *The Man-Eating Myth* questions why it is that first missionaries and later anthropologists always report that the South Pacific islanders have given up anthropophagy on their arrival, yet other habits, such as tattooing and dancing, are so difficult to repress. He wonders if cannibalism is easier to give up because it never existed in the first place. Arens writes: "Once having made the proper excuses for the benighted natives' former moral transgressions, the anthropological field-worker is also able to report, as we have so often seen, that contact with western civilization has immediately resulted in the demise of this custom which our culture views with such fascination and horror. Fortunately, but strangely enough, this is often the only trait which has been abandoned by the indigenes with such ease."[30] Arens adds, "A cynic might well suggest here that nothing disappears so easily as that which has never existed."[31]

Stewart writes as an earnest missionary in letter 9 in reference to the Taipis' vow to eat no more human flesh, but his comments on cannibalism and human sacrifice in the ninth letter from the Marquesas (letter 10) seem truer, more sincere, and far more visceral. His soul sickens at the sight of "altars of abomination and blood.... A few minutes here, were sufficient to sicken both the body and the soul, and we hastily turned from the revolting spectacle."[32] Stewart tells his correspondent: "The examination of a temple immediately adjoining the dwelling of the Taua, left impressions of deep melancholy at the degradation to which ignorance and superstition ... subject the mind and passions of man.... In a deep trough rudely sculptured at one end into a head, gaping hideously, as if to devour all who approach, lay a victim of cruelty, a single mass of putridity, above the surface of which, the green and discolored bones of the skull and chest only, were clearly discerned."[33] At the beginning of the eighth letter from the Marquesas (letter 9), Stewart tells his correspondent that he is "sadly dispirited just at present, and most cordially weary of the vileness of the Nukuhivans."[34] Although his view of the Marquesans throughout most of his letters has been generally evenhanded, if not at times deeply admiring, Stewart ends his last letter by stating, "In addition to other polluting qualities, [the Marquesans] most unquestionably are deceitful and treacherous, vindictive and blood-thirsty, delighting in devastation and war, and accustomed to riot on the flesh of their fellows."[35]

Stewart's presentation of cannibalism in the Marquesas is far more complex than Langsdorff's. He is ambivalent about the Marquesans, often admiring them and comparing individual Marquesan men to Apollo, Othello, and Adonis.[36]

Melville follows him in this comparison when he calls Marnoo "the Polynes-ian Apollo" (*Typee* 135). "Till now," Stewart tells his correspondent, "I had begun to doubt, from all I had seen at the sea side, whether the natives of this group are so decidedly a finer race and handsomer looking people than the Society and Sandwich Islanders, as they are generally accredited to be. But, judging from those seen on this occasion, I am fully persuaded they are—particularly in the fe-male sex."[37] Yet he believes them cannibals, although he himself never witnesses a cannibal act. The thought of such sin wearies and sickens him. Despite his weariness and sickness, he believes that they can be missionized and become true children of God. He also feels deep sympathy for the Marquesans because of the outrages committed upon them by Europeans. Letter 8, the seventh letter from the Marquesas, is entitled "Cruelty and Injustices of Foreigners to the Islanders." He is more and more fully persuaded, he tells his correspondent, "that the fierce and vindictive deportment, reported of [the Taipis] in some instances towards foreigners, is attributable, in a great degree at least, and in a majority of cases, to the ill treatment and wrong suffered by them from previous visitors; and often, is the direct consequence of the imprudent measures and violent usage of the very persons who publish their ferocity to the world."[38]

Stewart's response to the Marquesans is not a simple one. He admires their beauty, but he does not rest in that admiration, for he sees a dark underside. He cannot shake the idea of their cannibalism, and this overwhelms him with a sense of the sinfulness of the world. Finally, he feels profound sympathy for them and considers them deeply injured by Europeans. Yet even in his sympathy, he can-not excuse the Marquesans for the sin of cannibalism. Stewart's response, in other words, is that of a thinking human being who has seen too much and who has emerged, in the words of Samuel Taylor Coleridge, "like one that hath been stunn'd / And is of sense forlorn: / A sadder and a wiser man."[39]

David Porter sojourned in the Marquesas islands in 1813, nine years after Langsdorff's visit and sixteen years before Stewart's. The War of 1812 was raging, and Porter, like John Paul Jones before him, had gone into British territory to attack Britain's own ships. The British were astounded that their Pacific whale fishery should be threatened by an American vessel, and they sent out warships specifically to hunt down Porter. Porter ultimately lost his ship, the *Essex*, to the British warships *Phoebe* and *Cherub* in the bay of Valparaiso, Chile. For this loss, he was court-martialed, and his journal serves partially as an exoneration of his actions.

Porter disagrees with both Langsdorff and Stewart by concluding that the Marquesan islanders are *not* cannibals. In *Journal of a Cruise Made to the Pacific Ocean*, Porter writes: "I had been informed by the whites, on my arrival, and even by Wilson [a white man who had settled on Nuku Hiva, spoke Marquesan, and served as Porter's interpreter], that the natives of this island were cannibals: but, on the strictest inquiry, I could not learn that either of them had seen them in the act of eating human flesh."[40] Porter continues to ponder the question of whether or not Marquesans practice anthropophagy. He perceives the islanders as generous and benevolent, clean in their persons and in their mode of cooking and manner of eating, and wonders "whether they were really addicted to a practice so unnatural."[41] He continues: "How then can it be possible that a people so delicate, living in a country abounding with hogs, fruit, and a considerable variety of vegetables, should prefer a loathsome putrid human carcass, to the numerous delicacies their valleys afford? It cannot be: there must have been some misconception."[42]

Porter's questioning of the portrayal of Marquesans as cannibals should be examined against other explorers' accounts and in light of Melville's use of Porter as a source. Porter arrived at Nuku Hiva with the expectation that the islanders *were* cannibals. Indeed, he used the suggestion of cannibalism to instill fear into his crew before granting liberty ashore: "Let the fate of the many who have been cut off by the savages of the South Sea islands be a useful warning to us."[43] Here Porter both draws on and exploits cannibal talk.

At Nuku Hiva, Porter claimed the Marquesas for the fledgling United States and built Fort Collet to uphold his claim. During the building of the fort, with the Teii people as his allies, he fought a war first against the Ha'apa'a and then against the Taipi. To portray those he fought as cannibals seems to be in his best interest. Cannibalism has been used throughout history to justify aggression. Cannibalism is, in Porter's words, "a practice so unnatural" that cannibals must be conquered, even when the price is genocide. Yet Porter does not use cannibalism as a justification for violence. He *does* practice great violence against the Marquesan people, especially against the Taipi, but anthropophagy is not the excuse.

After Porter's description of his attack on the Taipi valley in 1813, during which he laid waste to the valley, burned ten villages, destroyed breadfruit trees, and killed and wounded great numbers of the Taipi, he fears the censure of the reader for his actions and attempts to justify those actions: "Many may censure my conduct as wanton and unjust. . . . They may question the motives of my conduct, and deny the necessity which compelled me to pursue it. But let such reflect a moment on our peculiar situation—a handful of men residing among numerous warlike tribes, liable every moment to be attacked by them, and all cut off; our only hopes of safety was in convincing them of our great superiority over them."[44] Interestingly, in the 1815 edition, Porter had appeared to contradict himself: he had written in his first sentence that the Taipi had "left us in quietness at our camp," a statement that seems at variance with his argument that his men were "liable every moment to be attacked by" the Taipi. Porter avoided this apparent contradiction by cutting the reference to quietness in the camp in the 1822 edition.

Porter could have strengthened his argument about the necessity of fighting the Taipi had he identified them as cannibals. Such an identification might have been used to justify extermination. Porter could have argued that cannibalistic savages would be even more "liable" to attack his troops at any moment, for such violence is inherent in their very natures—but he did not.

Porter ponders the question of Marquesan cannibalism throughout chapters 11–17 of his *Journal,* the chapters covering his time in the Washington Islands. He wonders whether the islanders resort to cannibalism because of hunger but questions whether they would prefer "a loathsome putrid human carcass, to the numerous delicacies their valleys afford?"[45] He then considers whether they eat enemies killed in battle. Such a thought deeply troubles him. After what Porter calls the Happah War, he goes to the Teii to claim the bodies of those killed so they can be buried and therefore not eaten. Upon his arrival, the Teii are thrown into confusion and snatch the bodies up in order to hide them in the bushes. Porter is overcome with horror, believing the Teii are hiding the bodies to conceal that they have been mutilated by cannibalism. He orders the Teii to reveal the bodies, but he is greatly surprised to find them unmutilated. The Teii claim that they hid the bodies because they feared that Porter would find them disagreeable. They entreat Porter to be allowed to keep two of the bodies to sing over and perform ceremonies, and Porter agrees. He notes that when the Teii recover the two bodies, they have a great aversion to touching either the dead bodies or even the blood on the poles used to carry the bodies. Porter writes: "This delicacy in concealing the wounded body of an enemy, and their caution in avoiding the touch of the blood or the dead carcasses, greatly staggered my belief of their being cannibals." He then adds, "Although they did not deny that they sometimes eat their enemies, at least so we understood them; *but it is possible we may have misunderstood.*"[46]

Porter posits the possibility that the identification of Marquesans as cannibals is both a misconception and a misunderstanding. Melville takes the very scenes in Porter's *Journal* that lead Porter to conclude that Marquesans are not cannibals and uses those exact materials to convey the opposite. Melville fixes on these scenes as some of the strongest and most direct evidence he presents in making the case that the Marquesans are in fact cannibals—and does this knowing that Porter reached the opposite conclusion. *Typee* is driven by the fear of cannibalism, but only in chapter 32 (of thirty-four chapters) does Tommo finally witness physical "evidence." The reader has anticipated the moment of Tommo's revelation throughout the book. Yet in Porter the same moment revealed the opposite: that Marquesans are *not* cannibals.

In *Typee* the confusion evinced by Marheyo and his family on Tommo's un-expected return from the Ti derives directly from the confusion of the Teii on Porter's appearance to claim the bodies of those slain in the Happah War. Porter writes: "At this moment my approach was discovered. They were all *thrown into the* utmost *confusion;* the dead bodies were in an instant snatched from the place where they lay, and hurried to a distance among the bushes, and shouting and hallooing evinced the utmost consternation. I now believed the truth of Wil-son's declaration [that the Marquesans are cannibals], and my blood recoiled with horror at the spectacle I was on the point of witnessing."[47] Melville echoes this sense of confusion and consternation, even repeating the phrase "throw[n] into the [utmost/greatest] confusion": "One day, returning unexpectedly from the 'Ti,' my arrival seemed to *throw* the inmates of the house *into the* greatest *con-fusion.* . . . The evident alarm the savages betrayed filled me with forebodings of evil, and with an uncontrollable desire to penetrate the secret so jealously guarded. . . . I forced my way into the midst of the circle, and just caught a glimpse of three human heads, which others of the party were hurriedly enveloping in the coverings from which they had been taken" (232; emphasis added). Porter has the power to direct the Teiis "in an authoritative manner" to return the bodies for him to see.[48] Because Porter can order the Teiis to uncover the bodies, he is able to see that there are no signs of cannibalism. Tommo does not have the authority Porter does, and so he continues to recoil in horror at what he perceives as evi-dence of anthropophagism. "Gracious God!" he thinks, "what dreadful thoughts entered my mind!" (233). Note here that even when Melville does not lift Porter's words directly, he paraphrases so closely that the origin of his source is evident.

Melville took from Porter not only the narrator's sense of alarm but also the packets in which the heads were concealed—and even the heads themselves. Tommo tells us, "I have already mentioned that from the ridge-pole of Marheyo's house were suspended a number of packages enveloped in tappa. . . . [Marheyo's family] was seated together on the mats, and by the lines which extended from the roof to the floor I immediately perceived that the mysterious packages were for some purpose or other under inspection" (232). These "mysterious packages" hold the heads that so appall Tommo. In Porter, the packages are completely in-nocent, hanging from the ceiling only to protect the contents from rats: "Their plumes and other articles of value, which would otherwise be injured by the rats, are suspended in baskets from the roofs of their houses, by lines passing through the bottom of an inverted calabash, to prevent those animals from descending them."[49]

Melville uses the heads that appear in Porter to direct the reader to an opposite conclusion from that which Porter reaches. In Porter, skulls and bones are a rec-ognized form of ancestor worship; they are "indeed the most precious relic."[50]

The keeping of skulls as a way to honor one's ancestors, especially within one's own domicile, is an old and recognized custom in many cultures and not necessarily a sign of cannibalism.[51] However, in *Typee*, Marheyo's family keeps heads, not skulls, which are preserved after the bodies to which they were attached were devoured.

Tommo's discovery that human heads are the contents of the mysterious packages hanging from the roof of Marheyo's house is the first of two pivotal scenes of cannibalism in *Typee*. The second occurs a week later (and within the same chapter). Tommo sees Typee warriors bearing the bodies of slain Happar warriors on long poles to the Ti. He is not permitted to stay at the Ti, but forced to leave. Two days later, he finally is allowed to return to the Ti and there finds a small canoe holding a human skeleton. Almost every description in the first part of this passage comes directly from chapter 13 of Porter's *Journal,* including the carrying of the bodies on poles, the stains of blood, the wrapping of the bodies in leaves, and the number of men—four—used to carry the bodies. Even the fact that the slain are Ha'apa'a is the same. Porter's description follows the "Happah War," and Melville's follows the "Second Battle with the Happars." As far as I have been able to discover, no French records document a battle between the Ha'apa'a and Taipi tribes during Melville's period of residence on Nuku Hiva, further evidence that Melville borrowed the description of this fight from Porter.

The second part of Melville's passage comes from a later chapter (16) in Porter's *Journal,* in which Porter sees the bodies of two slain Taipis in a canoe following the Typee War. Porter, like Tommo, is led to look into the canoe out of curiosity:

> The stench here was intolerable from the number of offerings which had been made: but, attracted by *curiosity,* I went to examine the canoes more minutely, and found the bodies of two of the Typees, whom we had killed, in a bloated state, at the bottom of that of the priest, and many other human carcasses, with the flesh still on them, lying about the canoe. . . . I asked them why . . . they put the bodies of the dead Typees in that [canoe] of the priest? they told me . . . that they were going to heaven, and that it was impossible to get there without canoes.[52]

The priest's canoe was large, so he needed ten bodies to propel it to heaven but as yet had only eight. Porter's attitude is nonchalant here, for he has by now concluded that the Marquesans are not cannibals, and therefore his interest in the bodies is only in why they have been put in that particular canoe. The answer he receives perfectly satisfies him.

Tommo's response to the same scene is very different. Once he is permitted back to the Ti, he sees a small canoe that had not been there before.

> Prompted by a *curiosity* I could not repress, in passing it I raised one end of the cover; at the same moment the chiefs, perceiving my design, loudly ejaculated, "Taboo! taboo!" But the slight glimpse sufficed; my eyes fell upon the disordered members of a human skeleton, the bones still fresh with moisture, and with particles of flesh clinging to them here and there! . . . All that night I lay awake, revolving in my mind the fearful situation in which I was placed. The last horrid revelation had now been made. (238; emphasis added)

For Porter, the bodies are stripped of horror. The flesh is still on the bone. Porter reports on the bodies as an ethnographic fact. They are placed in the priest's canoe to propel the canoe to heaven. Melville, however, invests the bodies with horror. That particles of flesh are still clinging to the bones here and there implies, at least in Tommo's imagination, that most of the flesh has been eaten off the bones. The bodies are the final revelation to Tommo that the Typees are indeed cannibals. Yet neither Porter nor Melville has witnessed cannibalism. Melville has none of the ocular proof of cannibalism that eighteenth- and nineteenth-century explorers were so eager to find.

Melville's method in *Typee* is very Hitchcockian. He elicits horror and fear from Tommo and from his readers with sound and glimpses and an overwhelming dread. Two days pass between when Tommo sees the bodies of the slain warriors borne to the Ti and when he is allowed to return. During those two days, "The sound of the drums continued, without intermission . . . and falling continually upon my ear, caused me a sensation of horror which I am unable to describe. On the following day hearing none of those noisy indications of revelry, I concluded that the inhuman feast was terminated" (237).

In his major written sources, Melville was presented with three very different views of cannibalism among the natives of one island, Nuku Hiva, within a period of thirty-five years (1804–39). One might expect a physician and naturalist such as Langsdorff to write with scientific detachment; a missionary such as Stewart to write with hope and faith; and a naval captain such as Porter, justifying his actions within his journal in response to a court-martial, to portray the Marquesans with savagery as a defense to justify his violence against them. Instead, Langsdorff relishes the thought that the Marquesans are cannibals and uses absurdity in his presentation of them as such, but he also advocates strongly the existence of anthropophagism. Stewart is ambivalent about Marquesans, both admiring them and feeling dejection and world-weariness at the thought of their violence and cannibalism. Porter questions whether Marquesans even are cannibals and finally concludes that they are not.

Geoffrey Sanborn asks, "*Why* were Western travelers to the Americas, Asia, the Pacific, and Africa so obsessed with the thought of cannibalism, even before their hosts provided them with a reason to think it?"[53] In his important work *The Sign of the Cannibal: Melville and the Making of a Postcolonial Reader,* Sanborn asks us to read *Typee, Moby-Dick,* and *Benito Cereno* from a postcolonial perspective. Sanborn cites the literary theory of Homi Bhabha as a principal influence on his work. The major claim of Sanborn's book, he tells us, is that "Bhabha's 'newness' existed as a *pattern* of interpretation within at least one colonial discourse [i.e., cannibalism], and this pattern was translated as a *challenge* to the structure of colonialism by at least one contemporary author," that is, Melville.[54] Sanborn quotes Bhabha's somewhat opaque definition of "newness" as "the mode of identity that emerges from 'the momentous, if momentary, extinction of the recognizable object of culture in the disturbed artifice of its signification, at the edge of experience.'"[55] Closer to my reading of *Typee* is Sanborn's assertion that "Especially in his representations of the encounters between white men and cannibals, [Melville] calls his readers back, again and again, to the 'afterthought' that haunts all efforts to ascertain and explain the existence of savagery."[56] Melville's calling back of his readers can be seen in the ways he draws on his major sources—Langsdorff, Stewart, and Porter—but ultimately does not follow the anthropophagic argument of any of them. Porter's ultimate denial of Marquesan cannibalism as a misconception and a misunderstanding might be expected to be closest to Melville's, but Melville rejects even this argument. Sanborn contends that Melville introduces the denial of cannibalism in *Typee* because he wants to make the entire discursive field an object of critical attention.[57] According to Sanborn, there is nothing particularly new in Melville's suggesting that the Taipis might not be cannibals: Melville is simply shifting from one established discursive position to another.[58] In *Typee,* Melville foregrounds questioning, just as he would later do in *Moby-Dick.* He questions the assertions of all his sources without coming to a final conclusion on whether the Marquesans were or were not cannibals.

Much of Sanborn's work resonates with mine, but I disagree with his argument about Melville's intentions in *Typee.* Sanborn wonders why Melville did not wage a stronger defense against the charge that Marquesans were cannibals. He argues that Melville worried that his narrative would be dismissed as untrustworthy because of its lack of dates and systematized explanations for customs and for its conclusions. For those reasons, Melville insists in *Typee* that his descriptions are drawn from memory and that his memory is perfectly exact and untainted by imagination. More importantly, Sanborn also believes that Melville was concerned that he would be attacked as a naive follower of discredited Rousseauian idealism. According to Sanborn, "those writers who denied the existence of cannibalism were very often stigmatized as deskbound theoreticians, incapable of accepting the fact that the world contained more than had been dreamed of in their philosophies."[59] As Sanborn notes, the word "theory" itself was stigmatized in this period because of its connections to the late Enlightenment idealization of the noble savage and to the perceived impact of that view on the horrific real-world events of the French Revolution. To avoid such a stigma, Melville backs away from the argument that Taipis are not cannibals.

I read the construction of *Typee* differently. While we know that Melville was brilliant, he had just spent four years at the farthest remove from intellectual discourse and the cultural perspectives of the literary world. He was casting about for a means of earning money and had been encouraged by those who heard them to turn his compellingly told tales into a written work. By the time *Typee* was published in 1846, Melville had spent four years telling the story of his adventures, first to his shipmates and then to his extended family. By reciting the story again and again, Melville learned what were its most effective parts and how to shape them into the final version. To preserve the threat of cannibalism throughout renders the story scarier, more dangerous, and more appealing. I agree completely with Sanborn that Melville "calls his readers back, again and again, to the 'afterthought' that haunts all efforts to ascertain and explain the existence of savagery."[60] But I see the oral quality of the tale shaping *Typee* far more than Melville's avoidance of criticism.

Melville left Nuku Hiva aboard the Australian whaleship *Lucy Ann* on August 9, 1842, so the first audience for his account of his sojourn in Nuku Hiva was his shipmates, fellow whalemen deeply versed in the related discourses of the South Seas. How better to establish his status as a new member of the crew than to spin a yarn in which he placed himself in the most sensational situation imaginable? By the last page of the first chapter of Melville's next book, *Omoo,* the sequel to *Typee,* the narrator is already called Typee, king of the cannibals. The narrator calls to his shipmate, who replies, "Halloa, who's that croaking? . . . Ay, Typee, my king of the cannibals, is it you!" (8). By his second book, Melville's narrator, loosely based on himself, is creating an aura that evokes his supposed time living among the Taipi cannibals. In 1824 the sociopath Samuel Comstock led the bloodiest mutiny in the history of the whale fishery aboard the whaleship *Globe.* His intent was to become the king of a cannibal island, but he failed miserably when he was murdered by his fellow mutineers within days of landing on Mili Island.[61] Melville metaphorically accorded himself the status Comstock aspired to by becoming Typee, the "king of the cannibals" in *Omoo.*

CANNIBAL CONTROVERSY

Any discussion of cannibalism must acknowledge the long-disputed question of whether cannibalism has ever existed. Even in the nineteenth century such questions arose. In *Voyages and Travels in Various Parts of the World*, Langsdorff writes: "Many persons of speculative and philosophic minds doubt, but upon insufficient grounds, the truth of anthropophagism. It is, however, incontrovertible, that almost all nations of the world have at one period or other been guilty of this crime."[62]

Melville was well aware of this controversy. In an important passage in *Typee*, he echoes Langsdorff before he comes to a middle ground between those who argue that cannibalism does not and never has existed and those who believe that anthropophagic epicureans can't wait to eat more human flesh:

> The reader will ere long have reason to suspect that the Typees are not free from the guilt of cannibalism; and he will then, perhaps, charge me with admiring a people against whom so odious a crime is chargeable. But this only enormity in their character is not half so horrible as it is usually described. According to the popular fictions, the crews of vessels, shipwrecked on some barbarous coast, are eaten alive like so many dainty joints by the uncivil inhabitants; and unfortunate voyagers are lured into smiling and treacherous bays; knocked in the head with outlandish war-clubs; and served up without any preliminary dressing. In truth, so horrific and improbable are these accounts, that many sensible and well-informed people will not believe that any cannibals exist; and place every book of voyages which purports to give any account of them, on the same shelf with Blue Beard and Jack the Giant-Killer; while others, implicitly crediting the most extravagant fictions, firmly believe that there are people in the world with tastes so depraved that they would infinitely prefer a single mouthful of material humanity to a good dinner of roast beef and plum pudding. But here, Truth, who loves to be centrally located, is again found between the two extremes; for cannibalism to a certain moderate extent is practised among several of the primitive tribes in the Pacific, but it is upon the bodies of slain enemies alone; and horrible and fearful as the custom is, immeasurably as it is to be abhorred and condemned, still I assert that those who indulge in it are in other respects humane and virtuous. (205)

Melville concludes that islanders of the South Pacific *are* cannibals "to a certain moderate extent" and only "among several of the primitive tribes"—and even then they feast on "the bodies of slain enemies alone."

In the controversy over the eating of human flesh, survival cannibalism is not under debate. It is unquestioned, understood, and accepted that humans in extreme conditions may be forced to eat the flesh of fellow humans in order to survive. After the sinking of the Nantucket whaleship *Essex* by a sperm whale in 1820, the survivors resorted to cannibalism. They were not condemned for their actions when they returned to Nantucket in 1821. Nor were the South American rugby players who survived an airplane crash in the Andes in 1972 and ultimately kept themselves alive by eating the bodies of those who died.

The fact that survival cannibalism exists is unquestioned. The reality of other forms of cannibalism, however, has long been debated. Cannibalism describes a large range of behaviors and motivations. These include the following:

Nutritional necessity (survival cannibalism)
Psychological imbalance (psychotic or criminal cannibalism)
Aggression (the hunting and eating of one's enemies)
Affection (the eating of one's friends or relatives)
Mortuary practice (funerary cannibalism)
Diet (gustatory cannibalism)
Health concerns (medicinal cannibalism)[63]

Cannibalism can be further divided into exocannibalism and endocannibalism. Exocannibalism refers to eating members of an enemy group, and endocannibalism to eating members of one's own group. Anthropologists and other social scientists have attempted to delineate ethnic groups by their practice of different forms of cannibalism.

The attempt at categorization was derailed with the more fundamental question of the existence of cannibalism posed in William Arens's *The Man-Eating Myth* in 1979. Arens's book brought this long-debated question to the public's attention. Arens, then associate professor of anthropology at the State University of New York at Stony Brook, argues that there are no unquestioned first-person accounts of ritual or gustatory cannibalism. Every report of cannibalism as a cultural phenomenon is second- or thirdhand. Native informants report to Europeans that they themselves are not cannibals, but that others are. Arens writes: "Given the time and effort, it might be possible to trace the path of such accusations in an unbroken chain across an entire continent. For example, the Baganda who live on the shores of Lake Victoria claim that inhabitants of the Sese Islands of this vast inland sea eat interlopers. The Sese deny this, but admit that the natives on the far shore are indeed cannibals. Unfortunately, the material trails off at this point, since the ethnographer failed to check with the latest suspects."[64] This same pattern can be seen in eighteenth-century newspapers. In 1796, *Mas-*

sachusetts Magazine, reporting on the European discovery of the northern Marquesas Islands by Captain Joseph Ingraham in the American brig *Hope* in 1791, stated: "There is every reason to suppose [the Marquesan islanders] cannibals. The inhabitants of Resolution-bay would not own it of themselves; but freely declared that the other islanders, and the inland people of their island, devoured human flesh."[65] Just as Arens suggests in his anecdote following cannibalism from one group to another, the broader sweep of accusations of cannibalism historically can be seen to move from region to region as Europeans make first contact.

Melville plays with this idea in *Typee.* Although the Typees are regarded by the other tribes of Nuku Hiva as cannibals, the Typees themselves claim that it is the Happars, and not themselves, who are the cannibals. When speaking to Toby and Tommo, the Typees "dwelt upon the cannibal propensities of the Happars, a subject which they were perfectly aware could not fail to alarm us; while at the same time they earnestly disclaimed all participation in so horrid a custom" (102).

Arens argues that the discipline of anthropology has not maintained the usual standards of documentation and intellectual rigor in its consideration of cannibalism. "Instead," he writes, "it has chosen uncritically to lend its support to the collective representations and thinly disguised prejudices of western culture about others. Indeed, I find it difficult to understand how learned debates could rage for decades on whether or not a particular marriage system actually exists, while we merely assume that people have eaten and continue to eat each other."[66]

Arens's arguments provoked a storm of controversy. Arens and Marshall Sahlins, a professor of anthropology at the University of Chicago, engaged in an exchange of letters printed in the *New York Review of Books* in 1979 over the question of Aztec cannibalism. Arens argues again that the lack of documentation of cannibalism is the important factor: "Liberal-minded scholars have taken upon themselves the responsibility of defending the savage mind and body without giving the matter of the evidence on this purported phenomenon even the minimal consideration."[67] Sahlins replies to Arens by quoting Bernal Diaz's purported firsthand account of the cannibalism he witnessed en route to Mexico City in 1519. "The Spanish chronicles," he states, "do not presuppose or allude to an *idea* of cannibalism; they quite plainly report the practice of it."[68] Unfortunately, at the end of his letter, Sahlins likens Arens's lack of belief in ritual cannibalism to a lack of belief in the Holocaust—"Professor X puts out some outrageous theory, such as the Nazis really didn't kill the Jews, human civilization comes from another planet, or there is no such thing as cannibalism"—and accuses Arens of presenting his argument as a publicity stunt to draw attention to his book.[69] Arens's attack on anthropology and Sahlins's attack on Arens thus undermine what is important scholarly disagreement with emotion and accusation.

Other anthropologists were drawn into the debate, as Lawrence Osborne ably points out in his 1997 *Lingua Franca* article, "Does Man Eat Man? Inside the Great Cannibalism Controversy." Peggy Reeves Sanday, professor of anthropology at the University of Pennsylvania, attempts to answer Arens mathematically in *Divine Hunger: Cannibalism as a Cultural System* (1986). She presents tables showing, for example, "Relationship between level of political sovereignty and cannibalism" and "Relationship between length of postpartum sex taboo and cannibalism in politically homogeneous and heterogeneous societies."[70] Nonetheless, she is still dependent on the same ethnographies that Arens so strongly criticized as the basis for determining the presence of cannibalism.

Sanday draws from a vast range of literature stretching back over millennia and then attempts to make it seem scientific by formulating this jumble of undifferentiated hearsay, historical documents (many of which have political, social, or other agendas peculiar to their very different times and places), and uncheckable accounts of travelers into tables. These tables do not address the force of Arens's arguments concerning the nature of the evidence for cannibalism.

"A search of the literature," Sanday writes, "convinces me that Arens overstates his case."[71] She does not, however, present that literature. Readers are dependent on her assertion that she searched the literature. Sanday continues:

> The fact that Arens overstates his case should not be taken to mean that the thirty-seven cases of cannibalism reported in Table 1 represent undisputed examples of actual cannibalism. The ethnographies upon which I relied are the best available for use in cross-cultural research based on a standard sample. The data on cannibalism, however, are uneven, ranging from lengthy descriptions of ritual cannibalism reconstructed from informants' recollections of the past to a few sentences describing the consumption of the hearts of enemies. Keeping in mind the problematic nature of the data, the reader is cautioned to look for suggestive trends in the tables rather than irrefutable demonstrations of relationships.[72]

After Arens, no scholar can simply accept the veracity of these ethnographies. Sanday's presentation of her information implies that she is imparting hard scientific fact in tabular form. But the same questions of reliability still dog those sources, and the ethnographies are, in Melville's words, "but boggy ground to build on" (*Billy Budd* 57).

If Sanday may be seen as allying herself with the Sahlins camp, Gananath Obeyesekere, emeritus professor of anthropology at Princeton University, is in the Arens camp. The University of Essex in Great Britain hosted a conference on cannibalism in 1995, out of which grew a collection entitled *Cannibalism and the*

Colonial World, to which both Arens and Obeyesekere contributed. Like Arens, Obeyesekere questions many of the sources on which assertions of cannibalism are based. Obeyesekere's interest in cannibalism culminated in *Cannibal Talk: The Man-Eating Myth and Human Sacrifice in the South Seas.* In that book, he investigates the discourses of cannibalism and the behaviors and practices associated with such talk in the interaction between natives of the South Pacific and Europeans after Captain James Cook's first voyage to the Pacific in 1768–72. He looks at what he calls dialogical misunderstandings in the South Seas. Misunderstanding extended in both directions. Europeans believed South Pacific islanders to be cannibals, and the islanders in turn believed Europeans to be cannibals. This misunderstanding resulted in what Obeyesekere calls "cannibal talk," talk that flowed in both directions.

Ultimately, the literary scholar does not have to solve this controversy—nor can she. Nonetheless, it is important to understand that questions about the existence of ritual cannibalism have arisen throughout history. They arose in Melville's day, and they continue to this day. Melville made little direct use of this controversy, but it underpins much of the narrative tension in the novel. As he wrote in the passage from *Typee* quoted above, "Many sensible and well-informed people will not believe that any cannibals exist . . . while others, implicitly crediting the most extravagant fictions, firmly believe that there are people in the world with tastes so depraved that they would infinitely prefer a single mouthful of material humanity to a good dinner of roast beef and plum pudding" (205). The controversy over the existence of cannibalism lurks in the background of Tommo's concerns over whether he will himself be eaten: the general informs the specific. Tommo is filled "with forebodings of evil" when he stumbles upon Marheyo and his family examining the mysterious packages that prove to contain human heads (232). He has an "expression of horror" when he sees the bones in the canoe with "particles of flesh clinging to them" (238). That night he cannot sleep out of fear. Earlier, he and Toby had mistaken a roasted juvenile pig at a midnight feast for a cooked baby. These incidents trigger Tommo's more overt statements of fear of cannibalism, although he in fact never witnesses anthropophagy. The uncertainty of Tommo's knowledge of whether he will be eaten or not parallels the uncertainty of whether ritual cannibalism has ever existed.

CANNIBAL CONVERSATION

That Melville traveled to the South Pacific during a historic moment has long been acknowledged. He arrived at the Marquesas in July of 1842 just as the French took possession of the islands. Over 165 years later, the French still retain possession of all of French Polynesia. Other claims to the Marquesas, including those by the Americans, British, and Russians, and earlier by the French, were short lived. But the historic moment of Melville's arrival in the South Pacific also coincides with a cultural moment. The romantic movement and the gothic strain within it that is an extreme version of romanticism dominated the first half of the nineteenth century. The gothic is obsessed with the morbid and the grotesque.

M. G. Lewis's *The Monk* (1796) and other gothic novels were published in Great Britain at the end of the eighteenth century; British gothicism culminated with Charlotte Brontë's *Jane Eyre* (1847) and Emily Brontë's *Wuthering Heights* (1847), published a year after *Typee*. Edgar Allan Poe's gothic stories were published in the United States beginning in the 1830s. Melville echoes Poe in his initial description of Taioha'e Bay in *Typee*. Melville writes: "Nothing can exceed the imposing scenery of this bay. Viewed from our ship as she lay at anchor in the middle of the harbor, it presented the appearance of a vast natural amphitheatre in decay, and overgrown with vines, the deep glens that furrowed its sides appearing like enormous fissures caused by the ravages of time" (24). This gloomy description evokes Edgar Allan Poe's "The Fall of the House of Usher" (1839) more than tropical paradise. Melville reinforces his subtextual reference to Poe with his use of Poe's words "decay" and "fissure." On his first approach to the House of Usher, Poe's narrator is oppressed by "an atmosphere which had no affinity with the air of heaven, but which had reeked up from the decayed trees, and the gray wall and the silent tarn—a pestilent and mystic vapor, dull, sluggish, faintly discernible, and leaden-hued."[73] Melville's reader, too, is oppressed by the decay of the vast, ravaged hillside.

At the end of the eighteenth century and in the first half of the nineteenth century, there is a cultural pattern that is perfectly geared to receive the image of cannibalism as the dark other side of tropical paradise. Books that charted the travels of early explorers during the 1800s almost invariably carry titles with the term "cannibal." The perception of the Marquesas is colored by cultural tropes that depict these dark, rain-shrouded islands as the habitation of the cannibal Other.

Some sense of the popular image of the South Seas cannibal can be seen in a newspaper piece on the Native American leader Joseph Brandt. To make his point, the writer states: "Many were mortified, that the appearance of Brandt did not inspire all the fantastic horrors of a chief of the Cannibal Islands."[74] Clearly, the public was enthralled by such horrors. The public held the image of a cannibal chief to be similar to Ishmael's first sight of Queequeg: squares of tattooing across his face and no hair on his head except "a small scalp-knot twisted up on his forehead." "Good heavens! what a sight! Such a face!" Ishmael tells us. "It was of a dark, purplish, yellow color, here and there stuck over with large, blackish looking squares" (*Moby-Dick* 21). Melville draws on the popular conception of the cannibal chief. Walt Disney Productions would do the same 150 years later in its depiction of cannibals in the film *Pirates of the Caribbean: Dead Man's Chest.* What Melville does that Disney does not, however, is subvert this popular image until Ishmael declares, "Better sleep with a sober cannibal than a drunken Christian," turns in with Queequeg, and "never slept better in my life" (24). One can certainly not imagine Will Turner (played by actor Orlando Bloom) or the pirate captain Jack Sparrow (played by actor Johnny Depp) blithely turning in with the cannibals portrayed in *Pirates of the Caribbean.*

Much of the cannibal talk that Melville heard evoked vivid images of the exotic, grotesque, and horrifying. Much was also unconscious, an unthinking comparison thrown out, unheeded by the speaker. For example, in a piece in the *New-York Mirror,* a master printer reports of his early life: "I had never seen a printing-press, or a metal type, and was as totally ignorant of the mode and manner by which the letters were arranged, and the impression given, as the natives of Captain Morrell's Cannibal Islands."[75] Melville later employs such offhandedness when he talks of the people of New Bedford staring "not at Queequeg so much for they were used to seeing cannibals like him in their streets,—but at seeing him and me" together (58). Here the term "cannibal" is simply a casual designation for a South Seas islander, a relatively meaningless label; it is not invested with horror, nor wonder, nor humor. In another offhand reference to cannibals, Lester Janes, writing for the *Western Christian Advocate,* tells us: "'The gospel,' then, as said Paul, 'Is the power of God unto salvation'—salvation from heathen ignorance and wretchedness, as also from sin—'to every one that believeth,' whether he be found in savage or civilized land, an Indian, a Hottentot, or a South Sea cannibal."[76] The Indian and the Hottentot are simply identified by ethnicity, but the South Sea islander is irrevocably paired with cannibalism. The Indian and the Hottentot are Others that have become known over a much longer period. Over time, as the Other becomes more familiar, the cannibal question recedes. By the 1830s, the image of Native Americans—the original subject of New World cannibal talk—had become freighted with a complex edifice of meaning based on extensive familiarity and interaction, but the association with cannibalism had vanished.

Not all cannibal talk was so unconscious. The *Catholic Telegraph* in 1838 ran a chauvinistic piece in a column entitled "Statistics 1" that is a classic statement of British imperialism and manifest destiny, with its overt ethnocentrism and contempt for most of the rest of humanity. Although the main objects of attack are native New Zealanders, all those who live from the Tropic of Capricorn south are included. "Whoever heard of the Polynesians learned," the writer asks, "or of any learning between Capricorn and the south pole?" Such chauvinism was part of the culture from which Melville emerged just before he left for the South Pacific in 1841.

[New Zealand natives] are cannibals from necessity. * * * * * Here, without the aid of "religious prejudices," we have the whole theory of cannibalism. Men tortured by insufferable hunger, cast "wolfish eyes" upon each other, and by degrees conquering the strong repugnance which all animals feel to prey upon their own species, exactly from the same cause which impelled the African hyenas mentioned by Bryce, to eat their companions. * * * There is no nation, however, so openly and disgustingly addicted to anthropophagy as the New Zealanders. Their unnatural and ferocious appetite delights in the taste of a human victim. . . .

It would be difficult to produce parallel instances of cannibalism in the temperate zone of the north, or even in the Arctic Circle. European Zealand, which gave the name to the South Sea Zealand, contained in former ages, pirates of the fiercest kind;—but we have no record of cannibals. Great Britain has been peopled by Pagans, by ferocious and war-like savages, but Cesar found no cannibals among the ancient inhabitants of that Island. The learned London Reviewers say, that the New Zealanders are cannibals from necessity. If so, with due deference let it be asked, does not the same, or even a greater degree of *necessity* exist within the limits of the Arctic Circle? Yet the Greenlander, the Samoides, and the Esquimaux are not man-eaters. . . .

Learning has flourished to some extent near the verge of the north frigid zone. Iceland and Lapland have had their learned men. Linnaeus was reckoned among the *hyperborean* learned, but whoever heard of the Australian learned? Whoever heard of the Polynesians learned, or of any learning between Capricorn and the south pole?

Great Britain alone, with her 24,000,000 of inhabitants, and her 10,000 square miles, (about half the size of Zealand) possesses and exercises more moral and physical force than the whole southern zone, with her 4,000,000 of square miles of land, and her uncounted millions of semi-barbarians, upon whose territory the sun never sets.[77]

Here as elsewhere cannibalism is a form of othering. The Esquimaux, although foreign to the "civilized" whites of the north, are not so foreign as the Polynesian—and therefore they are not labeled man-eaters.

In 1836, two years before the "Statistics 1" piece appeared, the *Catholic Telegraph* ran a short piece arguing the opposite of the 1838 piece: that cannibalism did exist in the north, even in Great Britain:

Cannibalism.—Cannibalism has existed among all savage nations. St. Jerome says some British tribes ate human flesh, and the Scots from Galloway killed and ate the English in the reign of Henry the 1st. Scythians were drinkers of human blood. Columbus found cannibals in America. The aborigines of the Carribbee [*sic*] Islands were cannibals; and some South American tribes, and most of the natives of the South Sea Islands, make it an open practice to eat human flesh;—while in some African cities it is openly sold by the pound.[78]

The two pieces from the *Catholic Telegraph* show the pervasiveness and arbitrary nature of cannibal talk. They also reassert its identification as "talk": in other words, as something that is transmitted verbally and that is inconsistent and fluid. *Typee* is filled with cannibal talk, everything from Ned's jocular statements to Melville's ponderings on whether the Marquesans eat human flesh or not to Tommo's use of the word as an identification rather than a judgment to the dread inspired by the term in Tommo's imagination as he is held captive in the Typee valley.

When the sailor Ned tells Tommo that the Typees "don't like sailor's flesh, it's too salt" (26), his statement resonates with Melville's written source, Langsdorff's *Voyages and Travels in Various Parts of the World,* in which Langsdorff tells his readers, "Englishmen are preferable to Frenchmen."[79] This taste for Englishmen can be found in Langsdorff's narrative as well as in the two-volume report of the expedition's leader, Adam Johann von Krusenstern, first published in 1811 and translated into English in 1813. Thirty years later, the Marquesan preference for Englishmen over Frenchmen entered popular culture. Two 1843 newspaper references contain no hints that knowledge of this preference originated in a Russian expedition to the Marquesas or that such knowledge was initially transmitted via the written word rather than orally.

By 1843 the cannibal targeting of Englishmen for their culinary superiority has become an oral story transmitted via speech and only set down in newspapers after it has been overheard. Lewis Gaylord Clarke, in his column "Gossip with Readers and Correspondents" in the *Spirit of the Times,* tells his readers:

> We do not know when we have been more "horrified" than on reading the following in a London journal: "Two natives of the cannibal islands of Marquesas have been carried to France. The story runs, that on the voyage one of their fellow-passengers asked them which they liked best, the French or the English? 'The English!' answered the man, smacking his lips; 'they are the *fattest.*' 'And a great deal more *tender,*' chimed in the woman, with a grin that exhibited two rows of pointed teeth as sharp as a crocodile's!"[80]

This story appeared one week earlier in a shortened version in the *Anglo American* under the subtopic "Flattering Preference" within the "Varieties" column: "Two natives of the Marquesas (cannibal) Islands have been carried to France.

The story runs, that on the voyage one of their fellow-passengers asked which they liked best, the French or the English? 'The English!' answered the man, smacking his lips, 'they are the *fattest.*'"[81]

Remarkably, in the thirty years between the publication of Langsdorff's book and the newspaper incarnations, the story has retained its Marquesan base. The cannibals who prefer Englishmen are still Marquesans. By 1843, however, the cannibals themselves affirm their preference in the first person and with a great deal of glee. The preference is no longer stated matter-of-factly in the third person by a naturalist. Additional details have accrued over time, including the fact that Englishmen are preferred for their fatness and that the cannibal woman has sharpened crocodile-like teeth. Sharpened teeth were popularly considered a certain sign of cannibalism; cannibals filed their teeth into points, it was argued, in order better to tear human flesh from bones and chew it. Melville gives Queequeg "filed teeth" in "The Cabin-Table," chapter 34 of *Moby-Dick* (152), but this is his only mention of Queequeg's teeth. No ethnographic account of the Marquesans in the nineteenth century mentions teeth sharpening as a cultural trait. Rather, sharpened teeth, characteristic of some native groups, are arbitrarily included here as a sign that these people are most certainly cannibals, which gives an "urban myth" quality to the story. And indeed, if sharpened teeth were necessary for consumption of flesh, why don't beefeaters cultivate the practice?

Melville's known encounter with the information that Marquesan cannibals prefer to eat Englishmen over Frenchmen in Langsdorff, and his possible encounter with the oral version of the same information, parallels his use of other sources in *Typee.* Melville was immersed in sailor talk during his almost four years at sea. He heard stories of cannibals from other sailors and told yarns to sailors as he moved from vessel to vessel. He sensationalizes the story of *Typee* in many ways. Yet Melville's presentation of his time "among the cannibals" is not so sensationalized or self-aggrandizing as other sailor narratives. He doesn't place himself joining or leading a war party, nor does he place himself next to the bonfire of a cannibal feast.

"S. R." (whoever he may be) published extracts from letters from a friend "now and for more than two years absent on a voyage to the South seas, on board of a Nantucket whaler," under the title "Incidents in a Whaling Voyage," in *Friend: A Religious and Literary Journal* in 1837. One of his extracts gives a sense of the cannibal talk that was indulged in by sailors shortly before Melville went to sea. The Marquesans "are tattooed horribly," the friend writes, "from crown to heel (the men),—look like so many fiends, and in some respects are not unworthy the association, since they are undoubtedly cannibals,—themselves avowing, and without shame, that they devour the bodies of their enemies slain or captured in battle."[82] Why undoubtedly? In what way did they avow their cannibalism? Was it in sign language? When so few sailors spoke any of the Polynesian languages, how were such important pieces of information conveyed? Indeed, who initiated discussion of the subject in these encounters?

Such questions arise in early encounters between Polynesians and Europeans. When Europeans first asked Polynesians if they were cannibals, they had no common language and so mimicked cannibalism by raising their arms and pretending to eat. Obeyesekere, among others, wonders how Polynesians interpreted such actions. Did they fear that the Europeans were signifying that they, the *Europeans*, were anthropophagists and were eager to eat the Polynesians? Obeyesekere writes of Cook's visit to the Sandwich Islands:

> Something curious was going on here—from the very first visit: Cook thought that the Hawaiians were cannibals; and the Hawaiians thought that it was the British who were out to eat them! . . . The Hawaiians' hypothesis was based on the "pragmatics of common sense" and empirical inference that characterizes the everyday thought of most peoples. Here was a ragged, filthy, half-starved bunch of people arriving on their island, gorging themselves on food and asking questions about cannibalism. Since Hawaiians did not know that the British inquiry was a scientific hypothesis, they must be forgiven for making the practical inference that these hungry people asking questions about cannibalism were cannibals themselves and might actually eat the Hawaiians.[83]

Melville posits this same misunderstanding in his description of Tommo and Toby's first encounter with members of the Typee tribe, two children presented as a savage Adam and Eve. "The frightened pair now stood still, whilst we endeavored to make them comprehend the nature of our wants. In doing this Toby went through with a complete series of pantomimic illustrations—opening his mouth from ear to ear, and thrusting his fingers down his throat, gnashing his teeth and rolling his eyes about, till I verily believe the poor creatures took us for a couple of white cannibals who were about to make a meal of them" (*Typee* 69). A little later, Kory-Kory reverses the sailor-Typee interaction when he attempts to make Tommo and Toby understand that the Happars are cannibals. He "explained himself by a variety of gestures, during the performance of which he would dart out of the house, and point abhorrently towards the Happar valley; running in to us again with a rapidity that showed he was fearful we would lose one part of his meaning before he could complete the other; and continuing his illustrations by seizing the fleshly part of my arm in his teeth, intimating by the operation that the people who lived over in that direction would like nothing better than to treat me in that manner" (*Typee* 103).

Arens notes that his interest in cannibalism was provoked when he was doing fieldwork in Tanzania in 1968. He was astonished to learn that Europeans were popularly seen as cannibals and were called by the African word for "bloodsucker." The locals believed that the blood was drained into a bucket and transported by fire engine to an urban hospital, where it was converted into red capsules taken by Europeans.[84] Arens locates the origin of this story in an unsuccessful British blood drive during World War II to provide blood for African troops fighting overseas. The most humanitarian of intents was thus transformed into an image of horror and fear, raising such questions as how do we see ourselves? How are we seen by others? What complex signs and signifiers shape these interactions?

THE DARK ISLANDS

Typee was written in a world in which the South Pacific islands were perceived as haunts of cannibals. The Marquesas, feared as they were, were eclipsed by the terror that gripped sailors at the mention of the word "Fiji." The words "Fiji" (in all its variant spellings) and "cannibal" are coupled throughout early nineteenth-century newspapers. The offhandedness with which this coupling occurs suggests its pervasiveness and acceptance. The Fijian is simply assumed to be a cannibal. In an 1845 column on "The Feejee Islands," for example, a writer from the *New York Observer and Chronicle* begins: "So beautiful was their aspect that I could scarcely bring my mind to the realizing sense of the well known fact, that they were the abode of a savage, ferocious, and treacherous race of cannibals."[85] In an 1847 article on Shakespeare in the *American Review,* the writer casually mentions that the "Brummel of Broadway may be no more exquisitely clad than the cannibal dandy of Feejee."[86] The writer means either to refer to the ornate headdresses and elaborate personal jewelry and decoration of some South Pacific tribes or to contrast the opulent clothing of Broadway to the relative nakedness of other South Pacific tribes, but he unthinkingly throws in the word "cannibal." The writer of an untitled 1848 article on the Irish famine discusses being driven by deep hunger to survival cannibalism then adds: "Such a man, placed in a position where the only food was human flesh, would have made his experiment a habit, and would have enjoyed his cannibal meals with as much relish as a chief of the Feejee Islands."[87] What is relevant here is not the matter of survival cannibalism but the unquestioning assumption of Fijian cannibalism. The geographic and economic range of the American merchant fascinates the author of an article on "The American Merchant": "The American merchant . . . sends his merchandise all over the earth, stocks every market; makes wants that he may supply them; covers the New Zealander with Southern cotton woven in Northern looms;

builds blocks of stores in the Sandwich Islands; swaps with the Feejee cannibals; sends the whale ship among the icebergs of the poles."[88] Note that only the description of the Fijian is pejorative, and the author seems completely unconscious of that fact. "Feejee" and "cannibal" are simply an accepted pairing.

Melville, too, exhibits a similar unconsciousness in equating Fijians with savagery throughout *Moby-Dick*. In "Cetology" (chapter 32), he writes of the killer whale that it "is very savage—a sort of Feegee fish" (143). In "The Shark Massacre" (chapter 66), the savagery is synonymous with paganism. Queequeg's hand is almost bitten off by a dead shark, and he agonizingly cries out, "Queequeg no care what god made him shark . . . wedder Fejee god or Nantucket god; but de god wat made shark must be one dam Ingin" (302). The god-creator of the shark is the ultimate savage: both a Fijian *and* an Indian. The tie between Indians and barbarity is made explicit—and deeply questioned—in the Indian-hating chapters of *The Confidence-Man* (1857). Finally, in "The Whale as a Dish" (chapter 65), Fijians are specifically tied to cannibalism: "Cannibals? who is not a cannibal? I tell you it will be more tolerable for the Fejee that salted down a lean missionary in his cellar against a coming famine; it will be more tolerable for that provident Fejee, I say, in the day of judgment, than for thee, civilized and enlightened gourmand, who nailest geese to the ground and feastest on their bloated livers in thy paté-de-foie-gras" (300). The anger in this passage is directed against intolerance, questioning those elites who eat the livers of geese nailed to the ground and yet condemn the savagery of others. Melville's anger at intolerance and cruelty is patent here, but Melville seems unaware that he, too, is dehumanizing the Fijians by labeling them cannibals.

Melville's references to Fiji and Fijians in *Moby-Dick* are not drawn from written sources, as so many of the references in *Moby-Dick* are. Instead, Melville's allusions to Fiji are a form of cannibal talk. Just as references to Fijian cannibals permeated contemporary nineteenth-century newspapers, so they filled the talk of sailors. When the crew of the whaleship *Grampus* bursts in to the Spouter Inn in chapter 3 of *Moby-Dick*, the landlord starts up, crying, "That's the Grampus's crew. I seed her reported in the offing this morning; a three years' voyage, and a full ship. Hurrah, boys; now we'll have the latest news from the Feegees" (15). There is much humor in this passage. How recent can the "latest news" be after a three-year voyage? And why would the citizens of a sober New England town such as New Bedford be interested in the news of an island half a world away? In fact, they would be—the Fiji Islands were a place of shipwreck and desertion, a dark and terrifying place in which the sailors were supremely interested. This passage illustrates how Fiji pervaded the speech of sailors.

How did Fijians acquire their reputation for cannibalism? All South Pacific islanders were supposed to be flesh-eaters, but the Fijians were considered the ultimate cannibals. The Fiji Islands were known as the Cannibal Islands. The islands of Fiji border Polynesia, but Fijians are *not* Polynesian. In early twentieth-century ethnographic terms, they are Melanesian, with much darker skin and more tightly curled hair than the light-brown skin and long black hair of the Polynesians. The first Melanesians encountered by early European voyagers traveling from the east were Fijians. Perhaps the darkness of their skin made Fijians even more Other than the islanders the Europeans had so far encountered.

As Obeyesekere notes, according to the reports of sea captains, missionaries, and beachcombers, Fiji was the "haunt of 'cannibals'" by the early nineteenth century.[89] The earliest accounts of Fijian cannibalism are from castaways, travelers, and traders. One sandalwood trader narrates a horrific account of Fijian cannibalism for *Gentleman's Magazine*, later reprinted in the July 15, 1820, issue of the *Atheneum*. The article begins uncompromisingly, "The people of these islands are cannibals."[90] The trader then tells a story of swindling and chicanery. Sandalwood was obtained by American vessels in Fiji and other South Pacific islands to be used as a trade item for China, but it had become scarce because demand was so high. When the trader arrives in Fiji, he is invited to join in eating an enemy chief recently killed in battle. "To enable me to have so intimate an intercourse with these people," he writes, "I had to encounter many dangers, and to conform to many of their disgusting customs. This horrible custom, however, of eating human flesh I had hitherto been able to avoid; but it was necessary that I should seem to acquiesce even in this, and, as the natives did, take a delight in it."[91] The trader comes up with a ruse by which the human flesh is to be brought to his vessel the next day. He then tells his mate that he will hide below and the mate is to pretend to be disgusted with the meat of cannibalism and order that it not be left on the ship. The ruse works, and the following day the trader goes ashore to demand the human flesh he was guaranteed. The natives try in vain to say that the meat was brought to the ship and refused by the mate. The trader feigns great anger, and one of the old women cowers in fear and tells him, "If *you* are angry, *me* shall die. She then demanded what could be done to pacify me? I told her I must have a certain quantity of sandel wood." The woman sends servants to cut the wood "which appeased me."[92] A hair-raising story of cannibalism becomes a nasty story of deception and exploitation. It is also important to note that the trader never actually witnesses cannibalism; this is yet another instance of cannibal talk.

The Fijians' cannibal reputation was only enhanced by reports of the United States Exploring Expedition (1838–42), which were widely reprinted in contemporary newspapers. The *Niles' National Register* reprints the following story, for example, from the *New York Tribune:* "In the Feejee Islands the inhabitants were found to be cannibals; and several of the natives came on board the Peacock with half eaten bones in their hands, and still eating the human flesh on deck as unconsciously as though it were a matter of the most ordinary occurrence."[93] If the islanders are eating human flesh onboard the *Peacock,* does this account constitute the ocular proof of cannibalism so desired by Europeans? Several factors arise, however, that cast doubt upon this "proof." First of all, the newspaper writer is clearly not aboard the vessel, and it is unclear whether the writer of the journal upon which the account is based was stationed aboard the *Peacock* or not. Second, what proof is there that the natives were carrying human bones, not pig bones with the meat still clinging to them? Again and again, it has been proved that what was thought to be human flesh was actually pork. Arens refers to the mistaken identity of pork as human flesh in *The Man-Eating Myth* and in "Rethinking Anthropophagy."[94] Melville illustrates a similar confusion in *Typee.* Tommo and Toby are woken in the middle of the night and urged to "ki ki," or eat. One of the Typees brings "a large trencher of wood, containing some kind of steaming meat" to them, and Toby is instantly suspicious. "A baked baby, I dare say! but I will have none of it, never mind what it is." A few moments later Toby tells Tommo, "A baked baby, by the soul of Captain Cook! . . . I tell you you are bolting down mouthfuls from a dead Happar's carcass, as sure as you live, and no mistake." Tommo feels instantly sick and demands that a light be brought. "When the taper came, I gazed eagerly into the vessel, and recognised the mutilated remains of a juvenile porker! 'Puarkee!' exclaimed Kory-Kory, looking complacently at the dish" (94–95). The confusion between pork and human flesh that Arens discusses in New Guinea in the twentieth century was thus a trope in the nineteenth century. In the newspaper piece on the United States Exploring Expedition, however, such a possibility is not acknowledged, and the assumption of cannibalism is instant and unquestioned. Tommo's allusion to Captain Cook refers to the still-debated question of whether Cook's body was cannibalized after he was killed in Hawaii on February 14, 1779, during his third voyage to the South Pacific.[95]

After sandalwood was depleted due to overharvesting throughout the Pacific, a trade arose in bêche-de-mer, or sea cucumbers, which were dried and sold to the Chinese. Mary Wallis, the pious wife of a sea captain involved in the bêche-de-mer trade, spent five years (1844–49) in the Fiji Islands. Her journal was published in 1851 as *Life in Feejee: Five Years among the Cannibals.* In the introduction, the Reverend C. W. Flanders, evidently the editor of the volume, tells us: "The natives of the Feejee Islands have, heretofore, been regarded as the Ishmaelites of the South Pacific Ocean. . . . Their natural ferocity and habits of cannibalism have discouraged all attempts even to civilize them."[96] Yet again the Fiji Islands are associated with cannibalism—as is, interestingly in the context of *Moby-Dick,*

Ishmael. But Wallis herself never saw the eating of human flesh. Like almost all reports of cannibalism, her account rests on hearsay.

Wallis's accounts of anthropophagy are vivid and visceral: "On one occasion, [Chief Thakombau] ordered a chief to be brought before him; he then commanded his tongue to be cut out, which he devoured raw, talking and joking with the mutilated chief at the same time."[97] This is a horrible story, but it occurred "several years ago,"[98] so Wallis only repeats what she has been told rather than witnessing anthropophagy herself. Later, she repeats another story, in which a beachcomber and his "native woman" are killed and eaten, but "the lives of the children were spared that they might be fattened before they should be killed."[99] Such horror stories invoke grim and violent fairy tales like *Hansel and Gretel*. To increase the dreadfulness, Wallis tells us, "Some part of the cooked bodies were offered [to the children] to eat."[100] In another instance, Wallis reports that the corpse of a murdered husband was sent to his wife, who "found his body exceedingly mutilated—the heart, liver and tongue had been devoured."[101]

Why does Wallis repeat such horrific stories? And why is her fascination with these stories so strong that she listens to and records them in detail? Again, in Sanborn's words, "*Why* were Western travelers to the Americas, Asia, the Pacific, and Africa so obsessed with the thought of cannibalism?"[102] Wallis's motivation seems threefold. First, stories of cannibalism obviously horrified and enthralled her at the same time. Second, she was meeting her audience's expectations, for they anticipated such stories from the Fiji Islands. For this reason, Wallis published her journal under the title *Life in Feejee* with the subtitle *Five Years among the Cannibals*. Third, and most importantly, Wallis believed that the Fijian islanders under the influence of Christianity were giving up their cannibal ways. Flanders, her 1851 editor, tells us that Wallis records a change in character among the islanders: "Here, the ferocious islander appears with his formidable war club—and there it is exchanged for the implement of husbandry. . . . Here, around the burning pile, feasting upon the flesh of their slaughtered captives— and there around the communion-table, celebrating the dying love of Him in whom they have believed."[103] Flanders seems astonishingly unaware of the irony in citing the "communion-table," at which Christians eat the flesh and drink the blood of Jesus Christ, as evidence of the islanders' reform. In his eyes, to show the depths from which the islanders have arisen only attests to the glory of Christianity.

The *Christian Register* and the *Missionary Herald* had made the same point in 1834. Both papers had printed a story of shipwreck in the Fiji Islands, then added, "A few years ago, if a vessel had been wrecked at any of these islands, every man would have been killed, and many of them eaten: this circumstance shows that the tone of the feeling at the Feejee group is improving; and that the Lord is caus-ing his great name to be known among this long lost part of the human family."[104] As an aside, neither newspaper considers what would actually happen had *every* man been killed. As Jack Sparrow asks in the 2003 film *Pirates of the Caribbean: The Curse of the Black Pearl*, "No survivors? Then where do the stories come from, I wonder?"

Wallis's enthusiasm for her Christian mission is undercut to some extent by the fact that her writing about the eating of human flesh is far more vivid than her writing about Christianity.[105] Flanders's pairing of the cannibal feast and Commu-nion also raises the whole conundrum of transubstantiation. Why do we under-stand and accept Holy Communion—eating the body and blood of Christ—as a deeply spiritual act while we view a cannibal feast as unnatural and inhuman?

The question of transubstantiation was raised in the *Gentleman and Lady's Town and Country* in 1784: "To be a thorough Roman catholic, a man must be a cannibal and gross idolater. A cannibal in the strictest sense; insomuch that at the sacrament of the Lord's Supper, nothing must satisfy him but eating the very flesh, and drinking the very blood of Christ his Saviour."[106] Despite its virulent anti-Catholicism, this piece does raise an interesting question. Why do Europeans understand and accept that the bread and wine of Holy Communion are transub-stantiated into the body and blood of Christ? A devout Catholic believes that he or she is actually partaking of the body and blood of Christ. Yet if a South Pacific islander eats pork and tells an anthropologist that he or she is eating a relative who has died—for example, if he or she states, "I am eating my mother"—why does the anthropologist not consider transubstantiation but rather unquestion-ingly interprets the islander's words literally?

The Wesleyan missionary the Reverend John Waterhouse visited the Fiji Is-lands in 1840 and later writes of the modesty and cleanliness of the Fijians and the eagerness with which they heard of their Savior Jesus Christ. He writes with joy, "They are remarkably modest," but then breaks off to add, "But, alas! there is an awfully dark shade." This refers not to the color of their skin but to a metaphoric darkness. Quoting the Bible, Waterhouse writes, "Their feet are swift to shed blood. Destruction and misery are in all their ways." He adds, "They eat each other's flesh, and glory in their shame."[107]

Another unnamed missionary was present in Fiji during the intertribal wars that Wallis describes. He writes in an 1846 piece entitled "What Can Be More Horrid?": "Some towns have been burned, and many persons have been killed and eaten, since we last wrote; and it is more than probable that hundreds more will follow them ere the war terminates. At Bau, perhaps, more human beings are now eaten than anywhere else. A few weeks ago they ate twenty-eight in one day. They had seized their wretched victims while fishing, and brought them alive to Bau, and there half-killed them, and then put them into their ovens."[108] His account is dramatic, shocking—and, like Wallis's and Waterhouse's, unwitnessed. Twenty-eight bodies would be a vast number of dead for a native conflict. The conflicts between natives and Europeans led to much higher numbers of dead and wounded, but those between native groups resulted in fewer deaths. In the Happah War fought by Porter and his men with his allies the Teii people against the Ha'apa'a people on the island of Nuku Hiva in the Marquesas in 1813, five Ha'apa'as were killed. As Porter states, "The number of dead which [the Teii] had borne off as trophies, had far exceeded that of any former battle within [the Teii leader Gattanewa's] recollection; as they fight for weeks, nay, for months sometimes, without killing any on either side."[109] Twenty-eight bodies, then, is both extravagant and preposterous.

Two of the qualities that make the accounts of Wallis and the unnamed missionary so overwhelming are precisely this extravagance and preposterousness. Not simply the body but the heart, liver, and tongue of the murdered husband were devoured. Twenty-eight corpses were eaten in one day. In *Moby-Dick*, Melville plays with similar exaggeration when he has Queequeg tell Ishmael of the stomachache he got from eating fifty slain enemies in one day (85).

Cannibal talk is innately extravagant. That extravagance is grounded in the nature of cannibalism itself. For one human being to eat another is so unthinkable and repulsive within most cultures that the talk about such actions must be extravagant. Cannibalism itself is larger than life; it is far beyond accepted modes of behavior. Melville sees the inherent humor, as well as the seriousness, of cannibalism. He incorporates exaggeration and the absurd level of horror that attaches to the subject in the scene of Queequeg's devouring of the fifty corpses. The excess corpses are "placed in great wooden trenchers, and garnished round like a pilau, with breadfruit and cocoanuts; and with some parsley in their mouths, were sent round with the victor's compliments to all his friends, just as though these presents were so many Christmas turkeys" (85). This description is both funny and revolting. The absurd level of horror associated with cannibal talk can be seen in Ishmael's response to Queequeg's discussion of the cannibal feast: "'No more, Queequeg,' said I, shuddering; 'that will do;' for I knew the inferences without his further hinting them" (85). Note, finally, that this is all cannibal talk. We do not see the corpses eaten: we only hear the story. It is a told story that grows from Ishmael's simple question to Queequeg whether he was ever troubled with dyspepsia. The exchange smacks of the oral, yarning nature of cannibal talk.

Wallis and the unnamed missionary rely, in contrast, on the vividness of their presentation of cannibalism rather than on the sound of the passages. Their vividness springs from the inherent exaggeration of cannibal talk. And this is exaggeration, not reportage. It is important to note that the scenes Wallis and the unnamed missionary describe are without European witness. The lack of such witness is one of the greatest concerns expressed by anthropologists such as Arens and Obeyesekere.

Obeyesekere has looked closely at the nineteenth-century works that purportedly established Fijians as cannibals. In his chapter on Fiji, he goes into great detail in order to question the suitability of three of the central Fijian cannibal narratives as ethnography. Obeyesekere writes: "In impeaching conventional cannibal testimonies I suggest that narratives such as Jackson's are totally unsuitable as an ethnographic resource and those who invent complicated relations between kinship and marriage and cannibalism on the basis of such evidence are simply refashioning in ethnographic terms the fantastic nature of the European construction of the cannibal."[110]

Obeyesekere deconstructs the cannibal narratives of William Endicott and Henry Fowler, John Jackson, and Peter Dillon. When feasible, he compares the published narratives with original logbooks or journals to show that it was impossible for the narrator to have been bodily present at the cannibal feast described. He also compares the language and situation of a fictional piece such as John Jackson's *Cannibal Jack* and an avowedly straightforward narrative such as John Jackson's earlier "Jackson's Narrative" and casts grave doubts on the accuracy of the latter. Finally, he looks at newspaper accounts and publication dates to determine the fictionality of the various narratives. A piece written many years after the event may not be as accurate as a contemporary piece.

According to Obeyesekere, many of these narratives were told and retold as oral pieces before being written down. He continues: "Once these stories were written or told and retold on ships and beaches, they produce their own progeny, such that many more tales of maritime adventures are created on these models."[111] This progeny has been used to support the truthfulness of the narratives. An event must be true, it is argued, because the narrative of the event is corroborated by a newspaper account of the same event penned by a different author. But what if one was the source for the other? What if the event never happened but was imagined by one shipmate and then retold by another? After Melville wrote *Typee*, Richard Tobias Greene published his account of the same events in the *Buffalo Commercial Advertiser*. Greene's newspaper account is the progeny of *Typee*, for Greene calls the whaleship *Dolly*, Melville's fictional name, rather than *Acushnet*, the vessel's true name.

Obeyesekere as an anthropologist uses his discussion of progeny to deconstruct cannibal narratives as part of the ongoing debate of whether or not Fijians are cannibals. To a certain extent, the question of whether or not Fijians are really cannibals is irrelevant to my argument establishing the connection between cannibal talk and Melville's use of it. In *Typee, Omoo,* and *Moby-Dick,* Melville embraces cannibal talk for many reasons. He employs it to propel the plot of *Typee,* for the action of the book is driven by the fear of cannibalism. He gleefully relishes it for the humor it evokes. With anger, he whips it on to the page to scourge hypocrisy and intolerance. He provokes his readers with it. He induces dread and horror from it. Finally, he uses it as a basis for his profound question, "Who is not a cannibal?" (*Moby-Dick* 300).

CHAPTER 4

∼ "Their Gestures Shame the Very Brutes"
Missionary Talk

> *I began.*
> *"Ah, Ideea, mickonaree oee?" the same as drawling out—"By the by, Miss Ideea, do you belong to the church?"*
> *"Yes, me mickonaree," was the reply.*
> *But the assertion was at once qualified by certain reservations; so curious, that I can not forbear their relation.*
> *"Mickonaree ena" (church member here), exclaimed she, laying her hand upon her mouth, and a strong emphasis on the adverb. In the same way, and with similar exclamations, she touched her eyes and hands. This done, her whole air changed in an instant; and she gave me to understand, by unmistakable gestures, that in certain other respects she was not exactly a "mickonaree." In short, Ideea was*
> *"A sad good Christian at the heart—*
> *A very heathen in the carnal part."*
> —Omoo *(178)*

TALK had a unique, formative role in the creation of missionaries. Sailor talk is predicated on action, or what Margaret Cohen calls "know-how."[1] Cannibal talk is predicated on perception. But missionary talk is above all *talk*. It was this talk that inspired men and women to travel to unknown places on the other side of the world to evangelize for their religion, and talk that formed the main means of carrying out this evangelization. The talk that frames the missionaries' whole reason for being is the heightened and absolute talk of spiritual revelation that is grounded in the complex metaphor of the Bible, the Book, the written word. Although the word of God is written, it was received by most people in the period before widespread literacy as heightened speech. Because both the terms— the language itself—and the purpose are heightened and understood as revealed truth, the potential for discrepancy between the talk and the actual experiences of missionaries is vast. The stakes are as high as they can be. The cost of failure: lost souls, damnation; the reward for success: eternal glory. The stakes are set by the missionaries themselves, and there is no room for flexibility or negotiation. As an observer, Melville, who shares an overarching cultural background with the missionaries, is nonetheless far more free to question and to identify contradictions. Because the missionaries are wedded to the absolute authority of their worldview, however, they are incapable of engaging in the sort of questing, questioning conversation that Melville relishes and upon which he thrives. Missionary talk is speech of another order, akin to prophecy. Melville adopted this authoritative, allusive language, freighted with complex meanings, as a vehicle for lifting his narratives into the realms of the metaphysical and the sublime.

The advent of organized missions to the South Pacific was recent enough that Melville observed societies in several stages of absorbing its impact. This chapter will first look at the early Protestant missionaries sent to the islands of what is now French Polynesia, then at the ways in which natives and missionaries responded to each other, then at the sailors, with whom both groups interacted. It will consider the missionaries' relationship with beachcombers, most often deserting or discharged sailors who lived for varying lengths of time on the beaches of the South Pacific. It will include an investigation of the overlapping forms of talk created by the interaction of these various groups and the suffering created by the misunderstandings that arose during this cross-cultural exchange.

As Niel Gunson, author of *Messengers of Grace: Evangelical Missionaries in the South Seas 1797–1860,* notes: "Silver-voiced preachers could often create a picture of the missionary life which would powerfully attract the young listener. The giants of this art were some of the missionaries who had already served in distant fields."[2] Missionaries returned from foreign stations and traveled throughout Great Britain and the United States to raise money and recruit new missionaries. The men and women they recruited then left to serve the Lord by preaching to the "heathen." Missionaries engendered talk not only through their sermons and the letters and reports they sent home but also through the responses of sailors and natives to their talk. Sailors were the means by which missionaries arrived at their distant stations, and natives were those they encountered there. Whenever missionaries were present on Pacific islands, sailors and natives were also present. All three groups came together as actors in the unfolding historical drama on the vast stage of the South Pacific.

Embedded in the question of talk is the really interesting question of language. When missionaries, especially in the earliest contacts, encountered native islanders, the spoken language of each group was mutually incomprehensible. Missionaries typically had faith in the power and persuasiveness of their own talk, believing they could convey a coherent image of Christianity to the islanders through it. Missionaries were frequently convinced that islanders had affirmed their comprehension of the missionaries' speech and their acceptance of

Christianity. The islanders seem to have understood fragments of what was being communicated and often recast them in the complex terms of their own cosmological views, believing in their turn that they had understood what was being said. This fundamental dissociation between talk and comprehension, coupled with the vast differences between European and island cultures, created a context in which multiple and often contradictory meanings coexisted. These contradictions resulted in distortion and breakdown of social structures on both sides and crises of identity for some individuals.

An amusing example of the disconnect between what missionaries thought they said and what they actually said is given by William Ellis, a member of the London Missionary Society. He spent the years 1816–24 as a missionary in Polynesia and set up the first printing press in Tahiti. His four-volume work *Polynesian Researches*, initially published in 1829, is the result of his observations and research. The second edition (1833) was Melville's most important written source for *Omoo*. During their passage to Tahiti aboard the missionary ship *Duff*, the first Protestant missionaries arranged a number of Tahitian words in sentences according to the English idiom. The words were taken from a vocabulary compiled by one of the *Bounty* mutineers. Ellis writes:

> One of these sentences, *Mity po tuaana,* often afterward amused the [Tahitian king Pomare II], when he came to know what they intended by it. *Maitai* is good, *po* is night, and *tuaana* brother. Good-night, brother, was the sentiment intended; but if the natives understood the English word *mighty*, it would mean, Mighty night, brother; or, if they understood *mity* as their word *maitai*, the phrase would be an assertion to this effect—Good (is the) night, brother. The simple declaration, Good-night, brother, would be unintelligible to the Tahitians, though the language were correct; a corresponding wish among them would be, *Ia ora na oe i teie nei po*—"May you have peace or life this night."[3]

Ellis gives this as an example of the difficulties encountered by the missionaries in their endeavors to learn Tahitian. Mistakes were made in the opposite direction as well. Tahitians trying to learn English stumbled over words and phrases. Ellis writes:

> It was not in words only, but also in their application, that the most ludicrous mistakes were made by the people. "Oli mani," a corruption of the English words "old man," is the common term for any thing old; hence a blunt, broken knife, and a threadbare or ragged dress, are called "oli mani." A captain of a ship at anchor in one of the harbours was once inquiring of a

native something about his wife, who was sitting by. The man readily answered his question, and concluded by saying, "Oli mani hoi," she is "also an old man."[4]

The missionaries' phrase "in the English idiom" takes an ironic twist when one considers the specific difficulty of translating idiomatic speech, as in the examples just given.

The pidgin that developed in Tahiti, like most pidgins, forms from elements of two or three languages to create a means of communication when there is no mutually understood language. Pidgins lack synonyms and, as in the example above, one term may be freighted with numerous meanings. This simplifies some sorts of interchanges, especially trade, but renders any sort of more sophisticated exchange regarding beliefs and ideas ambiguous and opaque.

Linguist Emanuel J. Drechsel notes that Melville "draws on two distinct pidgin languages, or grammatically reduced interlingual media—the first based on Polynesian languages, and now known as Maritime Polynesian Pidgin, and the second based on English, interspersed with occasional Polynesian words."[5] "Melville," Drechsel writes, "quoted Pacific Islanders principally in Maritime Polynesian Pidgin in *Typee* but used Pidgin English primarily in his sequel, *Omoo,* although there existed no temporal, spatial, or other sociolinguistic justification to warrant such a linguistic switch."[6] Ultimately, Drechsel finds Melville's use of Pidgin English "suspect" as accurate documentation of how islanders spoke.[7]

The zeal that inspired missionaries to leave their homes and embark on a voyage to the other side of the world was often all they had to sustain them through their journey and the initial encounters with the very different lands and peoples they had come to change. Expecting trials and hardship, they incorporated these factors into their understanding of the nature of their calling. Much more difficult to reconcile were the shortcomings of talk and the labyrinthine mirror house of linguistic, cultural, and social meanings into which talk often seemed to lead.

Missionary Ship *Duff* and the Early Missionaries to the South Pacific

The London Missionary Society began in 1794 as part of the evangelical revival that occurred among British and New England congregations in the second half of the eighteenth century. John Ryland, a Baptist minister in Britain, founded the society at the urging of his friend William Carey, an indigo planter recently arrived in India. In his correspondence with Ryland, Carey argued that the dissemination of Christianity required a sustained, widespread, and coordinated effort. A Scottish evangelical preacher, David Bogue, penned the announcement of the society for the *Evangelical Magazine*. The society began with eighteen members and continued to grow, meeting every two weeks in a room above the Castle and Falcon Inn in London. Two hundred people attended the first day of the initial public meeting in 1795, held at the Castle and Falcon, and paid a guinea each to become members. Thousands gathered for a public service at Whitfield's Tabernacle on Tottenham Court Road the next day.[8]

The Reverend David Bogue preached for "Christians of different denominations [to form] a society for propagating the gospel among the heathens."[9] Inspired by Captain James Cook's travels, the society decided to make the South Pacific its first missionary target. As Tom Hiney states in *On the Missionary Trail*, "The revelation of a 'lost' Polynesian culture, entirely cut off from any exterior force of civilisation, touched a chord with Cook's compatriots. The French and Spanish had both weighed anchor at Tahiti before Cook, but he was the first to stay there for any time and to record something of the Polynesian society."[10] Cook brought the Tahitian Omai back to England on his second voyage, and Omai was dressed by Cook's botanist Sir Joseph Banks, painted by Sir Joshua Reynolds, and conversed with by Samuel Johnson. Omai's visit as well as narratives of Captain Cook's voyages and accounts of the mutiny aboard HMS *Bounty* fired the British imagination.

The first official missionaries came to the South Pacific in 1797, only two years after the society was inaugurated. The London Missionary Society had been formed with the express purpose of sending godly men and women among the heathen. The missionary ship *Duff* took a complement of thirty male missionaries ranging in age from twenty to forty-eight, most of whom were in their early to mid-twenties; six missionary wives; and three children from England to the South Pacific.[11] Only four had received regular ordination. They established three missions in 1797: at Matavai in Tahiti, at Tongatapu in the Tonga Islands (terminated in 1800), and at Tahuata in the Marquesas (terminated in 1799). The Tahitian mission was temporarily abandoned in 1808 but resumed in 1811 and survived to become the nucleus of the London Missionary Society in the South Pacific.[12] William Pascoe Crook was the sole missionary left in the Marquesas by the *Duff*, but the other missions, especially that at Matavai in Tahiti, were more populous.

Melville mentions "the good ship Duff" in *Omoo* (163). The first three chapters of volume 2 of Ellis's *Polynesian Researches* tell the story of the early mission settlements, and Melville could have learned of the *Duff* there. Or he could have learned of it in the other narratives he perused as background for *Omoo*: Georg H. von Langsdorff's *Voyages and Travels in Various Parts of the World* (1813), David Porter's *Journal of a Cruise Made to the Pacific Ocean* (1815, 1822), Michael Russell's *Polynesia* (1843), Charles S. Stewart's *A Visit to the South Seas, in the U.S. Ship* Vincennes, *during the Years 1829 and 1830* (1831), or Charles Wilkes's *Narrative of the United States Exploring Expedition* (1844). Although Melville came to French Polynesia forty-five years after the initial arrival of the *Duff,* the story of the missionary ship was still vividly alive.

Most of the missionaries sent out on the *Duff* were of the mechanic class, which placed them at the level of the lower-middle class in the hierarchy of British social classes. Despite their relatively humble origin, mechanics were socially higher than laborers; they hoped to advance up the social hierarchy and deeply desired respectability. Although the fact of their having technical skills would seem to make them candidates for the establishment of Western technological culture in the islands as a groundwork on which to build, this was *not* a case of civilization preceding Christianity. Mechanic missionaries, like those who followed them, were sent to preach before all else.[13] Additionally, despite their mechanical skills, the educational level among the early missionaries was not high. Danish adventurer Jorgen Jorgensen savagely attacked the *Duff* missionaries as "illiterate and ruined tradesmen" who explained "to others what they [did] not comprehend themselves."[14] They were also characterized by a lack of humor.[15] The London Missionary Society later considered that the first group of missionaries may not have been intellectually as strong as subsequent groups, but in the earliest days the emphasis was on eagerness and dedication rather than religious learning or language skills.

Between 1797 and 1860, the London Missionary Society engaged 108 recognized missionaries along with their wives and children in the South Pacific.[16] Although other mission societies did not consider the South Pacific an important mission, the London Missionary Society chose to go to there from the beginning of its existence. In his account of the voyage, James Wilson, captain of the *Duff,* explains why:

> After a long and serious consideration of the subject, [the London Missionary Society, then known as the Missionary Society,] determined to commence with the islands of the southern ocean, as these, for a long time past, had excited peculiar attention. Their situation of mental ignorance and moral depravity strongly impressed on our minds the obligation we lay under to endeavour to call them from darkness into marvellous light. The miseries and diseases which their intercourse with Europeans had occasioned, seemed to upbraid our neglect of repairing, if possible, these injuries; but above all, we longed to send to them the everlasting gospel, the first and most distinguished of blessings which Jehovah has bestowed on the children of men.[17]

A mixture of guilt and desire draws them to the islands.

It was missionary talk in the form of preaching that above all convinced recruits to become disciples of the Lord. Charles Barff, one of the missionaries sent out on the *Duff*, recalls his conversion at age nineteen when he attended Surrey Chapel and sat "under the droppings of the word with delight."[18] John Williams confessed that before he heard the Reverend Timothy East preach, he was very wicked.[19] William Law noted that "a returned missionary was received with deafening applause. . . . Some modern Apollos electrified an assembly, with flashes of eloquence and wisdom."[20] Converts took the biblical passage "Go therefore and make disciples of all nations, baptizing them in the name of the Father and of the Son and of the Holy Spirit" (Matthew 28:16) as an injunction to extend knowledge of the revealed word of God to the "benighted heathen" and in so doing ensure the salvation of their own souls. Gunson states: "The missionaries who went out to convert the heathen were as much concerned with their own souls as with those of their coloured brethren."[21] It should not be forgotten that these Christians traveled more than halfway around the world for personal motives as well as altruistic ones.

The voyage from England to the Polynesian mission stations was often an extremely trying experience for the incipient missionaries, not only because of the discomfort of the journey itself but because of the distance and isolation the lengthy voyage represented. Young men and women had to leave their families with the knowledge that they might never see them again. They considered their dedication to mission work to last until death. They did not travel to the South Pacific for a set period of time; rather, they expected to be there the rest of their lives. Such a decision was noble but difficult to execute. Missionaries experienced deep emotional trauma during their long months aboard ship. They were also unfamiliar with conditions at sea and unprepared to accept the lower standard of living that such conditions demanded. Yet in the midst of the emotional wrenching they were experiencing, the missionaries aboard the *Duff* were conscious that they were making ecclesiastical and geographical history.[22]

DIFFICULTIES OF MISSIONARY LIFE

The earliest missionaries received scarcely any training or preparation for either their work as missionaries or the challenges of day-to-day life they would face in the places to which they were sent. Candidates such as John Williams, not only having been converted from being "very wicked" but swept headlong into becoming a missionary by the preaching of Timothy East, lacked a developed intellectual and rational component in their faith, relying solely on the fervor of conversion. When that intensity faded in the face of the challenges of their actual work, their resources proved meager. Without proper training, the preaching of these early missionaries was often crude and not always acceptable by European standards.[23] The apprentice missionaries, Methodist Walter James Davis writes, "cannot satisfy the *itching ears* of a Colonial congregation."[24] The missionary George Pratt later called the preaching of the Methodist teachers in Samoa "a mere jumble."[25] It was hoped and expected that these fledgling evangelists would make up in zeal and enthusiasm what they lacked in polish and experience. Yet even greater obstacles awaited them on arrival in the islands.

Necessarily, the difficulties of communication highlighted the shortcomings of their preparation in this regard. The early missionaries found it extremely daunting to learn Tahitian and the other native languages. Coming from a culture with a long history of using the written word as the basis for formal education, learning a foreign language entirely by ear was utterly strange to most of them. In *Polynesian Researches,* Ellis writes of the challenges of learning Tahitian: "The language was altogether oral; consequently, neither alphabet, spelling-book, grammar, nor dictionary existed, and its acquisition was a most laborious and tedious undertaking."[26] Not only was this language undocumented, but its vocabulary and structure were utterly unrelated to any language with which even educated missionaries were familiar.

The missionaries were grievously unprepared for preaching to native congregations, and they often found the circumstances into which they were thrust deeply disillusioning. The LMS missionary George Platt wrote to Ellis in 1838: "What wicked men *you officers* must be to deceive simple young people, and trepan them . . . into a service to which their hearts have no sympathy. You make them believe they are going to heaven. But when they arrive, instead of heaven, they find black men and fiends, and barbarized Missionaries and even the devil himself not cast out."[27] Platt's language is very vivid here, especially with the force and power of the verb "trepan" and the striking image of barbarized missionaries. This last bespeaks the apprehension that the writer himself may eventually fall prey to the temptation to "go native," a very real possibility that will be discussed below. The contempt for the "lower orders of humanity" by which the missionaries found themselves surrounded is also evident here. Black men, fiends, barbarized missionaries, and even the devil himself reside in the South Pacific. How does one contend with all these and continue preaching?

Such disillusionments as those to which Platt refers were not what the missionary societies back home in Great Britain or the United States wanted to hear. They wanted positive, enthusiastic letters sent home, not realistic ones, and so the perceptions of what missionaries could achieve were unrealistically high. "There was a marked disposition to regard the missionary who wrote home uncomplaining letters giving impressive figures as a successful and faithful servant of the Society, whereas a missionary whose reports attempted to give a full picture, frequently at the expense of his own success, was often regarded as a dissatisfied and unbalanced person."[28] Missionaries were thus stripped even of the psychological relief of reporting to their colleagues the true state of the conditions they encountered, furthering the cycle of unrealistic enthusiasm, hypocrisy, and crushing disillusionment.

The missionaries who did write to England with impressive figures of the number of converted heathens based their numbers—or so Melville argues—on enforced and coerced attendance at religious ceremonies. Melville writes: "The hypocrisy in matters of religion, so apparent in all Polynesian converts, is most injudiciously nourished in Tahiti, by a zealous, and in many cases, a coercive superintendence over their spiritual well-being" (*Omoo* 178–79).

The squalor and hardship of their daily lives as well as the clamor of their flocks for attention and judgment in petty disputes were often overwhelming to the missionaries. The irritation and distraction caused by heat, rain, mosquitoes, and flies interfered with the missionaries' ability to maintain their focus on their spirituality and to preach effectively. The Methodist missionary James Stephen Hambrook Royce wrote in his journal in 1860:

> How easy it is for a man however holy to lose his piety in Feejee. I feel this; a number of things take your thoughts from your proper work; so many affairs upon which you are called to give advice, both Chiefs and white men, then your domestic affairs, constantly a number of things on your mind, in addition to all the heat, or the rain, the wind, or the mosquitoes and flies to annoy you; it is difficult to keep in a spiritual frame under such circumstances, retire to prayer and meditation, and a host of things crowd your mind, try to make a sermon and you have a number of calls.[29]

Such seemingly insignificant elements exacted a far greater toll than missionary societies ever considered.

Longing for home and the comforts of familiar surroundings also sapped the missionaries' reserves. While married missionaries and their wives were lonesome and homesick, single missionaries were even more so. But above all, Gunson writes, "It was ill-health which was the canker within mission society."[30] Melville, writing of missionaries passing along Broom Road in Tahiti, calls them "sickly exotics" (*Omoo* 166). Disease and ill health plagued missionaries, especially missionary wives. The missionaries wore too much clothing for the climate and refrained from such healthful pursuits as bathing in seawater. The islanders were constantly in the water, and therefore, as far as this form of cleanliness could contribute, stayed healthy. Missionary wives often were in an almost continuous state of pregnancy. Mrs. Richard Armstrong, of the 1833 American mission to the Marquesas, arrived at Nuku Hiva pregnant, with a one-year-old daughter and a four-month-old son. She gave birth to her child before the missionaries left Nuku Hiva seven months later.[31] Thus scarcely two months passed between the birth of one child and the conception of the next. With childbirth as the greatest killer of women in the nineteenth century, it is no wonder then that so many missionaries married several times during the length of their stay in the islands. Other missionaries were forced to return to England or the United States because of ill health, either their own or more often that of their wives.

Missionaries occasionally faced situations that left them speechless, when words seemed inadequate to invoke the comforts of spirituality on which they relied so deeply. Gunson notes that hysterics were frequent in some households, especially where the women were directly confronted with traumatic sights, such as were associated with violent cultural practices in Fiji. Mary Wallis, who spent five years in the Fiji Islands as the wife of a sea captain involved in the bêche-de-mer trade, quotes a letter from Mr. Calvert, a missionary: "While we were absent at Bua, Navinde caught fourteen women and clubbed one man. News came to Vewa that the women were all to be clubbed the next day. Our wives could not rest, and procured a canoe and hastened to Bau with a whale's tooth to present to [the king] Tanoa to spare their lives. They were too late to save them all; nine had just been clubbed, but the others were saved at the intercession of the ladies, who approached the king with aching hearts and trembling frames."[32] The missionary wives trembled and their hearts ached at the sight of the clubbed Fijian women. Such trauma disrupted the equanimity of missionary households. In the face of the stresses induced by such trauma, the escapes of drunkenness and illicit sexual activity exposed the missionaries to charges of hypocrisy.

Alexander Simpson, who was evidently unpopular with the other missionaries, was the only LMS missionary dismissed for immorality. As Gunson suggests, "Not having recourse to a proper trial, Simpson was in many ways the victim of slander, intrigue and jealousy."[33] After he was dismissed, Simpson began to drink heavily, and such drinking further convinced the other missionaries of his debauchery. Gunson questions the extent of Simpson's transgressions: "He may have had affairs with Tahitian women, but he denied them, and his wife supported him. It is unlikely that he was the 'monster of depravity' which some missionaries represented him. The pathetic thing was that a man who fell into temptation and subsequently repented was a marked man. His preaching became ineffectual, and he spent his days between suffering and remorse."[34] Since the missionary enterprise is founded on talk, once such talk becomes ineffectual, the missionary has no recourse and spends his days in suffering or retreats, as Simpson did, into drunkenness.

Simpson is one of the few missionaries whom Melville mentions by name in a passage in which he sharply criticizes missionary attempts to keep their children from contact with Tahitians. The "Rev. Mr. Simpson and wife" run a seminary exclusively for missionary children so that "the two races are kept as far as possible from associating; the avowed reason being, to preserve the young whites from moral contamination." "And yet," Melville adds, "strange as it may seem, the depravity among the Polynesians, which renders precautions like these necessary, was in a measure unknown before their intercourse with the whites" (*Omoo* 188). While Melville is idealizing the state of precontact Tahitian society here, it is nonetheless ironic that several years later it was Simpson himself who was dismissed for immorality.

MISSIONARIES AND NATIVES: LANGUAGE

En route to the Pacific, the first missionaries sent out by the London Missionary Society attempted to learn the language and culture of Tahiti through ethnological and linguistic information collected from sailors and from the incarcerated mutineers of HMS *Bounty*. James Morrison, one of the mutineers, wrote a manuscript journal entitled *The Journal of . . . Boatswain's Mate of the Bounty describing the Mutiny and Subsequent Misfortunes of the Mutineers together with an account of the Island of Tahiti*.[35] The missionaries also acquired at least one vocabulary compiled by an unnamed mutineer.[36] Gunson notes:

> The first directors of the LMS believed that there would be little difficulty involved in learning Tahitian. This was largely due to the fact that [the Reverend Thomas Haweis, one of the founders of the LMS,] had supplied the missionaries of the *Duff* with a vocabulary drawn up by the *Bounty* mutineers. . . . This vocabulary was hopelessly inadequate, and it would seem that a considerable time passed before the missionaries realized that the grammatical and idiomatic differences between English and Tahitian were so marked.[37]

Again and again Ellis writes in *Polynesian Researches* of how elusive the acquisition of the Tahitian tongue proved to be for the missionaries. "In these embarrassments," he writes, "they had no elementary books to consult, no preceptors to whom they could apply, but were frequently obliged, by gestures, signs, and other contrivances, to seek the desired information from the natives; who often misunderstood the purport of their questions, and whose answers must as often have been unintelligible to the missionaries."[38]

Only a few missionaries mastered spoken Tahitian early on. These missionaries would author sermons that they then translated into phonetic Tahitian or, as the missionaries put it, rendered Tahitian in the English idiom. Other missionaries who had not yet mastered Tahitian would deliver these sermons, trying to sound out the Tahitian words using English letters without a sense of the meaning of what they were saying. Considering the vagaries of spelling at the time, the variety of accents, differing levels of literacy, and likely errors in the original understanding of Tahitian and the transcription of the sounds, it is no wonder, then, that although preaching to the heathen was a regular missionary pursuit, converts were rarely gained by it.

Melville gives a humorous rendition of this translation process in *Omoo* when the narrator attends a service at the Church of the Cocoa-nuts. Having heard that the missionaries' sermons were "of a rather amusing description to strangers" (173), he takes along a Hawaiian sailor named Jack to translate. Melville tells us: "Jack's was not, perhaps, a critical version of the discourse; and, at the time, I took no notes of what he said. Nevertheless, I will here venture to give what I remember of it; and, as far as possible, in Jack's phraseology, so as to lose nothing by a double translation" (173). The sermon was conceived in English; written out, either by the preacher himself or by another missionary, in Tahitian; sounded out by the preacher; translated from Tahitian back to pidgin English by a native Hawaiian; and then remembered by the narrator, before it even reaches us—and then the narrator claims that, first, Jack did not give a critical version of the sermon and, second, that the narrator himself did not take notes at the time. With all these layers, how can we trust any words of the sermon as we read it in *Omoo*, and even more importantly, how can we trust any of its words at all? Melville's subversion of the sermon through this multilayered rendition leads us to question the extent to which intended meaning is clearly conveyed at any point in this cycle. What, for instance, did the congregation make of the conflict between Catholicism and Protestantism as conveyed by "Wicked priests here, too; and wicked idols in woman's clothes, and brass chains" (173)?

Mark Twain mocks the errors inherent in such double translation in "The 'Jumping Frog': In English. Then in French. Then Clawed Back into a Civilized Language Once More, by Patient, Unremunerated Toil" (1875), in which he includes the full text of the original story, then the full text of the French translation, then his retranslation of the story from the French. The retranslation incorporates such hilarious passages as the following: "'I me demand how the devil it makes itself that this beast has refused. Is it that she had something? One would believe that she is stuffed.' He grasped Daniel by the skin of the neck, him lifted and said: 'The wolf me bite if he no weigh not five pounds.'"[39] While Twain uses the inherent humor in the difficulty of idiomatic translation to underscore his rebuttal of a poor review by the French critic who originally translated his work, Twain's piece clearly illustrates the difficulties of translating languages even as closely related as English and French. The linguistic hurdles faced by missionaries to Polynesia were far greater.

Eventually, with considerable effort, missionaries did learn the language. Nonetheless, preaching in Tahitian frequently meant reading a sermon written in Tahitian by another missionary; therefore, sermons in the native tongue were often too much the same: they were often simplistic and *boring*.

Much as the missionaries have been reviled for their destruction of Polynesian language and culture—and rightfully so—the fact remains that they were the first to transform many of the Polynesian languages, including Tahitian, into written form and therefore preserve those languages for future generations. The Bible was rendered into Tahitian at the beginning of the nineteenth century. Melville mentions the Tahitian Bible in chapter 45 of *Omoo* (173). Parts of the Tahitian Bible were published for the first time in 1818, the New Testament in 1829, and the complete Bible in 1838. The Tahitian Bible was principally translated by Henry Nott, a bricklayer without previous education in linguistic studies, who arrived in Tahiti aboard the *Duff* in 1797 and stayed until his death forty-seven years later.

One of the first tasks required of missionaries returning home to Great Britain or the United States was to create a vocabulary of the language native to the islands in which they had worked. When William Pascoe Crook and the Marquesan boy Temouteitei recorded such a vocabulary for the English linguist Samuel Greatheed, they were following a standard pattern. Catholic missionaries often compiled better vocabularies and ethnographies because they tended to stay longer in the islands. Many such documents were originally amassed by Jesuits. The importance of such vocabularies becomes increasingly evident when one considers that early missionary work consisted mostly of talk. Gunson writes: "Early mission work consisted mainly in collecting groups of people together and preaching to them, in having conversation with them in public meetings, and in giving them some form of catechetical instruction, so that they would know the form even if they were unable to feel the spiritual experience of religious worship."[40] For such talk, the missionaries needed words in the native tongue. For this reason, they collected words and gathered together in the evenings to translate sacred texts or to render sacred hymns into the language of the native people. This piecemeal work, word by word, chapter by chapter, stanza by stanza, belied the monumental nature of the task of translating the deeper meanings of these texts across not only linguistic but cultural borders.

MISSIONARIES AND NATIVES: CULTURE

Writing is no prerequisite for the existence of complex literature within a culture. Bear in mind that *The Iliad* and *The Odyssey* existed as spoken literature long before Homer dictated his versions to someone with knowledge of writing.

Navajo *hataalii* conduct curing ceremonies in which they perform ritual songs that last for several days. Polynesian cultures make use of lengthy songs in their cross-ocean navigation. Numerous other examples from throughout the world could be cited. In addition to such lore, cultures without writing often maintain extensive bodies of knowledge, including cosmology, as well as vast catalogs of plant and animal life and their interactions, genealogy, law, and custom, without the use of written records. The easy assumption of superiority by literate cultures ignores the sophistication and development of mental faculties that maintenance of these oral traditions implies. In the absence of writing, oral cultures maintain a sense of the relationship between clarity of expression, memory, and truth that literate cultures reserve for the written word.

The Christian missionaries were "people of the Book": members of a religion based on the Judeo-Christian scriptures. The cultural edifice they attempted to transmit to the Polynesians, assembled from a variety of sources over centuries and laden with many layers of interpretation and controversy, was remote from the missionaries' own culture in both time and place. It presented a tremendous challenge in translating to terms accessible to yet a third culture with a starkly different history and worldview.

The complications presented by speaking across language and cultural barriers are compounded when one party expects nothing less than the annihilation and replacement of the other's religion. Religion is one of the bases upon which a culture is built, and this was certainly true of Polynesian culture. The following questions asked by students at Malua in Samoa of George Turner of the London Missionary Society, while presenting humorous cultural misconstructions, serve to illustrate the vast gulf created by the difficulty in recognizing what one's own fundamental assumptions and body of knowledge are and how different the same sorts of knowledge base and assumptions can be for people in another culture.

"If we feel sleepy at prayer, should we open our eyes?"
"How tall was Zaccheus; how many feet do you suppose?"
"What is the meaning of cymbal? Is it an animal, or what?"
"Did Isaiah live before Christ, or after him?"[41]

Such questions are not much different from those asked of any teacher and, when asked in the context of a culture common to both teacher and student, often result in the teacher's recognition of his or her own shortcomings as an instructor and the resolve to explain more clearly and completely in the future. The early missionaries to the South Pacific had little experience of teaching or preaching and a tendency toward self-righteousness. Rather than leading the missionaries to reexamine either their assumptions or their pedagogical techniques, these questions often served to reinforce the contempt in which they held the islanders.

More seriously, islanders of the South Pacific questioned why they should swear allegiance to the Christian divinity and forswear their own. Methodist missionary Samuel Waterhouse reported the following interview with a Fijian chief. The chief asks: "Why should I worship Jehovah, as he was not my Father's God[?]" Waterhouse answers: "True, He was not your Father's God, in the sense that your father worshipped Him—but Jehovah was truly your father's God—Who else made him—who else decreed his death, and who else but Jehovah will judge him." To which the chief replies: "Look—Jehovah is not—cannot be our God—For you and we are different—He is the white man's God—but he is not the black man's God—if He were our God we also would have white skins."[42] Such questions were far harder for the missionary to answer. The conversation between the missionary and the Fijian chief grounds out on mutual incomprehension. One is reminded of the scene from Mark Twain's *Huckleberry Finn* (1884), in which Huck tries to convey to Jim the difference between the languages spoken by Englishmen and Frenchmen. Huck asks Jim if a cat and then a cow talk like we do, or if they talk like each other, and Jim replies to all three questions in the negative. Huck continues:

> "It's natural and right for 'em to talk different from each other, ain't it?"
> "'Course."
> "And ain't it natural and right for a cat and a cow to talk different from *us?*"
> "Why, mos' sholy it is."
> "Well, then, why ain't it natural and right for a *Frenchman* to talk different from us?—you answer me that."
> "Is a cat a man, Huck?"
> "No."
> "Well, den, dey ain't no sense in a cat talkin' like a man. Is a cow a man?—er is a cow a cat?"
> "No, she ain't either of them."
> "Well, den, she ain' got no business to talk like either one er the yuther of 'em. Is a Frenchman a man?"
> "Yes."
> "*Well*, den! Dad blame it, why doan he *talk* like a man?—you answer me *dat!*"
> I see it warn't no use wasting words—you can't learn a nigger to argue. So I quit.[43]

The mutual incomprehension of Huck and Jim is very similar to that of the missionary and the Fijian chief. But Huck's naïveté here serves as a reverse image, the photographic negative, of the knowing, scathingly ironic tone of Melville's narrator in *Omoo,* discussed more extensively in chapter 5.

Cultural misunderstanding and its consequences can be found in the keeping of a particular day for the Sabbath in *Omoo.* Melville recounts a missionary's attempt to clarify the confusion caused by the international date line. The question posed is "whether it was right and lawful for any one, being a native, to keep the European Sabbath, in preference to the day set apart as such by the missionaries, and so considered by the islanders in general" (163). The *Duff* missionaries, sailing eastward to Tahiti via the Cape of Good Hope, lost one day in their reckoning. Later vessels sailing via Cape Horn do not lose that day and so find it Sunday in Tahiti when according to their calculations it is Saturday. "But as it won't do to alter the log, the sailors keep their Sabbath, and the islanders theirs" (164).

> This confusion perplexes the poor natives mightily; and it is to no purpose that you endeavor to explain so incomprehensible a phenomenon. I once saw a worthy old missionary essay to shed some light on the subject; and though I understood but few of the words employed, I could easily get at the meaning of his illustrations. They were something like the following:
>
> "Here," says he, "you see this circle" (describing a large one on the ground with a stick): "very good; now you see this spot here" (marking a point in the perimeter): "well; this is Beretanee" (England), "and I'm going to sail round to Tahiti. Here I go, then" (following the circle round); "and there goes the sun" (snatching up another stick, and commissioning a bandy-legged native to travel round with it in a contrary direction). "Now then, we are both off, and both going away from each other; and here you see I have arrived at Tahiti" (making a sudden stop); "and look now, where Bandy Legs is!"
>
> But the crowd strenuously maintained, that Bandy Legs ought to be somewhere above them in the atmosphere; for it was a traditionary fact, that the people from the Duff came ashore when the sun was high overhead. And here the old gentleman, being a very good sort of man, doubtless, but no astronomer, was obliged to give up. (164)

The Tahitians' incomprehension is especially intriguing in light of Ellis's comment that the islanders' "extensive use of numbers," among other abilities, "warrant[s] the conclusion that they possess no contemptible mental capabilities."[44] According to *Polynesian Researches,* one of the foremost missionary accounts of the character and capacities of Tahitians, this is a subject that could be considered to be approachable and demonstrable. The Tahitians, like all Polynesians, have great skill as navigators. Their cultural framework provides them the means to understand and comprehend spatial relationships in a complex way. Yet here we see the missionary trying to explain something fairly basic and finding both gestures and language inadequate to the task because of cultural misunderstanding.

This anecdote is laden with ironic meaning in other ways as well. It serves as a metaphor for how far on the other side of the world the missionaries are. Keeping the Sabbath is a critical tenet of Christian faith, and yet which day is the true Sabbath? The one that the missionaries keep based on their personal reckoning, or the one the sailors keep? Sailor talk, missionary talk, and native talk are embroiled together: sailors recognize one Sabbath, and the missionaries another, and the natives are caught in the middle.

Another confounding state of affairs confronting natives as they attempted to parse European culture concerned the multiplicity of Christian denominations and especially the divide between Catholicism and Protestantism. Anti-Catholic talk among Protestant missionaries was vituperative. The Methodist missionary Joseph Waterhouse, writing from Ovalau, Fiji, in 1851, conflated Catholics with cannibals: "Here the popish chameleon *allows* the eating of human flesh, indecent songs, and gross immorality: it burns the bible: and injures the property of the English missionaries. . . . In Feejee [popery] is darkness and blackness itself."[45] Catholics were often considered by Protestant missionaries to be ten times *worse* than cannibals: "I would sooner trust ten cannibals than one Papist. I came to Feejee with very little prejudice against the Papists, but their conduct makes me conclude them to be worse than any heathen I ever met with or read of. The Lord save us from Popery!"[46]

In *Omoo*, Melville transfers the Protestant perception of Catholics to the Tahitians: "Such queer ideas as [the Tahitians] entertained, of the hated strangers [the Catholics]! Masses and chants were nothing more than evil spells. As for the priests themselves, they were no better than diabolical sorcerers" (141). To both Protestants and Tahitians, Catholic ritual is mysterious, impenetrable, and therefore diabolical. The hatred of Catholics is also tied to the long-standing English national dissonance with the French, for most Catholic missionaries in the South Pacific were French. An exception is, the Irish priest Father Murphy in *Omoo*, who visits the incarcerated mutineers from the *Julia* in the calaboose. Father Murphy is "pretty well known, and very thoroughly disliked, throughout all the Protestant missionary settlements in Polynesia" (142). The Protestant dislike of Father Murphy is tied to his Catholicism; to his love of drink, which the abstemious Protestants deplored; and to his Irish heritage. Tommo, free of such nationalist sentiments, relishes Father Murphy for his good humor and especially for the bread he sends to the calaboose's inmates.

In the South Pacific, linguistic and cultural misunderstanding could lead to war and death. The following wrenching story, which occurred in Tonga, illustrates what happens when the islanders take literally the injunction to make war upon the heathen.

> After the sack and massacre of Huli [Hule, January 25, 1837] the bodies of some of the dead were taken inside the Wesleyan Mission premises and stacked up there for inspection by the missionaries. The missionaries asked why the corpses were brought into their yard, and the natives replied by asking "was it not by your instructions that we made war upon the heathen?" "We have brought the corpses here that you may know how obedient we have been." The missionary said "We do not wish the corpses to be brought here", and asked the natives to remove them; when the natives again asked "Was it our wish to kill our relatives and friends?" "Was it not at your advice, and suggestion, and instigation that we did so?" Then they removed the corpses.[47]

The missionaries will not accept responsibility for the destruction their teachings have unleashed. Yet their sermons and the recitation of passages from Isaiah and the Psalms could be perceived as having instigated the bloody war that followed. Indeed, the missionaries were censured by the committee in London for their part in the wars.[48] The Tongan missionaries may or may not have invoked the martial language so common in the Bible as a conscious provocation to the violence that ensued. Certainly the censure they received suggests that that was at least suspected by their superiors. Yet military images were commonplace in nineteenth-century missionary talk. The well-known hymn "Onward Christian Soldiers" (the lyrics of which were written by Sabine Baring-Gould in 1864) is but the best-known example of a metaphor extensively employed to inspire a militant Christianity in the age of manifest destiny. This warlike imagery existed in tension with the exhortations to nonviolence and turning the other cheek central to the Christian message. In native eyes, these tensions reflected their variety of experiences with European visitors, ranging from benevolent kindness to genocidal violence.

Melville evokes the violent zeal of this brand of Christianity in his account of Porter's sojourn on Nuku Hiva in chapter 4 of *Typee*, equating Porter's naval force with the advent of Christendom in the islands: "The invaders, on their march back to the sea, consoled themselves for their repulse by setting fire to every house and temple in their route; and a long line of smoking ruins defaced the once-smiling bosom of the valley, and proclaimed to its pagan inhabitants the spirit that reigned in the breasts of Christian soldiers. Who can wonder at the deadly hatred of the Typees to all foreigners after such unprovoked atrocities?" (26).

Melville continues, specifically linking European retaliation for ships' crews "massacred" by islanders with Christendom: "On arriving at their destination, [the Europeans] burn, slaughter, and destroy, according to the tenor of written instructions, and sailing away from the scene of devastation, call upon all Christendom to applaud their courage and their justice" (27).

In *Polynesian Researches,* Ellis denies responsibility for the death and disease that followed in the wake of the European arrival in the islands. Despite his argument that such destruction comes from the licentiousness of sailors and natives combined, the natives blamed the missionaries in a passage seized upon by Melville. Ellis writes:

> The ravages of diseases originating in licentiousness, or nurtured by the vicious habits of the people, and those first brought among them by European vessels, appeared to be fast hastening the total desolation of Tahiti. The survivors of such as were carried off by these means, feeling the incipient effects of disease themselves, and beholding their relatives languishing under maladies of foreign origin, inflicted, as they supposed, by the God of the foreigners, were led to view the missionaries as in some degree the cause of their suffering; and frequently not only rejected their message, but charged them with being the authors of their misery, by praying against them to their God. When the missionaries spoke to them on the subject of religion, the deformed and diseased were sometimes brought out and ranged before them, as evidences of the efficacy of their prayers, and the destructive power of their God. The feelings of the people on this subject were frequently so strong, and their language so violent, that the missionaries have been obliged to hasten from places where they had intended to address the people.[49]

Earlier Ellis had written:

> The state of the people was at this time most affecting. Diseases, introduced by Europeans, were spreading, unmitigated, their destructive ravages, and some members of almost every family were languishing under the influence of foreign maladies, or dying in the midst of their days. The survivors, jealous of the missionaries, viewed them as the murderers of their countrymen, under the supposition that these multiplied evils were brought upon them by the influence of the foreigners with their God. They did not scruple to tell them that He was killing the people.[50]

The cultural dislocation and suffering caused by European presence and hegemony in the South Pacific are an ever-present subtext in *Omoo*. In chapter 56,

Melville attributes his own sufferings from swarms of mosquitoes to their introduction by an alleged act of petty vengeance by a Nantucket whaling captain whose name he gives as Nathan Coleman. "When tormented by the musquitoes [*sic*], I found much relief in coupling the word 'Coleman' with another of one syllable [F—— Coleman? D—— Coleman?], and pronouncing them together energetically" (215). More seriously, Melville blames drunkenness, smallpox, and venereal disease, all introduced by Europeans, for the depopulation of the Tahitian islands (191).

In *Typee,* Melville describes a leisurely life that, despite the foreboding background of Tommo's fear of cannibalism, is one of Edenic pleasure. Work in *Typee* is married to sociability. Consider, for example, the making of tapa or tattooing. What work is done is convivial, pleasant, and performed at a relaxed pace. One cannot imagine the inhabitants of the Typee valley bored or frustrated. One delight after another awaits them. The effort they put into their work is amply rewarded in both material and social benefits. In *Omoo,* the depiction of indolence stands in stark contrast. The indolent natives are bereft of the integrated social framework and simple economy that provides a supporting context for contented rest. The natives are winnowed by disease, harrowed by the missionaries' assertions that their beliefs and culture are inferior and evil, bewildered by the availability of material goods outside their previous experience, and tempted by alcohol as an escape from these jarring circumstances. In such a grim state it is remarkable that Melville encountered so much to admire in so many of the natives. Yet he does not flinch from portraying their degradation and pinning the blame for it squarely on the European presence. Unlike the missionaries, he does not single out sailors as the sole source of this degradation.

MISSIONARIES AND SAILORS

Sailors talked at length about missionaries, but unfortunately much of what they had to say is difficult to recover. Most of it was transmitted orally. In contrast, missionaries extensively used the written as well as the spoken word. They wrote in diaries and journals, sent letters to family and friends in Great Britain and the United States, compiled reports for the home office, created documents of all types, and contributed heavily to evangelical and other religious newspapers and journals. The historic record for the missionary response to sailors is rich, while that for the response of ordinary sailors to missionaries is scant.

Nonetheless, some documents do exist. The length of a whaling voyage was determined by how long it took to fill the hold with whale oil and whalebone. Captains occasionally transshipped oil and bone back to the United States from ports such as Honolulu, Hawaii. Sailors hated this practice because it meant that they had to begin filling the hold all over again, thereby lengthening the voyage. In 1853, ten men from the whaleship *Emerald* refused to work after a cargo of oil and bone was transshipped from their vessel and were consequently imprisoned in Honolulu. They wrote the American consul in a letter published in the local newspaper, the *Polynesian:* "We wish you, sir to understand that seamen are not always the poor, degraded class of beings you may have supposed. We, as well as yourself, have lived in the United States, under 'the banner of the free.'"[51] These men protest their worth in the face of the scorn heaped upon seamen by missionaries and the other European inhabitants of the islands.

As Briton Cooper Busch, author of *"Whaling Will Never Do for Me": The American Whaleman in the Nineteenth Century,* notes, interaction between missionaries and whalemen acted "in much the way that association with consuls did to show him the generally low esteem in which he was held. . . . Seldom, indeed, has there been so lengthy a quarrel between natural enemies, extending as it did from the arrival of both whalemen and missionaries to the virtual extinction of the former species."[52] Melville makes explicit the missionaries' attitude toward sailors in the sermon overheard by the narrator of *Omoo* and translated for him by the Hawaiian sailor Jack: "Good friends, many whale-ships here now; and many bad men come in 'em. No good sailors living—that you know very well. They come here, 'cause so bad they no keep 'em home" (173).

Two whalemen, James Chase and Thomas Turner, protested the missionary attitude in a letter to the London Missionary Society sent from Tahiti in 1841:

> The missionaries here represent Europeans that comes here in Whale Ships to be thieves and Robbers that cannot get a living at home here was a man run away from his ship and went into the mountains and the constables went over him but [LMS missionary Aaron] Busacott told them not to go near him but to stone him with stones untill he was down and here was another that was an unfortunate sailor caught in adultery and made his way to the Boat when the natives said let him go but Mr. Busacott told them to get him at any rate the[y] pushed on him and with clubs broke his arm. . . . Every farthing of money that arrives on the Island goes to them the island is governed by them the natives are ignorant and they do just as the [missionaries] tells them. . . . There are all afraid to let their own country man stop here Europeans because the[y] tell the Natives how they extort from them.[53]

This remarkable letter, written shortly before Melville arrived at Tahiti in 1842, documents how strongly sailors resented the way missionaries treated them.

Melville's narrator in *Omoo* encounters the scorn felt by missionaries toward sailors when the acting English consul, Charles Wilson, boards the *Julia* to adjudicate the differences between that vessel's officers and crew. George Pritchard, "the missionary consul," as the narrator tells us, "was absent in England; but his place was temporarily filled by one Wilson, an educated white man, born on the island, and the son of an old missionary of that name, still living" (75). Melville's Wilson is based on the real Charles B. Wilson, who was serving as acting English consul in 1842 when the sailors of the whaleship *Lucy Ann* rebelled and refused duty. Melville and ten other sailors were incarcerated at Wilson's directive. Charles B. Wilson was born into the missionary community on Tahiti; he was the son of Charles Wilson, who came to Tahiti as a mechanic missionary in 1801 and lived in the islands until his death in 1857.[54] English authority in Tahiti in 1842, then, rested in the hands of the missionaries.

In *Omoo* the crew of the *Julia* has thoroughly discussed their grievances and enumerated them in a time-honored document called a round robin, which is signed in a circular form so no one man can be singled out as the ringleader. This document, however, once presented to the officers, is never produced during Wilson's proceedings. Rather, the entire confrontation is conducted through talk. This allows the weight of authority to be brought to bear against the ephemeral words of the crew. The crew's careful formulation of their grievances and their designation of the cooper as their official spokesman all come to naught. A reasoned presentation and consideration of their circumstances become impossible, as the stereotypes and prejudices inherent in the tensions between sailor and missionary degenerate the interchange in increasingly heated language.

Wilson's first words underline the missionaries' predisposition of distrust and disdain toward sailors: "Mr. Jermin, tack ship, and stand off from the land" (75). He wishes to keep the sailors from corrupting the land. The sailors instinctively return the missionary's attitude: "Now, contempt is as frequently produced at first sight as love; and thus was it with respect to Wilson. No one could look at him without conceiving a strong dislike, or a cordial desire to entertain such a feeling the first favorable opportunity. There was such an intolerable air of conceit about this man, that it was almost as much as one could do to refrain from running up and affronting him" (76). These attitudes harden on both sides during the consul's interview of the crew, which quickly deteriorates to threats and insults. The cooper, selected by the crew as their spokesman, is quickly cowed by Wilson's bluster, which throws the outraged crew into an uproar. Finding that the complaints formulated in their round robin are to be ignored,

> Every one now turned spokesman; and [Wilson] was assailed by a perfect hurricane of yells, in which the oaths fell like hailstones.
> "How's this! what d'ye mean?" he cried, upon the first lull; "who told you all to speak at once? Here, you man with the knife, you'll be putting

some one's eyes out yet; d'ye hear, you sir? You seem to have a good deal to say, who are *you*, pray; where did *you* ship?"

"I'm nothing more nor a bloody *beach-comber*," retorted Salem, stepping forward piratically and eying him; "an if you want to know, I shipped at the Islands about four months ago."

"Only four months ago? And here you have more to say than men who have been aboard the whole voyage;" and the consul made a dash at looking furious, but failed. "Let me hear no more from *you*, sir. Where's that respectable, gray-headed man, the cooper? *he's* the one to answer my questions."

"There's no 'spectable, gray-headed men aboard," returned Salem; "we're all a parcel of mutineers and pirates!" (81)

Salem hurls Wilson's prejudices back at him like a gauntlet flung on the deck, and as the sailors anticipate, their entire argument is dismissed without a real hearing.

Missionaries were threatened by the moral, political, and economic disruption caused by sailors. Sailors came ashore after long months at sea eager to find alcohol and women, as attested by countless logbooks, consular records, newspaper articles, and letters to mission societies. Missionaries, who strongly advocated temperance and abstinence, believed that sailors' desires undermined the moral code they had imposed on islanders. Failure to restrain licentious behaviors by sailors undermined missionaries' standing and influence with native authorities. Finally, the missionaries wished to control trade with Europeans as a source of income for themselves, and when sailors directly traded with the islanders, they threatened the missionaries' domination of economic interaction.

MISSIONARIES AND BEACHCOMBERS

If missionaries felt threatened by sailors, they felt even more so by beachcombers. Beachcombers are those who crossed the beach, as Melville did when he deserted the *Acushnet* at Nuku Hiva in the Marquesas on July 9, 1842. Melville tells us in *Typee*: "To use the concise, point-blank phrase of the sailors, I had made up my mind to 'run away'" (20). A beachcomber was an anomalous person in a liminal space, belonging neither to the shipboard or mission world he had left nor to the island world he had entered.

In the sixty years after the arrival of Captain James Cook in 1774, no permanent European community was established in the Marquesas Islands. Mission stations were attempted in 1797 and 1833, but the missionaries grew discouraged and never stayed longer than eighteen months. Captain David Porter and the U.S.

Navy came and went within three months in 1813. Other European governments claimed the islands but departed shortly, leaving nothing but the memory of their violence. Beachcombers were thus the most consistent European presence in these islands. According to ethnohistorian Greg Dening, more than 150 white men came to live on the beach in the Marquesas between 1774 and 1842.[55] Dening compiled his list from ships' desertion documents, missionary records, "intelligences" reported in newspapers, and narratives penned by some of the men.

The ethnographies, dictionaries, and narratives written by missionaries and deserters are important as the earliest extensive written records of Marquesan life. William Pascoe Crook arrived on the missionary ship *Duff* in 1797. Captain James Wilson had brought two missionaries to the Marquesas aboard the *Duff*. The senior, William Harris, spent one terrified night ashore and refused to stay. Crook, only twenty-one years old, stayed alone until the end of 1798. He then returned to England with two Marquesans and a Tahitian. Crook and the Marquesan boy, Temouteitei, recorded an ethnography of the Marquesan people and a dictionary of their language for the English linguist Samuel Greatheed. Dening writes that Crook's description of what he saw is "a small masterpiece of ethnography."[56] It was, according to Dening, a very determined effort to see the land of the Marquesas as the Marquesans saw it.

Edward Robarts, a nineteen-year-old ship's cook, deserted the whaleship *New Euphrates* in the Marquesas in December 1798. Seven years later, in February 1806, he left the islands with his Marquesan wife, Ena, and their daughter Ellen. Robarts wandered the world with his wife and growing family, finally stranding in Calcutta, India. There his wife, all his children except Ellen, and he himself died. But before he died, at the instigation and with the varied support of English gentlemen Sir Thomas Stamford Raffles, Dr. Leyden, and Mr. T. Hare, Robarts recorded his experiences in the Marquesas. Together Crook's and Robarts's words rescue a record of the lives of the Marquesans.

Two months after Robarts's desertion, a Frenchman, Jean Baptiste Cabri, deserted the whaleship *London* and was greeted with hostility by Robarts. This hostility lasted throughout the four years of Cabri's stay in the Marquesas. Cabri is different from Crook and Robarts because of the extent to which he crossed the beach. He allowed himself to be heavily tattooed and even forgot his own language. Cabri only left the Marquesas by accident, when he was carried by the Russian expedition under Captain Adam Johann von Krusenstern to Kamchatka on the Siberian coast. His knowledge of the Marquesas is recorded in the works of Krusenstern and of Georg H. von Langsdorff, who sailed with Krusenstern as physician and naturalist. Cabri also published a small pamphlet in 1817 entitled *Précis historique et véritable du séjour de Joseph Kabris, natif de Bourdeaux, dans les îles de Mendoca situées dans l'océan Pacifique.*

These men created uniquely valuable records. Most beachcombers left no chronicle of their stay. Some beachcombers spent long lives on the beach; others departed with the next ship. Between twenty and thirty of the 150 beachcombers in the Marquesas between 1774 and 1842 died violent deaths. Thomas Clifton Lawson arrived on the beach at the age of forty-seven and stayed twenty years, eventually becoming an ethnographer and a guide. Two Hawaiians, servants of the abortive American mission at Nuku Hiva in 1833, stayed and taught the Marquesans to make liquor from the *ti* root.

Sometimes bands of seamen would steal a boat in order to escape to shore. Crews from the *New Euphrates* (1798), *Leviathan* (1805), *Lucy* (1806), *Sir Andrew Hammond* (1813), *Boy* (1837), *Sussex* (1840), *Conway* (1842), *George and Susan* (1843), and *Jones* (1850) all did so in the Marquesas.[57] If the deserters stole a boat, the captain would come looking for them—and almost always recover the boat *and* the deserters. The Marquesas were not an idyllic haven, but sailors still ran away.

The life of a beachcomber was often steeped in solitary regret. Melville gives some sense of this loneliness in *Typee* when Tommo mourns: "There was no one with whom I could freely converse; no one to whom I could communicate my thoughts; no one who could sympathise with my sufferings" (231). As Dening notes, the beach beckoned deserters from the prison of their ships and then mocked them with their pointless, meaningless lives.[58]

Beachcombers were caught between two worlds. Some, like Cabri, chose to be tattooed in order to integrate more fully into the Marquesan world. Melville's horror at such a decision leaps from the pages of *Omoo*. Entering Hanamenu Bay (Melville's "Hannamanoo") on Hiva Oa, the *Julia* is greeted by Lem Hardy, "a renegado from Christendom and humanity," tattooed across the face with a broad blue band with a blue shark tattooed on his forehead. "Some of us gazed upon this man with a feeling akin to horror, no ways abated when informed that he had voluntarily submitted to this embellishment of his countenance. What an impress! Far worse than Cain's—*his* was perhaps a wrinkle, or a freckle, which some of our modern cosmetics might have effaced; but the blue shark was a mark indelible. . . . He was an Englishman, Lem Hardy he called himself, who had deserted from a trading brig touching at the island for wood and water some ten years previous" (27; emphasis in original). Lem Hardy is a fictional character, but he is evidently based on real renegades whom Melville met or about whom he read, such as Cabri. Charles Roberts Anderson notes in *Melville in the South Seas* that Max Radiguet in *Les Derniers Sauvages* (originally published in 1860) gives a full account of his visit to Hanamenu, Hiva Oa, only two months before Melville's in 1842, but he makes no mention of a white man such as Lem Hardy living there.[59]

The indelibility of tattoos made them especially appalling. With such tattoos, the liminality of the beachcomber's life became permanent. This was so for Cabri. He forgot his own language. He never found a way to return to Nuku Hiva and became a sideshow in country fairs throughout Europe, an eternal alien.

Very few beachcombers learned the language of the islanders. In his one short month ashore on Nuku Hiva, Melville only picked up a form of pidgin Marquesan. Richard M. Fletcher ends his article on Melville's use of Marquesan, written for *American Speech:* "His fluency with the Marquesan language *per se* cannot be taken with any great seriousness."[60] Fletcher notes: "Whenever he was unable to remember an approximation of the proper word, Melville invented anything that happened to appeal to him. In *Typee* 'Tobi owlee permi' ('Toby has arrived here,' according to Melville) is patent gibberish, as is 'Oee tootai owree! ita maitai!' ('You are a good-for-nothing huzzy, no better than you should be!') in *Omoo*."[61] Although evidently unknown to Fletcher, many of the Marquesan words Melville uses were garnered from David Porter's *Journal of a Cruise* and from his other written sources. For example, Fletcher notes that *meitai* is more nearly correct as the Marquesan word for "good," but Melville's *mortarkee* is his rendering of Porter's *motakee*. Melville, as always, added the *r*, just as he did when he wrote "Happar" for Haʻapaʻa and "Tior" for Taiʻoa.

The clothing of beachcombers soon grew tattered in the tropical sun, and they often exchanged their sailor's outfits for native robes. With their disheveled hair and beards, tattoos, and native clothing, beachcombers became symbols of disaffection. They were undeniably Other. Even missionaries such as William Pascoe Crook often began to wear non-European clothing. As Dening notes, "Crook, musket in hand, dog at his side, a woman's *pareu* wrapped around his waist, aroused confused reactions among Enata [Marquesans]—as he certainly would also have done among the directors of the Missionary Society at home."[62]

Most beachcombers eventually became restless in the paradise they had entered and were eager to join another ship. Men deserted, spent time ashore, and then signed on another vessel. Crews of whaleships shifted throughout the voyage. The Master's Crew List carried onboard a vessel traveling overseas recorded all those who deserted, died, or were put ashore as well as those who signed on to replace them during the length of the voyage. Commonly fifty-five to seventy men would serve aboard a whaleship making a voyage two to five years in length and carrying a crew of thirty to thirty-five men. Sometimes the number of men serving on one voyage numbered over one hundred. As Busch notes, "Any sampling of logbooks soon shows that virtually every vessel making a whaling voyage, long or short, was prone to desertion; any voyage lasting over a single season could expect to turn over a substantial percentage of its crew before it reached home."[63]

Missionaries, like beachcombers, were *alien*. It was more usual for missionaries to be regarded as aliens than as accepted members of the society in which they worked, and early missionaries had a beachcomber-like experience. In fact, some, such as Thomas Lewis, Benjamin Broomhall, and George Vason, did become beachcombers.

It was hard for missionaries to retain their faith and to express it in words strong and eloquent enough to entice others to join them in that faith in the face of inadequate preparation, disillusionment, loneliness, ill health, native violence, and the mundane but cumulative annoyances of heat, rain, mosquitoes, and flies. Ultimately some missionaries deserted. Gunson enumerates: "Some were disillusioned. Some had had insufficient knowledge of the mission field. Some left because of personal danger, some because a false picture had been created by other missionaries, and others left because of disagreements in the field, persecution or scandal-mongering. Many left—especially the female missionaries—because of ill-health, nervous tension and climatic fatigue. Others left the missions after moral failings and backsliding."[64] Compare these reasons for desertion with those given by whalemen: insufficient or inedible food, poor living and working conditions, discouragement over the number of whales caught, and boredom. The missionaries were more troubled by moral considerations, but the reasons for desertion are not much different.

Thomas Lewis arrived in Tahiti on the *Duff* in 1797 and served faithfully for two years until he left the mission house to live with a *taio,* or Tahitian friend. "Three weeks afterward," Ellis tells us, "he intimated to his companions his intention of uniting in marriage with a native of the island, solemnly purposing to abide faithful towards her until death." Ellis continues: "Considering her an idolatress, the missionaries deemed this an inconsistent and unlawful act, and not only declined to sanction the proceeding, but endeavoured by every means to dissuade him from it; but Mr. Lewis persevering in his determination, they dissolved the connexion that had subsisted between him and themselves as members of a Christian church or society, and discontinued all religious and social intercourse with him."[65] Lewis was shortly afterward murdered by the islanders, and some of the missionaries "regretted that, after his separation, kindness and friendly intercourse were not continued, which might perhaps, without compromise of character, have been consistently maintained."[66] A true Ishmael, Lewis was shunned by the society from which he came, then murdered by the society that he entered.

Benjamin Broomhall was young, a great asset to the other missionaries, and respected by the natives. Several years after his arrival on the *Duff,* however, he "intimated his doubts as to the reality of Divine influence on the mind, and the immortality of the soul."[67] For this he was separated from the mission community and lived with a native woman as his wife until she, too, left him. He finally left the island. Years later, calling himself an "apostate missionary,"[68] he repented his doubts and resolved to resume his missionary work but was lost at sea en route.

Unlike Lewis and Broomhall, George Vason of the first Tongan mission, which arrived in Tonga aboard the *Duff* in 1797, defected completely. He adopted the dress and markings of the Tongans and took several wives.[69] With such actions, Vason's life seems to parallel Cabri's, but it did not end as badly. He later underwent a second conversion and became a Baptist and a respectable governor of Nottingham Gaol.[70] Unlike Cabri, Vason was able to recross the beach.

The intersection of the worlds of the beachcomber and the missionary are most evident in William Caw, a shipwright from England who served as a mechanic missionary on Tahiti in 1804–8.[71] Among other reasons, the missionaries snubbed Caw for his poor use of language. John Jefferson, the Tahitian missionary secretary, wrote: "We must acknowledge ourselves not a little surprized that a person of Mr Caw's advanced age, *impediment of speech* [evidently both physical and linguistic], and peculiarity of manners—should be thought a suitable character to be sent so many thousand miles to be an instructor of heathens of a *dark and strange speech* in the Christian religion and youth in the art of reading English."[72] Rejected by both missionaries and natives, Caw became friendly with the European beachcombers. Three months later, he was censured by the missionaries for "his intimacy with runaway seamen." Jefferson wrote: "It has been found necessary to come to the resolution of denying to br. Caw the right of attending when any publick business of any kind is in agitation among us: for it has been found that he makes so improper use of it as even to carry the account of some of our proceedings to the seamen that are living about here."[73] Caw became an utter outcast.

Missionaries had little good to say about beachcombers. Ellis notes that the missionaries "beheld with regret the baneful influence of unprincipled seamen on the minds and habits of the people."[74] J. S. H. Royce wrote far more forcefully of the beachcombers in Fiji: they were "a specimen of the devil's darlings, full of uncleanness, cursed children. . . . Their lives are drawn in flaming colours, lying, cursing, backbiting, fraud, murder, licentiousness, laziness, filth and foul deeds of the darkest dye fit only for some dark den in the bottomless pit."[75] As so often with missionary writing, the strength of Royce's feelings is shown in his use of alliteration, here on the letter *f,* but especially on the letter *d.* Royce's language echoes the diatribes against sailors themselves in contemporary newspapers discussed in chapter 2.

In 1826, the Tahitian parliament passed a regulation "Concerning Seamen who may leave their Vessels." As Ellis notes, "One of the greatest sources of annoyance to the natives, and inconvenience to foreigners, has been the conduct of seamen who have absconded from their ships, or been turned on shore by the masters of trading vessels."[76] Seamen who deserted as well as those who enticed them to desert or concealed them when they did so were to be punished with hard labor, either the building of fifty fathoms (three hundred feet) of road or eight yards (twenty-four feet) of stone pier or wall.[77]

The missionaries instigated the passing of the above regulation, as Melville discovered in his reading of Ellis. In *Omoo,* he states:

> The missionaries have prepared a sort of penal tariff to facilitate judicial proceedings. It costs so many days' labor on the Broom Road to indulge in the pleasures of the calabash; so many fathoms of stone wall to steal a musket; and so on to the end of the catalogue. The judge being provided with a book, in which all these matters are cunningly arranged, the thing is vastly convenient. For instance: a crime is proved,—say, bigamy; turn to letter B.—and there you have it. Bigamy:—forty days on the Broom Road, and twenty mats for the queen. Read the passage aloud, and sentence is pronounced. (300)

A native court metes out such a punishment to an adulterous couple—"some one's husband and another person's wife"—who had run off to the hills for ninety days. "They were subsequently condemned to make one hundred fathoms of Broom Road—a six months' work, if not more" (180). Melville mocks the reductive nature of making moral transgressions quantifiable in this manner. Despite the regulations on desertion and illicit sexual activity, seamen continued to desert in great numbers, and islanders continued to practice far more sexual freedom than the missionaries thought proper.

POLYNESIAN BEACHCOMBERS

In the character of Queequeg in *Moby-Dick,* Melville creates a beachcomber who has crossed the beach in the opposite direction, from the islands of the South Pacific to the decks of a whaleship. Much of what Melville tells us of Queequeg can be applied to Europeans on the beaches of Polynesia. Queequeg "was a creature in the transition state—neither caterpillar nor butterfly" (27). That liminality is the same experienced by European beachcombers. Both William Pascoe Crook and Queequeg do not grasp the technicalities of clothing in an alien culture. Crook wears Marquesan clothing, but it is a woman's pareu rather than the loin cloth of a man. His education, like Queequeg's, "was not yet completed. He was an undergraduate" (27). Queequeg puts his tall beaver hat on first and then, minus his trousers, crawls under the bed in order to be private in putting on his boots. Emerging from under the bed, Queequeg struts around the room with little but his hat and boots on, until Ishmael, embarrassed by the open window, begs him to "accelerate his toilet somewhat, and particularly to get into his pantaloons as soon as possible" (28).

In the years since leaving his native island of Kokovoko, Queequeg has not succumbed to the death that quickly engulfed so many of the Polynesians who left their island homes. He remains magnificent. In contrast, the Marquesans Temouteitei and Hekonaiki and the Tahitian Harraweia, who went to England with William Pascoe Crook in 1799, soon died of the cold and damp. Ahutoru, the first Tahitian to visit Europe, sailed to France in 1768 with the French navigator Louis-Antoine de Bougainville; he died in Madagascar in 1771 on his way back to Tahiti.[78] King Kamehameha II and Queen Kamamalu of Hawaii arrived in London in 1824 to visit King George IV. A little over a month later, before the meeting with the king could take place, they were both dead of measles. Many indigenous peoples, sent so hopefully by missionaries to the mission school in Cornwall, Connecticut, quickly died there. Lewis Keah, "a native of the Marquesas Islands, aged 17 years," and his "companion and countryman" of the same age died at the school in 1820. According to the account of the Reverend H. Daggett, the head of the school, "They were both in a feeble state of health when admitted to the school; on which they were ill prepared to endure the rigours of our climate." But the "youths were remarkably amiable and docile in their dispositions and manners, by which they secured the love of their instructors and fellow students."[79] Another Marquesan, Hami Patu, arrived at the school in March 1823 and was dead by the summer.

The Tahitian Omai, taken by Captain James Cook to London in 1774 on his second voyage, returned to Tahiti in 1776 during Cook's third voyage.[80] He lived to see his native land again, but his fate was not that of most of his countrymen.

In addition to the native South Pacific islanders taken to Europe to meet royalty or sent to mission schools, countless numbers of islanders joined ships, especially whaleships, as sailors. In 1846, the Hawaiian Ministry of Interior reported that three thousand Hawaiians were estimated to be at sea at that time; 651 had left the islands officially—and undoubtedly more unofficially—in the preceding year.[81] Most left no record. Their identities were lost when their names were mangled on crew lists or recorded simply as John Kanacka, Kanacka Joe, George Nukahiva, or such designations as Friday, Thursday, or October. For example, Temouteitei was known as John Butterworth: he was given the good Christian name "John," and since he had sailed to England on the whaleship *Butterworth*, he was given "Butterworth" for his surname. *Kanacka* derives from *Te Enata*, "the men," the term used by Polynesians for themselves; it was the most common sailor term for South Pacific islanders.[82] Like other Polynesians, Queequeg's name is mangled through what Melville calls "Captain Peleg's obstinate mistake touching his appellative" and he is listed in the ship's papers of the *Pequod* as Quohog (89). *Quohog* is the Algonquin word for a particular kind of large clam native to southern New England, an absurd misnomer for so experienced and magnificent a whaleman.

MISSIONARY INTERACTIONS WITH NATIVES

The attitude of missionaries toward those they came to Christianize was often one of repulsion and aversion. When we read their writings almost two centuries later, it is hard to reconcile this distaste with the missionaries' desire to save their souls and to see them as sisters and brothers in Christ. Such a seeming contradiction was difficult for missionaries to negotiate as well. In 1818 Hugh Thomas, a naval agent, advocated the Fijians as a people for prospective evangelization: "They are in one word the very *dregs of Mankind* or Human Nature, dead and buried under the primeval curse, and nothing of them alive but the *Brutal part,* yea far worse than the Brute-Savage quite unfit to live but far more unfit to die, and yet they are the Sons and Daughters of Adam, and destined to live for ever."[83] Within this one sentence, Thomas's argument veers back and forth between the belief that the souls of all human beings must be saved and that all humans are "destined to live for ever" and his repugnance toward these people in particular.

Such paradoxical feelings are also found in the private journals of missionaries. In August of 1833, the American mission to the Marquesas, consisting of six adults and four children and backed by the American Board of Commissioners for Foreign Missions, settled at Nuku Hiva. In her diary of private reflections, Mary Parker, one of the missionary wives, writes: "What a savage people—their looks strike terror—I cover my face to keep out the sight—Can they be human? Did humanity ever sink so below the brute? . . . [We are] surrounded by hundreds of these savages, their eyes glaring out on us. . . . Their words, their gestures shame the very brutes—Gracious God—can these be men and women! It seems impossible!"[84] Yet she explains in a journal letter to her family why she must turn away from the visual experience of the Marquesans and focus on their souls: "You would say to me come back, set not your foot on their shores should you look at them only—but remembering they are Christ's inheritance and that God is our Protector I know you would say go forward nothing doubting."[85] Parker's resolution to see Marquesans as God's creatures conflicts deeply with her physical abhorrence toward them.

Harriet Beecher Stowe makes damning literary use of this same conflict in the character of Miss Ophelia in *Uncle Tom's Cabin* (1852). A northern white woman, Miss Ophelia, cannot bear to touch the black slave girl Topsy or to be touched by her, and yet she believes her a child of God. Eva St. Clare, the young heroine of the story, tells Topsy to try to be good. Topsy answers: "Couldn't never be nothin' but a nigger, if I was ever so good. . . . If I could be skinned, and come white, I'd try then." Eva replies: "'But people can love you, if you are black, Topsy. Miss Ophelia would love you, if you were good.' Topsy gave the short, blunt laugh that was her common mode of expressing incredulity. 'Don't you think so?' said Eva. 'No; she can't bar me, 'cause I'm a nigger!—she'd 's soon have a toad touch her!'" Miss Ophelia overhears Topsy and admits to her cousin, Eva's father: "I've always had a prejudice against negroes . . . and it's a fact, I never could bear to have that child touch me; but, I didn't think she knew it."[86]

Mary Parker's private thoughts are echoed publicly by Richard Armstrong, another member of the 1833 American mission to the Marquesas. In a paper entitled "A Sketch of Marquesan Character," published in the *Hawaiian Spectator* in 1838, Armstrong writes: "Nothing we have ever beheld in the shape of human depravity in other parts of the world will compare for a moment with their shameful and shameless iniquities. The blackest ink that ever stained paper is none too dark to describe them. . . . Can such beings, without a change as great, and requiring as much power as a resurrection from the dead, ever dwell in a holy heaven, with a holy God?"[87] With such intolerance and initial disgust shaping the American mission, is it any wonder that the mission ended within a year?

But it was not only the Fijians and Marquesans, the two groups to which the accusations of cannibalism especially adhered, who were portrayed as brutes. John Whewell, a Methodist missionary, in a letter sent from Haʻapai, Tonga, can only denigrate Tongan character: "The Tonga character and 'gaahi Aga' (manners) is a source of continual trial and endurance to the missionary. They are naturally proud indolent forgetful dirty and ungrateful and I may add deceitful."[88] Fijians, Marquesans, Tongans—all are disparaged by those sent to evangelize them.

Missionaries were offended by all the signs of Otherness in the islanders whom they came to evangelize. They hated their dress, their curiosity, their sexual practices, and their dances. The tattoos that covered their skin were foreign and therefore terrifying. Ishmael reacts similarly on first seeing Queequeg's tattoos: "He turned round—when, good heavens! what a sight! Such a face! It was of a dark, purplish, yellow color, here and there stuck over with large, blackish looking squares. Yes, it's just as I thought, he's a terrible bedfellow; he's been in a fight, got dreadfully cut, and here he is, just from the surgeon" (*Moby-Dick* 21). Ishmael's language evokes the same horror and repugnance evident in Mary Parker's reaction to the Marquesans, yet in short order Ishmael has not only overcome this repugnance through his reflective and philosophical questioning but decided that it is "better [to] sleep with a sober cannibal than a drunken Christian" (24). Soon he and Queequeg are bosom friends.

Ishmael first mistakes Queequeg's tattoos for sticking plasters. When he understands that they are tattoos, he is reassured—until he realizes that Queequeg is not a white man. The color of Queequeg's skin, especially that of his scalp, is especially Other for Ishmael: "His bald purplish head now looked for all the world like a mildewed skull. . . . I am no coward, but what to make of this head-peddling purple rascal altogether passed my comprehension" (21). Ishmael finally comes to understand that "Ignorance is the parent of fear" (21). Few of the missionaries or their wives had this kind of understanding. Many continued to believe, as the American missionary Richard Armstrong did, that "The blackest ink that ever stained paper is none too dark to describe them."[89]

Yet the missionary view of natives as brutes and savages was not monolithic. The Methodist Thomas Williams has good words to say about Fijians: "Fijians are greatly wronged by being supposed to be a set of rough untutored brutes. They can feel as keenly, weep as sincerely, love as truly and laugh as heartily as any European. White men who call them brutes, devils and such-like find on better acquaintance that they have an elaborate system of etiquette, and that among themselves none but the very lowest are ill-behaved."[90] Certainly many of the missionaries grew to love and respect the islanders among whom they worked.

Some missionaries sought to control the Otherness of the islanders by banning many cultural practices. Melville deplores these restrictions in *Omoo*. He believes such laws lead to indolence and ultimately sickness and death among the native people.

> But the short kilts of dyed tappa, the tasseled maroes, and other articles formerly worn, are, at the present day, prohibited by law, as indecorous. . . . Many pleasant, and, seemingly, innocent sports and pastimes, are likewise interdicted. In old times, there were several athletic games practiced; such as wrestling, foot-racing, throwing the javelin, and archery. In all these they greatly excelled; and, for some, splendid festivals were instituted. Among their everyday amusements, were dancing, tossing the football, kite-flying, flute-playing, and singing traditional ballads; *now,* all punishable offenses. . . . Against tattooing, of any kind, there is a severe law. (182–83)

Missionary talk, for Melville, has become the talk of interdiction and deprivation. The missionaries wanted the islanders to conform, to become like them—with the caveat that the islanders, however, will never be *quite* like them: they will never attain the social standing of the missionaries. Melville's questioning and condemnation of missionary restrictions illustrates the pettiness and ineffectiveness of such restrictions. The complex web of cultural practices, interdependent upon each other, eventually breaks down when too many even seemingly insignificant elements are banned. The behaviors and material culture with which the missionaries attempted to replace some banned practices were at best irrelevant and at worst destructive. As Melville condemns the blind self-righteousness of the missionaries, he is all too aware of what these changes cost the islanders: alienation, indolence, apathy, disease, death.

In *Omoo,* Melville drenches us with facts and figures. For example, he tells us that Captain James Cook estimated the population of Tahiti in 1777 to be about two hundred thousand. By 1842, at the time of Melville's visit, the population was found to be only nine thousand. "All the wars, child murders, and other depopulating causes, alledged [*sic*] to have existed in former times, were nothing in comparison to [the evils that caused such a population decrease]. These evils, of course, are solely of foreign origin" (191). Melville blames drunkenness, smallpox, and venereal disease. The islanders respond to their deep loss in one of the most moving passages in *Omoo:* "Distracted with their sufferings, they brought forth their sick before the missionaries, when they were preaching, and cried out, 'Lies, lies! you tell us of salvation; and, behold, we are dying. We want no other salvation, than to live in this world. Where are there any saved through your speech? [The Tahitian king Pomare II] is dead; and we are all dying with your cursed diseases. When will you give over?'" (191). Here a sailor Other, who is called "Typee," the name of a native tribe, speaks for the alienated and dispossessed native Other, raising at least a ghost of the native voice that would, perhaps, otherwise be utterly lost. Melville creates a spoken response to the natives' suffering based on a description of their complaint that is not verbatim. Ultimately this speech is a forceful denunciation of missionary talk itself, couched in the missionary's own cadences and prophetic, sermonic style. Melville's ability to achieve the power and passion evident in this speech arises from his vast familiarity with and command of the missionary talk that permeated the South Pacific, a form of talk he increasingly incorporates in his early works and wields with astonishing subtlety and force in *Moby-Dick.*

$\sim$ "Cannibal Old Me"

The Development of Melville's Narrative Voice

Literature is invention. Fiction is fiction. To call a story a true story is an insult to both art and truth. Every great writer is a great deceiver. . . . There are three points of view from which a writer can be considered: he may be considered as a story-teller, as a teacher, and as an enchanter. A major writer combines these three—storyteller, teacher, enchanter—but it is the enchanter in him that predominates and makes him a major writer.

—Vladimir Nabokov

MELVILLE'S first words of the first chapter of his first book appear not as a statement, not as a description, but rather as a direct conversational address to his audience. "Six months at sea! Yes, reader, as I live" (*Typee* 3). It's as though you struck up a conversation with a stranger at a bar who begins forthwith to regale you with an account of his own remarkable doings. The ensuing paragraph maintains this tone as it touches on one vivid homely detail after another exoticized by its shipboard context. Exclamation points abound, creating the sense of the rise and fall of the speaker's voice. In fact, the tenor of the six paragraphs that comprise the first passage of this chapter as well as the first paragraph of the next passage can be characterized as exclamatory. The paragraphs maintain a lively, engaging, eager, conversational tone, drawing the reader in as a listener as much as or more than as a reader. Captivated by this compelling voice and the strange setting of the familiar details (bananas, oranges, breakfasting, lunching), we listen with increasing interest:

Six months as sea! Yes, reader, as I live, six months out of sight of land; cruising after the sperm-whale beneath the scorching sun of the Line, and tossed on the billows of the wide-rolling Pacific—the sky above, the sea around, and nothing else! Weeks and weeks ago our fresh provisions were all exhausted. There is not a sweet potatoe [*sic*] left; not a single yam. Those glorious bunches of bananas which once decorated our stern and quarter-deck have, alas, disappeared! and the delicious oranges which hung suspended from our tops and stays—they, too, are gone! Yes, they are all departed, and there is nothing left us but the salt-horse and sea-biscuit. Oh! ye state-room sailors, who make so much ado about a fourteen-days' passage across the Atlantic; who so pathetically relate the privations and hardships of the sea, where, after a day of breakfasting, lunching, dining off five courses, chatting, playing whist, and drinking champagne-punch, it was your hard lot to be shut up in little cabinets of mahogany and maple, and sleep for ten hours, with nothing to disturb you but "those good-for-nothing tars, shouting and tramping over head,"—what would ye say to our six months out of sight of land? (3)

By this point, the speaker has fully engaged our attention.

In these initial paragraphs, the reader encounters an unpracticed writer who achieves his fresh, vivid, and engaging effect through sentences that cry out to be read aloud. The phrasing, vocabulary, rhythm, punctuation, and above all tone of this passage derive from Melville's already highly developed skills as a storyteller. He is in conversation with himself as well as with his audience. Rhetorically he asks himself the questions that occur to us, to which he then furnishes the answers. Just as he enlivens his descriptions with his rich vocabulary, he personifies the last of the ship's poultry flock and heightens the humor of this personification by addressing the bird directly in archaic, formal language: "I wish thee no harm, Peter; but as thou art doomed, sooner or later, to meet the fate of all thy race; and if putting a period to thy existence is to be the signal for our deliverance, why— truth to speak—I wish thy throat cut this very moment; for, oh! how I wish to see the living earth again!" The personification continues in the next sentence: "The old ship herself longs to look out upon the land from her hawse-holes once more" (4). This personification persists until the end of the passage, set off by the odd, slightly mocking tone, the mix of folksy idiom and tongue-in-cheek formality, and the sharp ear for just the right adjective: "merry land," "some green cove," "boisterous winds" (5). From its inception, the narrative voice in Melville's prose demonstrates the author's long practice in telling stories as opposed to writing them.

Tommo, the narrator of *Typee*, almost immediately puts himself in the situation where he is a solitary outsider, essentially alien to the culture in which he thrusts himself. Once his companion Toby disappears, this alienation is complete. Even the charms of the lovely Fayaway provide no sure connection or refuge. Tommo's scant familiarity with the Marquesan language completes his isolation. In *Omoo*, Melville's narrator, now named Typee, goes ashore not as an individual but as part of a group, the crew of the *Julia*, with whom he has made common cause, thereby finding himself, along with the rest of the crew, pitted against not only the authorities but the societal conventions of his surroundings. His companion on this journey does not desert him. Here he maintains an implicitly political identity as a member of an outsider group with its own sly and at times coded language opposed to the conventional society he moves through as a skeptical observer. The shifting, phantasmagorical narrator of *Mardi* becomes submerged in the book's allegorical and philosophical ambitions. *Redburn* gives us the most straightforward narrator of Melville's first five books, recounting the conventional story of a young man's first voyage as a sailor, his induction into the seafaring world, and his observations of life in a foreign seaport. In *White-Jacket* the narrator finds himself a cog in the complex world of a man-of-war with its own formalized and structured language. He struggles with questions of the individual's role in society and the nature of human institutions and is troubled by a nagging but undefined sense that human institutions cannot answer all his questions. The narrator of *Moby-Dick*, Ishmael, thinks he is joining a community. Onboard the *Pequod* he encounters Ahab, whose overwhelming command of spoken language sways and compels all within its reach yet is finally ineffectual in the face of the existential human alienation from the universe. The trajectory from Tommo to Ishmael is mirrored in the development of the character of each narrator's voice. Essential to this development is the increasingly sophisticated and profound use of the oral sources and discourses that informed Melville's creative process.

The three forms of talk discussed in the preceding chapters—sailor talk, cannibal talk, and missionary talk—not only pervaded the South Pacific during Melville's time but were facets of the broader Western discourses of the civilized versus the savage, the character of human society, and humankind's place in nature. The vitality and complexity of these three forms are rooted in the extent to which they were carried on as talk. While the extant written record on these subjects is itself rich and complex, talk was the medium that allowed the fluidity, ubiquity, resilience, adaptability, persuasiveness, and variety of voices in which these overlapping discourses flourished. In the ferment produced by this lively interaction of talk and belief with his relation of his own experience and reflection, Melville's voice matured from the raw young wine of his told tales to the heady vintage we savor in *Moby-Dick*.

Melville's sense of fulfillment at becoming a published author stimulated huge ambition within him. His comfortable skill as a storyteller, challenged by the need to commit words to paper as a writer in *Typee*, was quickly superseded by a growing desire to be a literary artist of the first rank. He soon grew impatient with being seen as a journalist or a "romancer." His fictionalized account of his experiences on Nuku Hiva simultaneously generated widespread praise for the writing and skepticism as to its veracity. In his next book, *Omoo*, he combined an original and more developed and consistent narrative voice with more extensive research presented as his own observations. Frustrated by the limitations of writing what were essentially sold as travel books, he launched a hugely ambitious but failed literary experiment in *Mardi,* losing the focused narrative voice he had crafted in his first two books. Melville followed this with a determined effort to master a more conventional, conversational, and straightforward tone and form in *Red-burn,* establishing a much greater control of his use of language in that context. In *White-Jacket,* Melville combined this increased mastery with the ironic, mocking tone of his first two books to achieve a more subtle and complex effect, reaching for the higher order of literary achievement he finally grasped in his masterpiece, *Moby-Dick.*

Typee

Melville begins the preface to *Typee* by assuring us of the strangeness and yet the *truth* of the sailor's view of the world. "Sailors are the only class of men who now-a-days see anything like stirring adventure; and many things which to fire-side people appear strange and romantic, to them seem as common-place as a jacket out at elbows," he tells us at the beginning of the preface (xiii). The preface ends: "There are some things related in the narrative which will be sure to appear strange, or perhaps entirely incomprehensible, to the reader; but they cannot appear more so to him than they did to the author at the time. He has stated such matters just as they occurred, and leaves every one to form his own opinion concerning them; trusting that his anxious desire to speak the unvarnished truth will gain for him the confidence of his readers" (xiv). The sophisticated reader realizes that a good deal of what Melville says here is untrue. Melville has not stated matters as they occurred: much of *Typee* is borrowed from other narratives such as Georg H. von Langsdorff's *Voyages and Travels in Various Parts of the World,* Charles S. Stewart's *A Visit to the South Seas in the U.S. Ship* Vincennes, and David Porter's *Journal of a Cruise Made to the Pacific Ocean.* Melville does not leave everyone to form his or her own opinion: he ponders, analyzes, and questions at great length. *Typee* is not unvarnished truth: it is a carefully crafted work, published four years after Melville first began telling his story orally. Finally, no one who has read Melville's *The Confidence-Man* can ever again trust his use of the word "confidence."

Yet it is important to see that Melville is setting up the story as a true narrative told by a sailor who will speak plainly and without ornament or exaggeration. Thus, from the beginning, the narrator's voice is inextricably tied to sailor talk. The narrator will also knowingly speak as an outsider. He is outside the safe circle of firelight that encompasses his reader. He has gone beyond that circle just as surely as his elbows have passed through the fiber of his jacket.

By the time Melville penned *Typee,* the genre of maritime fiction had developed a set of conventions regarding form and narration. Often told in the first person, the standard works rely on a studied literary tone rooted in a moralistic viewpoint. The subtext is often the straying of the narrator from the upright society of his childhood. Witness Daniel Defoe's *Robinson Crusoe* (1719):

> I Was born in the Year 1632, in the City of *York,* of a good Family. . . . Being the third Son of the Family, and not bred to any Trade, my Head began to be fill'd very early with rambling Thoughts: My Father, who was very ancient, had given me a competent Share of Learning, as far as House-Education, and Country Free-School generally goes, and design'd me for the Law; but I would be satisfied with nothing but going to Sea, and my Inclination to this led me so strongly against the Will, nay, the Commands of my Father, and against all the Entreaties and Perswasions of my Mother, and other Friends, that there seem'd to be something fatal in that Propension of Nature tending directly to the Life of Misery which was to befal me.[1]

Jonathan Swift's *Gulliver's Travels* (1726) commences with a comparable statement of fact: "My Father had a small Estate in *Nottinghamshire;* I was the Third of Five Sons. He sent me to *Emanuel-Colledge* in *Cambridge,* at Fourteen Years old, where I resided three Years, and applyed my self close to my Studies. . . . My father now and then sending me Small sums of Money, I laid them out in learning Navigation, and other Parts of the Mathematicks, useful to those who intend to travel, as I always believed it would be some time or other my fortune to do."[2] Tobias Smollett's *The Adventures of Roderick Random* (1748) copies the beginning of *Robinson Crusoe* even more closely with its repetition of "I was born":

> Of my Birth and Parentage
> I was born in the northern part of this united kingdom, in the house of my grand father; a gentleman of considerable fortune and influence, who had, on many occasions, signalised himself in behalf of his country; and was remarkable for his abilities in the law, which he exercised with great success, in the station of a judge, particularly against beggars, for whom he had a singular aversion.[3]

Frederick Marryat's *Mr. Midshipman Easy* (1836), although told in the third person, similarly begins with straightforward information: "Mr. Nicodemus Easy was a gentleman who lived down in Hampshire; he was a married man, and in very easy circumstances."[4] Edgar Allan Poe consciously echoes his British literary antecedents in chapter 1 of *The Narrative of Arthur Gordon Pym* (1838): "My name is Arthur Gordon Pym. My father was a respectable trader in sea-stores at Nantucket, where I was born. My maternal grandfather was an attorney in good practice."[5] Arthur Gordon Pym's grandfather, like Roderick Random's, was distinguished in the law. But he, too, like the other protagonists before him, headed to sea.

The above works are all fiction and were all read by Melville.[6] Another work read by Melville, Richard Henry Dana Jr.'s nonfiction *Two Years before the Mast*, begins not with Dana's birth but with his departure on the brig *Pilgrim;* nonetheless, the tone is equally direct and factual: "The fourteenth of August was the day fixed upon for the sailing of the brig Pilgrim on her voyage from Boston round Cape Horn to the western coast of North America. As she was to get under weigh early in the afternoon, I made my appearance on board at twelve o'clock, in full sea-rig, and with my chest, containing an outfit for a two or three years' voyage."[7] In what is considered the first *true* sea novel, James Fenimore Cooper does not repeat the "I was born" formula, but *The Pilot* is nonetheless set in motion with factual statement. "A single glance at the map will make the reader acquainted with the position of the eastern coast of the island of Great Britain."[8]

Contrast the formality of all these with the abrupt conversational opening of *Typee*. Even though Melville is steeped in this literary genre as a reader, as a writer his template is not the conventions of the books he has read, but his own experience as a storyteller. Tommo assures us of his sailor credentials with his first words: "Six months at sea! Yes, reader, as I live, six months out of sight of land" (3). He is no coasting sailor who has only been out of sight of land for a few days, but a deepwater man who has seen no piece of earth for six months. Tommo derisively addresses those "state-room sailors" who would complain of a mere fourteen days crossing the Atlantic. If the sea is the space between lands and cultures, the space that Tommo has crossed is vast.

The vastness of the sea is contrasted with the smallness of the sailor's world aboard ship. During his six months at sea, Tommo has been submerged in sailor talk. That talk has shaped his expectations of the land they are about to encounter. Here sailor talk merges with cannibal talk. Tommo thinks to himself: "The Marquesas! What strange visions of outlandish things does the very name spirit up! Naked houris—cannibal banquets—groves of cocoa-nut—coral reefs—tatooed chiefs—and bamboo temples; sunny valleys planted with bread-fruit-trees— carved canoes dancing on the flashing blue waters—savage woodlands guarded by horrible idols—*heathenish rites and human sacrifices*" (5; emphasis in original).

Notice the rising hysteria in Tommo's voice. He stokes himself up until he cries out in fear at the vision of human sacrifice. Yet that vision clearly excites him.

Tommo's expectations of the Marquesas are in error, for the Marquesas have no coral reefs. They are not fringed with coral as other Polynesian islands are and therefore have neither the sapphire-blue water nor the white-sand beaches that so entrance visitors to the South Pacific. If Tommo's vision of Marquesan coral reefs, engendered by sailor talk, is wrong, perhaps his expectations of cannibalism are also in error. He calls his visions "strangely jumbled anticipations that haunted me during our passage from the cruising ground" (5). His anticipation and desire mixed with his fear recall Arthur Gordon Pym's statement at the beginning of Poe's *The Narrative of Arthur Gordon Pym* on why he wanted to go to sea:

> For the bright side of the painting I had a limited sympathy. My visions were of shipwreck and famine; of death or captivity among barbarian hordes; of a lifetime dragged out in sorrow and tears, upon some gray and desolate rock, in an ocean unapproachable and unknown. Such visions or desires—for they amounted to desires—are common, I have since been assured, to the whole numerous race of the melancholy among men—at the time of which I speak I regarded them only as prophetic glimpses of a destiny which I felt myself in a measure bound to fulfil [*sic*].[9]

Note again the formal literary quality of this passage compared with the earlier quotation from *Typee*. Melville's words are littered with exclamation points. The images tumble out, separated only by dashes, a single adjective sufficing to enliven each image—naked houris, bamboo temples, savage woodlands, horrible idols—the culminating phrase italicized for verbal emphasis. All these characteristics are designed to enhance the sense of spoken delivery: this passage is written as it would be spoken. In contrast, Poe's piece achieves a steady pulse through pairings: shipwreck and famine, death or captivity, sorrow and tears, gray and desolate, unapproachable and unknown. Poe's language is engrossing and evocative but decidedly not what you would hear a sailor utter in a bar. Poe's gothic romanticism is far more indebted to the literary tradition of the maritime novel than is Melville's. Melville imbibed his sailor talk directly from the source, Poe from a sickly child's ardor for armchair adventure through books. No true sailor such as Melville would ever romanticize shipwreck.

Visions haunt both Pym and Tommo and draw them to their respective destinies: Pym's to go to sea and be shipwrecked, Tommo's to live in a world of "tatooed chiefs . . . sunny valleys planted with bread-fruit-trees . . . [and] savage woodlands guarded by horrible idols," where the fear of cannibal banquets and human sacrifice is omnipresent. Tommo longs for the heathenish rites as much as he fears them.

Tommo's anticipations and desires are clear by the third page of chapter 1. Yet he still feels as if he must justify to us, his readers, why he deserts his ship. It is not the tug of his vision of heathenish rites but the "numberless instances" in which the captain has violated the ship's articles that causes him to run away—or so he tells us. Tommo speaks here as a sea lawyer skilled (even if only in his own mind) in the rights due to sailors. Perhaps best exemplified by the character of Donkin in Joseph Conrad's *The Nigger of the* Narcissus, a sea lawyer is a sailor with no legal training who advocates on shipboard the rights of seamen. "In numberless instances," Tommo tells us, "had not only the implied but the specified conditions of the articles been violated on the part of the ship in which I served. . . . The captain was the author of these abuses; it was in vain to think that he would either remedy them, or alter his conduct, which was arbitrary and violent in the extreme" (20–21). Tommo wants to win us to his side. He asks rationally, reasonably, "If one party fail to perform his share of the compact, is not the other virtually absolved from his liability?" (20). But we have already seen Tommo's deep-seated desire for heathenish rites, so we are not fully convinced by his arguments.

Tommo's voice is not Melville's. Tommo is a fictional character shaped by sailor talk as much as based upon Melville's own experiences. As is true of all of Melville's narrators, Tommo's voice is not consistent. The voice of excitement that is drawn to the vision of human sacrifice and throws the term "cannibal" about loosely is not the same one that only a few pages later makes us question our own inhumanity by probing our attitudes toward the kidnapping and murder of South Pacific islanders. "The enormities perpetrated in the South Seas upon some of the inoffensive islanders wellnigh pass belief," Tommo—or is it Melville?—tells us (26). He refers to the robberies, kidnappings, and murders inflicted on the islanders by visiting ships. He continues: "Sometimes vague accounts of such things reach our firesides, and we coolly censure them as wrong, impolitic, needlessly severe, and dangerous to the crews of other vessels. How different is our tone when we read the highly wrought description of the massacre of the crew of the Hobomak by the Feejees; how we sympathise for the unhappy victims, and with what horror do we regard the diabolical heathens" (27). This voice will again and again come forward throughout *Typee,* making us question many of our assumptions about civilization versus savagery, paganism versus Christianity, good versus evil.

In the next chapter, Tommo's recognized voice, with its slightly sardonic edge, its humor, and its conversational tone, returns. Tommo pictures himself after his escape from the ship then adds:

To be sure there was one rather unpleasant drawback to these agreeable anticipations—the possibility of falling in with a foraging party of these same bloody-minded Typees, whose appetites, edged perhaps by the air of so elevated a region, might prompt them to devour one. This, I must confess, was a most disagreeable view of the matter.

Just to think of a party of these unnatural gourmands taking it into their heads to make a convivial meal of a poor devil. (31)

Tommo's sailor talk, with its "anticipations" of what he will encounter, is here intrinsically entwined with cannibal talk. The reputation of the Taipi is that of most fearsome cannibals, and so they have become in Tommo's talk. Yet even Tommo's fear is charged with levity. Actually to be devoured would encompass a horror exceeding comprehension: it would be far beyond "most disagreeable." Tommo's joking references to "unnatural gourmands" and "a convivial meal of a poor devil" keep that horror at bay.

During Tommo's residence in the valley of the Typee, his remove first from the maritime environs of the ship and then from the companionship of his fellow sailor delineates a shift from the braggadocio and technical know-how of sailor talk to the exaggerations and helpless horror that characterize cannibal talk. Once Toby escapes, Tommo can give full rein to the delicious dread that increases throughout the latter part of the novel. His narrow escape from tattooing, which would have permanently marked him as a possession of the Typee, his glimpse of the morsels of flesh clinging to the bones in the canoe, and the mask of horror in the visage of Mow-Mow all enter when Tommo is the only outsider witness. The teasing, fleeting presence of Marnoo, who speaks some English, is the only straw at which he can grasp as his sense of security melts away. The tropes of the campfire ghost story are in full play as the book approaches its conclusion. Given that this has the feel of a told rather than a written account, Melville does not have the luxury of having us discover his manuscript in a bottle tossed into the sea—as occurs in Poe's "MS. Found in a Bottle" (1833)—just before Mow-Mow claws him back, leaving the reader to imagine for himself the horrors of the forbidden feast. The narrator must be present to tell his tale.

Since cannibalism is the overriding theme of *Typee,* and since the presence of missionaries on Nuku Hiva up to the point that both Melville and Tommo arrive was brief and abortive, Melville's overt discussion of missionaries plays a relatively minor role in his first book. Nonetheless, Melville develops one of his most powerful and essential uses of missionary talk in chapter 26 of *Typee:* his creation of what I will call the inverted sermon. Melville's employment of missionary language in the last five pages of chapter 26 is at its most subversive, for in this passage he appropriates from missionary sermons the form, cadences, and conventions used to structure an argument. He attacks the missionaries with their own talk. These five pages are forceful, persuasive, and exhortative; Melville makes a passionate moral appeal. Compare the last five pages of chapter 26 to chapter 27. There, as elsewhere in *Typee,* his tone ranges from pondering and pensive to occasionally bemused and jocular. The first part of chapter 26 is written in much the same tone. The chapter is generally ethnographic. Melville begins with the verbal crowning of Mehevi as king: "King Mehevi!—A goodly sounding title!—and why should I not bestow it upon the foremost man in the valley of Typee?" (188). He then writes of such topics as marriage, birth, funerary practices, geography, environs, customs, family ties—the standard fare of ethnographic description, delivered in a fairly dispassionate and objective, almost scientific, fashion.

The transitional paragraph from such ethnography to Melville's inverted sermon begins with a subtle evocation of the religious language employed by missionaries to contradict the Rousseauian ideal of the noble savage by painting these dwellers in a seeming Eden as children of Adam, the first fallen man. The paragraph begins: "The penalty of the Fall presses very lightly upon the valley of the Typee" (195). Melville then, like a matador confusing the bull with his cape, swings back into ethnographic description for the remainder of the paragraph. But the seed has been planted. Adam and Eve in Paradise had only to stretch forth their hands to pluck fruit. Part of their penalty for disobedience was having to work to produce food. The paragraph continues: "For, with the one solitary exception of striking a light, I scarcely saw any piece of work performed there which caused the sweat to stand upon a single brow. As for digging and delving for a livelihood, the thing is altogether unknown" (195). This subtle association again leads the mind of any lay Christian to the image of the original fallen man. Melville then swings back to Rousseau: "Nature has planted the bread-fruit and the banana, and in her own good time she brings them to maturity, when the idle savage stretches forth his hand, and satisfies his appetite" (195). Having juxtaposed the images of fallen man and the noble savage, he now launches with concentrated passion into his sermon. "Ill-fated people! I shudder when I think of the change a few years will produce in their paradisaical abode" (195). The first three words are a despairing cry, followed by the visceral verb "shudder," and Melville is off.

While sermons were often composed and written prior to being delivered, they are, as is true of drama or poetry, designed to be delivered orally and received aurally. The religious fervor that inspired the first and second Great Awakenings (1730s–1740s and 1820s–1830s) was most powerfully communicated in the revival meetings that centered on preaching. Other forms of formalized persuasive and informative speech characterized both the related social reform movements of the mid-nineteenth century and many public entertainments, such as the lyceum movement.

Compare the language that follows Melville's "Ill-fated people!" to the sermons taken down from Father Taylor, the Sailor Preacher, on whom the character Father Mapple in *Moby-Dick* is partly based. The editors of the 1872 collection of *Incidents and Anecdotes of Rev. Edward T. Taylor* write that "generally a playful or comical sentence was the prelude to some moving exhortation or some searching attack."[10] Melville often constructs his sermon-like addresses to his readers in much the same fashion. In a sermon given at Buffalo, New York, in 1860, Taylor urges his congregation:

> Let us have a funeral first, and then a rejoicing. Bury the dead and open the prisons. Throw wide the gates, and take the longitude off your faces. . . . No quibbling and hair-splitting brethren. Webster said once, "The country is tumbling to its ruin. Try to hold it up." God give you conviction till you do right. Will you go away from this place, and have dissension? Let us have a peace. . . . Brethren, you have signed a covenant; if you have, I will hold you to it. I hope you will not dabble with any thing but the gospel. Lord save the Church![11]

With similar cadence, Melville exhorts his readers: "Let the savages be civilized, but civilize them with benefits, and not with evils; and let heathenism be destroyed, but not by destroying the heathen" (195). Melville's words are not far from Taylor's—until he continues: "The Anglo-Saxon hive have extirpated Paganism from the greater part of the North American continent; but with it they have likewise extirpated the greater portion of the Red race. Civilization is gradually sweeping from the earth the lingering vestiges of Paganism, and at the same time the shrinking forms of its unhappy worshippers" (195). Unlike Taylor, Melville asks his readers indeed to dabble with something besides the Gospel.

Taylor often constructs his sermons around a central image or story. Such a story occurs in a bethel sermon given by Taylor in Boston in 1842 and narrated for the editors of the *Incidents and Anecdotes* by the Reverend Elijah Kellogg. A ship has caught fire and the passengers pour water onto it:

> It was all in vain. The fire increased instead of diminishing: the pitch began to melt from the seams of the planking; the lower parts of the hold-pumps were burned. . . . In short, after doing all that men could do to save the ship, they found themselves at their wits' end. . . . All work ceased: the captain called the crew and passengers together, and told them that it was hardly possible for the ship to continue afloat another day,—for she was leaky as well as on fire. . . . As if moved by a common impulse, they prostrated

themselves on the deck without uttering a word. Now, what do you think they prayed for? A little more Methodism, a little more Catholicism, a little more Presbyterianism, a little more Unitarianism, Universalism, or any other *ism?* No, no, brethren. A common danger had given them a common religion. Every soul communed with the same God. When they rose from the deck, a young sailor bounded aloft; and, when he reached the royal masthead, shouted with all his might, "Sail ho! steering in our wake." In a moment the ship was hove to.[12]

This story is a trope for the power of prayer. It supports the institution of Christianity and the power of essential religion to save us.

The central story of Melville's inverted sermon does the opposite. Melville's sermon is constructed around the image of the "robust, red-faced, and very lady-like personage, a missionary's spouse" who goes for daily airings in a go-cart drawn by two islanders (196). The islanders whom the missionaries have come to save have become draught horses. Melville's anger, and our own, at the missionary's spouse peaks when she cries, "Hookee! hookee!" and raps the elder of the two, "an old grey-headed man," on his skull with the heavy handle of her huge fan (197, 196).

Taylor ends his sermon with a strong lesson: "Did creeds give those rescued souls consolation in their hour of extreme peril? No: but the Word of God did; and that is my creed. I hold to the Bible, the whole Bible, as my creed, because it never grows old or needs repatching."[13] Melville builds the lesson at the end of his sermon in a similar way. He begins with a question, to which he gives a forceful answer:

Have not errors and abuses crept into the most sacred places, and may there not be unworthy or incapable missionaries abroad, as well as ecclesiastics of a similar character at home? . . . Those who from pure religious motives contribute to the support of this enterprise, should take care to ascertain that their donations, flowing through many devious channels, at last effect their legitimate object. . . . I urge this not because I doubt the moral probity of those who disburse these funds, but because I know that they are not rightly applied. (197–98)

The certainty of his final line equals Taylor's.

Unlike Melville, Taylor has no fear that he will be criticized for taking the Bible as his moral creed. Melville, however, knows the extent to which his sermon will be criticized. And indeed it was, in review after review. "As wise a man as Shakespeare has said," Melville writes, "that the bearer of evil tidings hath but a losing office; and so I suppose will it prove with me" (198). But Melville ends ringingly: "Those things which I have stated as facts will remain facts, in spite of whatever the bigoted or incredulous may say or write against them" (199).

Melville embarked on the writing of his first book with an enthusiasm and energy that belied his almost complete inexperience as literary author. Whether by accident or design, the narrative voice or rather voices in *Typee* are far more limited in variety and scope than Melville will later achieve. The arc of his plot dictated a narrowing of his choices in the variety of narrative modes. The fact that Tommo loses the companionship of the only other speaker of his language early in the book largely eliminates dialogue as a means of expression, leaving only description. Partly because they can only speak in such a limited way, the inhabitants of the Typee valley seem two-dimensional. Kory-Kory is not much more than a talking sedan chair; Mow-Mow a grotesque mask; and Mehevi, with his intermittent coldness toward Tommo, a stiff cardboard king. Even the beautiful Fayaway is more a woodland nymph than a flesh-and-blood young woman. We are told that she is sympathetic, rather than having it convincingly demonstrated. Toby, however, is more fully developed, as one would expect from the one character fluent in the narrator's own tongue. Toby is occasionally irritable, contrary, reckless, impulsive, and self-centered. These qualities lend a depth to the portrayal of his personality missing from almost all the other characters in *Typee*. Even with Toby, however, extensive dialogue occurs only in the escape chapters early in the book. Once Tommo and Toby arrive in the Typee valley, there are few scenes that include any verbal interchange between the two, the "baked baby" passage constituting one of the few. Toby's account of being attacked by the Happars is given as narration (100–2) rather than in dialogue. And then Toby is gone, just over one-third of the way through the book, after a final short speech in which he tells Tommo, "Should I succeed in getting down to the boats, I will make known the condition in which I have left you, and measures may then be taken to secure our escape" (106). Measures *may* be taken but are not, and Tommo never sees Toby again—at least, not until they meet in upstate New York after the publication of *Typee*. With so little dialogue, Melville maintains the spoken quality of *Typee* by directly addressing the reader. In his next book, Melville will find the opportunity to develop the most effective aspects of his narrative voice in a wider variety of contexts.

Omoo

In the preface to *Omoo*, Melville states explicitly that he is writing a sequel to *Typee*. The success of that first novel motivates him to continue, insofar as possible, with a story in the same vein. He adopts an identical formula for composition, relying on his own experiences, several written sources, and his familiarity with the over-lapping discourses of the South Seas. He commences *Omoo* with a nod to the conventions of the sailor narrative genre. The tale begins with the introduction, synopsizing very briefly the events in *Typee:* "In the summer of 1842, the author of this narrative, as a sailor before the mast, visited the Marquesas Islands in an American South Seaman. At the island of Nukuheva he left his vessel, which af-terward sailed without him" (3). The first three chapters are devoted largely to a description of ship and crew.

Yet scarcely is the narrator aboard the *Julia* when intimations of the precari-ous and fraught relationship between officers and crew evince themselves. In Melville's description of notable characters among the officers and crew, the bluff and unimaginative mate Jermin and the weak, indecisive captain Guy are coun-tered by the anomalous Doctor Long Ghost. Having quit the aftercabin and the companionship of the captain in favor of the fo'c's'le, this learned, cunning, ir-reverent, self-involved individual will become the narrator's companion—a far more complex and developed counterpoint to the narrator than Toby in *Typee*. The crisis in the little society aboard the *Julia* takes place when the narrator "had scarcely been aboard of the ship twenty-four hours" (16).

The conventions of shipboard custom and discipline place the fo'c's'le almost entirely off-limits to the officers without invitation, just as is true of the officers' residence in the after cabin for common sailors. Discipline has deteriorated on the *Julia* to the point that the first mate enters the fo'c's'le and ends up worsted in a struggle with the insubordinate carpenter. The captain, ineffectually attempting to smooth things over, talks into the fo'c's'le hatch and is ridiculed by Doctor Long Ghost, who "cries out in a squeak, 'Ah! Miss Guy, is that you? Now, my dear, go right home, or you'll get hurt'" (4). Captain Guy's remonstrance is followed by open defiance from the carpenter and physical assault: "As the captain once more dipped his head down the scuttle to make answer, from an unseen hand, he received, full in the face, the contents of a tin can of soaked biscuit and tea-leaves. The doctor was not far off just then" (18).

No consequences arise from this extraordinary departure from the norms of shipboard discipline. As the narrator makes clear, these events mark the incipient disintegration of the bonds that allow a shipboard society to function. Note the indirect way in which the narrator points to Doctor Long Ghost as the one who hurled the contents of the can in the captain's face. Ghostlike, he squeaks. Invis-ible, his "unseen hand" robs the captain of his remaining dignity. He is the spirit of rebellion, of the assertion of individuality, of irreverence—a trickster.

In *Typee*, the narrator's increasing horror of cannibalism mutes his jocu-lar tone more and more frequently as the book progresses. In *Omoo*, free of the menace of the cannibal Other and confronted at first with the more mundane annoyance of incompetent officers, the rebellious crew and especially the narrator, Typee, and his compatriot Doctor Long Ghost once again find this jocular voice. Their confrontation with authority and subsequent othering as a result of the confrontation establish this voice and the attitudes that accompany it as the predominant tone for the remainder of *Omoo.* By the time the narrator steps aboard the *Leviathan* at the end of *Omoo,* he has matured from the naive deserter we meet at the beginning of *Typee* into a far more worldly, observant, skeptical, and complex character. He has witnessed during his sojourn in the Society Islands a Vanity Fair of human types and foibles. The sailor who departs on *Leviathan* could never display the naive anticipation or dread that Tommo expresses in the early chapters of *Typee.*

The success of *Typee* both earned Melville much-needed income and confirmed his abilities as an author. It provided entry into the literary circles of New York City and created the opportunity to sell further writings. What better way to extend this success than to compose a sequel based on his experiences following his sojourn on Nuku Hiva? The result, published thirteen months later, was *Omoo.* In this novel, however, Melville faces a very different set of problems as a storyteller. His experiences aboard the *Lucy Ann* and his beachcomber wanderings around the island of Eimeo (now generally called Moorea) were neither particularly dramatic nor atypical.

The records of the revolt aboard the *Lucy Ann* establish that Melville shipped from Nuku Hiva on August 9, 1842, although they provide no evidence of a dramatic rescue. Melville served less than two months on the *Lucy Ann,* joining the revolters on September 27 or September 29 (the documentary evidence is exceedingly confusing in the matter of dates because of inconsistent testimony), when they were incarcerated ashore on the island of Tahiti. Melville himself, unlike Typee in *Omoo,* spent no time manacled aboard the French warship *La Reine Blanche.* Medical documentation from Melville's approximately three weeks in the Tahitian jail confirms that Dr. Francis Johnstone treated him for a leg injury. There is evidence that Melville and John B. Troy went to the island of Eimeo shortly after October 19, 1842, and worked briefly for two Westerners growing potatoes. They then wandered around the island. Melville spent at most nineteen days on Eimeo, unlike Typee and Doctor Long Ghost, who undergo two months of wandering in *Omoo.* He joined the Nantucket whaleship *Charles and Henry* at the beginning of November.[14]

As noted in the first and fourth chapters, desertion from whaleships in the South Pacific was commonplace, and beachcombers had by 1842 become a fixture of island life as well as a familiar nuisance to the authorities. Disgruntled and dissatisfied whalemen were proverbial, and missionary reports of their shortcomings were familiar reading in European and American journals and newspapers.

The refusal to work by the crew of the *Lucy Ann* constituted only a minor variation, and Melville's two weeks of beachcombing in the company of John B. Troy on the island of Eimeo were thoroughly unremarkable. As he had in *Typee*, Melville enhanced the drama and extended the length of time he spent on the island in the fictionalized version of his adventures. He likewise resorted to a number of earlier written accounts, notably that of William Ellis, to flesh out his second book. Yet these written sources are unlikely to account for other expansions of his experience of a more personal and anecdotal nature. Such expansions more likely had their source in sailor talk. Any number of mariners aboard Melville's ships who had spent time in similar pursuits would have regaled their shipmates with accounts of their rakish exploits on the islands and the foibles of islanders and missionaries. Certainly Melville recounts far more of this material than he could personally have experienced in two weeks ashore, and the nature of this material—suggestive stories and anecdotes—implies a very different source from the pages of accounts such as those of Ellis.

Once again crafting his work to sell as "useful knowledge"[15] but lacking both a theme as compelling as cannibalism and a dramatic plot, Melville structures the novel around his observations of the deterioration of two societies: the shipboard community of the *Julia* and the traditional culture of the Society Islands through interaction with missionaries and traders. In order to position his narrator as both participant in and observer of the events he describes, Melville further develops the wry, sardonic, jocular, mocking tone he first used in important sections of *Typee*.

Because there are numerous characters whose language the narrator understands, conversation plays a much greater role in *Omoo* than in Melville's first novel. Even in this sophomore work, Melville's command of a variety of spoken styles recalls Mark Twain's famous headnote at the beginning of *Huckleberry Finn* (1884).

> In this book a number of dialects are used. . . . The shadings have not been done in a hap-hazard fashion, or by guess-work; but pains-takingly, and with the trustworthy guidance and support of personal familiarity with these several forms of speech.
>
> I make this explanation for the reason that without it many readers would suppose that all these characters were trying to talk alike and not succeeding.
>
> THE AUTHOR.[16]

Dialect and pidgin, typical of the American humorist writing of the period, sharpen and illuminate Melville's characterizations. Often insight or wisdom is delivered in the vernacular. Pidgin also occasionally serves by its terse and un-ambiguous nature to strip the sophisticated pretensions from Western views.

> Kitoti, a depraved chief, and the pliant tool of Bruat,[17] was induced by him to give a great feast in the Vale of Paree, to which all his countrymen were invited. The governor's objective was to gain over all he could to his inter-ests; he supplied an abundance of wine and brandy, and a scene of bestial intoxication was the natural consequence. Before it came to this, however, several speeches were made by the islanders. One of these, delivered by an aged warrior[,] . . . was characteristic. "This is very good feast," said the reel-ing old man, "and the wine is also very good; but you evil-minded Wee-Wees (French), and you false-hearted men of Tahiti, are all very bad." (125)

Similarly the narrator has the Hawaiian sailor Jack translate the sermon of an old English missionary, given in Tahitian, into English. The missionaries, Typee tells us, have "much to say about steamboats, lord mayors' coaches, and the ways fire are put out in London," but what Jack gives us is straightforward pidgin, disrobed of its pretension so that the hypocrisy is laid bare. This sermon is steeped in the centuries-old animus between the French and the British. "Good friends, no you speak, or look at [the "wicked idols" of the Catholic French]—but I know you won't—they belong to a set of robbers—the wicked Wee-Wees [from the French *oui*]. Soon these bad men be made to go very quick. Beretanee ships of thunder come, and away they go" (173). The French imperialists, then, will be replaced by British ones.

The fictionalized account of the mutiny aboard the *Lucy Ann* depicts a world in which the misuse and abuse of authority provoke reactions ranging from mur-derous rage to debilitating apathy. The crew of the *Julia* cling to an innate sense of fairness and justice that they maintain even when some of their number succumb to threats or allow themselves to be seduced by false promises. The insubstan-tial nature of the spoken word plays an important role in the trajectory of events surrounding the mutiny. The consul's refusal to produce the round robin when he holds proceedings aboard the *Julia,* his dismissal at a later hearing of Typee's verbal argument that he had signed on for the passage and therefore technically his service was at a legal end, and his willful acceptance of only testimony that confirmed his previously held view of the mutiny all undercut the crew's efforts to obtain justice. Some of the sailors, "very justly regarding [the round robin] as an uncommon literary production, had been anticipating all sorts of miracles therefrom" (79), but it is not to be. The consul "despised" the written record of the men's complaints and so depends on an oral account, which he endows with no value and dismisses without thought.

Melville divides *Omoo* into two parts, the first of which coheres around the comic opera drama of the mutiny aboard the *Julia*. The ineffectual and badly applied authority of the officers of that vessel is augmented by the similar slipshod authority of the English missionary consul Wilson. The corrupt Doctor Johnson's visits to the Calabooza in order to obtain additional fees from the government, and the lackadaisical attitude of the native warden Captain Bob, emphasize the tenuous and arbitrary state of authority on Tahiti.

Melville uses his narrator's mordant, irreverent tone and Doctor Long Ghost's antics as a scalpel to expose the weakness and hypocrisy of both shipboard and island authorities. Navy Bob, one of the biggest and strongest of the sailors aboard the *Julia,* misses watch because he has snuck below to smoke his pipe and fallen asleep. In lieu of the mate punishing such a serious offense, the other men in the watch slip into the fo'c's'le and tie a rope to Navy Bob's ankle, meaning to hoist him aloft and so discomfit and embarrass him. Doctor Long Ghost steals from his bunk and ties the rope to a sea chest.

> Scarcely was the thing done, when lo! with a thundering bound, the clumsy box was torn from its fastenings, and banging from side to side, flew toward the scuttle. Here it jammed; and thinking that Bob, who was as strong as a windlass, was grappling a beam and trying to cut the line, the jokers on deck strained away furiously. On a sudden, the chest went aloft, and striking against the mast, flew open, raining down on the heads of the party a merciless shower of things too numerous to mention.
>
> Of course the uproar roused all hands, and when we hurried on deck, there was the owner of the box, looking aghast at its scattered contents, and with one wandering hand taking the altitude of a bump on his head. (43)

The antics of both Navy Bob's watchmates and the doctor violate proper shipboard authority in multitudinous ways. Bob should not sleep on watch, because by doing so he puts his shipmates in danger. His shipmates should have reported his absence to the mate. Instead, by their actions, as well as those of the doctor, they disrupt the sleep of the off-watch, pummel the men on deck, bruise the owner of the chest, and more importantly cause a loss to that seaman, innocent of any involvement, of goods that are irreplaceable at sea. If he lost his boots, for example, he might be condemned to frostbitten feet and the loss of toes; if his mittens, the loss of fingers.

The narrator's detailed and deeply felt personal observations regarding the breakdown of the conventions of authority aboard the *Julia* dovetail with his studied dissection of the weak and blustering Wilson and the false, grasping Doctor Johnson. For instance, Consul Wilson harangues the first mate, Jermin, after he brings the *Julia* to anchor off Papeetee, Tahiti: "'So the infernal scoundrels held out—did they? Very good; I'll make them *sweat* for it,' and he eyed the scowling men with unwonted intrepidity." Typee adds cynically, "The truth was, he felt safer *now*, than when outside the reef" (102).

The narrator then ventures into the new territory of the whole state and history of relations between missionaries, natives, and sailors. Much of this discussion derives from Melville's written sources, such as Langsdorff, Stewart, and Porter, but the narrator characteristically imbues it with a smoldering sense of personal indignation at the damage inflicted on native culture by the self-righteousness and easy superiority of the missionaries. "And yet, strange as it may seem, the depravity among the Polynesians ... was in a measure unknown before their intercourse with the whites" (188). Melville shows a heightened command of his narrator's tone as he intersperses material from written sources with a tempered and carefully measured criticism that achieves its force not in extravagant language but in this dry tone. "The majority [of the Tahitians] being unable to obtain European substitutes, for many things before made by themselves, the inevitable consequence is seen in the present wretched and destitute mode of life among the common people" (189). The dryness of his tone proves powerful as Melville details his argument.

In the second half of the novel, even the scant narrative continuity provided by the collapse of the shipboard community is gone, so that we find Typee and Doctor Long Ghost perambulating through a picaresque series of scenes. This lack of structure both calls forth a heightened descriptive power and forces the author to reach for more universal themes in an attempt to impart meaning and continuity to his tale. Ultimately this attempt is unsatisfying to both reader and author, but the questions framed in Melville's mind concerning society, authority, and the role of individuals when society is in a state of flux will haunt and overwhelm his next book and set his course toward his masterpiece.

Melville employs the picaresque mode more fully as the book progresses rather than the outraged moralism of his early chapters; he becomes more adept at conveying the effects of hodgepodge missionization and the inconsistencies in society and behavior that result through narrative and dialogue rather than through direct exegesis. Chapter 65, "The Hegira, or Flight," contains a rare example of Doctor Long Ghost actually talking. His words come pouring out until suddenly the imagined utopia/alternative universe he has created is shattered by *mickonarees*. "I'll put up a banana-leaf as physician from London," he tells Typee, "'—deliver lectures on Polynesian antiquities—teach English in five lessons, of one hour each—establish power-looms for the manufacture of tappa—lay out a public park in the middle of the village, and found a festival in honor of Captain Cook!' 'But surely not without stopping to take breath,' observed I" (245). The women of Tamai interrupt the doctor's pleasant vision by crying, "*Heree! heree!* (make our escape)," adding "something about the *mickonarees*" (245). The islanders are not truly missionized, because they hide from the missionaries rather than embrace them, but nor are they able—or willing?—to return to their pre-Christian state. A hodgepodge indeed.

One of the salient characteristics of the relationship between Typee and Doctor Long Ghost is their skill at verbal play. They use this skill as a weapon against authority. For example, Doctor Long Ghost mocks the captain in the passage quoted above by crying out in a squeak, "Ah! Miss Guy, is that you? Now, my dear, go right home, or you'll get hurt" (4). Zeke and Shorty, the potato farmers on Eimeo, think Doctor Long Ghost "nothing short of a prodigy" (230). The narrator tells us:

> My long companion employed such imposing phrases, that, upon one occasion, they actually remained uncovered while he talked.
>
> In short, their favorable opinion of Long Ghost in particular, rose higher and higher every day; and they began to indulge in all manner of dreams concerning the advantages to be derived from employing so learned a laborer. (230–31)

Possessing little or nothing in the way of material goods, the companions use their intellectual and verbal skills as their stock-in-trade, their defense, their means of obtaining a living. Their verbal skills, which come from within themselves, are served up in counterpoint to the talk of missionaries and authorities, which derives its power from documents and texts.

Interestingly, in *Omoo*, we never really get to know Doctor Long Ghost. In part, this is an offshoot of his "coolness," the detached irony with which he surrounds himself, but he is also drawn less vividly than characters in *Redburn*, *White-Jacket*, and *Moby-Dick*. Rarely do we hear Doctor Long Ghost speak. Far more often, his speech is described by the narrator. For example, early in the book, Typee and Doctor Long Ghost play chess aboard the *Julia* with pieces carved from bits of wood. Typee distinguishes his pieces with little scarves of black silk. "Putting them in mourning this way, the doctor said, was quite appropriate, seeing that they had reason to feel sad three games out of four" (36–37). The doctor's words are quite funny, but notice that we don't actually hear them: they are simply reported to us. Later, on the island of Eimeo, Typee and Doctor Long Ghost retreat to sleep in the ruin of a war canoe to escape the mosquitoes. Typee asks his comrade how it fares with him, and Doctor Long Ghost replies, "Bad enough. . . . Pah! how these old mats smell!" Typee then tells us: "As he continued talking in this exciting strain for some time, I at last made no reply, having resumed certain mathematical reveries to induce repose" (216). Most often Doctor Long Ghost is awarded a few words, the remainder of his speech being paraphrased by Typee.

The voice of Melville's narrator in *Omoo* is both ironic and comic. There is little in American literature preceding *Omoo* that partakes of this sardonic, knowing, ironic tone, the effect of which is enhanced by the conversational manner of its delivery. In British literature, *Don Juan* (1819–24), by George Gordon, Lord Byron, is perhaps closest to the narrative voice in *Omoo*. The novels of Henry Fielding, William Makepeace Thackeray, and Anthony Trollope imbibe to some extent in this tone. Charles Dickens's narrative voice and his comic characters are occasionally rendered in a tone somewhat resembling that of Melville's early narrators, and the implicit social criticism in many of his works likewise parallels the social criticism of *Typee*, *Omoo*, *Redburn*, and *White-Jacket*. All these writers, however, have a more consciously literary feel and their humor is rooted in the comedy of manners and the tensions inherent in the British class system. *Omoo* foreshadows a subgenre of American culture that partakes of a sort of irony that makes its first appearance in Melville's time. The materials for this subgenre began to be developed in the 1820s and 1830s with the advent of the figure of the comic backwoodsman. Personified in real life by Davy Crockett, who took advantage of the image in his congressional career, this "ring-tailed roarer" used exaggerated braggadocio and the yarn to create a distinctively American literary figure. Joined by regional variations such as the sly, greedy, deceptive Yankee trader; the laconic, deadpan farmer of the Arkansas Traveler skit; the stage Irishman; and the blackface comedian, these tropes provided the material for American humorists contemporary to Melville.

Melville's narrators, however, eschew the bragging in favor of a more subtle irony that foreshadows a more sophisticated and modern sensibility. This sensibility does not emerge fully as part of the widespread vernacular until the 1960s and has since become a staple of popular culture. The lineage from *Omoo* goes forward to John Steinbeck, Jack Kerouac, Bob Dylan, and the cool, sneering wit that characterized the counterculture of the 1960s. The tone of *Omoo* is much like the tone of Steinbeck's *Cannery Row* (1945), Kerouac's *On the Road* (1957), or Dylan's laconic interactions with earnest, conventional interviewers, especially as seen in the Martin Scorsese documentary *No Direction Home: Bob Dylan* (2005). In all these, the central characters are part of a group outside the mainstream whose motto is "If you have to ask, you'll never know."

Doctor Long Ghost and the narrator of *Omoo* create a circle beyond the bounds of society, spontaneously and unspokenly recognizing in each other an affinity of perspective, a removed "cool"—just as the bums of Cannery Row do, just as Dean Moriarty and Sal Paradise do, just as Bob Dylan and the musicians in his electric backup band do. They create their own ironic outsider language, tweaking the "squares" who stuffily go about their business without realizing that the beachcombers, bums, and beatniks they disdain are laughing at the hypocrisy and posing that characterize social norms.

Mark Twain skewers the absurdity of conventional society in *Huckleberry Finn*, but not with the ironic tone of *Omoo*. Huck is a naïf. The narrator of *Omoo* has a detachment that Huck cannot have. By contrast, the narrator of Twain's *Innocents Abroad* (1869), while indulging in a similar sardonicism, is less ironic than contemptuous and, perhaps more importantly, is in fact an insider, a member of an elite group of tourists serene in their sense of superiority as American democrats in the decadent Old World. Melville's narrator is a beachcomber, an outsider by definition. Like the bums of Cannery Row, he is not part of nor does he have a stake in society, whereas Huck accepts the legitimacy of immoral social convention and struggles unsuccessfully against his own natural morality in the face of it. The mocking tone that *Omoo*'s narrator and Doctor Long Ghost employ as they interact with those around them is foreign to Huck (although not of course to Twain himself, nor to the narrator of *Innocents Abroad*). That mocking tone is a gateway that invites the reader to share the narrator's ironic perspective on society. The reader can depart the conventions of society and join the beachcombers, bums, and beatniks.

In *Omoo* Melville's narrator brings to bear his ability to see several viewpoints simultaneously. The narrator's critique of the missionaries' deleterious effect on Tahitian society tells us that he is not a sailor seeking simply to entertain himself but also sets him apart from the earnestness of the missionaries, who see themselves as reformers. The "protest novel" aspect of *Omoo* is more than the "sailor's grudge" against the missionaries mentioned by Evert Duyckinck, when he wrote to his brother George: "Melville is in town with new MSS agitating the conscience of John Wiley and tempting the pockets of the Harpers. I have read it. . . . He owes a sailor's grudge to the Missionaries & pays it off at Tahiti."[18] Melville deplores the destruction caused by the interaction between Europeans and islanders and wants us to reconsider the cost of "civilizing" other nations. Yet he writes his protest in the face of his own skepticism that society is capable of either comprehending or responding effectively to the problems he relates.

Omoo is not simply a protest work. It is not solely autobiography nor a diatribe against the missionaries nor a comic piece with a quixotic protagonist. All these elements are present, but Melville is interested in his art as well as his subject. Doctor Long Ghost is loosely based on John Troy, the steward of the *Lucy Ann*, but he is also a figure of Melville's art and imagination and can be relished as such. In Doctor Long Ghost, Melville has created a worldly, ironic, very comic character. Through this character he can consider the absurdities of social hierarchy and convention, the foibles of human nature, and the destruction of native culture. Doctor Long Ghost is an important step toward the creation of Ishmael in *Moby-Dick*. He is educated, well read, jaded, cocky, and occasionally reckless and self-centered. The narrator is also educated, but neither as jaded nor as cocksure. He possesses a moral sense from which springs his capacity for both sympathy and empathy, and he also displays a strong questioning intelligence. Elements of these two characters will mesh in Ishmael, a former schoolmaster turned wanderer who is ready to sign as a fo'c's'le hand.

The sailors, missionaries, and natives Melville encountered in Polynesia in 1842 had restricted visions of the world. The sailors were not reflective, looking only for physical comfort and relative ease. The missionaries were reflective, but only within channels formed by their religious viewpoint and the elaborate social conventions to which they adhered. The natives observed and reacted within the dictates of their own customs. Melville gives his narrator a wider view. This larger vision, encompassing his observations of both native and European customs, his questioning of both worldly and religious authority, and his eye for a lovely woman, a good time, and a practical joke even in the midst of his passionate concern with the devastation of native culture, is the quality that allows Melville to transform his material and become a great artist.

MARDI AND REDBURN

In the writing of *Mardi* and *Redburn*, Melville experiments, fails, and compromises in true journeyman fashion. His third book, *Mardi*, is his first attempt to grapple with the existential phantoms he so much more successfully makes immanent in *Moby-Dick*. The mechanism of allegory he employs limits and confines the free flow of his thought and the lively naturalness of his language as he attempts to build a systematic correspondence. Much of this book reminds a reader far more of J. R. R. Tolkien's *The Silmarillion* (published posthumously in 1977), with its stilted formal language and consciously archaic tone, than of *The Hobbit* (1937), with its warmly drawn characters and swiftly moving plot. Perhaps both *Mardi* and *The Silmarillion* owe something to Ossian.

The first paragraph of *Mardi* commences with the same storyteller's quality found at the beginning of *Typee*, and although the three-word opening sentence is far inferior to the famed first line of *Moby-Dick*, the exclamation point punctuating the end signals the author's intention to take us on a lively romp. Yet by the end of that paragraph, an arch literary presentation of a simile belies the oral quality that characterized Melville's first two works. "We are off! The courses and topsails are set: the coral-hung anchor swings from the bow: and together, the three royals are given to the breeze, that follows us out to sea like the baying of a hound. Out spreads the canvas—alow, aloft—boom-stretched, on both sides, with many a stun' sail; till like a hawk, with pinions poised, we shadow the sea with our sails, and reelingly cleave the brine" (3). The narrator then poses a rhetorical question to himself in archaic, formal language, but without the humorous effect of Tommo's address to the rooster in the opening of *Typee*: "But whence, and whither wend ye, mariners?" (3).

The first part of *Mardi* has been labeled an adventure story, yet as the author indulges his "longing to plume my pinions for a flight,"[19] his exuberant, extravagant language obscures the effect that his earlier leaner prose achieved in *Typee* and *Omoo*. The narrative voice becomes a jumble almost instantly. While Melville revels in his vocabulary, his vivid, descriptive images, and his penchant for allusion, his lack of both control and sense of proportion results in prose that is overwrought, dense, and occasionally opaque. Whereas in both earlier and later works a line such as "Now, round about those isles, which Dampier once trod, where the Spanish bucaniers once hived their gold moidores, the Cachalot, or sperm whale, at certain seasons abounds" (3) would have been placed in a setting where the elaborate vocabulary would achieve a pointed humorous effect, here it is simply a descriptive passage. The introduction of colloquial terms juxtaposed with this elaborate language more often than not strikes a false note instead of giving the reader a sense of having been included in the narrator's detached ironic viewpoint.

Largely because of this overwrought language with its obfuscated terms, obscure references, and over-artful constructions, the narrator is not nearly as likable or sympathetic as the narrators of Melville's other early works. In *Mardi* the narrator considers neither the crew nor the captain to be his social and intellectual equals: "The sailors were good fellows all. . . . Nevertheless, they were not precisely to my mind. There was no soul a magnet to mine; none with whom to mingle sympathies" (4). Even the captain is beneath him: "Could he talk sentiment or philosophy? Not a bit. His library was eight inches by four: Bowditch, and Hamilton Moore" (5).[20] This narrator is a far cry from the sociable fellow who sounds out Toby regarding desertion or makes common cause with Doctor Long Ghost and the crew of the *Julia*. It is even less possible to imagine him sharing a bed with and finding a soul mate in Queequeg. He is, in point of fact, a snob.

Mardi was the first book Melville constructed out of whole cloth. He wrote to the English publisher John Murray: "My object in now writing to you . . . is to inform you of a change in my determinations. To be blunt: the work I shall next publish will in downright earnest a 'Romance of Polynisian Adventure'— But why this? The truth is, Sir, that the reiterated imputation of being a romancer in disguise has at last pricked me into a resolution to show those who may take any interest in the matter, that a *real* romance of mine is no Typee or Omoo, & is made of different stuff altogether."[21] With *Mardi,* ambition outran experience. Melville wrote a novel of over 650 pages full of artistic and intellectual aspirations with little sense of how to proportion them to reach his artistic goals. The exuberance of his language reflects the intellectual ferment that resulted from his intense engagement with New York literary society and his voluminous reading. Here we see both the positive and the negative aspects of having "a whale-ship [for his] Yale College and [his] Harvard" (*Moby-Dick* 112). Melville's lack of formal higher education frees him from the stultifying effects of literary convention and fashion; at the same time, his writing lacks the discipline and structure lent by academic perspective and experience. Melville attempts to make up in energy what he lacks in coherence.

A striking contrast can be seen in a comparison of chapter 121 of *Mardi,* "They regale themselves with their Pipes," with chapter 30 of *Moby-Dick,* "The Pipe." Chapter 121 of *Mardi* begins with a riff on pipes and the various forms of tobacco: "Nothing so beguiling as the fumes of tobacco, whether inhaled through hookah, narghil, chibouque, Dutch porcelain, pure Principe, or Regalia. . . . Now, the leaf called tobacco is of divers [*sic*] species and sorts. Not to dwell upon vile Shag, Pigtail, Plug, Nail-rod, Negro-head, Cavendish, and misnamed Lady's-twist, there are the following varieties:—Gold-leaf, Oronoco, Cimaroza, Smyrna, Bird's-eye, James-river, Sweet-scented, Honey-dew, Kentucky, Cnaster, Scarfalati, and famed Shiraz, or Persian" (371). Much of the information on the types of tobacco can be found under "Tobacco" in volume 25 of *The Penny Cyclopædia of the Society for the Diffusion of Useful Knowledge* (1843). Melville, of course, borrowed again from *The Penny Cyclopædia:* for the passage on beards in *White-Jacket,* for "Cetology" in *Moby-Dick,* for many of the passages in *Israel Potter.* The listing of the types of tobacco is not much more than classification. In contrast, Melville uses the lists of whales in "Cetology," ostensibly only a statement of classification, to question the very nature of knowledge itself. All forms of knowledge—scientific, cultural, and religious—ultimately fail. Melville questions Linnaeus's declaration "I hereby separate the whales from the fish" when he replies: "But of my own knowledge, I know that down to the year 1850, sharks and shad, ale-wives and herring, against Linnaeus's express edict, were still found dividing the possession of the same seas with the Leviathan" (*Moby-Dick* 136). He submits Linnaeus's arguments that the whale is a mammal, rendered in Latin to avoid speaking of sex in English, to two Nantucket whalemen, "and they united in the opinion that the reasons set forth were altogether insufficient. Charley profanely hinted they were humbug" (136). Melville *knows* that the whale is a mammal, he knows that Simeon Macey and Charley Coffin are the ones who are humbug, and yet he asserts, "Be it known that, waiving all argument, I take the good old fashioned ground that the whale is a fish, and call upon holy Jonah to back me" (136), thus challenging the religious belief in the infallibility of the Bible.

Chapter 121 continues with more and more descriptions of the various pipes smoked by those present. The humor that would later enliven *Moby-Dick* is certainly here: Media's pipe is described as showing like "the turbaned Grand Turk among his Bashaws. It was an extraordinary pipe, to be sure; of right royal dimensions" (372). But in *Mardi* Melville exerts little control. His instinct is to take an idea and expand on it in multiple variations to the point of redundancy in a poorly controlled flow of verbiage.

Set against "They regale themselves with their Pipes" is "The Pipe." Melville centers the latter chapter on a concrete object, the pipe, that gives a clear visual image to the reader. But he lifts this image into the realm of philosophy that at the same time stays true to the human character he has developed. Ahab soliloquizes to his pipe: "Oh, my pipe! hard must it go with me if thy charm be gone! Here have I been unconsciously toiling, not pleasuring. . . . What business have I with this pipe? This thing that is meant for sereneness, to send up mild white vapors among mild white hairs, not among torn iron-grey locks like mine. I'll smoke no more—" (129). Then, in an action weighed down with profound woe, an action that imbues the reader with sadness and dark foreboding, Ahab "tossed the still lighted pipe into the sea. The fire hissed in the waves; the same instant the ship shot by the bubble the sinking pipe made. With slouched hat, Ahab lurchingly paced the planks" (130). The wording of "The Pipe" is concise and laden; in "They regale themselves with their Pipes," as even the title shows, many words are used over and over again to the point that the chapter loses focus and the images become diffuse.

In *Mardi,* Melville uses many of the same mechanisms that he used to achieve the oral tone in *Typee* and *Omoo,* but the overwrought content is ludicrous at times—no one *ever* talked as he has both his narrator and characters speak. The first bit of dialogue in the book occurs between the narrator and the captain a few pages into chapter 1. When the narrator states, "It's very hard to carry me off this way to purgatory. I shipped to go elsewhere," the captain replies, "Yes, and so did I. . . . But it can't be helped. Sperm whales are not to be had. We've been out now three years, and something or other must be got; for the ship is hungry for oil, and her hold a gulf to look into" (6). No sea captain in real life—or in *Typee* or *Omoo*—would say, "The ship is hungry for oil, and her hold a gulf to look into." The dialogue becomes stilted through awkward grammatical constructions that are decidedly not oral delivery. Melville, self-consciously trying to bring his artistic vision to fruition, has moved away from the wonderful oral quality of his first two books.

As the tale progresses, the jarring mismatch of spoken tone and stilted language continues. Media cries at the beginning of chapter 144, "Of the Sorcerers in the Isle of Minda": "Up, comrades! and while the mat is being spread, walk we to the bow, and inhale the breeze for an appetite. Hark ye, Vee-Vee! forget not that calabash with the sea-blue seal, and a round ring for a brand. Rare old stuff, that, Mohi; older than you: the circumnavigator, I call it" (461). Just as the structure of the plot breaks down as the book progresses, so too does the oral quality of the characters' voices. Taji is a step on the way to Ishmael, but finally only a blundering one.

The captain of the *Arcturion* in *Mardi,* like the captain of the *Pequod* in *Moby-Dick,* heads out to sea in search of something he's not supposed to pursue. In *Moby-Dick,* of course, Ahab is in pursuit of the great white whale and all it symbolizes. In *Mardi,* more prosaically, the captain is in pursuit of right whales instead of the sperm whales he had set out to hunt. The narrator tells us: "Now, this most unforeseen determination on the part of my captain to measure the arctic circle was nothing more nor less than a tacit contravention of the agreement between us. . . . Here, Heaven help me, he was going to carry me off to the Pole! And on such a vile errand too! For there was something degrading in it. Your true whaleman glories in keeping his harpoon unspotted by blood of aught but Cachalot. By my halidome, it touched the knighthood of a tar. Sperm and spermaceti! It was unendurable" (6). *Moby-Dick* is tightly constructed around Ahab's pursuit of the white whale. The plot of *Mardi,* like its uncontrolled language, is a hodgepodge. The narrator literally abandons the captain when he heads out in an open boat. His peregrinations through the allegorical islands of the world make up the bulk of the book, but because the book is a fiction, his wanderings are even more disjointed than Typee's perambulations in *Omoo.*

The contemporary reviews of *Mardi* praised the early parts of the book—those parts that were most like *Typee* and *Omoo*—and criticized the rest. The *Athenaeum* wrote harshly: "If this book be meant as a pleasantry, the mirth has been oddly left out—if as an allegory, the key of the casket is 'buried in ocean deep'—if as a romance, it fails from tediousness—if as a prose-poem, it is chargeable with puerility," and the *Spectator* proclaimed that Melville "has neither the mind nor the mental training requisite for fiction."[22]

In the face of such reviews, Melville consciously retrenched. In *Redburn,* he returns once more to fictionalized autobiography, which gives him a ready-to-hand plotline and places his narrator in a far more gregarious situation. This is by far Melville's most conventional sea story and rides the wave of works inspired by the success of Richard Henry Dana Jr.'s *Two Years before the Mast,* published only nine years earlier. *Redburn* is a bildungsroman that nonetheless reinvigorates

Melville's observant eye, reawakens his sympathy for the underdog, and allows him to sharpen and polish his skills at characterization, dialogue, and description. In this book, he recaptures his storyteller's voice and achieves far greater and more subtle control over his language.

At the age of nineteen, Melville sailed aboard the merchant vessel *St. Lawrence* from New York to Liverpool, England, and back to New York. He served as a "boy," or greenhand, the lowest rank of sailor. Melville's experiences in the merchant service provided the basis for his fourth book, which he subtitled *Being the Sailor-boy Confessions and Reminiscences of the Son-of-a-Gentleman, in the Merchant Service.* He was in fact the son of a gentleman thrust through poverty into work normally done by men of lower social rank. Early Melville biographers and scholars took *Redburn* as largely, if not completely, autobiographical. In fact, Raymond Weaver in his biography, *Herman Melville: Mariner and Mystic* (1921), quotes large sections of *Redburn* verbatim. In *Redburn,* one sailor jumps overboard en route to Liverpool; on the return voyage, a second man dies of spontaneous combustion and a third falls to his death from the topsail yard. However, the crew list of the *St. Lawrence* shows that no member of the ship's company died during either passage. There certainly are connections, such as a seaman named Jackson serving on both the actual *St. Lawrence* and the fictional *Highlander.*[23] But the five-foot, six-inch seaman of light complexion who deserted before returning to New York pales next to Melville's vicious, spiteful character of the same name.

For the first time in *Redburn,* Melville has the opportunity to make extensive use of realistic dialogue, both to establish character and to carry on elements of the plot. He is far more likely to present dialogue than to summarize a conversation, as was the case with Doctor Long Ghost in *Omoo,* and the dialogue itself rings far truer than the overheated and elaborate mouthings of the two-dimensional characters that inhabit much of *Mardi.* Even the more realistic characters in *Typee* and *Omoo* are not as convincingly drawn nor as deeply felt as the vile Jackson or the melancholic Harry Bolton of *Redburn.*

In a nod to the accepted patterns of maritime narrative, Melville opens *Redburn* with an account of his narrator's personal history and the circumstances that sent him to sea. The Melvillean touch of the narrator's brother speaking to him in the first sentence is a variation from this standard trope. Melville's instinct is always to open with talk. After this initial talk, however, the first few pages of *Redburn* partake of the literary quality of most sea narratives. As he warms to his tale, however, the narrative voice becomes more and more oral in quality: vernacular, idiomatic, conversational, and employing vocabulary and grammatical formulation appropriate to speech, even in descriptive passages. The occasional incursion of a more literary descriptive voice is diluted sufficiently that the overall impression created is that of a told tale. This spoken quality creeps back in through the second chapter and by the third is predominant. In chapter 1, Wellingborough Redburn begins his story in a formal way: "I was then but a boy. Some time previous my mother had removed from New York to a pleasant village on the Hudson River" (3). The first line of chapter 2 is even more Crusoesque: "It was with a heavy heart and full eyes, that my poor mother parted with me" (10). Wellingborough's brother accompanies him to the steamboat, but as soon as he is gone, little glimmerings of Redburn's oral voice appear. By chapter 3, this oral voice is ascendant. Redburn tells us: "As soon as I clapped my eye on the captain, I thought to myself he was just the captain to suit me. He was a fine looking man, about forty, splendidly dressed, with very black whiskers, and very white teeth" (15). This passage is vernacular, idiomatic, and slangy. Note the shortness of the words and the speech-like quality of "very black whiskers, and very white teeth." The captain does not have luxuriant whiskers and gleaming teeth. The narrator goes on to tell us, with an exaggeration common to the spoken word, "I liked him amazingly" (15). Then the captain and the narrator engage in dialogue. This exchange does not have the stilted, literary quality of the exchange between the captain and narrator at the beginning of *Mardi*. Here the narrator conveys in the tone of the dialogue a slight wink: looking back, he now knows what a naïf he was at the outset of the voyage. Dialogue is used here to much better effect than in Melville's earlier books.

In *Redburn* Melville is determined to present realistic dialogue. The sentences are of a length that an actual person would speak. The interchange between Wellingborough and the owner of the pawn shop in chapter 4 is a fine example. There is no excess verbosity, no unusual vocabulary, and no awkward grammatical constructions. Throughout *Redburn,* dialogue intercut with the more vernacular descriptive narrative voice once again succeeds in creating the oral feel that permeates *Omoo.* But in *Redburn* the narrator mildly mocks his own naïveté rather than mocking and satirizing others. The degree of self-mockery is perfectly calibrated to include the reader in the narrator's own knowledge of the extent of his naïveté at the outset of the tale without demeaning the narrator's remembered self.

Humor serves a variety of purposes throughout the book. Melville pokes fun at the attention shown by the ill-dressed captain toward the beautiful "anonymous nymph" who ships as a passenger aboard the *Highlander.* "No gentleman ever pretends to save his best coat when a lady is in the case; indeed, he generally thirsts for a chance to abase it, by converting it into a pontoon over a puddle, like Sir Walter Raleigh, that the ladies may not soil the soles of their dainty slippers" (110). The alliteration in this passage serves to highlight its humor. This nymph evokes such a strong response in the sailors that one of them creates his own vocabulary concerning her: "spandangalous" (111).

While talk does return with *Redburn,* Melville is writing a book that is modeled on the literary genre of which it is a part. Melville made clear to his English
publisher Richard Bentley that he was restricting his scope and writing a conventional book for a conventional audience: "I have now in preparation a thing
of a widely different cast from 'Mardi':—a plain, straightforward, amusing narrative of personal experience—the son of a gentleman on his first voyage to sea as a
sailor—no metaphysics, no conic-sections, nothing but cakes & ale."[24] Yet he had
written to his father-in-law Lemuel Shaw only a month and a half earlier:

> I see that Mardi has been cut into by the London Atheneum, and also burnt
> by the common hangman in the Boston Post. . . . These attacks are matters
> of course, and are essential to any building up of any permanent repu-
> tation—if such should ever prove to be mine.—"There's nothing in it!"
> cried the dunce, when he threw down the 47th problem of the 1st Book of
> Euclid—"There's nothing in it!—"—Thus with the posed critic. But Time,
> which is the solver of all riddles, will solve "Mardi."[25]

Melville's sense of his own prodigious abilities as not yet fully appreciated by
the wider world is evident when he compares himself to Euclid—who is after all
known as the father of geometry!

Nonetheless, Melville disciplines himself in *Redburn.* The buoyancy of speech
infiltrates the language of the book, but not the extravagance and exuberance
found in *Mardi.* Melville is determined to master his materials. His deconstruction of the narrator's reaction to the ship advertisements in chapter 1 falls into the
exclamatory mode that we noted in *Typee;* the narrator then reminisces about
that element of sailor talk that is the image of sailors held by non-sailors and
its effect on him in describing his motivations to go to sea. "I remembered," he
tells us, "The *yo heave ho!* of the sailors, as they just showed their woolen caps
about the high bulwarks. I remembered how I thought of their crossing the great
ocean; and that that very ship, and those very sailors, so near to me then, would
after a time actually be in Europe" (4–5). On the first waterborne stage of the
narrator's journey—his passage down the river, even before he steps aboard the
Highlander—Wellingborough finds himself shedding his civilized trappings and
becoming the raw savage material from which sailors are made. When he stares
down his fellow passengers aboard the steamboat, he goes back to the primal
undifferentiated stuff that can be a savage or a cannibal or a sailor, but he goes as
a naïf, someone uninitiated into the world of sailors. He has no way of channel-
ing the force of that primal power in his negotiations with a maritime world
that runs on that power. His brother's friend's negotiation with the captain on

Wellingborough's behalf illustrates the pitfalls of entering an alien world in which one does not know the talk. Wellingborough does not get his three-dollar advance because Mr. Jones wants to make it appear as if he comes from a wealthy family.

The main form of talk on the *Highlander* is sailor talk, and in fact *Redburn* represents by far Melville's most extensive use of sailor talk up to that time. As Wellingborough becomes steeped in this new language, so does the reader. Wellingborough receives an order to "slush down the main-top mast" (29).

> This was all Greek to me, and after receiving the order, I stood staring about me, wondering what it was that was to be done. But the mate had turned on his heel, and made no explanations. At length I followed after him, and asked what I must do.
>
> "Didn't I tell you to slush down the main-top mast?" he shouted.
>
> "You did," said I, "but I don't know what that means."
>
> "Green as grass! a regular cabbage-head!" he exclaimed to himself. "A fine time I'll have with such a greenhorn aboard. Look you, youngster. Look up to that long pole there—d'ye see it? that piece of tree there, you timber-head—well—take this bucket here, and go up the rigging—that rope-ladder there—do you understand?—and dab this slush all over the mast, and look out for your head if one drop falls on deck." (30)

The sailor talk heard on the *Highlander* is often technical, but not always. Sailors swore with great gusto. Wellingborough is taken aback by the sailors' foul language when he first joins the crew. The sailors "swore so," he tells us, that "it made my ears tingle, and used words that I never could hear without a dreadful loathing" (34).

The dark side of the sailors that comes out in their swearing is the same dark side that comes out in Redburn himself when he threatens a fellow steamboat passenger with his gun. He later reflects on his action with horror. "I could hardly believe that I had really acted that morning as I had, for I was naturally of an easy and forbearing disposition; though when such a disposition is temporarily roused, it is perhaps worse than a cannibal's" (15). Even though Melville has "shifted his ground from the South Seas to a different quarter of the globe—nearer home," as he wrote to Bentley,[26] the discourse of cannibalism in which he is steeped has crept in.

Tommo's contention regarding cannibals in *Typee* is echoed by the sailor Larry, a former whaleman, in *Redburn*. Larry argues in the vernacular that despite the calumny heaped upon cannibals and by extension all islanders, theirs was in many ways an ideal life. His speech is especially interesting for its commingling of sailor talk and cannibal talk:

> "Why," said Larry, talking through his nose, as usual, "in *Madagasky* [the island of Madagascar in the Indian Ocean] there, they don't wear any togs at all, nothing but a bowline round the midships; they don't have no dinners, but keeps a dinin' all day off fat pigs and dogs; they don't go to bed any where, but keeps a noddin' all the time; and they gets drunk, too, from some first rate arrack they make from cocoa-nuts; and smokes plenty of 'baccy, too, I tell ye. Fine country, that! Blast Ameriky, I say!" (100)

"Snivelization" (101), as Larry calls it, has been the downfall of all. The word "civilization," and by implication its meaning, has become especially unpleasant with its rendering as "snivelization." "Sn" produces a nasty sound, and many words that begin with those letters signify something disagreeable: snit, snip, snippy, snappy, snide, snicker, snaggletooth, snake, snaky, sneak, snarl, sneer, snigger, snivel, sniffle, snob—even the character of Snape in the Harry Potter series by J. K. Rowling. In this passage, Tommo has been resurrected in the nose-talking character of Larry.

Just as cannibal talk pierces *Redburn* despite its North Atlantic setting, so too does missionary talk. The mate gives Wellingborough a sailor name, just as the missionaries gave the island natives "Christian" names. In both cases, the giving of the new name is overtly designated a baptism. The chief mate asks the narrator his name, and he answers first "Redburn," then "Wellingborough." "Worse yet," the chief mate replies to the latter. "Who had the baptizing of ye? Why didn't they call you Jack, or Jill, or something short and handy. But I'll baptize you over again. D'ye hear, sir, henceforth your name is *Buttons*" (28). Missionary talk entwines itself with sailor talk.

Missionary talk is more overtly present in the Melvillean sermons found in chapters 29, 33, and 35–38. Chapter 29, "Redburn Deferentially Discourses concerning the Prospects of Sailors," becomes more sermonic as it progresses, building with the narrator's ringing questions: "And yet, what are sailors? What in your heart do you think of that fellow staggering along the dock? Do you not give him a wide berth, shun him, and account him but little above the brutes that perish? Will you throw open your parlors to him; invite him to dinner? or give him a season ticket to your pew in church?" (140). The chapter ends at its most sermonic when the narrator tells us, "Yet we feel and we know that God is the true Father of all, and that none of his children are without the pale of his care" (140).

In *Redburn*, although the vessel and its crew are far from the South Pacific, sailor talk, cannibal talk, and missionary talk commingle, creating language that is more powerful than any of its separate parts. Within the confines of the established form of the maritime bildungsroman, Melville successfully develops and elaborates a distinctive narrative voice that attests to his newfound discipline and control and shows glimmerings of the greater artistic achievements that lie just ahead.

White-Jacket

The opening of *White-Jacket* is so oral that it begins mid-paragraph as though the reader happens to have tuned into an interesting conversation at the next table. "It was not a very white jacket, but white enough, in all conscience, as the sequel will show" (3). And the conversation that follows justifies the catching of the reader's attention. All the techniques and mannerisms that Melville used to begin his earlier books are here in full force: the interjections, exclamation points, rapid-fire descriptive phrases, rhetorical questions, and direct address to the reader. Melville intermixes an ironic, mocking, jocular tone with surprising, vivid vernacular metaphors: "I dripped like a turkey a' roasting; and long after the rain storms were over, and the sun showed his face, I still stalked a Scotch mist; and when it was fair weather with others, alas! it was foul weather with me" (4). The narrator's white jacket in Melville's fifth book is prefigured in Wellingborough Redburn's shooting jacket in his fourth book. Both narrators are nicknamed in relation to their jackets: Redburn becomes "Buttons" after the oversized fancy buttons on his coat; White-Jacket is named for the incomplete, ambiguous "quilted grego" (4) that he makes for himself. Both tone and content of this overheard conversation hint at deeper meanings beneath the surface.

For the first time in *White-Jacket*, Melville has created not an allegory but a freighted symbol: a symbol that is rich, complex, and elusive rather than allusive. White-Jacket is the title of the book and the name of the narrator, yet Melville doesn't belabor the symbolism of the jacket itself. It is in the title, in the background, and often on the narrator's mind; therefore, the jacket takes on multiple meanings and becomes a touchstone in relation to which many aspects of the book can be seen. The white jacket is a major step for Melville as an artist, a step that will bring him to the white whale of *Moby-Dick*.

In *White-Jacket*, Melville also takes the narrative voice much further than in *Omoo* or *Redburn*. Talk returns in *Redburn*, but it is not until *White-Jacket* that the fledgling ambitions underlying *Mardi* are married to the growing mastery of craft that characterizes *White-Jacket*. In his fifth book, Melville returns to and extends the narrative voice he had developed in *Omoo* rather than to the straightforward voice of *Redburn* or the overwrought voice of *Mardi*. The narrative voice in *White-Jacket* tends toward direct address to the reader rather than to a boon companion such as Doctor Long Ghost provides in *Omoo*. Still conversational in tone, the voice of *White-Jacket* allows the reader to view and analyze events along with the narrator. For example, White-Jacket's internal contemplation of simultaneous murder and suicide at the climactic moment when it seems Captain Claret will have him flogged pulls the reader in. "I can not analyze my heart," he tells us, "though it then stood still within me. But the thing that swayed me to my purpose was not altogether the thought that Captain Claret was about to degrade me, and that I had taken an oath with my soul that he should not. No, I felt my man's manhood so bottomless within me, that no word, no blow, no scourge of Captain Claret could cut me deep enough for that. I but swung to an instinct in me" (280). The distortion and abuse Melville condemns throughout the book conspire to drive White-Jacket beyond the pale, and only the nobility of character of Colbrook, the corporal of marines, and of Jack Chase, who both speak on his behalf, deflects his gathering determination literally to throw himself and the captain out of the world. Because the reader partakes of the narrator's inner thoughts, White-Jacket's passion is visceral and enveloping.

In this book Melville achieves a far more systematic, detailed, and unified vision of humanity than in any of his earlier works, enlivened and thrown into relief through his more fully developed abilities of description, dialogue, and characterization. This is in part due to the nature of his subject: the ordered, hierarchical world of a naval vessel. The contrast between the theoretical system aboard the ship and the human foibles displayed by individuals provides much of the richness of this work. Still wary of overdependence on his penchant for incorporating philosophical and metaphysical perspectives, Melville nonetheless elevates his narrative of a relatively uneventful voyage to a studied societal critique. The vast complexity and large population of a man-of-war provides voluminous material with which he establishes the context of his critiques.

Melville himself served as an ordinary seaman aboard a man-of-war, the naval frigate *United States,* for fourteen months, sailing from Honolulu, Hawaii, back to Boston. With a crew of 470, the *United States* was the flagship of the American Pacific Squadron under the command of the controversial Thomas ap Catesby Jones. During Melville's time onboard, the frigate engaged in no sea battles and encountered few storms. However, Melville was forced 163 times to "witness punishment," the flogging of a seaman. He based *White-Jacket* on his time in the naval service, and the book rings with his absolute hatred of flogging. But *White-Jacket,* like all his earlier works, is a piece of fiction. Jack Chase was a real sailor and the man to whom Melville dedicated *Billy Budd,* but the Jack Chase of *White-Jacket* is nonetheless a fictional character, ennobled—and questioned—in Melville's portrayal of him.

Nabokov tells us in the epigraph to this chapter: "There are three points of view from which a writer can be considered: he may be considered as a storyteller, as a teacher, and as an enchanter. A major writer combines these three—storyteller, teacher, enchanter—but it is the enchanter in him that predominates and makes him a major writer." Melville could be seen as a storyteller in *Typee*, as a teacher in *Omoo*, and as a failed enchanter in *Mardi*. An enchanter creates a believable, intuitive world, which Melville does not succeed in doing in *Mardi*. He retreats in *Redburn*, combining the functions of storyteller and teacher. In *White-Jacket*, Melville achieves mastery of the roles of teacher and storyteller and touches successfully on the role of enchanter without fully embracing it. *White-Jacket* nonetheless represents a harmonious blend of the three roles that allows the author to approach his potential as an artist.

The subject of *White-Jacket* is the world of a man-of-war. Part of Melville's goal is to describe the intricate workings of a large naval vessel. In this sense, he is a teacher, vividly conveying the details of living conditions, work, and the functioning of the hierarchy in such a ship, as well as technical information. He also presents a tableau of finely sketched characters that interrelate in dramatic ways as the *Neversink* proceeds from Callao, Peru, to Norfolk, Virginia, providing the narrative that highlights his skill as a storyteller. But in *White-Jacket*, Melville uses these two elements as a platform from which to observe the human condition and to make profound observations about what is to be learned from the interactions between human personality, social order, the tension between individual and community, and the pressures on both individuals and communities dedicated to serving an outside purpose. He ruminates on the distortions of human character produced in this hothouse environment: men are both pushed to heroic acts that seem beyond their individual capacity and bestialized by unchecked power and subservience. The enchanter reaches beyond the didactic and the narrative by means of an inanimate magical familiar: the white jacket.

Throughout the book, the narrator's white jacket flits hauntingly as an inchoate metaphor. The first chapter of the book is devoted to a description of the jacket and ends with a tantalizing comparison of the garment to Walter Scott's ghostly White Lady of Avenal, but it is in the second chapter that the reader glimpses the amorphous changeling quality that Melville invests in it. The following passage that ends chapter 2 demonstrates the descriptive power Melville brings to bear in his accounts of working the ship. The final mention of the jacket places the reader simultaneously far aloft with the narrator and on deck gazing up at him, evoking the Ancient Mariner, crossbow in hand in the moment before he calls down disaster.

"All hands up anchor!"

When that order was given, how we sprang to the bars, and heaved round that capstan; every man a Goliath, every tendon a hawser!—round and round—round, round it spun like a sphere, keeping time with our feet to the time of the fifer, till the cable was straight up and down, and the ship with her nose in the water.

"Heave and pall! unship your bars, and make sail!"

It was done:—bar-men, nipper-men, tierers, veerers, idlers and all, scrambled up the ladder to the braces and halyards; while like monkeys in Palm-trees, the sail-loosers ran out on those broad boughs, our yards; and down fell the sails like white clouds from the ether—top-sails, top-gallants, and royals; and away we ran with the halyards, till every sheet was distended.

"Once more to the bars!"

"Heave, my hearties, heave hard!"

With a jerk and yerk, we broke ground; and up to our bows came several thousand pounds of old iron, in the shape of our ponderous anchor.

Where was White-Jacket then?

White-Jacket was where he belonged. It was White-Jacket that loosed that main-royal, so far up aloft there, it looks like a white albatross' wing. It was White-Jacket that was taken for an albatross himself, as he flew out on the giddy yard-arm! (7)

This passage is rooted in the concrete description of sailor talk. The men march around the capstan to the music of a fife. They cease their marching at the cry of "Heave and pall [pawl]!" when the anchor lies directly below the bow of the ship and the anchor cable is "straight up and down." After the men run aloft and loose the sails, they return to deck to push once more on the capstan bars until they raise the anchor to the bow of the ship. These are the accurate and standard actions of a crew getting a large vessel underway. The quoted commands are appropriate and timely. But the chapter concludes not with the ponderous anchor, but with the giddy yardarm. The chapter literally soars, to the metaphorical and the metaphysical. Such a Melvillean lift ends almost every one of the "cetological" chapters of *Moby-Dick*. In *White-Jacket*, however, it remains peripheral. Melville has not yet figured out how to incorporate fully such an element. In his fifth book, the Melvillean lift occurs most often at the conclusion of chapters devoted to the jacket. Chapter 19, "The Jacket Aloft," for instance, ends with the refusal of the first lieutenant to spare some black paint with which the narrator could darken and waterproof his jacket. Melville soars from this refusal into contemplation of sin and forgiveness and of the making of a ghost into a man. "I fear it will not be well with me in the end," White-Jacket tells us, "for if my own sins are to be forgiven only as I forgive that hard-hearted and unimpressible First Lieutenant, then pardon there is none for me." He continues: "What! when but one dab of paint would make a man of a ghost, and a Mackintosh of a herring-net—to refuse it!" (78). The mention of a ghost evokes Shakespeare's *Hamlet* just as the allusion to a herring net conjures up the biblical metaphor of Christ as fisherman. Like Hamlet's father, White-Jacket has been stripped of his humanity by being forced to become a ghost: literally in the case of Hamlet's father, metaphorically—and almost literally—in the case of White-Jacket. The metaphor of Christ as fisherman also raises questions of what it means to be human. Christ is God made man, and he was incarnated to raise the people of the earth from animalistic urgings to an understanding of the divinity within them that makes them fully human. The many layers of this short passage at the end of chapter 19 are a glimmering of what Melville will fully achieve in *Moby-Dick*.

As the discussion of chapter 2 illustrates, *White-Jacket* is rife with sailor talk. Missionary talk also infuses Melville's fifth book. In many ways, the whole of *White-Jacket* is a sermon. The central image around which Melville constructs his homily is "The World in a Man-of-War." Just as Father Taylor condemns sin in his sermons, Melville denounces the institutional cruelty practiced by the American navy. His task is not to approve of the navy, for, as he tells us, "hardly one syllable of admiration . . . has been permitted to escape me." No, for "the office imposed upon me is of another cast; and, though I foresee and feel that it may subject me to the pillory in the hard thoughts of some men, yet, supported by what God has given me, I tranquilly abide the event, whatever it may prove" (385). This is missionary talk indeed. Absolutely certain that he is right, Melville remains tranquil, even when confronting pillory. God supports him, and that is all the comfort he needs.

That *White-Jacket* includes both sailor and missionary talk is not surprising considering its subject and thesis. What is more surprising is that even here, in this book set aboard an American ship cruising mainly on the Atlantic Ocean, cannibal talk appears. When Melville reaches for a term that encompasses his condemnation of the entire nature of a naval vessel, he turns again to the Fiji Islands: "But as the whole matter of war is a thing that smites common sense and Christianity in the face; so every thing connected with it is utterly foolish, unchristian, barbarous, brutal, and savoring of the Feejee Islands, cannibalism, saltpetre, and the devil" (315). Just as Melville wanted to send pagans and cannibals to missionize Christians in *Typee,* he wants to "christianize Christendom" in *White-Jacket:*

And yet, fellow-Christians, what is the American frigate Macedonian, or the English frigate President, but as two bloody red hands painted on this poor savage's blanket?

Are there no Moravians in the Moon, that not a missionary has yet visited this poor pagan planet of ours, to civilize civilization and christianize Christendom? (267)

Here, as in his earlier books, missionary talk is inextricably tied together with cannibal talk.

A more extensive use of cannibal talk occurs in the Cadwallader Cuticle section of *White-Jacket,* at once the most comic and most appalling and therefore most difficult chapters to read. In his portrait of the surgeon, Melville fixes on his penchant for collecting examples of "Morbid Anatomy" (249), including the cast of the head of an old woman with a horn growing downward out of her forehead, on which Cuticle hangs his cap at night. Melville ascribes the surgeon's fascination with his collection to a scientific coldness: cold passion and unbridled enthusiasm. But Cuticle himself is an example of morbid anatomy. "The withered, shrunken, one-eyed, toothless, hairless Cuticle; with a trunk half dead" (259) is an almost blasphemous inversion of that paragon of mariners, Horatio Nelson, who was blinded in one eye, had his right arm amputated, and was badly wounded in his back, stomach, and head. With his wig, false teeth, and glass eye, Cuticle's assemblage of parts is similar to Frankenstein's monster, and his cold passion to that of Frankenstein himself. Cuticle also has a Melvillean antecedent in the character of Mow-Mow in *Typee.* Mow-Mow, too, is one eyed and a specimen of morbid anatomy: "His cheek had been pierced by the point of a spear, and the wound imparted a still more frightful expression to his hideously tattooed face, already deformed by the loss of an eye" (236). Cuticle is part of a continuum that goes from Mow-Mow to Ahab. The humanity of all three characters is permanently marred by their dismemberment.

The discourse of cannibalism occurs metaphorically in *White-Jacket* in Cuticle's dismemberment and literally in the cruel practical joke the wardroom officers play on the surgeon. When Cuticle is ashore, the officers make up a parcel of the "bluish-white, firm, jelly-like" sago pudding they had for dessert and leave a note for the surgeon purporting to come from an eminent physician in Rio de Janeiro and offering the pudding as "an uncommonly fine specimen of a cancer" (250). Cuticle is beside himself with glee when he sees the contents of the package, and horrified when one of the lieutenants wants to eat it. The lieutenant tells him: "I'm fond of the article. . . . It's a fine cold relish to bacon or ham. You know, I was in New Zealand last cruise, Cuticle, and got into sad dissipation there among the cannibals; come, let's have a bit, if it's only a mouthful" (250). The ubiquity of cannibal talk as a discourse in Western civilization renders the joke effective. The joke is also set up as a yarn—the lieutenant fell into bad habits in New Zealand—and partakes of the grisly exaggerated humor common to cannibal talk. Yet the underlying intent of the joke is to make an implied statement regarding the officers' view of Cuticle's moral stature, to hold up a mirror to Cuticle wherein he can see how others view him, but it does *not* succeed in humanizing Cuticle, nor in bringing him to repentance. Ultimately it is a cruel joke. Cruelty begets cruelty and attracts similar behavior. Cuticle remains untouched· by the "moans and shrieks" of his patients, by "features distorted with anguish inflicted by himself" (251). The inhumanity of Cuticle's insistence on amputation despite the fact that such an operation will almost inevitably lead to the death of the patient prefigures Ahab's inhumanity in his obsession with the white whale. Of course ultimately Ahab is far more sympathetic than Cuticle, for we see how much his obsession costs him. Cuticle's fixation has cost him his humanity, but that seems to him to be of as little importance as his false teeth, false hair, and false eye, all of which he discards before each operation.

In *White-Jacket,* Melville consciously pursues not an allegory but a straightforward depiction of "The World in a Man-of-War." He presents this naval world in a time of peace with no battles to distract us. We must concentrate on the world isolated aboard an American frigate carrying a crew of five hundred men. There is significance in the fact that in his second book Melville writes about the *Society* Islands; by his fifth book, he writes about the *world* in a man-of-war. *White-Jacket* marks the last stage in Melville's development as a journeyman writer, wherein he assembles the tools and materials with which he will create his "master-piece," in the fine old sense of a medieval craftsman applying to his guild for the rank of master.

Melville dashed off an astounding nine hundred pages in four months in the writing of *Redburn* and *White-Jacket.* As he wrote his father-in-law, "They are two *jobs,* which I have done for money—being forced to it, as other men are to sawing wood."[27] His impatient, questing mind and highly artistic temperament seem to have caused him to take his elevated craftsmanship as a writer almost entirely for granted. Even as he saw these two books through the press, his next monumental, timeless work was taking shape within him. In White-Jacket's most desperate moment, believing he is about to be flogged and resolving to kill both himself and Captain Claret, he says, "But the thing that *swayed me to my purpose* was not altogether the thought that Captain Claret was about to degrade me, and that I had taken an oath with my soul that he should not. No, I felt my man's manhood so bottomless within me" (*White-Jacket* 280; emphasis added). Proclaiming the value of an individual set against the workings of a mechanical social order, White-Jacket nonetheless only advocates justice within the system. This relatively conventional morality will be questioned beyond its limits in *Moby-Dick.* Note both the echoes of this moment in the two uses of "sway me to my" and the reach for something beyond the horizon in the final paragraphs of "Loomings," the first chapter of Melville's masterpiece. These paragraphs describe not only Ishmael's mental state, but also that of Melville himself as he ponders the risky, dangerous, blasphemous, unfathomable, luminous book he is writing.

> Chief among these motives was the overwhelming idea of the great whale himself. Such a portentous and mysterious monster roused all my curiosity.

Then the wild and distant seas where he rolled his island bulk; the undeliverable, nameless perils of the whale; these, with all the attending marvels of a thousand Patagonian sights and sounds, helped to *sway me to my* wish. With other men, perhaps, such things would not have been inducements; but as for me, I am tormented with an everlasting itch for things remote. I love to sail forbidden seas, and land on barbarous coasts. Not ignoring what is good, I am quick to perceive a horror, and could still be social with it—would they let me—since it is but well to be on friendly terms with all the inmates of the place one lodges in.

By reason of these things, then, the whaling voyage was welcome; the great flood-gates of the wonder-world swung open, and in the wild conceits that *swayed me to my* purpose, two and two there floated into my inmost soul, endless processions of the whale, and, midmost of them all, one grand hooded phantom, like a snow hill in the air. (*Moby-Dick* 7; emphasis added)

MOBY-DICK

In what is perhaps one of the most famous and widely quoted openings in the history of literature, the narrative voice of *Moby-Dick* begins with a three-word sentence that simultaneously evokes sailor talk, cannibal talk, and missionary talk—"Call me Ishmael" (3). The Ishmael of the Old Testament is the bastard son fathered by Abraham on Hagar, his slave, before Abraham's wife Sarah, thought to be barren, conceived his legitimate son Isaac through divine intervention. Hagar and her offspring are cast into the wilderness, estranged from God and the rest of humanity, along with all their descendants, the Ishmaelites. The name Ishmael suggests the wanderer as outsider, the "children of darkness," and the mystery of divine judgment. The sailor/beachcomber, the native/cannibal, and the missionary confronted by the incomprehensible all live in this complex metaphor.

Once again, as was true in *Typee*, we meet a narrator who rivets us with a deceptively understated conversational opening. But the bar at which we meet this stranger is not the bright, airy bar of *Typee*, full of gaily chattering sailors spending their recently earned money; no, this bar is grim, dark, and morose, with only a few broken-down solitary drinkers, each privately nursing his rum. If we hadn't already plunked our money down on the counter, we would have left before the weather-beaten man in the threadbare jacket addressed us. "Call me Ishmael," he says, embarking on an epic, fantastical tale that plumbs the depths of the human condition.

Beyond the fact that Melville went to sea on a whaleship, beyond the fact that he was a schoolteacher, beyond the fact that Ishmael himself is an interesting and compelling narrator, Ishmael *does* to some extent stand in for Melville. We all present versions of ourselves as we tell stories and create narratives that define us. We almost invariably shape our accounts of important events, significantly distorting experience or exaggerating because those distortions and exaggerations resonate with who we are, even if the event itself did not occur exactly as stated. Ishmael is not Melville, but a creature of Melville's intellect and imagination. Nonetheless, as is true of all Melville's narrators—even the narrator of *Mardi*— he is to a certain degree based on Melville himself, with his personality and perspective. Melville's portrayal of Taji as a snob undoubtedly represents, at least fractionally, his own experience. The acknowledgment that his narrators partially represent Melville leads to insights into his own experience and the way it shaped his writing. During his time at sea, Melville wasn't meeting people who were likely to make the same sort of analysis or have the same degree of self-awareness that someone of his intellectual stature would bring to the experience, which led to two important results: his motivation to present the story in a way commensurate with his intellectual abilities and, more importantly, his practiced development of relating the significance of his experience in a vernacular accessible to his original audience—his shipmates.

Perhaps the most fantastical element of *Moby-Dick* is the far-fetched but true basis for its ending, the sinking of the whaleship *Essex* by a giant sperm whale. By the time Melville went to sea, this 1820 incident had become a commonplace of sailor talk, especially among whalemen. Melville is believed to have encountered the son of Owen Chase, first mate of the *Essex*, during his sojourn in the South Seas. The story, now once again well known since the 2000 publication of Nathaniel Philbrick's *In the Heart of the Sea: The Tragedy of the Whaleship* Essex, is steeped in the ironic results of the cannibal talk prevalent among sailors at the time. So convinced was the *Essex*'s crew that they would be devoured if they touched on the relatively nearby islands that lay downwind that they opted to struggle against the wind and strong current for over two thousand miles toward the coast of South America, the survivors only managing by eating their shipmates. Melville did not really need to make the cannibals in *Moby-Dick* islanders, although the image was convenient and pointed. Underlying their presence is the nascent awareness that we could any of us be shipmates—or cannibals.

Moby-Dick contains far more cannibal talk than Queequeg's story of eating fifty slain enemies in one day (85). For example, Ishmael tells us, "New Bedford beats all Water street and Wapping. In these last-mentioned haunts you see only sailors; but in New Bedford, actual cannibals stand chatting at street corners; savages outright; many of whom yet carry on their bones unholy flesh" (31). The richness of this passage is reinforced with its alliteration on *w*, its contrast between the horrors of cannibalism and the fact that these men stand *chatting* at street corners, and the echoes of not only cannibal talk but also missionary talk in the wonderful phrase "many of whom yet carry on their bones unholy flesh." Melville has always been praised for his ear for language. The critic Richard Brodhead calls *Moby-Dick* "a book in love with language."[28]

Spoken language is as important a source for Melville as written works, especially in his early books and *Moby-Dick*. Even when his language derives from written sources, those sources are often intended to be read aloud or declaimed. Melville's three foremost written sources for his major books are, in ascending order, the works of John Milton, the works of William Shakespeare, and the Bible. *Paradise Lost* was meant to be heard, as Milton's prefatory note "The Verse" tells us. Shakespeare's plays were obviously meant to be performed, not merely read (*pace* Charles Lamb). For most people before Melville's generation, when the literacy rates finally climbed as a result of movements in education and the lower cost of producing readable materials such as newspapers, the Bible was a heard rather than a read experience. Even readers of the Bible heard it in church. The rolling, declamatory cadences of the King James Bible have informed English-language literature since it first appeared in 1611. Similarly, the richness of the Shakespearean resonances in Ahab's speeches lies with the sound as well as the meaning of the language. Melville was first an oral storyteller and then a writer, and he relied on that oral quality to produce some of his most compelling work.

Biblical cadence and language appear in the Quaker speech of the leading officers of the *Pequod*. All three of the captains—Ahab, Bildad, and Peleg—are Nantucket Quakers, as is Starbuck. In fact, the captain (Valentine Pease Jr.) and the first mate (Frederic Raymond) of Melville's own whaleship, the *Acushnet*, were born on Nantucket. Melville may have had the experience of hearing the archaic form of address prevalent among Quaker speech aboard the *Acushnet*. Whether or not he did, Quakerism gives him the license to use archaic language in the mouths of several of his characters without sounding awkward or unnatural. When Ishmael goes to sign aboard the *Pequod*, Peleg tells his fellow captain-owner: "'He says he's our man, Bildad.... He wants to ship.' 'Dost thee?' said Bildad, in a hollow tone, and turning round to me. 'I *dost*,' said I unconsciously, he was so intense a Quaker" (75; emphasis in original). Melville's use of archaic Quaker speech evokes all three of his major written sources, especially the King James Bible and Shakespeare.

Scholars have long observed and discussed the multiple voices that develop throughout *Moby-Dick*. The vaulting ambition Melville brings to his sixth book requires a flexible complex of narrative voices to achieve its ends. Yet all these voices remain rooted in fundamentally oral forms of composition. While Ishmael's clear first-person storyteller's voice dominates the early part of the book as well as the very end and occasionally surfaces in the intervening chapters, the second most common voice is still a first-person narrator who addresses the reader directly, referring to himself as "I." Many of the chapters wherein the narrative voice does not use the first-person pronoun maintain a conversational tone, using such devices as rhetorical questions, exclamations, and interjections, and often addressing the reader as "you" when the narrative voice does not self-refer as "I." This second narrative voice, even when it is employed purely for description, often derives its form and trajectory from sermons and accesses the heightened speech founded in biblical and prophetic utterance. The third form, or rather set of forms, that the narrative voice takes is based in drama. Soliloquies and dialogues are frequently employed. This, of course, allows Melville to reveal the inner thoughts of his characters or important personal interactions not as description, but as talk. Certainly on occasion the narrator recedes into third-person description with dialogue interspersed, but the reader's overall sensation of being addressed directly is by this time so firmly established that this change does not unseat the sensation.

Melville's utter command of the technical details, physical sensations, attitudes, and relationships comprised in sailor talk allows him to transcend simple description and put this discourse fully in service of his art. Maritime writers of a lower order may convey a clear picture of the excitement, tension, sociability, boredom, or danger of shipboard life and the personal significance of these conditions to the characters they depict and even hint at the larger significance implied. In contrast, Melville in *Moby-Dick* and to some extent in *White-Jacket* regularly makes the leap from mundane detail through vivid imagery to the great existential questions gracefully, naturally, and breathtakingly. This sets him apart not only from the writers of maritime adventure stories such as Jack London, C. S. Forester, and Patrick O'Brian but also from writers of greater literary ambition such as James Fenimore Cooper and Joseph Conrad. Melville's command of both the variety of narrative voices he employs and sailor talk allows him access to this discourse whenever he needs it.

Melville's first foray into sailor talk in *Moby-Dick* occurs in "Loomings" when Ishmael, speaking in the first person, ruminates on the prospect of going to sea as a sailor, "right before the mast, plumb down into the forecastle, aloft there to the royal mast-head" (5–6). This passage flows naturally into a contemplation of human dignity, the role of an individual in a community, the function of hierarchy, and the inscrutability of fate. "Who aint a slave? Tell me that. . . . However they may thump and punch me about[,] . . . everybody else is one way or other served in much the same way—either in a physical or metaphysical point of view, that is; and so the universal thump is passed round, and all hands should rub each other's shoulder-blades, and be content" (6). This is but the first of numerous instances wherein Melville puts sailor talk into the service of his art by grounding his loftier ruminations in the assured, detailed, concise, concrete language of the sailor.

The following passage, given in the third-person descriptive voice, is reminiscent at its beginning of the famous scene in Richard Henry Dana Jr.'s *Two Years before the Mast,* where Dana, sitting well out on the bowsprit at the front of the vessel, looks back at the pyramid of perfectly filled sails and revels in their beauty in the moonlight and the sense of the vessel's motion as they drive the vessel forward ("How quietly they do their work!").[29] But Dana attaches no further significance to the sight or sensation. In the beginning of the following passage, Ahab orders a similar press of sails set:

> Walking the deck with quick, side-lunging strides, Ahab commanded the t'gallant sails and royals to be set, and every stunsail spread. The best man in the ship must take the helm. Then, with every mast-head manned, the piled-up craft rolled down before the wind. The strange, upheaving, lifting tendency of the taffrail breeze filling the hollows of so many sails, made the buoyant, hovering deck to feel like air beneath the feet; while still she rushed along, as if two antagonistic influences were struggling in her—one to mount direct to heaven, the other to drive yawingly to some horizontal goal. And had you watched Ahab's face that night, you would have thought that in him also two different things were warring. While his one live leg made lively echoes along the deck, every stroke of his dead limb sounded like a coffin-tap. On life and death this old man walked. (233)

This passage seamlessly and sublimely combines occupational knowledge, Melville's own experience of the physical sensations he describes, and the breathtaking leap to the metaphysical implications in one of the most extraordinarily drawn characters in all of literature. It is the accuracy of the sailor talk—occupational knowledge and remembered sensation—that grounds the flight into the metaphysical realm and thus renders it convincing and accessible to the reader.

Chapter 120, "The Deck towards the End of the First Night Watch," serves to exemplify Melville's use of dramatic dialogue in a passage that packs a tremendous range of meaning into a few short sentences:

> (*Ahab standing by the helm. Starbuck approaching him.*)
> "We must send down the main-top-sail yard, sir. The band is working loose, and the lee lift is half-stranded. Shall I strike it, sir?"
> "Strike nothing; lash it. If I had sky-sail poles, I'd sway them up now."
> "Sir?—in God's name!—sir?"
> "Well."

"The anchors are working, sir. Shall I get them inboard?"

"Strike nothing, and stir nothing, but lash everything. The wind rises, but it has not got up to my table-lands yet. Quick, and see to it.—By masts and keels! he takes me for the hunchbacked skipper of some coasting smack. Send down my main-top-sail yard! Ho, gluepots! Loftiest trucks were made for wildest winds, and this brain-truck of mine now sails amid the cloud-scud. Shall I strike that? Oh, none but cowards send down their brain-trucks in tempest time. What a hooroosh aloft there! I would e'en take it for sublime, did I not know that the colic is a noisy malady. Oh, take medicine, take medicine!" (509)

Note the full employment of dramatic form in this chapter, given here in its entirety. It commences with dramatic direction, consists of nothing but dialogue, and uses internal rhyme in its last sentences:

Oh, none but cowards send down their brain-trucks in tempest time.
What a hooroosh aloft there! I would e'en take it for sublime[.]

The final repetition for emphasis at the end of a speech, as seen in the repeating of "take medicine," is likewise Shakespearean. See, for example, Lear's final lament for the death of Cordelia: "Do you see this? Look on her,—look,—her lips,—/ Look there!—look there!"[30]

This chapter once again begins with mundane and accurate detail of nautical terminology. The main topsail is the second sail up the middle mast of the three masts on the ship. It is one of the largest and most frequently set sails on the vessel and provides a disproportionate share of driving power and stability. The main topsail yard is attached to the mast by means of a loose collar, or band, around the mast. When the sail is set, the yard is raised up the mast by means of a line called the main topsail halyard, which can be slacked to lower the yard back down when the sail is to be furled, or put away. The lee lift is one of two lines attached to either end of the yard angling up to join the mast at a higher point, there passing through pulleys and leading to the deck, allowing the horizontal attitude of the yard to be adjusted by way of tightening one of the lifts while slacking the other. Which lift is to the lee depends on the direction from which the wind is coming in relation to the ship—the direction the wind blows *from* is windward or weather, while the direction the wind blows *toward* is leeward. Starbuck informs Ahab that the rope from which the lee lift is made has frayed in one of its strands and is no longer dependable, partly because of the increased stress induced by the band itself working loose. He asks permission to bring the yard to the deck in order to make repairs—a considerable undertaking not normally part of setting and furling sails. But before this operation can be effected, the sail must first be furled, or "struck." Ahab responds with a reckless refusal of permission to make this highly necessary repair in the circumstances, ordering instead that the yard be lashed in place. And more, he tells Starbuck that if he had the equipment to set sails above the already-set highest sails on the mast, the royal sails, he would "sway up" skysail poles, or spars to hold the yet higher skysails.

The discerning reader will of course note that the long preceding paragraph explains only the first two sentences of chapter 120. The concise efficiency of sailor talk is clearly demonstrated here, but even without providing the reader with this detailed understanding, Melville forcefully conveys the urgency of the situation to the uninitiated in this interchange. Starbuck's reaction to the refusal— "Sir?—in God's name!—sir!"—confirms this sense and provides the leaping-off point from which Ahab's soliloquy takes flight.

The soliloquy itself is laden with yet more sailor talk. Deepwater sailors crossing oceans looked down upon sailors who carried on trade along the shore, hence "the hunchbacked skipper of some coasting smack." The truck is the very top of the mast; the word "top" in sailor talk refers to the platform at the joint where the lowest two sections of mast overlap. Ahab coins the term "brain-truck" to indicate the heights to which his mental state has extended and glories in the wild winds now buffeting both his thought and the ship. Yet he then collapses the vaulting language and imagery in which he has indulged with a sly, rude, self-mocking scatological joke that turns the wild winds he gloried in a moment before into intestinal gas produced by colic: "What a hooroosh aloft there! I would e'en take it for sublime, did I not know that the colic is a noisy malady. Oh, take medicine, take medicine!" Here we see Ahab lurch from manic rapture to earthy self-deprecation. The extraordinary sweep of complex moods and meanings in this miniscule chapter is conveyed entirely through sailor talk.

Missionary talk enters *Moby-Dick* most obviously in "The Sermon" (chapter 9). One of the most striking aspects of "The Sermon" is the profusion of sailor talk. The crude stereotype of the sailor addicted to shipboard language is in full sway throughout this chapter. Father Mapple's exhortation to the scattered crowd to draw close is rendered: "Starboard gangway, there! side away to larboard— larboard gangway to starboard! Midships! midships!" (41). These stereotypical devices continue unabated: "he seemed kneeling and praying at the bottom of the sea"; "in prolonged solemn tones, like the continual tolling of a bell in a ship that is foundering at sea in a fog"; Father Mapple's continually addressing the congregation as "shipmates"; and his endless employment of technical nautical metaphors such as "Shipmates, this book, containing only four chapters—four yarns—is one of the smallest strands in the mighty cable of the Scriptures. Yet what depths of the soul does Jonah's deep sea-line sound!" (41–42). The bulk of the sermon inverts Melville's practice: rather than have a sailor-narrator discuss shipboard subjects in sermonic form, Father Mapple delivers his sermon in the form of a yarn, peppered with nautical phrases and vernacular slangy language. Father Mapple depicts Jonah in the standard terms used by newspaper writers and others to describe the moral depravity of mariners. Sailors were feared because of the danger of moral contagion and pestilence they represented, and Jonah, too, is portrayed in these terms.

As the spiritual crisis in the yarn approaches, the language steadily flows back into the more formalized language of oration, until it thunders out in biblical rhythms, finally blending sailor talk and missionary talk seamlessly in heightened speech: "Woe to him who seeks to pour oil upon the waters when God has brewed them into a gale"; "Yea, woe to him who, as the great Pilot Paul has it, while preaching to others is himself a castaway!"; "But oh! shipmates! on the starboard hand of every woe, there is a sure delight; and higher the top of that delight, than the bottom of the woe is deep. Is not the main-truck higher than the kelson is low?" and "Delight is to him, whom all the waves of the billows of the seas of the boisterous mob can never shake from this sure Keel of the Ages" (48). This sermon is laid out in standard form despite its use of yarning language early on. Its arc and lesson remain conventional until the hidden double meaning in the final question, perhaps unconscious on Father Mapple's part: "for what is man that he should live out the lifetime of his God?" (48). Certainly for Father Mapple this is a rhetorical question, but it may not be for Ishmael, and it foreshadows the central question posed by Ahab.

The two chapters that precede "The Sermon" engage missionary talk in a more complex and troubled way. The doubts and perplexities Ishmael entertains make it seem unlikely that the straightforward simplicity of Father Mapple's exegesis can possibly satisfy the narrator's profoundly questioning mind. In the first of these, "The Chapel" (chapter 7), Ishmael contemplates the marble tablets "masoned into the wall" of the chapel (34). These memorialize whalemen lost at sea, and the chapel serves as a touchstone for grieving relatives deprived of the comfort provided by the nearness of the physical remains of lost loved ones. "Oh! ye whose dead lie buried beneath the green grass; who standing among flowers can say—here, *here* lies my beloved; ye know not the desolation that broods in bosoms like these. What bitter blanks in those black-bordered marbles which cover no ashes! What despair in those immovable inscriptions! What deadly voids and unbidden infidelities in the lines that seem to gnaw upon all Faith, and refuse resurrections to the beings who have placelessly perished without a grave" (36). Ishmael's musings on the implications of these memorials gradually take shape as an anti-sermon. In death the fact of the absence of the sailor's body is the ultimate form of othering. Sailors who died suddenly at sea were isolated from last rites and had no chance for final conversion or to purify their souls. Ishmael begins by questioning the justice of refusing resurrection to such men. As was true in his sermonic critique of missionaries in *Typee*, Melville employs the form and language of sermons to advance an argument that veers back and forth between the accepted Christian understanding of life, death, and resurrection and subversion of conventional Christian doctrine until its final striking sentence, in which he denies God's ultimate authority over his soul:

> Yes, there is death in this business of whaling—a speechlessly quick chaotic bundling of a man into Eternity. But what then? Methinks we have hugely mistaken this matter of Life and Death. Methinks that what they call my shadow here on earth is my true substance. Methinks that in looking at things spiritual, we are too much like oysters observing the sun through the water, and thinking that thick water the thinnest of air. Methinks my body is but the lees of my better being. In fact take my body who will, take it I say, it is not me. And therefore three cheers for Nantucket; and come a stove boat and stove body when they will, for stave my soul, Jove himself cannot. (37)

These are the words of one who contemplates deeply and is not prone to accept dogmatic authority. The repetition of the word "Methinks" drives home this independent philosophizing. He will look behind and beyond appearances and make his own judgments.

In the beginning of chapter 8, "The Pulpit," Ishmael continues this reverie when Father Mapple makes his dramatic larger-than-life entrance, instantly commanding the attention of everyone in the room in the manner of a great actor striding onto the stage. He exudes vitality in his old age and is costumed for his role, eschewing the parson's umbrella in favor of a tarpaulin hat and pilot-cloth jacket, the theatrical effect heightened by the melting sleet dripping from them. These articles of clothing removed, he assumes the form of a preacher "arrayed in a decent suit" and quietly approaches the pulpit (38). Suddenly, the salty mariner reappears as he ascends by means of "a perpendicular side ladder, like those used in mounting a ship from a boat at sea" with a "truly sailor-like but still reverential dexterity, hand over hand . . . as if ascending the main-top of his vessel" (39). Father Mapple then pulls up the side ladder, isolating himself in the pulpit.

Ishmael responds to Father Mapple's action: "I pondered some time without fully comprehending the reason for this. Father Mapple enjoyed such a wide reputation for sincerity and sanctity, that I could not suspect him of courting notoriety by any mere tricks of the stage" (39). He posits that there must be an unspoken spiritual symbolism for this isolation, indicating Father Mapple's absolute reliance on spiritual rather than earthly nourishment. Yet Ishmael seems himself unconvinced by this rather thin hypothesis. He immediately proceeds to describe the chapel in terms that make it clear that the chapel functions as an elaborate stage set, perfectly designed to enhance the effect of Father Mapple's carefully constructed role—a persona that is further developed through the exaggerated use of sailor talk discussed earlier. Father Mapple may indeed be sincere and sanctified, but Ishmael's eagerness to absolve him of indulging in theatricality seems disingenuous, especially in light of the subversive nature of his earlier musings.

Father Mapple's sermon is in fact only one of a number of sermons delivered throughout *Moby-Dick*. Fleece's sermon to the sharks in chapter 64 has long been recognized, as has Ishmael's brief sermon in chapter 18. The other sermons, however, have not been identified as such. "The Line" (chapter 60) is perhaps the most fully indebted to the sermon form. In the ten paragraphs of this chapter, a piece of essential gear rather than a biblical verse is held up for examination and exegesis. Here it is a "line"—not a line of scripture, but "the magical, sometimes horrible whale-line" (278). The examination begins with the matter-of-fact physical description of the whale line. Its material, color, thickness, strength, number of yarns, length, and manner of storage as well as the precise pattern in which it is placed in the boat are described in careful, thorough detail, leavened with occasional flashes of Melvillean wit in the form of personification and whimsical metaphor. This exact technical description parallels the way in which a preacher paraphrases and clarifies the meaning of the biblical text on which his sermon is based.

Toward the end of the fourth paragraph and again in the sixth paragraph, hints of the danger posed by the line appear. These are, however, vivid and visceral: "As the least tangle or kink in the coiling would, in running out, infallibly take somebody's arm, leg, or entire body off, the utmost precaution is used in stowing the line in its tub" (279); "were the lower end of the line in any way attached to the boat, and were the whale then to run the line out to the end almost in a single, smoking minute as he sometimes does, he would not stop there, for the doomed boat would infallibly be dragged down after him into the profundity of the sea; and in that case no town-crier would ever find her again" (279). Note the repetition of the word "infallibly." The consequences described are not to be avoided unless the precautions also described are meticulously followed. The sense of inevitable consequence begins to build with these two lines and lays the groundwork for the sermon's lesson. The seventh paragraph details and emphasizes the extent to which every man in the boat is involved in the coils of the line.

With this groundwork laid, the eighth, ninth, and tenth paragraphs soar. The clear, concise, almost terse tone in the earlier part of the chapter gives way to the ringing delivery of a preacher warming to his subject. Metaphors, emotional adjectives, and rhetorical questions along with the telltale exclamation points and interjections indicate the quality of oral delivery. The metaphysical metaphor is revealed through dramatic physical examples: "for, when the line is darting out, to be seated then in the boat, is like being seated in the midst of the manifold whizzings of a steam-engine in full play, when every flying beam, and shaft, and wheel, is grazing you" (280). The ultimate paragraph unleashes the full power of Melville's mastery of this form. The remorseless pressing of the increasingly complex and interconnected metaphor, the effortless allusions, the reinforcing alliteration, and the devastating inevitability of the conclusion are accomplished with powerful, perfect language and logic. One is reminded of the accounts of Jonathan Edwards's auditors writhing in the aisles as he delivered his brilliantly constructed sermons in a quietly reasonable voice.

The middle chapters of *Moby-Dick* that deconstruct the whale and whaling all follow this sermon-like pattern to some extent. Taking some part of the whale or a particular aspect of whaling as the "text," Melville subjects it to an exegesis, lards it with humor, and culminates his discussion of it with a lift into metaphysics. "The Mat-Maker" (chapter 47), "Brit" (chapter 58), "The Tail" (chapter 86), and "A Squeeze of the Hand" (chapter 94) are good examples of this. Even "Cetology" (chapter 32), the most maligned chapter in the book and the one most directly based on written sources (the "Whales" entry in volume 27 of *The Penny Cyclopædia*), strays into this pattern, ending with Melville's transcendent invocation: "For small erections may be finished by their first architects; grand ones, true ones, ever leave the copestone to posterity. God keep me from ever completing anything. This whole book is but a draught—nay, but the draught of a draught. Oh, Time, Strength, Cash, and Patience!" (145). Taken as an example of one of Melville's anti-sermons, the pompous, pedantic, prolix language in this chapter lampoons an all-too-familiar trope: the long-winded boring sermon. One is reminded of the passage in *Typee* in which Mehevi subjects Tommo to "a long, and I have no doubt a very learned and eloquent exposition of the history and nature of the 'taboo'" in Marquesan, a language Tommo does not understand except for the most basic of phrases, "employing a variety of most extraordinary words, which, from their amazing length and sonorousness, I have every reason to believe were of a theological nature" (133).

At the end of the "Cetology" chapter, the narrator himself, positing the endlessness of the subject, prays for "Patience!" But the end of chapter 32 also speaks to the universality of the human need for more time, more strength, more cash, and more patience and to the fact that truth is sprawling and eternally unfinished, unable to be contained in a small erection.

Contrast the elegant flow of the language in these chapters (especially "The Line," discussed in detail earlier), the intricately layered meanings, and the irresistible force of the arguments with Father Mapple's sermon in chapter 10. Father Mapple's reading of Jonah is far more conventional and straightforward. This simplicity is belied by the highly colored dramatic expansion of the tale that Father Mapple presents. The force of the sermon lies therein: the theatrical retelling, the imagined conversations, the carefully chosen adjectives and verbs (Jonah has a "*slouched* hat and *guilty* eye, *skulking* from his God; *prowling* among the shipping like a *vile* burglar" [43; emphasis added]). Father Mapple renders the characters in familiar, believable form, realizing them further by putting vernacular dialogue in their mouths. "One whispers to the other—'Jack, he's robbed a widow;' or, 'Joe, do you mark him; he's a bigamist;' or, 'Harry lad, I guess he's the adulterer that broke jail in old Gomorrah, or belike, one of the missing murderers from Sodom'" (43). He gives us the captain's inner judgment of Jonah, characterizes the captain's own moral shortcomings, and tells us repeatedly that he is imparting "a weighty lesson" (46). Yet what is the matter of this lesson? "Sin not; but if you do, take heed to repent of it like Jonah" (47). He goes on to tell us that he is about to give us a "more awful lesson which Jonah teaches to *me*, as a pilot of the living God" (47; emphasis in original). And what is this more awful lesson? That God is everywhere, and therefore "Woe to him who would not be true, even though to be false were salvation! Yea, woe to him who, as the great Pilot Paul has it, while preaching to others is himself a castaway!" (48). And delight is to him who remains faithful. This is barely exegesis. It is more on the level of the moral to one of Aesop's fables. And it certainly fails even to begin the approach to the profound questions Ishmael has just raised in "The Chapel."

This reading shows in stark relief the subversive and ironic subtext to the last paragraph in chapter 8: "What could be more full of meaning?—for the pulpit is ever this earth's foremost part; all the rest comes in its rear; the pulpit leads the world. From thence it is the storm of God's quick wrath is first descried, and the bow must bear the earliest brunt. From thence it is the God of breezes fair or foul is first invoked for favorable winds. Yes, the world's a ship on its passage out, and not a voyage complete; and the pulpit is its prow" (40). Having absorbed extensive negative reviews for his critiques of missionaries in *Typee* and *Omoo*, Melville slyly incorporates this apparently straightforward presentation of conventional Christianity. The full force of Melville's subversive irony will not become apparent until the very end of the book when all the ship's crew save Ishmael disappear into the metaphoric belly of the whale. And only Ishmael is spewed back out. The entire iconoclastic text of *Moby-Dick* is Ishmael's answer to Jonah. He stands on the streets of Nineveh and utters his existential anguish as prophecy without the authority of the divine voice speaking through him.

One must always approach Melville's use of religious language and imagery bearing in mind his immense ambivalence and the ability his towering intellect gives him to perform feats of legerdemain with his meanings. On the surface,

Ishmael has acted as the missionaries hope a devout sailor Christian would act: attended chapel and heard the sermon of a great sailor preacher on the eve of his departure, thereby taking with him the comforts of faith. But Ishmael enters the chapel only to be profoundly troubled by the questions it raises and leaves the sermon to seek out his bosom friend, the almost ghostly apparition whom he is surprised to see on entering the chapel: "affected by the solemnity of the scene, there was a wondering gaze of incredulous curiosity in his countenance. This savage was the only person present who seemed to notice my entrance; because he was the only one who could not read, and, therefore, was not reading those frigid inscriptions on the wall" (36). Ishmael returns to the Spouter Inn to join his bosom friend, whose empty coffin will be the means of his survival, if not salvation: the cannibal.

The friendship between Ishmael and Queequeg is the single most thoroughly elaborated relationship in *Moby-Dick*. Far more space is devoted to this than to the interactions between Ahab and Starbuck or Ahab and Pip, the next most thoroughly explored relationships. All the other characters have only intermittent and fleeting contacts. This relationship fixes the nature of the cannibal as an essential and central metaphor in the book. One-fifth of the book, almost entirely at the beginning, is devoted to developing the character of Queequeg and the narrator's reaction to him. The centrality of the cannibal is obscured by Queequeg's long periods of absence once the voyage commences.

I will posit two important reasons for this absence, both rooted in sailor talk. The first arises from Melville's personal experience aboard whaleships, an experience deeply internalized. The physical spaces of a whaleship define and articulate the rigid hierarchy necessarily maintained on a voyage of the length and nature of a whaling cruise. The separation of officers from common sailors and the relative importance of the officers within the hierarchy are literally built into the ship. Ahab's grand isolation and his ability to hide his whaleboat crew occur because the captain of a whaleship has as much private space reserved to himself as nearly two dozen men might share in the fo'c's'le. The first mate commanded a fraction of that private space in his own cabin, but the other boatheaders shared cabins, and all the harpooneers were ensconced in a single room. These officers all lived in the stern of the ship in an area called the aftercabin. Hence, Queequeg lived in complete isolation from Ishmael, who bunked with fifteen to twenty-three other common sailors in the bow of the vessel in the forecastle (or fo'c's'le). The only direct communication between these two spaces occurred by means of the open upper deck. No doorways or passages below gave access through the solid bulkheads that separated each of these end spaces from the central blubber room. In addition to this hierarchical separation, a whaleship's crew was divided in two other ways. First, the crew and officers were divided evenly into two watches. The only people onboard not included in a watch were the captain and the "idlers": the cabin boy, steward, cook, carpenter, and blacksmith. Each of these two divisions would alternate being on duty or watch every four hours. In addition, the men in those watches were distributed among the boat's crews, each boat requiring a crew of six, including a boatheader and a harpooneer. A boat's crew was not necessarily all on the same watch. This complicated hierarchy and division meant that, once at sea, even if they were on the same watch, Ishmael and Queequeg would have little opportunity for purely social time together.

The second reason is analogous to the metaphor employed by Father Mapple in the final passage of the sermon: "Is not the main-truck higher than the kelson is low?" (48). This bit of sailor talk refers to the structural fact that the top of the tallest, or main, mast is far higher above the water than the bottom of the keel, or backbone, of the ship is below it. When a ship is being built on the sloping ways at the edge of the water, the keel is the timber laid first. The rib-like frames arise from the keel and define the shape of the vessel, and the planking enclosing those frames is then sealed with hemp and tar caulking to ensure that the vessel floats. The lower masts having been installed, the vessel is launched, after which the upper masts and rigging complete the structure. Sails are bent, provisions brought aboard, and a crew hired. Only then is the vessel ready to embark on its voyage. Once the vessel is launched, the keel is out of sight under the surface. It is, however, far weightier than the towering masts, which it must counterbalance. Melville constructs *Moby-Dick* with the metaphor of the cannibal as the keel. We see this metaphor when the vessel is onshore. Once launched, the weight of that metaphor counterbalances the entire metaphorical structure we see above the surface. Although out of sight, it is never out of Melville's mind.

When Ishmael returns from the chapel, he finds Queequeg "quite alone . . . holding close up to his face that little negro idol of his; peering hard into its face, and with a jack-knife gently whittling away at its nose, meanwhile humming to himself in his heathenish way" (49). Interrupted by Ishmael, Queequeg takes up "a large book" and begins to count fifty-page sections (49). What other book than the Bible would Queequeg find with so many multiples of fifty pages? Good Christians, people of the Book, have their beliefs fixed in a written text. As controversial and subject to dispute as the meaning of that text is, it is nonetheless relatively fixed compared to talk. Queequeg is not one of the people of the Book. His beliefs are mutable, transmitted orally as talk, and his god, too, is mutable. He is reshaping his god—just as his face itself has been marred and reshaped. That does not matter, for Queequeg's essential nature shines through.

As Ishmael contemplates Queequeg's visage, the virtues evident there remind him of "General Washington's head, as seen in the popular busts of him. It had the same long regularly graded retreating slope from above the brows, which were likewise very projecting, like two long promontories thickly wooded on top. Queequeg was George Washington cannibalistically developed" (50). Consider the reverence in which Washington was held at this period in American history. A mythic Colossus, Father of His Country, the larger-than-life, too-good-to-be-true character out of Parson Weems's widely read biography (c. 1800)[31] was incapable of falsehood, the embodiment of selfless courage, at once a natural aristocrat and the first citizen of a democratic republic. Melville's audacity in pairing him with Queequeg is extreme and bespeaks the significance Melville intends for Queequeg in the novel. As Ishmael continues to contemplate the impression Queequeg creates in him, he experiences something like conversion: "I began to be sensible of strange feelings. I felt a melting in me. No more my splintered heart and maddened hand were turned against the wolfish world" (51). Queequeg's presence heals him, makes him whole. "And those same things that would have repelled most others, they were the very magnets that thus drew me. I'll try a pagan friend, thought I, since Christian kindness has proved but hollow courtesy" (51). Remember that Ishmael has just returned from hearing a sermon by the celebrated Father Mapple, which seems to have had no effect on him whatsoever. Only three paragraphs later, Ishmael the Presbyterian has decided that "consequently, I must then unite with [Queequeg] in his [form of worship]; ergo, I must turn idolator. So I kindled the shavings; helped prop up the innocent little idol; offered him burnt biscuit with Queequeg; salamed before him twice or thrice; kissed his nose; and that done, we undressed and went to bed, at peace with our own consciences and all the world" (52). The grim misanthropic Ishmael who introduces himself at the beginning of the novel has been redeemed, and by a cannibal.

Throughout the development of Ishmael and Queequeg's friendship, the tension between Christianity and paganism pivots on Queequeg's cannibal identity. Ishmael's first awareness of Queequeg comes about through Peter Coffin's macabre teasing in his deliberate vagueness over both Queequeg's origins and the fact that he's selling embalmed New Zealand heads. Exasperated, Ishmael finally lashes out a long diatribe exhorting the landlord to speak plainly—a speech the landlord characterizes as "a purty long sarmon for a chap that rips a little now and then" (19). After Coffin explains himself more fully, Ishmael wonders, "What could I think of a harpooneer who stayed out of a Saturday night clean into the holy Sabbath, engaged in such a cannibal business as selling the heads of dead idolators?" (19). Thus, before he is even aware of Queequeg's origins in the Pacific islands, Ishmael has associated Queequeg with the tension between cannibalism and Christianity.

The cannibal Queequeg is a complex layering of reversals. Whereas a sailor leaves the ship and crosses the beach to go native as a beachcomber, Queequeg leaves the native beach to go to sea. Rather than missionaries coming to Koko-voko, Queequeg leaves his native island, of which he is a royal prince, in order to learn more of Christendom. In counterpoint to the expected optimistic letters sent home by missionaries, Queequeg's experience of Christians and Christendom has so disillusioned him that "he was fearful Christianity, or rather Christians, had unfitted him for ascending the pure and undefiled throne of thirty pagan Kings before him. But by and by, he said, he would return,—as soon as he felt himself baptized again" (56). Queequeg turns this sort of reversal to his own purposes in the next chapter, "Wheelbarrow," when Ishmael scolds him upon hearing Queequeg's self-deprecating account of lashing his sea chest to a wheelbarrow and then carrying both on his shoulders. "Queequeg, you might have known better than that, one would think. Didn't the people laugh?" (59). Queequeg counters this with a tale of a merchant ship captain attending a wedding on Kokovoko who, having seen the high priest consecrate the punch by dipping his fingers in it, self-importantly washes his own hands in the punch bowl, "taking it I suppose for a huge finger-glass. 'Now,' said Queequeg, 'what you tink now?—Didn't our people laugh?'" (59). Similarly, the bumpkin who mimics Queequeg aboard the schooner *Moss* on passage to Nantucket, on being tossed in the air by Queequeg, calls him a devil, and the captain of the *Moss* calls him a cannibal, threatening to kill him "if you try any more of your tricks aboard" (61). At that moment, the bumpkin is swept overboard when the sheet attached to the main boom parts, and Queequeg proves not a devil but the bumpkin's guardian angel. Angel-like, he is unconscious of any extraordinary merit in this act. Ishmael observes that Queequeg seems to be thinking, in the often-quoted line, "It's a mutual, joint-stock world, in all meridians. We cannibals must help these Christians" (62).

This line establishes the centrality of the image of the cannibal in *Moby-Dick*. It is tied here to another metaphor Melville employs in several crucial places, illustrating Ishmael's view of the fundamental nature of community, that of the joint-stock company. This pairing of metaphors openly places the cannibal on equal footing with the Christian, recognizing the cannibal's equal stake in and value to their shared interests. This is an extraordinary inversion of the significance of the cannibal Other. The tension produced by this inversion sounds in subsequently presented characters, events, and ponderings whenever these approach its vibrational frequency—the novel is tuned to this key. Once Ishmael and Queequeg embark on the *Pequod,* the movements and variations in this composition may seem to stray from this strongly elaborated original theme, but the cannibal leitmotif emerges sporadically at crucial points and swells forth again hauntingly in the chapter that precedes the final crescendo in "The Chase"—"The Symphony."

At the end of chapter 10, "A Bosom Friend," Ishmael, through Queequeg's benign influence, becomes a convert to paganism, an "idolator," joining Queequeg in his worship of Yojo. The malleable Yojo nonetheless proves to be an inscrutable and jealous god and demands an act of faith of Ishmael: he must choose the whaleship on which they are to embark without Queequeg's advice and experience. Examining the whaleships in Nantucket harbor readying for their cruises, Ishmael fastens on the doomed *Pequod*. And what manner of ship is this? "She was apparelled like any barbaric Ethiopian emperor, his neck heavy with pendants of polished ivory. She was a thing of trophies. A *cannibal of a craft*, tricking herself forth in the chased bones of her enemies. All round, her unpanelled, open bulwarks were garnished like one continuous jaw, with the long sharp teeth of the sperm whale, inserted there for pins, to fasten her old hempen thews and tendons to" (69–70; emphasis added). The as-yet-unseen captain of this vessel is described by Captain Peleg as "a grand, ungodly, god-like man. . . . Ahab's above the common; Ahab's been in colleges, as well as 'mong the cannibals; been used to deeper wonders than the waves; fixed his fiery lance in mightier, stranger foes than whales" (79).

The captain of this "cannibal craft" has been "'mong the cannibals." He is, of course, not the first important character in one of Melville's works to have lived among the cannibals. Both Tommo in *Typee* and Typee in *Omoo* are similarly experienced. Indeed, Typee, at the beginning of *Omoo*, is referred to as the "king of the cannibals" (8). This phrase could also characterize Ahab. It will crop up later in chapter 57, "Of Whales in Paint; in Teeth; in Wood; in Sheet-Iron; in Stone; in Mountains; in Stars": "Long exile from Christendom and civilization inevitably restores a man to that condition in which God placed him, *i.e.* what is called savagery. Your true whale-hunter is as much a savage as an Iroquois. I myself am a savage, owning no allegiance but to the King of the Cannibals; and ready at any moment to rebel against him" (270). Despite Peleg's assurances, once Ahab appears on the deck of the *Pequod*, he quickly reveals himself to be just such a savage. After *Typee* and the early Ishmael-Queequeg chapters of *Moby-Dick*, the reader realizes that the terms "savagery" and "civilization" are always in tension in Melville's works. Melville writes that he owes no allegiance but to the "King of the Cannibals"—but he is ready at any moment to rebel even against him. The whale hunter in Melville embraces savagery but at the same time refuses to be confined by it. Melville leaves open the possibility of rebellion. However, the possibility of rebellion is ambiguous. Would such rebellion lead back to civilization or so far beyond savagery that there is no frame of reference? That unknown is what is being reached for throughout *Moby-Dick*. The entire book revolves around the narrator's attempt to articulate something that is not possible to articulate, embodied in Ahab's famous exhortation to "strike through the mask!" (164).

In the following chapter, "The Ramadan," Ishmael returns to find Queequeg so deeply in communion with Yojo that he seems catatonic, a condition that persists until the following dawn. This circumstance arouses all of Ishmael's deeply felt doubts about religion in general, and he attempts to persuade Queequeg that this extreme behavior is "stark nonsense; bad for the health; useless for the soul; opposed, in short, to the obvious laws of Hygiene and common sense" (85). He posits the religious vision of hell in "hereditary dyspepsias nurtured by Ramadans" (85). The exchange that follows includes some of the most arrant cannibal talk in all of *Moby-Dick* and blends it first with sailor talk and then with a striking inversion of missionary talk. Ishmael asks Queequeg whether he has ever been troubled with dyspepsia, and Queequeg responds that he has been only on the occasion of a great battle "wherein fifty of the enemy had been killed by about two o'clock in the afternoon, and all cooked and eaten that very evening" (85). *Fifty* bodies are eaten between 2 P.M. and the evening of the same day. Such exaggeration is a central feature of cannibal talk. Cannibal talk combines with sailor talk in the ludicrous details *told* to Ishmael by a sailor who has visited the island: the bodies are prepared, garnished, stuffed with parsley, and sent around as though they were "so many Christmas turkeys" (85). The image of Christmas turkeys entwines these cannibalized bodies with Christian custom. The whole story has an elaborate yarn-like appeal.

Ishmael returns to his attempt to convert Queequeg from his pagan practices, but Queequeg "somehow seemed dull of hearing on that important subject, unless considered from his own point of view" (85). Melville here depicts Queequeg as the mirror image of the stuffy, self-righteous missionary, serene in the absolute authority of his dogma and unable to hear anybody else's point of view. He has "no doubt that he knew a good deal more about the true religion than I did," Ishmael tells us, and Queequeg looks at Ishmael "with a sort of condescending concern and compassion, as though he thought it a great pity that such a sensible young man should be so hopelessly lost to evangelical pagan piety" (86). Here Melville inverts missionary talk as he did in the sermon in *Typee* discussed above. This passage is a compact blending of cannibal, sailor, and missionary talk, as they existed in the South Pacific, which is used by Melville for his own artistic purposes.

The complex intertwining of sailor, cannibal, and missionary talk developed in these early chapters culminates in chapter 18, "His Mark." Significantly, this is the point at which Ishmael and Queequeg finally commit themselves to sailing aboard the *Pequod*. Peleg and Bildad will not allow a *cannibal* to become a *sailor* unless he proves that the *missionaries* have converted him to the Christian church. They insist that this be confirmed in writing. "I mean," Peleg replies, "he must show his papers" (87). Bildad confirms this. "'He must show that he's converted. Son of darkness,' he added, turning to Queequeg, 'art thou at present in communion with any christian church?'" (87). The captains want positive visual proof, written documentation.

Ishmael immediately responds that Queequeg is a member of the First Congregational Church. "'First Congregational Church,' cried Bildad, 'what! that worships in Deacon Deuteronomy Coleman's meeting-house?'" (87). Eyeing Queequeg, both Bildad and Peleg express doubt. Ishmael presses on, asserting that "Queequeg here is a born member of the First Congregational Church. He is a deacon himself, Queequeg is" (88). They press for further explanation.

> "I mean, sir, the same ancient Catholic Church to which you and I, and Captain Peleg there, and Queequeg here, and all of us, and every mother's son and soul of us belong; the great and everlasting First Congregation of this whole worshipping world; we all belong to that; only some of us cherish some queer crotchets noways touching the grand belief; in *that* we all join hands."
>
> "Splice, thou mean'st *splice* hands," cried Peleg, drawing nearer. [Note the reentry of sailor talk in this dialogue.] "Young man, you'd better ship for a missionary, instead of a foremast hand; I never heard a better sermon. Deacon Deuteronomy—why Father Mapple himself couldn't beat it, and he's reckoned something. Come aboard, come aboard; never mind about the papers." (88)

Ishmael's "sermon," his subversive use of talk, sways the captains in the absence of the written word. Queequeg's employment is confirmed when he demonstrates his savage ability to inflict deadly violence with his harpoon, unerringly striking a tiny spot of tar in the water. To borrow a metaphor from Father Mapple, the three strands of sailor talk, cannibal talk, and missionary talk are laid up into a single line here. Ishmael, already hired as a sailor, is told he should ship as a missionary. Queequeg, tabooed for his heathen status, has religious legitimacy conferred upon him by an inverted sermon. Peleg paraphrases Ishmael's exegesis in the form of sailor talk. The captains hasten to sign Queequeg aboard, upon completion of which Bildad earnestly attempts to evangelize him using language in which "something of the salt sea yet lingered," but he is immediately enjoined to cease his evangelization by Peleg, who cries: "Pious harpooneers never make good voyagers—it takes the shark out of 'em; no harpooneer is worth a straw who aint pretty sharkish" (89).

The cannibal metaphor develops in front of our eyes as we would see a ship in the ways being built, but once the vessel slides down the ways, is rigged, and departs, the hull of the ship submerges and the keel becomes invisible. Chapter 19,

"The Prophet," and chapter 21, "Going Aboard," wherein Queequeg and Ishmael encounter the mystifying Elijah, speak to the quality of concealment and hidden significance that attaches to the *Pequod* as it leaves port. We have one last glimpse of Queequeg the cannibal before he is absorbed into the workings of the ship. Sitting on and then, at Ishmael's urging, next to a sleeping sailor, Queequeg lights his tomahawk pipe, passing it back and forth to Ishmael. "Every time Queequeg received the tomahawk from me, he flourished the hatchet-side of it over the sleeper's head. 'What's that for, Queequeg?' 'Perry easy, kill-e; o! perry easy!'" (100). This menacing image of Queequeg flourishing a weapon that is also the mark of friendship between himself and Ishmael and that "had in its two uses both brained his foes and soothed his soul" (100) is our last clear view of Queequeg for a long time. The fateful journey is about to begin. Up until now Queequeg has appeared as "the cannibal," but he has now boarded the "cannibal craft" captained by a man who has lived "'mong the cannibals," and the significance of the term "cannibal" overflows and infuses every aspect of the vessel and voyage to the point that it becomes unspoken. The cannibal craft is leaving shore. We will glimpse the cannibal surfacing occasionally throughout the journey in various images and actions foreshadowed in these early chapters. The ubiquitous cannibal permeates the voyage, not least in the as-yet-unseen Captain Ahab, who, already aboard, "remained invisibly enshrined within his cabin" (101).

The surfacings of the cannibal metaphor occur in a variety of subtle and overt ways, ranging from Melville's self-referential "cannibalization" of his own earlier work to the direct evocation of the cannibal in the epigrammatic codas in some of his sermon chapters. The building tension and apprehension caused by Ahab's mysterious lurking, shadowy presence offstage when the *Pequod* first goes to sea replicate the technique Melville used in *Typee* to build tension through the mounting fear of cannibalism. When Ahab finally appears on deck, Ishmael tells us: "Reality outran apprehension" (123). The tension breaks. Ahab's first appearance on deck presents vague echoes of both Mehevi and Mow-Mow. His commanding but initially mute presence and classical aspect, "like Cellini's cast Perseus" (123), recall Mehevi, while the scar marring that face evokes Mow-Mow. Yet Ahab is of course a far more complex and developed character than either of these and far more subtly and skillfully drawn—one cannot imagine either of the earlier cannibals putting "forth the faint blossom of a look, which, in any other man, would have soon flowered out in a smile" (125).

While the harpooneers are all described as heathens, pagans, and savages, Daggoo and Tashtego are cannibals only through their association with Queequeg. Queequeg's past "murderous convivial indiscretions" terrify the steward Dough-Boy, as does his "mortal, barbaric smack of the lip in eating—an ugly sound enough—so much so, that the trembling Dough-Boy almost looked to see if any marks of teeth lurked in his own lean arms. And when he would hear Tashtego singing out for him to produce himself, that his bones might be picked, the simple-witted Steward all but shattered the crockery" (153). Melville depicts the simple Dough-Boy as a victim of the fears induced as much by Tashtego's use of cannibal talk as by the presence of the actual cannibal Queequeg. The effective menace of cannibal talk suffices to cast a dark enchantment around all the harpooneers—an enchantment that will later attach to Fedallah and his shadowy boat crew.

The tension between the cannibal and the missionary here and there surfaces overtly, notably in this passage: "a crew . . . chiefly made up of mongrel renegades, and castaways, and cannibals—morally enfeebled also, by the incompetence of mere unaided virtue or right-mindedness in Starbuck, the invulnerable jollity of indifference and recklessness in Stubb, and the pervading mediocrity in Flask" (186–87). The permeating power of the cannibal image subsumes the preceding characterizations of the crew as "mongrel renegades, and castaways." One cannot have "just a touch" of the cannibal about him: the cannibal is wholly other. Mongrel renegades and castaways may be redeemable by unaided virtue or right-mindedness, but these qualities are incompetent in redeeming cannibals. Melville casts Starbuck in this role of ineffectual missionary throughout *Moby-Dick*. He is a foil against which the engrossing quality of the cannibal propensity is displayed. Notable also in this passage is the concise thumbnail sketch of Stubb's character, which calls to mind the earlier portraits of both Toby in *Typee* and Doctor Long Ghost in *Omoo*. Ishmael, however, is very different from the narrators of those two earlier books, and Stubb's ironic remove, which he knowingly erects to insulate himself from the profounder implications of Ahab's quest, renders him an unfit companion for Ishmael. This narrator, unlike those in *Typee* and *Omoo*, exhibits the stunning range of intellectual, moral, and spiritual curiosity required to frame *Moby-Dick,* and the ironic voice is but one of many he employs.

Melville once again touches on cannibalism in chapter 58, "Brit," and alludes to the submerged nature of the metaphor in that chapter's penultimate paragraph. "Consider the subtleness of the sea; how its most dreaded creatures glide under water, unapparent for the most part, and treacherously hidden beneath the loveliest tints of azure. Consider also the devilish brilliance and beauty of many of its most remorseless tribes, as the dainty embellished shape of many species of sharks. Consider, once more, the universal cannibalism of the sea; all whose creatures prey upon each other, carrying on eternal war since the world began" (274). The narrator asks us to consider this in light of the "green, gentle, and most docile earth," there to find "a strange analogy to something in yourself" (274). Here we find finally the universal, the ubiquitous cannibal emerging fully revealed at almost the exact halfway point in the book. This is the image on which all pivots:

cannibal talk delivered by a sailor in the sermonic voice of a missionary. "For as this appalling ocean surrounds the verdant land, so in the soul of man there lies one insular Tahiti, full of peace and joy, but encompassed by all the horrors of the half known life. God keep thee! Push not off from that isle, thou canst never return!" (274). Ishmael issues this warning, emphasized by his slide into biblical diction, far too late for himself, for Ahab, for Queequeg, for the *Pequod*'s crew, and not least of all for us, the readers. To be halfway into a voyage is to be as far as one can go. From there it is just as long a journey to return unsatisfied as it is to press on to the unknown end. Lest we think of returning, the cannibal stew of the sea immediately issues forth a phantom image of Moby Dick, mistaken for the thing itself by Daggoo at the masthead. It is the first time the white whale is cried from the masthead: "There! there again! there she breaches! right ahead! The White Whale, the White Whale!" (275). What is seen, however, is not the white whale at all but its food, the giant squid, which Starbuck dreads as an omen of doom in a sentence that is a classic of sailor talk: "The great live squid, which, they say, few whale-ships ever beheld, and returned to their ports to tell of it" (276). Again we are reminded of Captain Jack Sparrow's line in the film *Pirates of the Caribbean: The Curse of the Black Pearl:* "No survivors? Then where do the stories come from, I wonder?"

One of the most lengthy, elaborated, and overt minglings of sailor talk, cannibal talk, and missionary talk occurs in chapters 64, 65, and 66, "Stubb's Supper," "The Whale as a Dish," and "The Shark Massacre." Melville compares the shark and the cannibal frequently. Peleg's assertion that a harpooneer must have a sharkish quality and the sharks mentioned in "Brit" (chapter 58) prefigure the full development of the pairing in these three chapters. In sailor talk, sharks share with cannibals the voracious desire for human flesh. In "Stubb's Supper," Melville constructs a sequence of similitudes, first likening Stubb to a shark because of their shared desire for whale's flesh, then by extension identifying Stubb with the cannibal, since sharks likewise desire human flesh. Stubb's taste for whale's meat, which he shares with the shark, implies the cannibalistic quality inherent in his sharkishness. The connection between Stubb and the cannibal is emphasized by an adroit sleight of hand with metaphors when the narrator expands on the role of sharks during naval battles:

Though amid all the smoking horror and diabolism of a sea-fight, sharks will be seen longingly gazing up to the ship's decks, like hungry dogs round a table where red meat is being carved, ready to bolt down every killed man that is tossed to them; and though, while the valiant butchers over the deck-table are thus cannibally carving each other's live meat with carving-knives all gilded and tasselled, the sharks, also, with their jewel-hilted mouths, are quarrelsomely carving away under the table at the dead meat;

and though, were you to turn the whole affair upside down, it would still be pretty much the same thing, that is to say, a shocking sharkish business enough for all parties. (293)

Aboard the *Pequod,* this symbolic inversion has been effected. Stubb embodies the shark when he devours the whale. Like any good cannibal, he has killed his enemy in battle and is now going to cook and eat him.

As chapter 64, "Stubb's Supper," continues, Stubb tells the black cook Fleece, in an inversion of missionary talk: "You must go home and be born over again; you don't know how to cook a whale-steak yet," to which Fleece replies, "Bress my soul, if I cook noder one" (296). Stubb wants Fleece to be born again to serve him, *not* Christ. Fleece replies by blessing himself, but his blessing is far from sacred: it is at best just an expression, and at worst a curse. Stubb follows this exchange with an inversion of the sacrament of Communion when he forces Fleece to taste the cooked whale then asks him the question Bildad posed of Queequeg: "Do you belong to the church?" (296). Stubb ritualizes his cannibalism with the sermon to the sharks. In this reversal, Stubb, the cannibal, asks Fleece, who is Other because of his race and because of his non-sailor role onboard ship, to act the part of the missionary. Here, Fleece is an Other, but less of an Other than Stubb. It is not one of the pagan harpooneers—not Queequeg, Tashtego, or Daggoo—who is the cannibal here, but *Stubb.* The hunger of the cannibal is not to be assuaged—even a whale is not enough to fill it. In pressing Fleece to preach to the sharks, Stubb will not relent until Fleece has achieved the ironic, sardonic tone of which he himself is so fond. Finally, Stubb gives the benediction, and Fleece erupts in a curse. Cannibal talk and missionary talk are inextricably entwined.

Sailor talk, too, lards this scene. Stubb uses sailor talk in ordering the comings and goings of his subordinates: "cook, you cook!—sail this way, cook!" (294). He wants to eat at his private table, the capstan, in an inversion of transubstantiation: he's going to eat raw flesh, the flesh of the whale, after it has been blessed by Fleece. As a good cannibal, Stubb wants Fleece to collect the tips of the fins and flukes for the next day's meal, for as Langsdorff said, cannibals consider the hands and feet most delectable: here we see the continued exaggeration of cannibal talk. These incredible complex interminglings of the three forms of talk end not with a dog biting a man, but a shark (and a dead one at that!) biting a cannibal. Who is not a cannibal?

The set of chapters beginning with "Brit" and ending with "Of Whales in Paint; in Teeth; in Wood; in Sheet-Iron; in Stone; in Mountains; in Stars" rises into an upwelling of the cannibal metaphor. This triptych of chapters sets the pin in the hinge on which the novel turns.

"The Symphony," which appears immediately before the final three chapters delineating the three days of the *Pequod*'s chase of Moby Dick, is Ahab's last chance to turn back from the object of his monomania, and it is at this point that Ahab calls himself "cannibal old me" (544). Now, his goal seemingly within reach, is the moment when Ahab seems most human and when he acknowledges the cost of his obsession. He reflects on his many years at sea and on his wife and son, figuratively widowed and orphaned by his need to hunt Moby Dick. This scene is a haunting inversion of Christ in the Garden of Gethsemane. Starbuck sees Ahab weeping into the sea, a disconcerting sight both for Starbuck and for us. Ahab turns and sees Starbuck watching him and launches into an elegiac lament for his life: "When I think of this life I have led; the desolation of solitude it has been; the masoned, walled-town of a Captain's exclusiveness, which admits but small entrance to any sympathy from the green country without—oh, weariness! heaviness! Guinea-coast slavery of solitary command!" (543). Ahab pours out an extraordinary language of lamenting into Starbuck's ears, and Starbuck responds with his final plea: "Oh, my Captain! my Captain! noble soul! grand old heart, after all! why should any one give chase to that hated fish! Away with me! let us fly these deadly waters! let us home! Wife and child, too, are Starbuck's—wife and child of his brotherly, sisterly, play-fellow youth; even as thine, sir, are the wife and child of thy loving, longing, paternal old age! Away! let us away!" (544). It is here that Ahab calls himself a cannibal. "About this time," he tells Starbuck, "—yes, it is his noon nap now—the boy vivaciously wakes; sits up in bed; and his mother tells him of me, of cannibal old me" (544). In this most poignantly human moment, contemplating his most intimate connections and the son he has fathered in his own image, Ahab thrusts his wife and son from him as he confronts his own cannibal nature. Recall the exaggerated cannibal talk wherein cannibals are said to feed on their own wives and children. Simultaneously stimulated and horrified by his irrevocable acceptance of the cannibal within, Ahab eats his own heart. He is completely othered. He dons the mask of inhumanity and will not remove it. He refuses Starbuck's plea, and "blanched to a corpse's hue with despair" (545), Starbuck steals away. Starbuck cries to him during the second day of the chase, "Great God! but for one single instant show thyself" (561), but Ahab will not. Ahab is no longer Ahab the human being, but Ahab the Fates' lieutenant. He has become the cannibal.

METHODOLOGY AND POLITICS

As stated in the introduction, this is a study of the aesthetic, linguistic, ethical, cultural, and political implications of Melville's borrowing. Melville filched not only from written sources but also from oral sources, especially those he had heard during his sojourn in the South Pacific. I have attempted to assemble a set of tools and methods that, taken together, provide a mechanism with which to consider the more ephemeral sources on which Melville drew. I have identified and investigated the evidence for oral sources Melville brought to bear in his work, including relevant vernacular material such as newspaper accounts, logs and journals, letters, sermons, and songs. I have examined and deconstructed Melville's use of occupational aspects of sailor talk. By using tools of traditional source study, I have analyzed what evidence is extant regarding the way that the discourses discussed were carried on verbally. I have also employed relevant analytical techniques from folklore, ethnomusicology, and anthropology. It testifies to Melville's astounding literary achievement in *Moby-Dick* that elements of all these disparate disciplines can be brought to bear on this text and its meanings remain inexhaustible.

Questions of authenticity, veracity, and authorship dogged Melville from the inception of his literary career. While it was not until long after his death that the extent of his almost verbatim taking from written sources was recognized and analyzed, the skepticism regarding *Typee* anticipated the whole confounding range of questions raised by the techniques he employed in his literary art, many of which have to do with provenance. These same questions have immense currency today in an age in which not only texts but a variety of other creative forms exist in digital format. It is remarkable to contemplate the parallels between Melville's creative process and digital remix culture. The creation of musical works through the sampling of other works, the ability to digitally alter and combine images, and the creation of interactive online novels, musical performances, other artworks, and games are now commonplace.

The concept of intellectual property in the creation of art rests on the illusion that any artist, ever, creates "wholly original" works. Any work that owes nothing to the cultural context in which it was created would be meaningless, without reference, save as a Rorschach ink blot on which each viewer projects his or her own assemblage of culturally shaped meanings. Originality in art consists of creating or revealing hitherto unrecognized relations of meaning among culturally significant referents or in intensifying existing significances. The materials available to artists, therefore, necessarily comprise the entire cultural lexicon. Melville found the materials for his early books in an arena characterized by rapid cultural change and the interaction of vastly different groups. Part of his genius was his ability to draw from this uncentered theater of cultural interaction themes that transfix us with their evident universal truth. In order to realize his vision, Melville developed a complex narrative voice that allowed him to synthesize disparate discourses and examine them from a multitude of perspectives. The elusive shifting quality of the narrative voice in *Moby-Dick* is necessitated by both the material and the author's ambitious use of it.

Melville's originality is inextricable from his indebtedness to his sources. The fact that much of the material Melville assembled in *Moby-Dick* and his earlier works is lifted, borrowed, appropriated, stolen, plagiarized, and used without attribution or a hint of conscience is in fact an enduring testament to the writer's originality. His use of William Shakespeare's *King Lear,* cannibal talk, and sailor talk in the creation of Ahab in *Moby-Dick* is a triumph of manipulation of preexisting cultural referents, remixed to create a remarkable character recognized as one of the great originals in the history of literature. In contemporary culture, this process is paralleled in works such as DJ Danger Mouse's *Grey Album* (2004) and the countless interchanges, gifts, imitations, appropriations, and thefts that have formed the stuff of popular culture in every artistic discipline.

The *Grey Album* is a digital remix of the Beatles' classic and technically untitled *White Album* (1968), one of the band's more experimental works, with the *Black Album* (2003) of hip-hop artist Jay-Z. Hip-hop itself relies almost entirely on the creative recombination of earlier recordings blended with live performance or electronic sound. In its earliest incarnation, the music depended on DJs with multiple turntables spinning two or more records simultaneously and physically "scratching" them by manually manipulating either the record or the tonearm. With the advent of digital recording technology, hip-hop artists created digital samples from earlier recordings and looped them in increasingly complex ways to achieve remarkable effects. This art form derives meaning not only from the sound of the music itself but also from the layered cultural allusions implicit in the contextual background of the samples. The *Grey Album* juxtaposes the *White Album* by a group of English musicians who achieved worldwide renown for their mastery of a commercial musical form with roots in past African American musical forms with the *Black Album* exemplifying current African American musical culture as practiced by an acknowledged hip-hop master. As a consequence of such mixing, this work both celebrates the common ground achieved by the counterculture in the 1960s and throws into relief the continuing racial tension in American society.

The extent to which Melville borrowed and combined sources and literary forms and interlaced them with his own luminous revelations not only sets his work apart from that of any of his contemporaries but places him far ahead of his time. Indeed, it is not until the advent of electronic media creates the potential for combining moving images, sound recording, and text that the tools for such a technique to become a general artistic practice exist. The currency of Melville's technique is evident in controversies over the *Grey Album* and over other recent works such as Bob Dylan's *Modern Times* (2006).

Martin Scorsese's documentary *No Direction Home: Bob Dylan* and the release of *Modern Times,* combined with Dylan's reconfiguration as a radio DJ in his 2006 XM satellite weekly radio show "Theme Time Radio Hour," marked his reemergence as a significant cultural force. Like Melville, Dylan manipulated his biography when he first came to public attention in order to establish "authentic" credentials.[32] He used his first years as a performer to master a range of traditional material in both repertoire and technique. He moved on to create his early original works by emulating his musical hero Woody Guthrie and borrowed melodies and phrases from his already vast repertoire of traditional song to create powerful new pieces. For instance, Dylan borrowed the melody of what is perhaps his best-known early song, "Blowing in the Wind," from the antebellum slave song "No More Auction Block for Me." As he grew as a writer, Dylan's incorporation of source material became increasingly layered and complex. His embrace of electric music and rejection of his identity as a topical songwriter as seen in the Scorsese documentary marked his determination to follow his own artistic muse, even at the risk of losing his original audience.

The controversy over Dylan's wholesale lifting of phrases and lines from Henry Timrod, the "poet laureate of the Confederacy," who died in 1867 just shy of his thirty-ninth birthday, eerily echoes questions about Melville's similar borrowing technique. Many of the lyrics on Dylan's *Modern Times* album come directly from Timrod's poetry—Timrod, "Two Portraits": "how then, O weary one! explain/ The sources of that hidden pain?"; Dylan, "Spirit on the Water": "can't explain/ The sources of this hidden pain"; Timrod, "Sonnet 13": "Things which you neither meant nor wished to say"; Dylan, "When the Deal Goes Down": "Things I never meant nor wished to say"; Timrod, "A Vision of Poesy— Part 01": "A childish dream is now a deathless need"; Dylan, "Tweedle Dee & Tweedle Dum": "Well a childish dream is a deathless need"; Timrod, "Retirement": "There is a wisdom that grows up in strife"; Dylan, "When the Deal Goes Down": "Where wisdom goes up in strife."[33] The online Dylan pool discussion lists several more examples.[34] In an op-ed piece for the *New York Times*, the songwriter Suzanne Vega ponders Dylan's alleged plagiarism.

> These days if a sample of music is taken, you have to acknowledge the original artists and pay them. . . . Shouldn't the same courtesy be extended to all intellectual property? In other words, is [Dylan] really "a thieving little swine" as one "fan" puts it?
>
> Well, I guess he is. But I am trying to imagine a Bob Dylan album with footnotes, asterisks, ibid.'s and nifty little anecdotes about the origins of each song. It's not going to happen. He's never pretended to be an academic, or even a nice guy. He is more likely to present himself as, well, a thief. Renegade, outlaw, artist. That's why we are passionate about him.[35]

No one has ever called Melville "a thieving little swine," although many of his borrowings are even more wholesale than those of Dylan. One only has to compare Melville's *Benito Cereno* to chapter 18 of Amasa Delano's *A Narrative of Voyages and Travels* to see how extensive his lifting can be. Both Melville and Dylan are great enough artists that their Midas touch transforms the material they appropriate by incorporating it into their singular artistic visions. J. Ross Browne was incapable of writing *Moby-Dick,* although he, too, wrote a description of a "whaling cruise." Timrod's phrases fit seamlessly into Dylan's work, but the songs are fully and unquestionably Bob Dylan songs. The strength and character of Dylan's poetic voice function as a beautiful but not overstated setting for the jeweled phrases he lifts from Timrod, displaying their intrinsic beauty far better than the over-elaborate, ornate, and sentimental context from which they are lifted. As John Dryden wrote of Ben Jonson, "He invades Authours [*sic*] like a Monarch, and what would be theft in other Poets, is onely [*sic*] victory in him."[36]

The question of whether such borrowings are theft or not remains politically fraught. Intellectual property law is one of the most controversial and active areas of the legal system. In Melville's lifetime, copyright protection was extended from twenty-eight to forty-two years; it now, as of 1998, extends to seventy years beyond the author's death. Some legal scholars argue that laws governing digital works on the Internet effectively eliminate the concept of fair use. Advocates for limiting the effect of copyright law often cite the following passage by Thomas Jefferson in an 1813 letter to Isaac McPherson:

> If nature has made any one thing less susceptible than all others of exclusive property, it is the action of the thinking power called an idea, which an individual may exclusively possess as long as he keeps it to himself; but the moment it is divulged, it forces itself into the possession of every one, and the receiver cannot dispossess himself of it. Its peculiar character, too, is that no one possesses the less, because every other possesses the whole of it. He who receives an idea from me, receives instruction himself without lessening mine; as he who lights his taper at mine, receives light without darkening me. That ideas should freely spread from one to another over the globe, for the moral and mutual instruction of man, and improvement of his condition, seems to have been peculiarly and benevolently designed by nature, when she made them, like fire, expansible over all space, without lessening their density in any point, and like the air in which we breathe, move, and have our physical being, incapable of confinement or exclusive appropriation. Inventions then cannot, in nature, be a subject of property.[37]

Whatever one thinks of the current state of copyright law, it is certain that *Moby-Dick* and many of Melville's other works would have received a very different scrutiny and reception had they been published under the current regime.

A second political aspect of Melville's writing is the degree to which he used his works as vehicles for social protest. One of the most important questions for Melville is the fragility of the structures of human community and the influences that render them brittle. His early years at sea introduced him to several communities in which he could observe this process, ranging from the fairly standard disaffection aboard the *Acushnet* to his observations of the establishment of French hegemony on Nuku Hiva, an island already altered forever in the aftermath of earlier outside incursions, most notably that of David Porter. He witnessed much more advanced deterioration in the Society Islands, the collapse of the accepted structures of shipboard life aboard the *Lucy Ann*, and the distorting, deadening effect of flogging in the military hierarchy aboard the *United States*.

In a time when oratory was one of the most important and effective means of advancing social justice, Melville incorporated elements of several forms of this verbal art into his written work, notably in several of his "sermons" and soliloquies. However, even in *Typee*, his artistic vision elevates him beyond the merely topical. His heroes, unlike those in Cooper's novels for example, are far more likely to advance the plot and deepen the significance by talk than they are by action. As much as Ahab is modeled on King Lear, Ishmael owes more to Hamlet, constantly observing, pondering, and reexamining, although unlike Hamlet, he is unable to act not because he cannot make up his mind to do so but rather because the choice is not his to make. In *Moby-Dick*, Melville demands so much of his characters that social criticism recedes into the background, obscured by the more timeless questions on which the book centers.

The Chase—Third Day

Herman Melville's reputation as a storyteller flourished among his family, friends, and acquaintances before he ever set pen to paper as an author. His confidence in his ability to spin a good yarn sustained his early efforts to develop a story into a novel. Once committed to completing his first work, however, he found he must flesh it out with material from other sources, and his restless intellect caused him to compare and contrast what he read with his own experiences and insights.

From the inception of his literary career, Melville is always at the center of a conversation with his readers and his sources. In the manner of any great teacher, he invites his readers to engage him in the same way that he engages his sources: by arguing, questioning, and examining from multiple points of view. Melville filled his copy of his Hilliard & Gray edition of *The Poetical Works of John Milton* (1836) with fierce jottings that reveal the extent to which he ponders, disputes, and revels in the images, arguments, and language of the book.[38] He interacts with all his sources in the same way. Evidence for this lies in the uses to which he puts this material, inverting its meanings, placing it in starkly different contexts, mocking and parodying, and sometimes emulating his most important sources with such sure mastery that he rivals or surpasses them.

By means of the knowing wink implied in his narrator's sardonic tone, Melville summons readers to a removed perspective that allows a free play of ideas. Throughout his early works, he employs this increasingly supple and flexible voice. By the time he commences writing *Moby-Dick,* the narrator's voice carries the spellbinding force of an incantation, sweeping the reader on to an enchanted sea in which currents of hidden meanings tug like undertow beneath the clearly visible surface waves. Melville's evolving narrative voice influences his deepening exploration of meaning. Once he has adopted a slightly skeptical, mocking tone as a literary device, the tone itself leads him to examine and question the world he has experienced. This intersection of narrative voice and the materials encountered in the rich and interconnected talk produced in the South Pacific in the 1840s provides the basis for Melville's increasingly profound questioning. Thus, his memories of his own seafaring experiences, the tone and attitude of sailor talk, the strangeness of the cannibal Other, and the deceptive certainty of the missionary lead Melville's narrators deeper into elusive questions of identity, community, morality, humanity, knowledge, truth, and the very roots of being.

ᴄ᷉ Notes

Introduction

1. The Melville Revival is usually dated from the publication of Raymond Weaver's *Herman Melville: Mariner and Mystic* (New York: George H. Doran, 1921). In November of the same year, H. M. Tomlinson published "A Clue to 'Moby Dick,'" about Melville's use of Sir Thomas Browne (Literary Review, *New York Evening Post* [Nov. 5, 1921], 141–42). Fifteen months later, Whitney Hastings Wells published a note on "Moby Dick and Rabelais" in *Modern Language Notes* 38 (Feb. 1923), 123.

2. Roger P. McCutcheon, "The Technique of Melville's Israel Potter," *South Atlantic Quarterly* 27 (Apr. 1928), 161–74, and Harold H. Scudder, "Melville's *Benito Cereno* and Captain Delano's Voyages," *Publications of the Modern Language Association* 43 (June 1928), 502–32.

3. According to Nathaniel Philbrick, the Wampanoag word *townor* means that a whale has been sighted for a second time. See *In the Heart of the Sea: The Tragedy of the Whaleship* Essex (New York: Viking, 2000), 13.

4. Richard D. Altick, *The Scholar Adventurers* (New York: Macmillan, 1950).

5. More information on the Barouallie whalemen can be found in Roger D. Abrahams, *Deep the Water, Shallow the Shore: Three Essays on Shantying in the West Indies* (first published as number 60 of American Folklore Society Monographs, Austin: Univ. of Texas Press, 1974; Mystic, CT: Mystic Seaport Museum, 2002).

6. *Tusitala* is a Samoan word that can be translated as "storyteller" or "teller of tales." As a Polynesian language, Samoan is closely allied with Tahitian and Marquesan.

7. William Shakespeare, *The Tempest*, ed. Louis B. Wright and Virginia A. LaMar (New York: Washington Square Press, 1961), 1.2.131.

8. Charles Roberts Anderson, *Melville in the South Seas* (New York: Columbia Univ. Press, 1939), 307.

9. Ida Leeson, "The Mutiny on the *Lucy Ann*," *Philological Quarterly* 19 (Oct. 1940): 370–79.

10. Robert S. Forsythe, review of *Melville in the South Seas* by Charles Roberts Anderson, *American Literature* 11 (Mar. 1939), 85–92. The earlier pieces referred to are "Herman Melville in Honolulu," *New England Quarterly* 8 (Mar. 1935): 99–105; "Herman Melville in the Marquesas," *Philological Quarterly* 15 (Jan. 1936): 1–15; "Herman Melville in Tahiti," *Philological Quarterly* 16 (Oct. 1937): 344–57; "More upon Herman Melville in Tahiti," *Philological Quarterly* 17 (Jan. 1938): 1–17.

11. Heflin's work first appeared in his 1952 dissertation and then in his posthumously published book. Wilson Heflin, "Herman Melville's Whaling Years" (PhD diss., Vanderbilt University, 1952); *Herman Melville's Whaling Years,* ed. Mary K. Bercaw Edwards and Thomas Farel Heffernan (Nashville, TN: Vanderbilt Univ. Press, 2004).

12. Harrison Hayford, editors' introduction and explanatory notes to *Omoo,* by Herman Melville, ed. Harrison Hayford and Walter Blair (New York: Hendricks House, 1969), xvii–lii, 341–438; Harrison Hayford, note on the text and afterword to *Typee,* by Herman Melville, ed. Harrison Hayford (New York: Signet, 1964), 303–20; Herman Melville, *Typee,* ed. Harrison Hayford, Hershel Parker, and G. Thomas Tanselle, with historical note by Leon Howard (Evanston and Chicago: Northwestern Univ. Press and the Newberry Library, 1968); Herman Melville, *Omoo,* ed. Harrison Hayford, Hershel Parker, and G. Thomas Tanselle (Evanston and Chicago: Northwestern Univ. Press and the Newberry Library, 1968).

13. Greg Dening, *Islands and Beaches: Discourse on a Silent Land: Marquesas 1774–1880* (Honolulu: Univ. Press of Hawaii, 1980).

14. Greg Dening, *Beach Crossings: Voyaging across Times, Cultures, and Self* (Philadelphia: Univ. of Pennsylvania Press, 2004).

15. Robert C. Suggs, *The Hidden Worlds of Polynesia: The Chronicle of an Archaeological Expedition to Nuku Hiva in the Marquesas Islands* (New York: Harcourt, Brace & World, 1962).

16. Robert C. Suggs, "Melville's Flight to Taipi: Topographic, Archeological, and Historic Considerations," *ESQ: A Journal of the American Renaissance* 51.1–3 (2005), 47–86; John Bryant, "Taipi, Tipii, *Typee:* Place, Memory, and Text," *ESQ: A Journal of the American Renaissance* 51.1–3 (2005): 137–68.

17. T. Walter Herbert Jr., *Marquesan Encounters: Melville and the Meaning of Civilization* (Cambridge, MA: Harvard Univ. Press, 1980), 22.

18. The missionary documents that Herbert studied are Mary Charlotte Alexander, *William Patterson Alexander in Kentucky, the Marquesas, Hawaii* (Honolulu, 1934); William Patterson Alexander to Rufus Anderson, journal letter, Sept. 4, 1833, to May 13, 1834, in the Houghton Library, Harvard University, Cambridge, MA; Robert Armstrong, "Journal Written at the Island of Nuuhiva," entries from Aug. 21, 1833, to Mar. 22, 1834, in the Houghton Library; and Benjamin Wyman Parker, "Joint Communication of Messrs. Alexander, Armstrong & Parker," Apr. 10, 1834, in the Houghton Library.

19. Herbert cites the first edition of David Porter's *Journal of a Cruise Made to the Pacific Ocean* (Philadelphia, 1815), although most Melville scholars cite the second edition, published in 1822. See my discussion of the two editions of Porter in note 64 of chapter 1.

20. Caleb Crain, "Lovers of Human Flesh: Homosexuality and Cannibalism in Melville's Novels," *American Literature* 66 (Mar. 1994), 28.

21. Ibid., 31.

22. William Arens, *The Man-Eating Myth: Anthropology and Anthropophagy* (New York: Oxford Univ. Press, 1979); William Arens, "Rethinking Anthropophagy," *Cannibalism and the Colonial World*, ed. Francis Barker, Peter Hulme, and Margaret Iversen (Cambridge: Cambridge Univ. Press, 1998), 39–62; Gananath Obeyesekere, "Cannibal Feasts in Nineteenth-Century Fiji: Seamen's Yarns and the Ethnographic Imagination," *Cannibalism and the Colonial World*, ed. Francis Barker, Peter Hulme, and Margaret Iversen (Cambridge: Cambridge Univ. Press, 1998), 63–86; Gananath Obeyesekere, *Cannibal Talk: The Man-Eating Myth and Human Sacrifice in the South Seas* (Berkeley: Univ. of California Press, 2005).

23. Marshall Sahlins, "Artificially Maintained Controversies: Global Warming and Fijian Cannibalism," *Anthropology Today* 19 (June 2003), 3–5; Joan-Pau Rubiés, "Virtual Suppers," *Times Literary Supplement*, Mar. 17, 2006. See also Robert Borofsky, "CA Forum on Theory in Anthropology: Cook, Lono, Obeyesekere, and Sahlins," *Current Anthropology* 38 (Apr. 1997), 255–82. Borofksy's essay is followed by comments by Herb Kawainui Kane, Gananath Obeyesekere, and Marshall Sahlins and a reply by Borofsky.

24. Geoffrey Sanborn, *The Sign of the Cannibal: Melville and the Making of a Postcolonial Reader* (Durham, NC: Duke Univ. Press, 1998), xiii.

25. Ibid.

26. Ibid., xii.

27. Melville wrote to Nathaniel Hawthorne in early May 1851: "To go down to posterity is bad enough, any way; but to go down as a 'man who lived among the cannibals'!" This letter is dated June 1?, 1851, by Lynn Horth in *Correspondence* (Evanston and Chicago: Northwestern Univ. Press and the Newberry Library, 1993), 193, but Hershel Parker, in *Herman Melville: A Biography* (Baltimore, MD: Johns Hopkins Univ. Press, 1996), 1:841–44, redates it early May based on evidence that has come to light since *Correspondence* was published.

1. "WHERE THE WILD THINGS ARE"

1. According to Andrew Delbanco in *Melville: His World and Work* (New York: Alfred A. Knopf, 2005), "after several exhausting days, having lost their bearings and much of their morale, [Melville and Richard Tobias Greene] found themselves among the dreaded Typees" (43). Hershel Parker, in *Herman Melville: A Biography*, writes: "Melville's narrative of the desertion in *Typee* is not the unvarnished truth, but true in much of its substance and grand items, truth a good deal varnished" (1:214). Laurie Robertson-Lorant states in *Melville: A Biography* (New York: Clarkson Potter, 1996): "After climbing from peak to valley and valley to peak and valley once again, Herman and Toby reached a village whose inhabitants seemed friendly. . . . The natives turned out to be the Typees" (107–8). An example of unquestioning acceptance is Leon Howard's historical note to *Typee* in the Northwestern-Newberry edition of *The Writings of Herman Melville*, considered the standard edition of Melville's works. Howard writes: "Herman Melville's first book, *Typee*, was the literary result of the most exciting adventure of his life—his escape from an American whaling vessel in the Marquesas Islands of the South Pacific and his residence in the valley of cannibals where he was kept captive until an Australian whaler came to his rescue" (277).

2. Herman Melville to Nathaniel Hawthorne, May 1851, in *Correspondence*, 193.

3. Bryant, "Taipi, Tipii, *Typee*," 147–48.

4. For much of the evidence cited in this chapter, I am indebted to my work as co-editor of the posthumous edition of Wilson Heflin's *Herman Melville's Whaling Years.*

5. *Typee* was published in London on Feb. 26, 1846, and in New York City on Mar. 17, 1846 (Howard, historical note to *Typee*, 285). Melville's birth date is Aug. 1, 1819; he was twenty-six years old when *Typee* was published.

6. John Murray to Gansevoort Melville, Oct. 17, 1846, in *The Melville Log: A Documentary Life of Herman Melville 1819–1891*, ed. Jay Leyda (New York: Harcourt, Brace, 1951), 1:199.

7. Frederick Douglass, *Narrative of the Life of Frederick Douglass, An American Slave. Written by Himself*, *The Frederick Douglass Papers*, 2nd series, ed. John W. Blassingame, John R. McKivigan, and Peter P. Hinks (1845; New Haven, CT: Yale Univ. Press, 1999), 31.

8. Ibid., 37.

9. Gansevoort Melville to John Murray, Oct. 21, 1846, in *Melville Log*, 1:199.

10. [Charles F. Daniels], Review of *Typee*, *Morning Courier and New-York Enquirer*, Apr. 17, 1846, in Melville *Log*, 1:211–12.

11. Herman Melville to Alexander W. Bradford, May 23, 1846, in *Correspondence*, 38.

12. Melville writes in the last lines of *Typee*: "The mystery which hung over the fate of my friend and companion Toby has never been cleared up. I still remain ignorant whether he succeeded in leaving the valley, or perished at the hands of the islanders" (253).

13. Richard Tobias Greene, "To the Editor of the Buffalo Com. Adv.," *Buffalo Commercial Advertiser*, July 1, 1846.

14. Melville had written to Evert Duyckinck, the editor at his American publishers Wiley and Putnam: "Seriously, My Dear Sir, this resurrection of Toby from the dead . . . can not but settle the question of the book's genuineness" (July 3, 1846, in *Correspondence*, 50).

15. Herman Melville to Nathaniel Hawthorne, May 1851, in *Correspondence*, 193.

16. Evert Duyckinck to George Duyckinck, Mar. 18, 1848, in *Melville Log*, 1:273.

17. Anderson, 35.

18. Glenn Grasso, "Valentine Pease, Jr. and Melville's Literary Captains" (paper delivered at the Second International Melville Conference, "Melville and the Sea," Mystic, CT, June 18, 1999).

19. When recaptured runaway seamen were questioned by British and American consuls in foreign ports about their reasons for deserting, the most common answer they gave was the lack of quality and quantity of shipboard food. See, for example, the complaints of deserters from Pease's earlier command, the *Houqua*, now in the British consular papers, Tahiti, vol. 8, in the collection of the Mitchell Library, State Library of New South Wales, Sydney, Australia, reference number ML MSS 24/8: FM4/582.

20. Logbook of the *Florida*, entry for Jan. 29, 1859, ODHS 763, New Bedford Whaling Museum, New Bedford, MA, quoted in Briton Cooper Busch, *"Whaling Will Never Do for Me": The American Whaleman in the Nineteenth Century* (Lexington: Univ. Press of Kentucky, 1994), 104.

21. Quoted in Granville Allen Mawer, *Ahab's Trade: The Saga of South Seas Whaling* (New York: St. Martin's Press, 1999), 110. Additionally, the prevalence of desertion is discussed in Elmo P. Hohman's seminal work, *The American Whaleman: A Study of Life and Labor in the Whaling Industry* (New York: Longmans, Green, 1928), 62–69 and Appendix B, "Desertions, Discharges, and Deaths in Relation to the Size of Whaling Crews," 316–17, and in Margaret S. Creighton, *Rites and Passages: The Experience of American Whaling, 1830–1870* (Cambridge: Cambridge Univ. Press, 1995), especially 144–46. It is also supported by a study of the crew lists of the thirty-seven voyages (1841–1921) of the whaleship

Charles W. Morgan: see John F. Leavitt, *The Charles W. Morgan,* 2nd ed. (Mystic, CT: Mystic Seaport Museum, 1998), 108–16.

22. Certificate of John Stetson, Lahaina, June 2, 1843, New Bedford Whaling Museum, New Bedford, MA. For information on Stetson, see documents filed in "Miscellaneous Letters 1838–1846" (box 30), Consular Posts: Honolulu, HI, RG84: Records of Foreign Service Posts, National Archives, Washington, DC, and Heflin, *Herman Melville's Whaling Years,* 191.

23. Logbook of the *Potomac,* entries for July 4, 7, 11, and 13, 1842, Peabody-Essex Institute, Salem, MA.

24. Thomas Farel Heffernan extensively studied Greene's time on the *London Packet* for "Toby Greene," Appendix I, in Heflin, *Herman Melville's Whaling Years.* No document exists supporting Greene's claim that he shipped on the *London Packet* in Nuku Hiva, but his description of the vessel's movements in his *Buffalo Commercial Advertiser* account matches the known movements of the *London Packet.* See Heffernan, "Toby Greene," 209–10.

25. Logbook of the *Charles,* entry for July 13, 1842: "PM The Acushnet appears of[f] the harbour sends in a boat gets 2 out of the 4 men that deserted from him 5 days prev[ious]," in the Kendall Collection of the New Bedford Whaling Museum, New Bedford, MA.

26. The crew list of the *Lucy Ann* records that Herman Melville signed on as an able seaman at the 120th lay as witnessed by J. German, the first mate of the *Lucy Ann.* The notes of Charles B. Wilson, HBM acting consul at Tahiti, record that Melville signed on at Nuku Hiva on Aug. 9, 1842. See the British consular records of the revolt aboard the *Lucy Ann,* in the Mitchell Library, State Library of New South Wales, Sydney, Australia, reprinted as "Revolt Documents," and edited by Harrison Hayford in the Hendricks House edition of *Omoo,* 313, 318.

27. Heflin, *Herman Melville's Whaling Years,* 137.

28. Heflin himself considered that Melville might never have left the beach. See Heflin, *Herman Melville's Whaling Years,* 157.

29. Richard Tobias Greene, "Typee. Toby's Own Story," *Buffalo Commercial Advertiser,* July 11, 1846: 2. Melville visited Greene in upstate New York between July 15 and 22, 1846. From their conversation came "The Story of Toby," first published separately in England and then as part of the revised edition of *Typee* in the United States. "The Story of Toby" follows Greene's account in the *Buffalo Commercial Advertiser* in a general way, but there are differences that are typically Melvillean. Melville wants to maintain the level of excitement and suspense with which *Typee* ends. Melville makes additions and alters some of Greene's statements. For a study of the differences between Greene's newspaper account and "The Story of Toby," see Heflin, *Herman Melville's Whaling Years,* 152–55.

30. Heffernan, 207.

31. Heflin, *Herman Melville's Whaling Years,* 157.

32. Vivien de Saint-Martin and Louis Rousselet, *Nouveau dictionnaire de géographie universelle* (Paris: Hachette et Cie., 1887), 3:684. The late Karl Steinmayer translated the passage for me before he died on Oct. 3, 2002.

33. Titus Coan, *Life in Hawaii. An Autobiographic Sketch of Mission Life and Labors* (New York: Anson D. F. Randolph, 1882), 199–200. André Revel, in "*Typee:* In the Footsteps of Herman Melville" (*Melville Society Extracts,* 90 [Sept. 1992], 2–6), suggests the path Melville followed to enter the Taipi valley, but Robert C. Suggs, in "Topographic, Archeological and Historical Considerations Relevant to Melville's Flight to Taipi" (paper delivered at the Kendall Institute, New Bedford Whaling Museum, New Bedford, MA, Aug. 19,

2003), strongly disagrees with Revel's identification. Suggs's "Melville's Flight to Taipi" is a longer version of the paper delivered in New Bedford.

34. Bryant, "Taipi, Tipii, *Typee*," 161.

35. Ibid., 149–50, 165.

36. This discussion is based on Heflin, *Herman Melville's Whaling Years*, 155–57.

37. *Annales maritimes et coloniales* (Paris: Imprimerie Royale, 1844), 3:337–40, 347.

38. Heflin, *Herman Melville's Whaling Years*, 156.

39. Max Radiguet, *Les Derniers Sauvages aux îles Marquises 1842–1859* (1860; Paris: Éditions Phébus, 2001), 95. Originally published under the title *Les derniers sauvages: souvenirs de l'occupation française aux îles Marquises, 1842–1859* (Paris: Hachette, 1860).

40. The first time the name Mohi-a-Taipis is given in Heflin's dissertation, it is spelled "Mohi-a-Taiipiis"; two pages later, it is spelled "Mohi-a-Taipis" ("Herman Melville's Whaling Years," 350, 352).

41. Heflin, *Herman Melville's Whaling Years*, 156. If the name "Mehevi" is based on "Mataheva," it is based on the name of a real person—but that individual is a member of the Tai'oa, not of the Taipi.

42. Charles S. Stewart, *A Visit to the South Seas, in the U.S. Ship* Vincennes, *during the Years 1829 and 1830* (New York: John P. Haven, 1831), 247; see discussion below.

43. Robert C. Suggs, private correspondence, Jan. 31, 2004. I am grateful to Suggs for his great kindness in reading over this chapter and offering many corrections and suggestions.

44. The ship *George and Susan* departed New Bedford on Oct. 17, 1841, and returned on July 12, 1845, with 1,600 barrels of sperm oil. See Alexander Starbuck, *History of the American Whale-Fishery from Its Earliest Inception to the Year 1876* (Waltham, MA: Author, 1878), 374–75.

45. *Annales maritimes et coloniales*, 3:337–38.

46. Logbook of *La Reine Blanche*, entry for July 6, 1842, Archives Nationales, Paris.

47. Radiguet, 94–95.

48. Bryant, "Taipi, Tipii, *Typee*," 149.

49. Hayford, editors' introduction to *Omoo*, xx.

50. Herman Melville to John Murray, Jan. 29, 1847, in *Correspondence*, 78: "You will perceive that there is a chapter in the book which describes a dance in the valley of Tamai. This discription [*sic*] has been modified & adapted from a certain chapter which it was thought best to exclude from Typee. In their dances the Tahitians much resembled the Marquesans (the two groups of islands are not far apart) & thus is the discription faithful in both instances."

51. The official records of the revolt aboard the *Lucy Ann* are in the Mitchell Library, State Library of New South Wales, Sydney, Australia. Their existence was first revealed in 1940 by Ida Leeson, a librarian at the Mitchell Library, in "The Mutiny on the *Lucy Ann*."

52. See Hayford, editors' introduction to *Omoo*, xxviii.

53. Ibid., xxv.

54. As a contributing scholar to the Northwestern-Newberry editions of *Israel Potter* (1982) and *The Piazza Tales and Other Prose Pieces 1839–1860* (1987), I keyed the original pieces by Trumbull and Delano to *Israel Potter* and *Benito Cereno*, respectively.

55. See Mary K. Bercaw, *Melville's Sources* (Evanston, IL: Northwestern Univ. Press, 1987), for verification of information found throughout this paragraph.

56. John Bryant discussed Melville's use of Porter in a study of imperial discourse in "'A Work I Have Never Happened to Meet': Revision and Appropriation in *Typee* and the

Shaping of Imperial Discourse" (paper delivered at the Fourth International Melville Conference, "Melville and the Pacific," Lahaina, Maui, HI, June 7, 2003). This paper was revised and published as "'A Work I Have Never Happened to Meet': Melville's Versions of Porter in *Typee*," *"Whole Oceans Away": Melville and the Pacific,* ed. Jill Barnum, Wyn Kelly, and Christopher Sten (Kent, OH: Kent State Univ. Press, 2007), 83–97.

57. Stewart, 323.

58. *Typee,* 77; Stewart, 247.

59. Stewart, 247–48. The words *abrus precatorius* are italicized in the original.

60. *Typee,* 78; Stewart, 248–49.

61. *Typee,* 77, 78; Stewart, 247.

62. Georg H. von Langsdorff, *Voyages and Travels in Various Parts of the World during the Years 1803, 1804, 1805, 1806, and 1807* (London: Henry Colburn, 1813), 158–59.

63. Langsdorff, 172–73; *Typee,* 145.

64. David Porter, *Journal of a Cruise Made to the Pacific Ocean* (1815; New York: Wiley and Halsted, 1822), 2:37. This quotation comes from chapter 13 and appears on p. 328 of Porter, *Journal of a Cruise Made to the Pacific Ocean,* ed. R. D. Madison and Karen [Alexander] Hamon with an introduction by R. D. Madison (Annapolis, MD: Naval Institute Press, 1986). Hereafter, all references to Porter will be given first to chapter number, then to volume and page number of the 1822 second edition, designated "1822," and finally to page number of the 1986 edition, designated "NIP," which reprints the first edition as well as the entirely new chapters from 1822.

Scholars have wondered which version of Porter's *Journal of a Cruise* Melville consulted, since there is no external evidence of Melville having owned or read a particular copy. Porter's *Journal* was published in 1815 and reprinted in 1822. The second edition was cleaned up: its grammar and spelling were brought into conformity with genteel usage and, most importantly, any passage considered offensive was altered or cut. As R. D. Madison, editor of the 1986 Naval Institute Press edition, writes in the introduction to that volume, the question of which edition Melville used "has perplexed informed readers and scholars ever since [Melville wrote of Porter in *The Encantadas*]—did the sometimes racy Melville have the good fortune to have the first edition of Porter's *Journal* before him as he wrote of the delicious Fayaway? Or was he studying the later edition, with its unique map of the Galapagos? Could he perhaps have seen both?" (xxiii). Madison finally leans toward Melville's use of the 1822 edition with its map for *The Encantadas.* Wilson Heflin himself used the 1822 edition for his early work on *Herman Melville's Whaling Years,* perhaps because the 1822 was the only edition to which he had access. Australian scholar Ruth Blair also used the 1822 edition of Porter in her 1996 Oxford University Press edition of *Typee.* In a paper given at the "Melville and the Pacific" conference in Lahaina in June 2003, John Bryant argued that Melville used the 1822 edition of Porter for *Typee,* based on Melville's use of words found only in that edition ("A Work I Have Never Happened to Meet"). For this work, I have quoted from the 1822 edition. The question of which edition Melville used is not yet settled, however. Melville writes in *Typee* that Porter "is said to have been vastly smitten by the beauty of the ladies" (184)—a notion he could have received from the second edition of 1822, but that would have been much clearer in the first edition of 1815. The engraving of the lovely "Woman of Nooaheevah" only appeared in the first edition (352 [NIP]). This lovely engraving could have inspired the creation of the character of Fayaway. Did Melville track down the 1815 edition? Did he see both? Madison comments: "It would be perfectly in line with Melville's known habits of reading for him to follow up Porter's rebuttal of the English reviewer in the 1822 edition by searching out the racier 1815 edition for a 'first-hand' peep" (personal communication to the author, Apr. 18, 2006).

65. Porter, ch. 13, 2:47 (1822), 339 (NIP).

66. Ibid., ch. 14, 2:69 (1822), 364 (NIP).

67. Ibid., ch. 14, 2:70 (1822), 364 (NIP).

68. The burning of the villages is found in Porter, ch. 15, 2:103 (1822), 401 (NIP).

69. Ibid., ch. 15, 2:98–99 (1822), 397 (NIP). In the first edition, the last line reads: "for the necessity which compelled me to punish a happy and heroic people."

70. Ibid., ch. 15, 2:105 (1822), 403 (NIP).

71. Ibid., ch. 15, 2:99 (1822), 397 (NIP).

72. Ibid., ch. 15, 2:100 (1822), 398 (NIP). "However I may regret . . . incorrigible people" was added in the second edition.

73. Ibid., ch. 13, 2:38 (1822), 329 (NIP).

74. Dening, *Islands and Beaches,* 28.

75. For contemporary descriptions of the Marquesans, see Radiguet. In *The Hidden Worlds of Polynesia,* Suggs writes: "The society described by Melville is not much different from that seen by Porter in Taiohae" (53). See also Anderson's chapter 7, "The Noble Savages of Typee Valley," 117–78.

76. Dening, *Beach Crossings,* 95.

77. Ibid., 95.

78. Radiguet, 98. My thanks to my sister-in-law Gabrielle Hecht for translating this passage for me.

79. Information on the historical James Fitz can be found in the Public Record Office, London: logbook of the HMS *Carysfort,* ADM 57/3714; muster book of HMS *Carysfort,* ADM 38/600, Accountant General's Department, Muster Series 3; and description book of HMS *Carysfort,* ADM 38/7769.

80. Porter, ch. 13, 2:16 (1822), 303 (NIP).

81. Anderson, 115–16, and Ruth Blair, explanatory notes to *Typee* (Oxford: Oxford Univ. Press, 1996), 324. Anderson observes, "Of course it is possible that here, as elsewhere, Melville may have drawn from Porter's experience rather than from any real experience of his own. In default of better proof to the contrary, however, we must assume that Melville finally made his way into this danger-beset paradise [the Taipi valley] about the fifteenth of July, 1842" (116). In his afterword to the Signet Classic edition of *Typee,* Harrison Hayford, like Anderson, ultimately decides to believe the factual basis of the story: "Although we have misgivings about the veracity of many parts of the story, we do know that he visited the Marquesas Islands for one month, though we do not know exactly how he spent that time, and the general outlines of Melville's story may still be credited. After deserting the ship he did cross the mountains with Toby, did descend into the Typee valley and live there for a while" (314).

82. *Typee,* 49; Porter, ch. 15, 2:98 (1822), 397 (NIP).

83. Stewart, in just one example, visits the Taipi valley by sea; noting this, the Ha'apa'a try "to excite a panic [among the Taipi] . . . by spreading the intelligence that Porter's ship [the *Vincennes,* called "Porter's ship" because it was American] was coming up to attack them by water" (314).

84. Bryant repeats this twice, first telling us, "the chapters dealing with Melville's escape (chaps. 6–9) are, to my knowledge, devoid of source borrowings," then later, "But what is telling is that . . . the subsequent chapters 6–9, which relate Melville's escape, are devoid of source borrowings" ("Taipi, Tipii, *Typee,*" 144, 147).

85. Porter, ch. 15, 2:94 (1822), 392 (NIP). Compare the reeds in *Typee,* 37.

86. Ibid., ch. 15, 2:94 (1822), 392 (NIP).

87. Ibid., ch. 15, 2:95 (1822), 393 (NIP).

88. Ibid., ch. 13, 2:24 (1822), 312 (NIP).

89. Stewart tells us that the skin of Piaroro, a Haʻapaʻa chief, "is so perfectly covered with tatau . . . [that] his whole face and head, chest and shoulders, are, from this cause, as black as ever an Othello is pictured to be" (140–41); a large, fat islander described by Stewart is "tataued from head to foot till as black as the darkest of the Congo race" (185). Langsdorff notes: "We saw some old men of the higher ranks, who were punctured over and over to such a degree, that the outlines of each separate figure were scarcely to be distinguished, and the body had an almost negro-like appearance" (119).

90. Porter, ch. 13, 2:46, 337 (NIP).

91. Ibid., ch. 13, 2:46 (1822), 337 (NIP); *Typee*, 88.

92. *Typee* 208; Porter, ch. 13, 2:43 (1822), 335 (NIP).

93. *Typee* 209; Porter, ch. 13, 2:43–44 (1822), 335 (NIP).

94. Porter, ch. 13, 2:38 (1822), 330 (NIP); *Typee*, 154.

95. Porter, ch. 13, 2:39 (1822), 330 (NIP); *Typee*, 154.

96. Porter, ch. 13, 2:39 (1822), 330 (NIP); *Typee*, 154.

97. This statement was deleted in the revised edition of July 1846 (Howard, historical note to *Typee*, 289).

98. Porter, ch. 16, 2:111 (1822), 410 (NIP).

99. Dening, *Islands and Beaches*, 148.

100. Henry A. Wise, *Los Gringos* (New York, 1849 [1850]), 399n. I examined this book myself, but see also Heflin, *Herman Melville's Whaling Years*, 282, n. 84; Anderson, 227–28; and *Melville Log*, 1:149–150.

101. Samuel Garman, *The Galapagos Tortoises*, vol. 30 of *Memoirs of the Museum of Comparative Zoology at Harvard College* (Cambridge, MA: Printed for the Museum, Jan. 1917), 265.

102. Porter, ch. 17, 2:159 (1822), 447 (NIP); *Moby-Dick*, 3.

103. Edward Robarts, *The Marquesan Journal of Edward Robarts*, ed. Greg Dening (Canberra: Australian National Univ. Press, 1974); Jean Cabri, *Précis historique et véritable du séjour de Joseph Kabris, natif de Bordeaux, dans les iles de Mendoca situées dans l'océan Pacifique* (Paris, 1817); Langsdorff, *Voyages and Travels*; Stewart, *A Visit to the South Seas*; Radiguet, *Les Derniers Sauvages* .

104. Herman Melville to Nathaniel Hawthorne, May 1851, in *Correspondence*, 193.

105. Vladimir Nabokov, *Lectures on Literature*, ed. Fredson Bowers (New York: Harcourt Brace Jovanovich, 1980), 5. See beginning of this chapter.

106. T. S. Eliot, "Philip Massinger," *The Sacred Wood: Essays on Poetry and Criticism* (1920; London: Methuen, 1932), 125.

107. John Dryden, "An Essay of Dramatick Poesie," *Prose 1668–1691*, ed. Samuel Holt Monk (Berkeley: Univ. of California Press, 1971), 57.

2. "Six Months at Sea! Yes, Reader, as I Live"

1. Shakespeare, *The Tempest*, 1.1.36–37.

2. Ibid., 1.1.14.

3. Ibid., epilogue, lines 11–12.

4. Heflin, *Herman Melville's Whaling Years*, 10.

5. Rudyard Kipling, *Captains Courageous* (New York: Century, 1897), 88.

6. Ibid., 92–93.

7. Margaret Cohen, "Traveling Genres," *New Literary History* 34 (2003), 486–87. She cites Gilbert Ryle's "Knowing How and Knowing That," in *The Concept of Mind* (London,

1949), 25–61. My thanks to Steve Mentz of St. Johns College, Queens, for first calling my attention to Cohen's article.

8. First published in Samuel Johnson, "Preface to Dryden," *Prefaces Biographical and Critical to the Works of the English Poets* (now known as *The Lives of the English Poets*), vol. 3 (London: J. Nichols, 1779).

9. Greg Dening, *Mr. Bligh's Bad Language: Passion, Power and Theatre on the Bounty* (Cambridge: Cambridge Univ. Press, 1992), 56.

10. Ibid.

11. Sena Jeter Naslund, *Ahab's Wife: Or, The Star-Gazer: A Novel* (New York: William Morrow, 1999). Naslund's lack of knowledge about whaling and seafaring in general leads her to make many mistakes. In the five pages of chapter 30, for example, I count nine errors, everything from serving the crew of a whaleship with thirty platters on deck (crew's meals were served in buckets carried into the fo'c's'le, where each crewman would serve himself, dishing the food into a container that he provided) to describing a whaleship as slender (whaleships were notoriously tubby to provide stability and durability during multiyear voyages) to eating catfish at sea far from land (where on the open ocean would a cook find this freshwater fish?).

12. James Fenimore Cooper, *The Pilot: A Tale of the Sea,* ed. Kay Seymour House, *The Writings of James Fenimore Cooper* (Albany: State Univ. of New York Press, 1986), 5–6.

13. Stan Hugill, *Shanties and Sailors' Songs* (New York: Frederick A. Praeger, 1969), 210. I wish to thank my husband, Craig Edwards, a Wesleyan University–trained ethnomusicologist who served for twenty-one years as a staff musician and later director of music programs at Mystic Seaport, for his assistance with my discussion of sea music.

14. Richard Tobias Greene, letter, *Sandusky Register,* Jan. 13, 1855; reprinted in Clarence Gohdes, "Melville's Friend 'Toby,'" *Modern Language Notes* 59 (Jan. 1944), 53. The story is, in fact, a motif of sailor talk, and versions of it appear throughout the literature. A folkloric trope that reinforces the separation between inexperienced and experienced seamen, it is similar to an "urban legend."

15. Stan Hugill, *Shanties from the Seven Seas* (London: Routledge & Kegan Paul, 1961), 359. In *Moby-Dick,* the line is used in a capstan chantey. But "the girls in Booble Alley" is a floating verse line that can be put in any chantey in which the chanteyman sings about girls, as long as it scans.

16. Quoted in Leonard Huxley, ed., *Jane Welsh Carlyle: Letters to Her Family, 1839–1863* (New York: Doubleday, Page, 1924), v, and quoted again in Janet Ray Edwards, "A Life in Letters: Jane Welsh Carlyle, 1801–1866" (paper delivered at the conference of the Society for Values in Higher Education, Naperville, IL, July 20, 2006), 5. My deep thanks to my mother-in-law, the Carlyle scholar Janet Ray Edwards, who first presented the idea of coterie speech to me and then shared her writings on the subject. For further discussion of coterie speech, see Christopher Stray, ed., *Contributions Towards a Glossary of the Glynne Language by George William, Lord Lyttelton* (Newcastle, UK: Cambridge Scholars Press, 2005), especially vii–xxix, and Christopher Stray, ed., *The Mushri-English Pronouncing Dictionary: A Chapter in 19th-Century Public School Lexicography* (Berkeley, UK: Department of Typography & Graphic Communication, Univ. of Reading, 1996), especially 2–35.

17. "The Eight Famous Fishermen," collected by Helen Creighton from Edward Deal of Seabright, Nova Scotia, in Aug. 1950, in Helen Creighton, *Maritime Folk Songs,* Canada's Atlantic Folklore and Folklife Series 5 (1961; St. John's, Newfoundland, Canada: Breakwater Books 1979), 192. Reference is to Breakwater edition.

18. "Shearing Day," written Charles Murphy in 1832 and collected by Gale Huntington, *Songs the Whalemen Sang* (Barre, MA: Barre, 1964), 154.

19. The bunting chantey "Paddy Boyle's Boots" also contains coterie speech. The reference in the first verse line of the chantey, "We'll pay Paddy Doyle for his boots," has been lost. Nobody knows with certainty what the boots signify. While the phrase itself has became widespread to the point of ubiquity, nobody knows what it means.

20. Joseph Conrad, *The Nigger of the* Narcissus (1897; New York: Doubleday, Doran, 1928), 81.

21. Ibid., 84.

22. Richard Henry Dana, Jr., *Two Years Before the Mast,* ed. Thomas L. Philbrick (1840; New York: Library of America, 2005), 314.

23. Ibid., 316.

24. Conrad, 31.

25. Dana, 99; emphasis in original.

26. Hugill, *Shanties from the Seven Seas,* 477.

27. Ibid., 385.

28. Ibid., 340.

29. Huntington, 149–51.

30. Frederick Pease Harlow, *Chanteying aboard American Ships* (Barre, MA: Barre Gazette, 1962), 207–8. Harlow collected most of the songs in this collection in the 1870s, but the book was not published until ten years after his death on Sept. 10, 1952.

31. Jack London, *The Sea Wolf,* ed. Donald Pizer (1904; New York: Library of America, 1982), 511–12.

32. Frederick Pease Harlow, *The Making of a Sailor or Sea Life aboard a Yankee Square-Rigger* (Salem, MA: Marine Research Society, 1928), 128. Although not published until the end of his life, *The Making of a Sailor* records Harlow's time at sea in the 1870s and is written from his journal, now in the collection of Mystic Seaport Museum.

33. Richard Tobias Greene to Herman Melville, Jan. 4, 1860, in *Correspondence,* 679.

34. Julian Hawthorne, *Nathaniel Hawthorne and His Wife: A Biography* (Boston: Osgood, 1884), 1:407.

35. Society for the Diffusion of Useful Knowledge, "Whales," *The Penny Cyclopædia of the Society for the Diffusion of Useful Knowledge* (London: Charles Knight, 1833–43), 27:272.

36. Philbrick, *In the Heart of the Sea,* 98–99.

37. "Mariner's Cause," *Boston Recorder,* Oct. 18, 1823: 165.

38. "Anecdotes of the Hindoos," *Port-Folio,* Nov. 1, 1827: 377. Originally printed in the *London Weekly Review,* and later reprinted in the *Museum of Foreign Literature, Science, and Art,* May 1828: 17.

39. "The American Seamen's Friend Society," *New-York Mirror,* June 27, 1828: 407.

40. "American Seamen's Friend Society," *New-York Evangelist,* May 14, 1836: 80.

41. "The Neglected Sailor," *Christian Reflector,* Dec. 28, 1842: 2.

42. "Seamen's Cause," *New York Observer and Chronicle,* May 30, 1846: 88.

43. "Mariner's Cause," 165.

44. "American Seamen's Friend Society," 80.

45. "Editorial Gleanings," *Christian Reflector,* May 24, 1843: 81.

46. "Seamen's Cause," 88.

47. "American Seamen's Friend Society," 80.

48. "Editorial Gleanings," 81.

49. "American Seamen's Friend Society," 80.

50. Ibid.

51. Delivered orally by Stan Hugill at the Sea Music Festival, Mystic Seaport Museum, Mystic, CT, in June 1992.

52. Samuel Samuels, *From Forecastle to Cabin* (New York: Harper and Brothers, 1887), 266.

53. Eugene O'Neill, *The Hairy Ape, Plays of Eugene O'Neill* (1922; New York: Boni & Liveright, 1925), 119; scene 1.

54. "Mariner's Cause," 165.

55. Thomas Philbrick discusses the various attitudes toward sailors in his seminal work on sea literature, *James Fenimore Cooper and the Development of American Sea Fiction* (Cambridge, MA: Harvard Univ. Press, 1961).

56. Cooper, 203, 204.

57. Ibid., 285, 287.

58. Conrad, 89.

59. Ibid., 98–99.

60. Ibid., 168.

61. James Russell Lowell, *A Fable for Critics* (1848; Boston: Ticknor and Fields, 1859), 48–49.

62. Evert Duyckinck to George Duyckinck, Mar. 18, 1848, in *Melville Log*, 1:273.

3. "They Say They Don't Like Sailor's Flesh, It's Too Salt"

1. Herodotus, *The History of Herodotus,* book 4, trans. George Rawlinson, Internet Classics Archive, http://classics.mit.edu/Herodotus/history.4.iv.html (accessed Sept. 5, 2007).

2. Pliny the Elder, *Natural History of Pliny,* trans. John Bostock and H. T. Riley (London: George Bell and Sons, 1900), 2:36.

3. I wish to thank my father-in-law, the Reverend Carl Edwards, for first directing me to Pliny the Younger.

4. William Shakespeare, *Othello,* ed. Louis B. Wright and Virginia A. LaMar (Washington, DC: Folger Library, [1957]), 1.3.158–66.

5. Christopher Columbus, *The Journal of Christopher Columbus,* trans. Cecil Jane (New York: Bramhall House, 1960), 52.

6. The CBC reported on Feb. 14, 2005: "The Carib Indians of Dominica are upset over a Walt Disney film that would portray them as cannibals. The film is a sequel to 2003's *Pirates of the Caribbean: The Curse of the Black Pearl,* which starred Johnny Depp and Orlando Bloom. According to Dominica's government, Disney planned to shoot the picture there. A Carib Indian leader told the BBC's website that he objects because there is 'a strong element of cannibalism in the script which cannot be removed.' The Caribs dispute the notion that they descended from cannibals. 'Our ancestors stood up against early European conquerors and because they stood up . . . we were labelled savages and cannibals up to today,' said Carib chief Charles Williams. 'This cannot be perpetuated in movies.'" The indigenous Caribs (Garifuna) issued a press release on June 17, 2006, urging readers to boycott the showing of *Pirates of the Caribbean: Dead Man's Chest* for its denigration of the Garifuna people. Thanks to Dan Lanier for bringing this information to my attention. See CBC, "Carib Indians Protest 'Pirates' Sequel," Feb. 14, 2005, http://www.cbc.ca/story/arts/national/2005/02/14/Arts/pirates050214.html (accessed Aug. 2006).

7. D. Carleton Gajdusek, "Unconventional Viruses and the Origin and Disappearance of Kuru," *Science* 197 (1977), 956; quoted in Arens, "Rethinking Anthropophagy," 51.

8. As discussed in Lawrence Osborne, "Does Man Eat Man? Inside the Great Cannibalism Controversy," *Lingua Franca,* Apr.–May 1997: 32; emphasis in original.

9. Ibid., 32–33.

10. "The Mystery of Kuru," 2008, http://learn.genetics.utah.edu/features/prions/ kuru.cfm (accessed Mar. 2008); "The Sad Tale of Kuru," Oct. 23, 1996, Why Files, http:// whyfiles.org/012mad_cow/6.html (accessed May 2006).

11. Interestingly, in the film *Pirates of the Caribbean: Dead Man's Chest,* the cannibals resemble the popular conception of the natives of New Guinea far more than they do the Caribs, on whom they supposedly are based.

12. Paul Raffaele, "Sleeping with Cannibals: Our Intrepid Reporter Gets up Close and Personal with Remote New Guinea Natives Who Say They Still Eat Their Fellow Tribesmen," *Smithsonian* 37 (Sept. 2006), 57. I wish to thank my mother-in-law, Janet Ray Edwards, and my friend and colleague Dan Lanier, who both sent me copies of this article. The April 2006 issue of *Smithsonian* features an article on artist Caroline Mytinger, whose sojourns to paint natives in the Solomon Islands and New Guinea resulted in portraits of islanders and two books entitled *Headhunting in the Solomon Islands* (1942) and *New Guinea Headhunt* (1946). Although the article never mentions even a claim that she witnessed cannibalism, it casually uses the word "cannibal" to describe natives and claims that the subject of the portrait featured on her second book was "part of a group that had been taken prisoner by the authorities for allegedly beheading and eating 39 [!] members of a neighboring village" (Tessa Decarlo, "A Gibson Girl in New Guinea," *Smithsonian,* 37 [Apr. 2006], 87). Thanks to Priscilla Wells for giving me a copy of this article. It is quite intriguing that within five months *Smithsonian* ran two articles on New Guinea that used cannibal talk without any proof of cannibalism.

13. Raffaele, 53.

14. Ibid., 48; emphasis added. Such headnotes are usually written by an editor rather than by the author.

15. Langsdorff, 143.

16. Ibid., 145–46.

17. Michel de Montaigne, "Of Cannibals," *The Complete Works of Michael de Montaigne,* ed. William Hazlitt (London: John Templeman, 1842 [1845]), [3].

18. Ibid.

19. Ibid., [4].

20. See Aretta J. Stevens (Sister Mary Dominic), "Melville: Sceptic" (PhD diss., Loyola University Chicago, 1967), passim. Other scholars who have studied Melville's use of Montaigne are listed in Bercaw, 104. See also Merton M. Sealts Jr., *Melville's Reading: Revised and Enlarged Edition* (Columbia: Univ. of South Carolina Press, 1988), 199, for a discussion of the edition acquired by Melville.

21. Sanborn, 130; emphasis in original.

22. Langsdorff, 94.

23. Ibid.

24. Ibid., 141.

25. Richard Pryor, *Richard Pryor: Live in Concert* (1979). Filmed at Terrace Theater, Long Beach, CA, Jan. 1979. Directed by Jeff Margolis.

26. Langsdorff, 141.

27. Ibid., 145.

28. Stewart, 276.

29. Ibid., 319.

30. Arens, *Man-Eating Myth,* 168.

31. Ibid.

32. Stewart, 333.

33. Ibid., 331–32.

34. Ibid., 309.

35. Ibid., 356.

36. Ibid., 228, 228, and 259, respectively.

37. Ibid., 255.

38. Ibid., 317.

39. Samuel Taylor Coleridge, "The Rime of the Ancyent Marinere," *The Annotated Ancient Mariner*, ed. Martin Gardner (New York: Meridian, 1965), 208. Originally published in *Lyrical Ballads* in 1798. The lines quoted are 655–57.

40. Porter, ch. 13, 2:41 (1822), 332 (NIP).

41. Ibid., ch. 13, 2:42 (1822), 333 (NIP).

42. Ibid.

43. Ibid., ch. 11, 2:4 (1822), 284 (NIP).

44. Ibid., ch. 15, 2:99 (1822), 397 (NIP). This passage appeared in the 1815 edition as: "Many may censure my conduct as wanton and unjust; they may inquire what necessity could compel me to pursue [the Taipis] into their valley; where, in fact, was any necessity for hostilities with them so long as they left us in quietness at our camp: But let such reflect a moment on our peculiar situation—a handful of men residing among numerous warlike tribes, liable every moment to be attacked by them and all cut off; our only hopes of safety was in convincing them of our great superiority over them."

45. Ibid., ch. 13, 2:42 (1822), 333 (NIP).

46. Ibid., ch. 13, 2:45 (1822), 337 (NIP); emphasis added.

47. Ibid., ch. 13, 2:44 (1822), 335 (NIP); emphasis added.

48. Ibid.

49. Ibid., ch. 16, 2:117–18 (1822), 419 (NIP).

50. Ibid., ch. 16, 2:114 (1822), 415 (NIP).

51. For instance, unusual markings on 160,000-year-old human skull fragments, discovered by paleontologists in Ethiopia and pieced together by physical anthropologist Tim White, as reported in 2003 on National Public Radio and in many newspapers, indicate, according to White, a form of ancestor worship. White claims that similar practices were observed as late as the early twentieth century among tribes in New Guinea. See Terry Gross, interview with Tim White, *Fresh Air*, June 18, 2003, http://www.npr.org/templates/story/story.php?storyId=1301741 (accessed Oct. 6, 2006).

52. Porter, ch. 16, 2:110–11 (1822), 410 (NIP); emphasis added.

53. Sanborn, 17; emphasis in original.

54. Ibid., 16; emphasis in original.

55. Ibid., 9. The Bhabha quotation is from Homi K. Bhabha, *The Location of Culture* (New York: Routledge, 1994), 126.

56. Sanborn, 14.

57. Ibid., 89.

58. Ibid., 86.

59. Ibid., 88.

60. Ibid., 14.

61. For an account of the *Globe* mutiny, see Thomas Farel Heffernan, *Mutiny on the Globe: The Fatal Voyage of Samuel Comstock* (New York: Norton, 2002), and Gregory Gibson, *Demon of the Waters: The True Story of the Mutiny on the Whaleship* Globe (Boston: Little, Brown, 2002).

62. Langsdorff, 141.

63. This list is based on information found in James Cole, "Consuming Passions: Reviewing the Evidence for Cannibalism within the Prehistoric Archaeological Record,"

Assemblage: The Sheffield Graduate Journal of Archaeology 9 (2006), http://www.assemblage .group.shef.ac.uk/issue9/cole.html#keywords (accessed Oct. 6, 2006).

64. Arens, *Man-Eating Myth*, 142; Arens cites H. Johnston, *The Uganda Protectorate* (London: Hutchinson, 1902), 693, as the source of his information.

65. Josiah Roberts and Bernard Magee, "Original Communications," *Massachusetts Magazine*, Mar. 1796: 130.

66. Arens, *Man-Eating Myth*, 10.

67. William Arens, "Cannibalism: An Exchange," with reply by Marshall Sahlins, *New York Review of Books*, Mar. 22, 1979: [45].

68. Ibid., [46]; emphasis in original.

69. Ibid., [47].

70. Peggy Reeves Sanday, *Divine Hunger: Cannibalism as a Cultural System* (Cambridge: Cambridge Univ. Press, 1986), 12–13.

71. Ibid., 9.

72. Ibid., 10.

73. Edgar Allan Poe, "The Fall of the House of Usher," *Collected Works of Edgar Allan Poe*, ed. Thomas Ollive Mabbott, 2 (1839; Cambridge, MA: Belknap Press of Harvard Univ. Press, 1978), 399–400.

74. "Anecdote of Brandt, the Indian Chief," *Museum of Foreign Literature, Science, and Art*, Jan. 1831: 33.

75. Peregrine, "Original Auto-Biography," *New-York Mirror*, Nov. 23, 1833: 165. The sealing captain and explorer Benjamin Morrell published *A Narrative of Four Voyages* in 1832. His account served as the basis for a melodrama entitled "Cannibal Islands" that was produced the following year. The *New-York Mirror* reports: "A melo-drama, taken from 'Morrell's Voyages,' is in rehearsal at this establishment. It is by a well-known writer of this city, whose numerous contributions to the boards have hitherto met with universal favor. The new piece is called the 'Cannibal Islands'" ("The Drama," *New-York Mirror*, Feb. 23, 1833: 271).

76. Lester Janes, "Missionary Intelligence," *Western Christian Advocate*, July 6, 1838: 42.

77. "Statistics 1," *Catholic Telegraph*, Mar. 29, 1838: 121. Asterisks are in the original.

78. "Article 1," *Catholic Telegraph*, June 16, 1836: 231.

79. Langsdorff, 141.

80. Lewis Gaylord Clarke, "Gossip with Readers and Correspondents," *Spirit of the Times*, Oct. 7, 1843: 376.

81. "Flattering Preference," subtopic in column entitled "Varieties," *Anglo American*, Sept. 30, 1843: 548.

82. S. R., "Incidents in a Whaling Voyage," *Friend: A Religious and Literary Journal*, Oct. 14, 1837: 9.

83. Obeyesekere, *Cannibal Talk*, 26–27.

84. Arens, *Man-Eating Myth*, 12.

85. "The Feejee Islands," *New York Observer and Chronicle*, July 12, 1845: 1.

86. "Shakespeare versus Sand," *American Review: A Whig Journal of Politics, Literature, Art and Science*, May 1847: 470.

87. G. A. H., "Article 3," *Littell's Living Age*, Feb. 19, 1848: 356.

88. "The American Merchant," *Prisoner's Friend: A Monthly Magazine Devoted to Criminal Reform*, Nov. 16, 1850: 22.

89. Obeyesekere, *Cannibal Talk*, 155.

90. "Voyage to the Feejee Islands," *Atheneum; or, Spirit of the English Magazines*, July 15, 1820: 401.

91. Ibid.

92. Ibid.

93. "The U.S. Exploring Expedition," *Niles' National Register,* May 20, 1843: 190.

94. Arens, *Man-Eating Myth,* 114–15; Arens, "Rethinking Anthropophagy," 56–61.

95. This question is discussed in Borofsky.

96. C. W. Flanders, introduction to Mary Wallis, *Life in Feejee: Five Years among the Cannibals: A Woman's Account of Voyaging the Fiji Islands aboard the "Zotoff" (1844–49)* (1851; Santa Barbara, CA: Narrative Press, 2002), 5.

97. Wallis, 21–22.

98. Ibid., 21.

99. Ibid., 37.

100. Ibid.

101. Ibid., 55.

102. Sanborn, 17; emphasis in original.

103. Flanders, introduction to Wallis, 8.

104. "Miscellaneous," *Christian Register,* Oct. 18, 1834: 40; "Proceedings of Other Societies," *Missionary Herald,* Oct. 1834: 381.

105. On a much more profound level, William Blake wrote of John Milton in *The Marriage of Heaven and Hell:* "Note. The reason Milton wrote in fetters when he wrote of Angels & God, and at liberty when of Devils & Hell, is because he was a true Poet and of the Devils party without knowing it" (*The Poetry and Prose of William Blake,* ed. David V. Erdman [Garden City, NY: Doubleday, 1970], 35).

106. C., "Some Unconnected Reflections and Remarks," *Gentleman and Lady's Town and Country,* Dec. 1784: 339.

107. "Wesleyan (Eng.) Missionary Society," *Baptist Missionary,* Aug. 1841: 265.

108. "What Can Be More Horrid?" *Trumpet and Universalist,* Sept. 19, 1846: 54.

109. Porter, ch. 13, 2:38 (1822), 329 (NIP).

110. Obeyesekere, *Cannibal Talk,* 156.

111. Ibid., 166.

4. "Their Gestures Shame the Very Brutes"

1. Cohen, 486. See the discussion of "know-how" in chapter 2.

2. Niel Gunson, *Messengers of Grace: Evangelical Missionaries in the South Seas 1797–1860* (Oxford: Oxford Univ. Press, 1978), 60.

3. William Ellis, *Polynesian Researches,* 2nd ed. (New York: J. & J. Harper, 1833), 2:18–19.

4. Ibid., 2:19.

5. Emanuel J. Drechsel, "Sociolinguistic-Ethnohistorical Observations on Pidgin English in *Typee* and *Omoo,*" *"Whole Oceans Away": Melville and the Pacific,* ed. Jill Barnum, Wyn Kelley, and Christopher Sten (Kent, OH: Kent State Univ. Press, 2007), 49.

6. Ibid., 59.

7. Ibid., 50.

8. The information found in this paragraph and those following is based on Tom Hiney, *On the Missionary Trail: A Journey through Polynesia, Asia, and Africa with the London Missionary Society* (New York: Atlantic Monthly Press, 2000), chapter 1.

9. Ibid.

10. Ibid. Note Hiney's incorrect use of sailor talk. The term should be "dropped anchor," not "weighed anchor."

11. James Wilson, *A Missionary Voyage to the Southern Pacific Ocean Performed in the Years 1796, 1797, 1798, in the Ship* Duff (London: Printed by S. Gosnell for T. Chapman, 1799), 5–6.

12. Gunson, 12.

13. Ibid., 270.

14. Jorgen Jorgensen, *State of Christianity in the Island of Otaheite* (London, 1811), 98–101; quoted in Gunson, 97.

15. Gunson, 109.

16. Ibid., 35.

17. Wilson, 3.

18. Charles Barff, candidates' papers, London Missionary Society, 1816; quoted in Gunson, 53.

19. John Williams, candidates' papers, London Missionary Society, July 1816; quoted in Gunson, 50.

20. William Law, candidates' papers, London Missionary Society, 1851; quoted in Gunson, 62.

21. Gunson, 48.

22. Ibid., 332.

23. Ibid., 80.

24. Walter James Davis, Aug. 9, 1856, missionaries' letters, Australian Wesleyan Methodist Missionary Society, Tonga, in Methodist overseas missions (Sydney); quoted in Gunson, 100, with emphasis added.

25. George Pratt, Sept. 6, 1841, London Missionary Society, South Seas letters; quoted in Gunson, 325.

26. Ellis, 2:17.

27. George Platt, Apr. 12, 1840, London Missionary Society, South Seas letters; quoted in Gunson, 61, with emphasis in the original.

28. Gunson, 121.

29. J. S. H. Royce, journal, Feb. 19, 1860, Methodist overseas missions (Sydney); quoted in Gunson, 150.

30. Gunson, 162.

31. See Herbert, 27.

32. Wallis, 346.

33. Gunson, 157.

34. Ibid.

35. The *Journal* was partially written as Morrison awaited trial for mutiny in 1792, and completed after he was acquitted. It was later edited by Owen Rutter and published by the Golden Cockerell Press in London in 1935. See Dening, *Mr. Bligh's Bad Language,* 74.

36. See Gunson, 112.

37. Ibid., 255.

38. Ellis, 2:19.

39. Mark Twain, "The 'Jumping Frog': In English. Then in French. Then Clawed Back into a Civilized Language Once More, by Patient, Unremunerated Toil," *Collected Tales, Sketches, Speeches, & Essays: 1852–1890,* ed. Louis J. Budd (1875; New York: Library of America, 1992), 602–03.

40. Gunson, 237.

41. George Turner, *Nineteen Years in Polynesia: Missionary Life, Travels and Researches in the Islands of the Pacific* (London, 1861), 138–39; quoted in Gunson, 221.

42. Samuel Waterhouse, copy of diary, correspondence from S. Waterhouse, Mitchell Library, State Library of New South Wales, Sydney, Australia; quoted in Gunson, 217–18.

43. Mark Twain, *The Adventures of Huckleberry Finn,* ed. Thomas Cooley, Norton Critical 3d ed. (1884; New York: Norton, 1999), 89–90.

44. Ellis, 1:77.

45. Joseph Waterhouse to G. M. Waterhouse and T. Padman, Dec. 12, 1851, Waterhouse correspondence, Mitchell Library, State Library of New South Wales, Sydney, Australia; quoted in Gunson, 178; emphasis in original.

46. Joseph Waterhouse to T. Padman, Aug. 30, 1852, Waterhouse correspondence; quoted in Gunson, 179.

47. Anonymous, MS history of Tonga, copy in the Department of Pacific and Southeast Asian History, Australian National Univ., Canberra; quoted in Gunson, 298, with editorial insertion and ellipsis in Gunson.

48. See Gunson, 392, n. 67.

49. Ellis, 2:63–64.

50. Ibid., 2:56.

51. *Polynesian,* Nov. 26, 1853; quoted in Busch, 17.

52. Busch, 105.

53. James Chase and Thomas Turner to the London Missionary Society, Mar. 26, 1841; quoted in Busch, 107.

54. Gunson, 351.

55. Dening, *Islands and Beaches,* 130. Much of the following discussion of beachcombers is based on Dening.

56. Ibid., 142.

57. The names of all these vessels except the *George and Susan* come from Dening, *Islands and Beaches,* 136. The information on the *George and Susan* comes from the work I did editing Wilson Heflin's *Herman Melville's Whaling Years.*

58. Dening, *Islands and Beaches,* 137.

59. Anderson, 467, n. 15.

60. Richard M. Fletcher, "Melville's Use of Marquesan," *American Speech* 39 (May 1964), 138. For a related discussion of Melville's use of pidgin, see Drechsel. Just as Fletcher finds some of Melville's Marquesan renderings "patent gibberish" (137), Drechsel finds Melville taking "literary license" (59) in his use of pidgin, especially in *Omoo.*

61. Ibid., 137. Interestingly, Fletcher misquotes *Typee.* Melville wrote: "'Toby pemi ena' (Toby has arrived here)" (245). This misquotation most likely occurs in the 1892 edition that is Fletcher's source. Fletcher does not tell us which edition of *Omoo* he has consulted, but the only differences between his quotation and that in the Northwestern-Newberry edition are minor punctuation variants.

62. Dening, *Islands and Beaches,* 105.

63. Busch, 92. See chapter 1, note 21, for further discussion of desertion.

64. Gunson, 152.

65. Ellis, 2:35.

66. Ibid., 2:36.

67. Ibid., 2:42.

68. Quoted in Ellis, 2:43.

69. George Vason, *An Authentic Narrative of Four Years' Residence at Tongataboo* (London, 1810); recounted by Gunson, 154.

70. Ibid.

71. Ellis mentions Caw on 2:59.

72. John Jefferson, July 25, 1804, London Missionary Society, South Seas journals, 22; quoted in Gunson, 98, with emphasis added.

73. John Jefferson, Oct. 22, 1804, London Missionary Society, South Seas journals, 22; quoted in Gunson, 169.

74. Ellis, 2:31.

75. J. S. H. Royce, journal, May 3 and 19, 1857, Methodist Overseas missions (Sydney); quoted in Gunson, 168.

76. Ellis, 3:159.

77. Ibid.

78. Melville mentions Aotooroo (Ahutoru) in *Omoo*, 66.

79. "Lewis Keah," *Religious Intelligencer,* Dec. 23, 1820: 496; reprinted in *Religious Remembrancer,* Jan. 6, 1821: 79.

80. Melville mentions Omai in *Omoo*, 66.

81. Ministry of Interior to king, Aug. 1, 1846, Ministry of Interior Misc., Archives of Hawaii, Honolulu; quoted in Busch, 46.

82. Dening, *Islands and Beaches,* 3.

83. Hugh Thomas, June 18, 1818, London Missionary Society, South Seas letters; quoted in Gunson, 197; emphasis in original.

84. Mary Elizabeth Parker, Aug. 10, 1833, "Intimate Diary of Religious Thoughts," vol. 1, Hawaiian Mission Children's Society; quoted in Herbert, 136.

85. Mary Elizabeth Parker, Aug. 12, 1833, journal letter, Nov. 23, 1832, to Aug. 18, 1833, Houghton Library, Harvard University, Cambridge, MA; quoted in Herbert, 136.

86. Harriet Beecher Stowe, *Uncle Tom's Cabin,* ed. Elizabeth Ammons, Norton Critical ed. (1852; New York: Norton, 1994), 245–46.

87. Richard Armstrong, "A Sketch of Marquesan Character," *Hawaiian Spectator* (1838), 11; quoted in Gunson, 198.

88. John Whewell, Aug. 4, 1856, Australasian Wesleyan Methodist Missionary Society, Tonga, Missionaries' letters, Methodist Overseas missions (Sydney); quoted in Gunson, 317.

89. Armstrong, "A Sketch," 11; quoted in Gunson, 198.

90. Thomas Williams, 1850, quoted by G. C. Henderson, ed., *The Journal of Thomas Williams, Missionary in Fiji, 1840–1853,* 2 vols., Sydney, and in turn quoted in Gunson, 212.

5. "CANNIBAL OLD ME"

1. Daniel Defoe, *The Life & Strange Surprizing Adventures of Robinson Crusoe* (1719; Oxford: Blackwell, 1927), 1–2.

2. Jonathan Swift, *Gulliver's Travels,* ed. Albert J. Rivero, Norton Critical ed. (1726; New York: Norton, 2002), 15.

3. Tobias Smollett, *The Adventures of Roderick Random* (1748; London: J. M. Dent & Sons, 1927), 9.

4. Frederick Marryat, *Mr. Midshipman Easy* (1836; London: J. M. Dent & Sons, 1928), 3.

5. Edgar Allan Poe, *The Narrative of Arthur Gordon Pym, of Nantucket, The Imaginary Voyages,* ed. Burton R. Pollin (1838; Boston: Twayne, 1981), 57.

6. See Bercaw, items 196 (Defoe), 683 (Swift), 654 (Smollett), 480 (Marryat), 561 (Poe), 189 (Dana), 167 (Cooper).

7. Dana, 5.

8. Cooper, 11.

9. Poe, *Pym*, 65.

10. Gilbert Haven and Thomas Russell, eds., *Father Taylor, the Sailor Preacher: Incidents and Anecdotes of Rev. Edward T. Taylor* (Boston: B. B. Russell, 1872), 151.

11. Ibid., 217.

12. Ibid., 180.

13. Ibid., 182.

14. The chronology of Melville's time aboard the *Lucy Ann,* incarcerated on Tahiti, and wandering on Eimeo is set out and documented in chapter 17, "The Troublesome Crew of the Lucy Ann," and the beginning of chapter 18, "Nantucket Whaler," of Heflin, *Herman Melville's Whaling Years,* 158–78.

15. The Society for the Diffusion of Useful Knowledge was founded in 1826 to give the rapidly expanding reading public the "right" kind of knowledge. It disbanded in 1848 but during its years of existence published *The Penny Cyclopædia of the Society for the Diffusion of Useful Knowledge* (1833–43), which was the encyclopedia used by Melville.

16. Twain, *Huckleberry Finn,* 5.

17. Armand Bruat was governor of Tahiti after the island became a French protectorate in 1843.

18. Evert Duyckinck to George Duyckinck, Dec. 15, 1846, *Melville Log,* 1:230.

19. Herman Melville to John Murray, Mar. 25, 1848, in *Correspondence,* 106.

20. The obituary notice of John Hamilton Moore that appeared in *Gentleman's Magazine* on Dec. 30, 1807 lists Moore as "late teacher of Navigation on Tower-Hill, author of Moore's Navigation" (1174). He was the author of *The Practical Navigator, and Seaman's New Daily Assistant,* originally published in England in 1722.

21. Herman Melville to John Murray, Mar. 25, 1848, in *Correspondence,* 106.

22. London *Athenaeum* 117 (Mar. 24, 1849): 296–98; quoted in Elizabeth S. Foster, historical note to *Mardi,* by Herman Melville, ed. Harrison Hayford, Hershel Parker, and G. Thomas Tanselle (Evanston and Chicago: Northwestern Univ. Press and the Newberry Library, 1970), 665.

23. The crew list of the *St. Lawrence* lists Robert Jackson, born in New York; residence New York; age thirty-one; height five feet, six inches; complexion light; hair brown. According to a certificate attached to the crew list signed by Francis B. Ogden, American consul at Liverpool, Aug. 6, 1839, Jackson was one of five men who deserted before the return voyage. See crew list of the *St. Lawrence,* "This Port In: Aug. 1839 to Sept. 1839" (box 3), crew lists, 1803–1919, New York, NA-RG36 (New York).

24. Herman Melville to Richard Bentley, June 5, 1849, in *Correspondence,* 132.

25. Herman Melville to Lemuel Shaw, Apr. 23, 1849, in *Correspondence,* 130.

26. Herman Melville to Richard Bentley, June 5, 1849, in *Correspondence,* 132.

27. Herman Melville to Lemuel Shaw, Oct. 6, 1849, in *Correspondence,* 138.

28. Richard H. Brodhead, ed., *New Essays on "Moby-Dick"* (New York: Cambridge Univ. Press, 1986), 6.

29. Dana, 319.

30. William Shakespeare, *King Lear,* ed. Horace Howard Furness, New Variorum Edition, 7th ed. (Philadelphia: Lippincott, 1880), 5.3.311–12.

31. Mason Locke Weems, *The Life and Remarkable Actions of George Washington,* ed. Peter S. Onuf (c. 1800; Amonk, NY: M. E. Sharpe, 1996).

32. Rachela Permenter discussed the Melville-Dylan connection in "Modern Times: The Never-Ending Melville/Dylan Connection" (paper delivered at the Sixth International

Melville Conference, "Hearts of Darkness: Melville and Conrad in the Space of World Cultures," Szczecin, Poland, Aug. 6, 2007), which I heard after I had written the above, but she focuses on different elements than I do.

33. "More Henry Timrod Lines on *Modern Times*" (accessed Sept. 5, 2006), scottw .alby.qwest.net.

34. "Dylan Pool Discussion," http://pool.dylantree.com (accessed Sept. 5, 2006).

35. Suzanne Vega, "The Ballad of Henry Timrod," *New York Times,* Sept. 17, 2006.

36. Dryden, "An Essay of Dramatick Poesie," 57.

37. Thomas Jefferson to Isaac McPherson, Aug. 13, 1813, *The Life and Selected Writings of Thomas Jefferson,* ed. Adrienne Koch and William Peden (New York: Random House, 1944), 630.

38. See Robin Grey, ed., *Melville and Milton,* special issue of *Leviathan: A Journal of Melville Studies* 4.1–2 (2002), which includes a complete transcription of Melville's marginalia (117–204).

⁓ Works Cited

Melville Texts

Correspondence. Ed. Lynn Horth. Evanston and Chicago: Northwestern University Press and the Newberry Library, 1993.
Israel Potter. Ed. Harrison Hayford, Hershel Parker, and G. Thomas Tanselle. Evanston and Chicago: Northwestern University Press and the Newberry Library, 1982.
Mardi. Ed. Harrison Hayford, Hershel Parker, and G. Thomas Tanselle, with historical note by Elizabeth S. Foster. Evanston and Chicago: Northwestern University Press and the Newberry Library, 1970.
The Melville Log: A Documentary Life of Herman Melville 1819–1891. Ed. Jay Leyda. 2 vols. New York: Harcourt, Brace, 1951.
Moby-Dick. Ed. Harrison Hayford, Hershel Parker, and G. Thomas Tanselle. Evanston and Chicago: Northwestern University Press and the Newberry Library, 1988.
Omoo. Ed. Harrison Hayford, Hershel Parker, and G. Thomas Tanselle. Evanston and Chicago: Northwestern University Press and the Newberry Library, 1968.
The Piazza Tales and Other Prose Pieces 1839–1860. Ed. Harrison Hayford et al. Evanston and Chicago: Northwestern University Press and the Newberry Library, 1987.
Redburn. Ed. Harrison Hayford, Hershel Parker, and G. Thomas Tanselle. Evanston and Chicago: Northwestern University Press and the Newberry Library, 1969.
Typee. Ed. Harrison Hayford, Hershel Parker, and G. Thomas Tanselle, with historical note by Leon Howard. Evanston and Chicago: Northwestern University Press and the Newberry Library, 1968.
White-Jacket. Ed. Harrison Hayford, Hershel Parker, and G. Thomas Tanselle. Evanston and Chicago: Northwestern University Press and the Newberry Library, 1970.

Archival Documents

Alexander, William Patterson. Journal Letter to Rufus Anderson. September 4, 1833, to May 13, 1834. Houghton Library, Harvard University, Cambridge, MA.

Annales maritimes et coloniales. Vol. 3. Paris: Imprimerie Royale, 1844.

Armstrong, Robert. "Journal Written at the Island of Nuuhiva." Entries from August 21, 1833, to March 22, 1834. Houghton Library, Harvard University, Cambridge, MA.

Barff, Charles. Candidates' Papers. London Missionary Society. 1816. Quoted in Niel Gunson, *Messengers of Grace: Evangelical Missionaries in the South Seas 1797–1860.* Oxford: Oxford University Press, 1978.

British Consular Papers, Tahiti, vol. 8. Reference number ML MSS 24/8: FM4/582. Mitchell Library, State Library of New South Wales, Sydney, Australia.

British Consular Records of the Revolt aboard the *Lucy Ann.* Mitchell Library, State Library of New South Wales, Sydney, Australia. Reprinted as "Revolt Documents" and edited by Harrison Hayford. *Omoo.* By Herman Melville. Ed. Harrison Hayford and Walter Blair. New York: Hendricks House, 1969. 309–39.

Certificate of John Stetson, Lahaina, June 2, 1843. New Bedford Whaling Museum, New Bedford, MA.

Chase, James, and Thomas Turner. Letter to the London Missionary Society. March 26, 1841. Council for World Mission Archives, University of London. Quoted in Briton Cooper Busch. *"Whaling Will Never Do for Me": The American Whaleman in the Nineteenth Century.* Lexington: University Press of Kentucky, 1994.

Crew List of the *St. Lawrence.* "This Port In: Aug. 1839 to Sept. 1839." Box 3. Crew Lists, 1803–1919, New York. NA-RG36. National Archives Regional Office, New York.

Davis, Walter James. August 9, 1856. Missionaries' Letters. Australian Wesleyan Methodist Missionary Society, Tonga. Methodist Overseas Missions, Sydney. Quoted in Niel Gunson, *Messengers of Grace: Evangelical Missionaries in the South Seas 1797–1860.* Oxford: Oxford University Press, 1978.

Description Book of HMS *Carysfort.* ADM 38/7769. Public Record Office, London.

History of Tonga. Manuscript. Copy in the Department of Pacific and Southeast Asian History. Australian National University, Canberra. Quoted in Niel Gunson, *Messengers of Grace: Evangelical Missionaries in the South Seas 1797–1860.* Oxford: Oxford University Press, 1978.

Jefferson, John. July 25, 1804. London Missionary Society, South Seas Journals. Quoted in Niel Gunson, *Messengers of Grace: Evangelical Missionaries in the South Seas 1797–1860.* Oxford: Oxford University Press, 1978.

———. October 22, 1804. London Missionary Society, South Seas Journals. Quoted in Niel Gunson, *Messengers of Grace: Evangelical Missionaries in the South Seas 1797–1860.* Oxford: Oxford University Press, 1978.

Law, William. Candidates' Papers. London Missionary Society. 1851. Quoted in Niel Gunson, *Messengers of Grace: Evangelical Missionaries in the South Seas 1797–1860.* Oxford: Oxford University Press, 1978.

Logbook of the HMS *Carysfort.* ADM 57/3714. Public Record Office, London.

Logbook of the *Charles.* Kendall Collection. New Bedford Whaling Museum, New Bedford, MA.

Logbook of the *Florida,* ODHS 763, New Bedford Whaling Museum, New Bedford, MA. Quoted in Briton Cooper Busch. *"Whaling Will Never Do for Me": The American Whaleman in the Nineteenth Century.* Lexington: University Press of Kentucky, 1994.

Logbook of *La Reine Blanche.* Archives Nationales, Paris.

Logbook of the *Potomac.* Peabody-Essex Institute, Salem, MA.

Ministry of Interior. Letter to King. August 1, 1846. Ministry of Interior Miscellaneous, Archives of Hawaii, Honolulu. Quoted in Briton Cooper Busch. *"Whaling Will Never Do for Me": The American Whaleman in the Nineteenth Century.* Lexington: University Press of Kentucky, 1994.

"Miscellaneous Letters 1838–1846." Box 30. Consular Posts: Honolulu, HI. RG84: Records of Foreign Service Posts. National Archives, Washington, DC.

Muster Book of HMS *Carysfort*. ADM 38/600, Accountant General's Department, Muster Series 3. Public Record Office, London.

Parker, Benjamin Wyman. "Joint Communication of Messrs. Alexander, Armstrong & Parker." April 10, 1834. Houghton Library, Harvard University, Cambridge, MA.

Parker, Mary Elizabeth. August 10, 1833. "Intimate Diary of Religious Thoughts." Volume 1. Hawaiian Mission Children's Society. Quoted in T. Walter Herbert, Jr. *Marquesan Encounters: Melville and the Meaning of Civilization*. Cambridge, MA: Harvard University Press, 1980.

Platt, George. April 12, 1840. London Missionary Society, South Seas Letters. Quoted in Niel Gunson, *Messengers of Grace: Evangelical Missionaries in the South Seas 1797–1860*. Oxford: Oxford University Press, 1978.

Pratt, George. September 6, 1841. London Missionary Society, South Seas Letters. Quoted in Niel Gunson, *Messengers of Grace: Evangelical Missionaries in the South Seas 1797–1860*. Oxford: Oxford University Press, 1978.

Royce, J. S. H. Journal. February 19, 1860. Methodist Overseas Missions, Sydney. Quoted in Niel Gunson, *Messengers of Grace: Evangelical Missionaries in the South Seas 1797–1860*. Oxford: Oxford University Press, 1978.

———. Journal. May 3 and 19, 1857. Methodist Overseas Missions, Sydney. Quoted in Niel Gunson, *Messengers of Grace: Evangelical Missionaries in the South Seas 1797–1860*. Oxford: Oxford University Press, 1978.

Thomas, Hugh. June 18, 1818. London Missionary Society, South Seas Letters. Quoted in Niel Gunson, *Messengers of Grace: Evangelical Missionaries in the South Seas 1797–1860*. Oxford: Oxford University Press, 1978.

Waterhouse, Joseph. Letter to G. M. Waterhouse and T. Padman. December 12, 1851. Waterhouse Correspondence. Mitchell Library, State Library of New South Wales, Sydney. Quoted in Niel Gunson, *Messengers of Grace: Evangelical Missionaries in the South Seas 1797–1860*. Oxford: Oxford University Press, 1978.

———. Letter to T. Padman. August 30, 1852. Waterhouse Correspondence. Mitchell Library, State Library of New South Wales, Sydney. Quoted in Niel Gunson, *Messengers of Grace: Evangelical Missionaries in the South Seas 1797–1860*. Oxford: Oxford University Press, 1978.

Waterhouse, Samuel. Copy of Diary. Correspondence from S. Waterhouse. Mitchell Library, State Library of New South Wales, Sydney. Quoted in Niel Gunson, *Messengers of Grace: Evangelical Missionaries in the South Seas 1797–1860*. Oxford: Oxford University Press, 1978.

Whewell, John. August 4, 1856. Missionaries' Letters. Australian Wesleyan Methodist Missionary Society, Tonga. Methodist Overseas Missions, Sydney. Quoted in Niel Gunson, *Messengers of Grace: Evangelical Missionaries in the South Seas 1797–1860*. Oxford: Oxford University Press, 1978.

Williams, John. Candidates' Papers. London Missionary Society. July 1816. Quoted in Niel Gunson, *Messengers of Grace: Evangelical Missionaries in the South Seas 1797–1860*. Oxford: Oxford University Press, 1978.

EIGHTEENTH- AND NINETEENTH-CENTURY NEWSPAPER PIECES

"The American Merchant." *Prisoner's Friend: A Monthly Magazine Devoted to Criminal Reform*. November 16, 1850: 22.

"The American Seamen's Friend Society." *New-York Mirror*. June 27, 1828: 407.

"American Seamen's Friend Society." *New-York Evangelist*. May 14, 1836: 80.

"Anecdote of Brandt, the Indian Chief." *Museum of Foreign Literature, Science, and Art*. January 1831: 33.

"Anecdotes of the Hindoos." *Port-Folio*. November 1, 1827: 377. Originally printed in the *London Weekly Review*, and later reprinted in the *Museum of Foreign Literature, Science, and Art*, May 1828: 17.

Armstrong, Richard. "A Sketch of Marquesan Character." *Hawaiian Spectator*. 1838: 11. Quoted in Niel Gunson, *Messengers of Grace: Evangelical Missionaries in the South Seas 1797–1860*. Oxford: Oxford University Press, 1978.

"Article 1." *Catholic Telegraph*. June 16, 1836: 231.

C. "Some Unconnected Reflections and Remarks." *Gentleman and Lady's Town and Country*. December 1784: 339.

Clarke, Lewis Gaylord. "Gossip with Readers and Correspondents." *Spirit of the Times*, October 7, 1843: 376.

[Daniels, Charles F.] Review of *Typee*. *Morning Courier and New-York Enquirer*. April 17, 1846. Reprinted in *Melville Log*, 1:211–12.

"The Drama." *New-York Mirror*. February 23, 1833: 271.

"Editorial Gleanings." *Christian Reflector*. May 24, 1843: 81.

"The Feejee Islands." *New York Observer and Chronicle*. July 12, 1845: 1.

"Flattering Preference." Subtopic in column entitled Varieties. *Anglo American*. September 30, 1843: 548.

G. A. H. "Article 3." *Littell's Living Age*. February 19, 1848: 356.

Greene, Richard Tobias. Letter. *Sandusky Register*. January 13, 1855. Reprinted in Clarence Gohdes. "Melville's Friend 'Toby.'" *Modern Language Notes* 59 (January 1944), 52–55.

———. "To the Editor of the Buffalo Com. Adv." *Buffalo Commercial Advertiser*. July 1, 1846.

———. "Typee. Toby's Own Story." *Buffalo Commercial Advertiser*. July 11, 1846: 2.

Janes, Lester. "Missionary Intelligence." *Western Christian Advocate*. July 6, 1838: 42.

"Lewis Keah." *Religious Intelligencer*. December 23, 1820: 496. Reprinted in *Religious Remembrancer*. January 6, 1821: 79.

"Mariner's Cause." *Boston Recorder*. October 18, 1823: 165.

"Miscellaneous." *Christian Register*. October 18, 1834: 40.

"The Neglected Sailor." *Christian Reflector*. December 28, 1842: 2.

Obituary Notice of John Hamilton Moore. *Gentleman's Magazine*. December 30, 1807: 1174.

Polynesian. November 26, 1853. Quoted in Briton Cooper Busch. *"Whaling Will Never Do for Me": The American Whaleman in the Nineteenth Century*. Lexington: University Press of Kentucky, 1994.

Peregrine. "Original Auto-Biography." *New-York Mirror*. November 23, 1833: 165.

"Proceedings of Other Societies." *Missionary Herald*. October 1834: 381.

Review of *Mardi*. London *Athenaeum*, 177. March 24, 1849: 296–98. Quoted in Elizabeth S. Foster, historical note to *Mardi* by Herman Melville. Ed. Harrison Hayford, Hershel Parker, and G. Thomas Tanselle. Evanston and Chicago: Northwestern University Press and the Newberry Library, 1970.

Roberts, Josiah, and Bernard Magee. "Original Communications." *Massachusetts Magazine*. March 1796: 130.

"Seamen's Cause." *New York Observer and Chronicle*. May 30, 1846: 88.

"Shakespeare versus Sand." *American Review: A Whig Journal of Politics, Literature, Art and Science*. May 1847: 470.

S. R. "Incidents in a Whaling Voyage." *Friend: A Religious and Literary Journal*. October 14, 1837: 9.

"Statistics 1." *Catholic Telegraph*. March 29, 1838: 121.

"The U.S. Exploring Expedition." *Niles' National Register*. May 20, 1843: 190.

"Voyage to the Feejee Islands." *Atheneum; or, Spirit of the English Magazines*. July 15, 1820: 401.

"Wesleyan (Eng.) Missionary Society." *Baptist Missionary*. August 1841: 265.

"What Can Be More Horrid?" *Trumpet and Universalist*. September 19, 1846: 54.

Published Works

Abrahams, Roger D. *Deep the Water, Shallow the Shore: Three Essays on Shantying in the West Indies*. Mystic, CT: Mystic Seaport Museum, 2002. Originally published as Number 60. American Folklore Society Monographs. Austin: University of Texas Press, 1974.

Alexander, Mary Charlotte. *William Patterson Alexander in Kentucky, the Marquesas, Hawaii*. Honolulu, 1934.

Altick, Richard D. *The Scholar Adventurers*. New York: Macmillan, 1950.

Anderson, Charles Roberts. *Melville in the South Seas*. New York: Columbia University Press, 1939.

Arens, William. "Cannibalism: An Exchange." With Reply by Marshall Sahlins. *New York Review of Books*. March 22, 1979: 45–47.

———. *The Man-Eating Myth: Anthropology and Anthropophagy*. New York: Oxford University Press, 1979.

———. "Rethinking Anthropophagy." *Cannibalism and the Colonial World*. Ed. Francis Barker, Peter Hulme, and Margaret Iversen. Cambridge: Cambridge University Press, 1998. 39–62.

Bercaw, Mary K. *Melville's Sources*. Evanston, IL: Northwestern University Press, 1987.

Bhabha, Homi K. *The Location of Culture*. New York: Routledge, 1994. Quoted in Geoffrey Sanborn, *The Sign of the Cannibal: Melville and the Making of a Postcolonial Reader*. Durham, NC: Duke University Press, 1998.

Blake, William. *The Marriage of Heaven and Hell*. *The Poetry and Prose of William Blake*. Ed. David V. Erdman. Garden City, NY: Doubleday, 1970. 33–44.

Blair, Ruth. Explanatory Notes. *Typee*. Ed. Ruth Blair. Oxford: Oxford University Press, 1996. 318–35.

Borofsky, Robert. "CA Forum on Theory in Anthropology: Cook, Lono, Obeyesekere, and Sahlins." *Current Anthropology* 38 (April 1997), 255–82.

Brodhead, Richard H., ed. *New Essays on "Moby-Dick."* New York: Cambridge University Press, 1986.

Bryant, John. "Taipi, Tipii, *Typee*: Place, Memory, and Text." *ESQ: A Journal of the American Renaissance* 51.1–3 (2005), 137–68.

———. "'A Work I Have Never Happened to Meet': Melville's Versions of Porter in *Typee*." *"Whole Oceans Away": Melville and the Pacific*. Ed. Jill Barnum, Wyn Kelley, and Christopher Sten. Kent, OH: Kent State University Press, 2007. 83–97.

———. "'A Work I Have Never Happened to Meet': Revision and Appropriation in *Typee* and the Shaping of Imperial Discourse." Paper delivered at the Fourth International Melville Conference, "Melville and the Pacific," Lahaina, Maui, HI, June 7, 2003.

Busch, Briton Cooper. *"Whaling Will Never Do for Me": The American Whaleman in the Nineteenth Century*. Lexington: University Press of Kentucky, 1994.

Cabri, Jean. *Précis historique et véritable du séjour de Joseph Kabris, natif de Bordeaux, dans les iles de Mendoca situées dans l'océan Pacifique*. Paris, 1817.

CBC. "Carib Indians Protest 'Pirates' Sequel." February 14, 2005. http://www.cbc.ca/story/arts/national/2005/02/14/Arts/pirates050214.html. Accessed August 2006.

Coan, Titus. *Life in Hawaii. An Autobiographic Sketch of Mission Life and Labors*. New York: Anson D. F. Randolph, 1882.

Cohen, Margaret. "Traveling Genres." *New Literary History* 34 (2003), 481–99.

Cole, James. "Consuming Passions: Reviewing the Evidence for Cannibalism within the Prehistoric Archaeological Record." *Assemblage: The Sheffield Graduate Journal of Archaeology* 9. http://www.assemblage.group.shef.ac.uk/issue9/cole.html#keywords. Accessed October 6, 2006.

Coleridge, Samuel Taylor. "The Rime of the Ancyent Marinere." *The Annotated Ancient Mariner*. Ed. Martin Gardner. New York: Meridian, 1965. 185–208. Originally published in *Lyrical Ballads* in 1798.

Columbus, Christopher. *The Journal of Christopher Columbus*. Trans. Cecil Jane. New York: Bramhall House, 1960.

Conrad, Joseph. *The Nigger of the* Narcissus. New York: Doubleday, Doran, 1928. Originally published in 1897.

Cooper, James Fenimore. *The Pilot: A Tale of the Sea*. Ed. Kay Seymour House. *The Writings of James Fenimore Cooper*. Albany: State University of New York Press, 1986. Originally published in 1824.

Crain, Caleb. "Lovers of Human Flesh: Homosexuality and Cannibalism in Melville's Novels." *American Literature* 66 (March 1994), 25–53.

Creighton, Helen. *Maritime Folk Songs*. Canada's Atlantic Folklore and Folklife Series 5. St. John's, Newfoundland, Canada: Breakwater Books, 1979. Originally published in 1961.

Creighton, Margaret S. *Rites and Passages: The Experience of American Whaling, 1830–1870*. Cambridge: Cambridge University Press, 1995.

Dana, Richard Henry, Jr. *Two Years Before the Mast*. Ed. Thomas L. Philbrick. New York: Library of America, 2005. Originally published in 1840.

Decarlo, Tessa. "A Gibson Girl in New Guinea." *Smithsonian* 37 (April 2006), 80–89.

Defoe, Daniel. *The Life & Strange Surprizing Adventures of Robinson Crusoe*. Oxford: Blackwell, 1927. Originally published in 1719.

Delbanco, Andrew. *Melville: His World and Work*. New York: Alfred A. Knopf, 2005.

Dening, Greg. *Beach Crossings: Voyaging across Times, Cultures, and Self*. Philadelphia: University of Pennsylvania Press, 2004.

———. *Islands and Beaches: Discourse on a Silent Land: Marquesas 1774–1880*. Honolulu: University Press of Hawaii, 1980.

———. *Mr. Bligh's Bad Language: Passion, Power and Theatre on the Bounty*. Cambridge: Cambridge University Press, 1992.

Douglass, Frederick. *Narrative of the Life of Frederick Douglass, An American Slave. Written by Himself. The Frederick Douglass Papers*. 2nd series. Ed. John W. Blassingame, John R. McKivigan, and Peter P. Hinks. New Haven, CT: Yale University Press, 1999. Originally published in 1845.

Drechsel, Emanuel J. "Sociolinguistic-Ethnohistorical Observations on Pidgin English in *Typee* and *Omoo*." *"Whole Oceans Away": Melville and the Pacific*. Ed. Jill Barnum, Wyn Kelley, and Christopher Sten. Kent, OH: Kent State University Press, 2007. 49–62.

Dryden, John. "An Essay of Dramatick Poesie." *Prose 1668–1691*. Ed. Samuel Holt Monk. Berkeley: University of California Press, 1971. 57.

"Dylan Pool Discussion." http://pool.dylantree.com. Accessed September 5, 2006.

Edwards, Janet Ray. "A Life in Letters: Jane Welsh Carlyle, 1801–1866." Paper delivered at the conference of the Society for Values in Higher Education, Naperville, Illinois, July 20, 2006.

Ellis, William. *Polynesian Researches.* 2nd ed. 4 vols. New York: J. & J. Harper, 1833.

Eliot, T. S. "Philip Massinger." *The Sacred Wood: Essays on Poetry and Criticism.* London: Methuen, 1932. Originally published in 1920.

Fletcher, Richard M. "Melville's Use of Marquesan." *American Speech* 39 (May 1964), 135–38.

Forsythe, Robert S. "Herman Melville in Honolulu." *New England Quarterly* 8 (March 1935), 99–105.

———. "Herman Melville in Tahiti." *Philological Quarterly* 16 (October 1937), 344–57.

———. "Herman Melville in the Marquesas." *Philological Quarterly* 15 (January 1936), 1–15.

———. "More upon Herman Melville in Tahiti." *Philological Quarterly* 17 (January 1938), 1–17.

———. Review of *Melville in the South Seas* by Charles Roberts Anderson. *American Literature* 11 (March 1939), 85–92.

Gajdusek, D. Carleton. "Unconventional Viruses and the Origin and Disappearance of Kuru." *Science* 197 (1977). Quoted in William Arens, "Rethinking Anthropophagy." *Cannibalism and the Colonial World.* Ed. Francis Barker, Peter Hulme, and Margaret Iversen. Cambridge: Cambridge University Press, 1998.

Garman, Samuel. *The Galapagos Tortoises.* Vol. 30 of *Memoirs of the Museum of Comparative Zoology at Harvard College.* Cambridge, MA: Printed for the Museum, January 1917.

Gibson, Gregory. *Demon of the Waters: The True Story of the Mutiny on the Whaleship Globe.* Boston: Little, Brown, 2002.

Gohdes, Clarence. "Melville's Friend 'Toby.'" *Modern Language Notes* 59 (January 1944), 52–55.

Grasso, Glenn. "Valentine Pease, Jr. and Melville's Literary Captains." Paper delivered at the Second International Melville Conference, "Melville and the Sea," Mystic, CT, June 18, 1999.

Grey, Robin, ed. *Melville and Milton.* Special issue of *Leviathan: A Journal of Melville Studies* 4.1–2 (2002).

Gross, Terry. Interview with Tim White. *Fresh Air.* June 18, 2003. www.npr.org/templates/story/story.php?storyId=1301741. Accessed October 6, 2006.

Gunson, Niel. *Messengers of Grace: Evangelical Missionaries in the South Seas 1797–1860.* Oxford: Oxford University Press, 1978.

Harlow, Frederick Pease. *Chanteying aboard American Ships.* Barre, MA: Barre Gazette, 1962.

———. *The Making of a Sailor or Sea Life aboard a Yankee Square-Rigger.* Salem, MA: Marine Research Society, 1928.

Haven, Gilbert, and Thomas Russell, eds. *Father Taylor, the Sailor Preacher: Incidents and Anecdotes of Rev. Edward T. Taylor.* Boston: B. B. Russell, 1872.

Hawthorne, Julian. *Nathaniel Hawthorne and His Wife: A Biography.* Vol. 1. Boston: Osgood, 1884.

Hayford, Harrison. Afterword. *Typee.* By Herman Melville. Ed. Harrison Hayford. New York: Signet, 1964. 309–20.

———. Editors' Introduction. *Omoo.* By Herman Melville. Ed. Harrison Hayford and Walter Blair. New York: Hendricks House, 1969. xvii–lii.

———. Explanatory Notes. *Omoo*. By Herman Melville. Ed. Harrison Hayford and Walter Blair. New York: Hendricks House, 1969. 341–438.

———. A Note on the Text. *Typee*. By Herman Melville. Ed. Harrison Hayford. New York: Signet, 1964. 303–8.

Heffernan, Thomas Farel. *Mutiny on the* Globe: *The Fatal Voyage of Samuel Comstock*. New York: Norton, 2002.

———. "Toby Greene." Appendix I. In Wilson Heflin. *Herman Melville's Whaling Years*. Ed. Mary K. Bercaw Edwards and Thomas Farel Heffernan. Nashville, TN: Vanderbilt University Press, 2004.

Heflin, Wilson. "Herman Melville's Whaling Years." PhD diss., Vanderbilt University, 1952.

———. *Herman Melville's Whaling Years*. Ed. Mary K. Bercaw Edwards and Thomas Farel Heffernan. Nashville, TN: Vanderbilt University Press, 2004.

Herbert, T. Walter, Jr. *Marquesan Encounters: Melville and the Meaning of Civilization*. Cambridge, MA: Harvard University Press, 1980.

Herodotus. *The History of Herodotus*. Book 4. Trans. George Rawlinson. Internet Classics Archive. http://classics.mit.edu/Herodotus/history.4.iv.html. Accessed September 5, 2007.

Hiney, Tom. *On the Missionary Trail: A Journey through Polynesia, Asia, and Africa with the London Missionary Society*. New York: Atlantic Monthly Press, 2000.

Hohman, Elmo P. *The American Whaleman: A Study of Life and Labor in the Whaling Industry*. New York: Longmans, Green, 1928.

Hugill, Stan. *Shanties and Sailors' Songs*. New York: Frederick A. Praeger, 1969.

———. *Shanties from the Seven Seas*. London: Routledge & Kegan Paul, 1961.

Huntington, Gale. *Songs the Whalemen Sang*. Barre, MA: Barre Publishers, 1964.

Huxley, Leonard, ed. *Jane Welsh Carlyle: Letters to Her Family, 1839–1863*. New York: Doubleday, Page, 1924.

Jefferson, Thomas. Letter to Isaac McPherson. August 13, 1813. *The Life and Selected Writings of Thomas Jefferson*. Ed. Adrienne Koch and William Peden. New York: Random House, 1944.

Johnson, Samuel. "Preface to Dryden." *Prefaces Biographical and Critical to the Works of the English Poets* (now known as *The Lives of the English Poets*). Vol. 3. London: J. Nichols, 1779.

Johnston, H. *The Uganda Protectorate*. London: Hutchinson, 1902. Cited in William Arens, *The Man-Eating Myth: Anthropology and Anthropophagy*. New York: Oxford University Press, 1979.

Jorgensen, Jorgen. *State of Christianity in the Island of Otaheite*. London, 1811. Quoted in Niel Gunson, *Messengers of Grace: Evangelical Missionaries in the South Seas 1797–1860*. Oxford: Oxford University Press, 1978.

Kipling, Rudyard. *Captains Courageous*. New York: Century, 1897.

Langsdorff, Georg H. von. *Voyages and Travels in Various Parts of the World during the Years 1803, 1804, 1805, 1806, and 1807*. London: Henry Colburn, 1813.

Leavitt, John F. *The Charles W. Morgan*. 2nd ed. Mystic, CT: Mystic Seaport Museum, 1998.

Leeson, Ida. "The Mutiny on the *Lucy Ann*." *Philological Quarterly* 19 (October 1940), 370–79.

London, Jack. *The Sea Wolf*. Ed. Donald Pizer. New York: Library of America, 1982. Originally published in 1904.

Lowell, James Russell. *A Fable for Critics*. Boston: Ticknor and Fields, 1859. Originally published in 1848.

Marryat, Frederick. *Mr. Midshipman Easy.* London: J. M. Dent & Sons, 1928. Originally published in 1836.

Mawer, Granville Allen. *Ahab's Trade: The Saga of South Seas Whaling.* New York: St. Martin's Press, 1999.

McCutcheon, Roger P. "The Technique of Melville's Israel Potter." *South Atlantic Quarterly* 27 (April 1928), 161–74.

Montaigne, Michel de. "Of Cannibals." *The Complete Works of Michael de Montaigne.* Ed. William Hazlitt. London: John Templeman, 1842 [1845].

"More Henry Timrod Lines on *Modern Times.*" scottw.alby.qwest.net. Accessed September 5, 2006.

"The Mystery of Kuru." 2008. http://learn.genetics.utah.edu/features/prions/kuru.cfm. Accessed March 2008.

Nabokov, Vladimir. *Lectures on Literature.* Ed. Fredson Bowers. New York: Harcourt Brace Jovanovich, 1980.

Naslund, Sena Jeter. *Ahab's Wife: Or, The Star-Gazer: A Novel.* New York: William Morrow, 1999.

Obeyesekere, Gananath. "Cannibal Feasts in Nineteenth-Century Fiji: Seamen's Yarns and the Ethnographic Imagination." *Cannibalism and the Colonial World.* Ed. Francis Barker, Peter Hulme, and Margaret Iversen. Cambridge: Cambridge University Press, 1998. 63–86.

———. *Cannibal Talk: The Man-Eating Myth and Human Sacrifice in the South Seas.* Berkeley: University of California Press, 2005.

O'Neill, Eugene. *The Hairy Ape. Plays of Eugene O'Neill.* New York: Boni & Liveright, 1925. Originally published in 1922.

Osborne, Lawrence. "Does Man Eat Man? Inside the Great Cannibalism Controversy." *Lingua Franca,* April–May 1997: 28–38.

Parker, Hershel. *Herman Melville: A Biography.* 2 vols. Baltimore, MD: Johns Hopkins University Press, 1996, 2002.

Permenter, Rachela. "Modern Times: The Never-Ending Melville/Dylan Connection." Paper delivered at the Sixth International Melville Conference, "Hearts of Darkness: Melville and Conrad in the Space of World Cultures," Szczecin, Poland, August 6, 2007.

Philbrick, Nathaniel. *In the Heart of the Sea: The Tragedy of the Whaleship* Essex. New York: Viking, 2000.

Philbrick, Thomas. *James Fenimore Cooper and the Development of American Sea Fiction.* Cambridge, MA: Harvard University Press, 1961.

Pliny the Elder. *Natural History of Pliny.* Vol. 2. Trans. John Bostock and H. T. Riley. London: George Bell and Sons, 1900.

Poe, Edgar Allan. "The Fall of the House of Usher." *Collected Works of Edgar Allan Poe.* Ed. Thomas Ollive Mabbott. Volume 2. Cambridge, MA: Belknap Press of Harvard University Press, 1978. Originally published in 1839.

———. *The Narrative of Arthur Gordon Pym, of Nantucket. The Imaginary Voyages.* Ed. Burton R. Pollin. Boston: Twayne, 1981. Originally published in 1838.

Porter, David. *Journal of a Cruise Made to the Pacific Ocean.* New York: Wiley and Halsted, 1822. Originally published in 1815.

———. *Journal of a Cruise Made to the Pacific Ocean.* Ed. R. D. Madison and Karen [Alexander] Hamon, with introduction by R. D. Madison. Annapolis, MD: Naval Institute Press, 1986.

Pryor, Richard. *Richard Pryor: Live in Concert.* 1979. Filmed at Terrace Theater, Long Beach, CA. January 1979. Directed by Jeff Margolis.

Radiguet, Max. *Les Derniers Sauvages aux îles Marquises 1842–1859.* Paris: Éditions Phébus, 2001. Originally published in 1860.

Raffaele, Paul. "Sleeping with Cannibals: Our Intrepid Reporter Gets up Close and Personal with Remote New Guinea Natives Who Say They Still Eat Their Fellow Tribesmen." *Smithsonian* 37 (September 2006), 48–60.

Revel, André. "*Typee:* In the Footsteps of Herman Melville." *Melville Society Extracts* 90 (September 1992), 2–6.

Robarts, Edward. *The Marquesan Journal of Edward Robarts.* Ed. Greg Dening. Canberra: Australian National University Press, 1974.

Robertson-Lorant, Laurie. *Melville: A Biography.* New York: Clarkson Potter, 1996.

Rubiés, Joan-Pau. "Virtual Suppers." *Times Literary Supplement.* March 17, 2006.

Ryle, Gilbert. *The Concept of Mind.* London, 1949. Cited in Margaret Cohen, "Traveling Genres." *New Literary History* 34 (2003), 486–87.

"The Sad Tale of Kuru." Why Files. October 23, 1996. http://whyfiles.org/012mad_cow/6.html. Accessed May 2006.

Sahlins, Marshall. "Artificially Maintained Controversies: Global Warming and Fijian Cannibalism." *Anthropology Today* 19 (June 2003), 3–5.

Saint-Martin, Vivien de, and Louis Rousselet. *Nouveau dictionnaire de géographie universelle* Vol. 3. Paris: Hachette et Cie., 1887.

Samuels, Samuel. *From Forecastle to Cabin.* New York: Harper and Brothers, 1887.

Sanborn, Geoffrey. *The Sign of the Cannibal: Melville and the Making of a Postcolonial Reader.* Durham, NC: Duke University Press, 1998.

Sanday, Peggy Reeves. *Divine Hunger: Cannibalism as a Cultural System.* Cambridge: Cambridge University Press, 1986.

Scudder, Harold H. "Melville's *Benito Cereno* and Captain Delano's Voyages." *Publications of the Modern Language Association* 43 (June 1928), 502–32.

Sealts, Merton M., Jr. *Melville's Reading: Revised and Enlarged Edition.* Columbia: University of South Carolina Press, 1988.

Sendak, Maurice. *Where the Wild Things Are.* New York: HarperCollins, 1963.

Shakespeare, William. *King Lear.* Ed. Horace Howard Furness. New Variorum Edition. 7th ed. Philadelphia: Lippincott, 1880.

———. *Othello.* Ed. Louis B. Wright and Virginia A. LaMar. Washington, DC: Folger Library, [1957].

———. *The Tempest.* Ed. Louis B. Wright and Virginia A. LaMar. New York: Washington Square Press, 1961.

Smollett, Tobias. *The Adventures of Roderick Random.* London: J. M. Dent & Sons, 1927. Originally published in 1748.

Society for the Diffusion of Useful Knowledge. *The Penny Cyclopædia of the Society for the Diffusion of Useful Knowledge.* London: Charles Knight, 1833–43.

Starbuck, Alexander. *History of the American Whale-Fishery from Its Earliest Inception to the Year 1876.* Waltham, MA: Author, 1878.

Stevens, Aretta J. (Sister Mary Dominic). "Melville: Sceptic." PhD dissertation, Loyola University Chicago, 1967.

Stewart, Charles S. *A Visit to the South Seas, in the U.S. Ship* Vincennes, *during the Years 1829 and 1830.* New York: John P. Haven, 1831.

Stowe, Harriet Beecher. *Uncle Tom's Cabin.* Ed. Elizabeth Ammons. Norton Critical ed. New York: Norton, 1994. Originally published in 1852.

Stray, Christopher, ed. *Contributions Towards a Glossary of the Glynne Language by George William , Lord Lyttelton.* Newcastle, UK: Cambridge Scholars Press, 2005.

———, ed. *The Mushri-English Pronouncing Dictionary: A Chapter in 19th-Century Public School Lexicography.* Berkeley, UK: Department of Typography & Graphic Communication, University of Reading, 1996.

Suggs, Robert C. *The Hidden Worlds of Polynesia: The Chronicle of an Archaeological Expedition to Nuku Hiva in the Marquesas Islands.* New York: Harcourt, Brace & World, 1962.

———. "Melville's Flight to Taipi: Topographic, Archeological, and Historic Considerations." *ESQ: A Journal of the American Renaissance* 51.1–3 (2005), 47–86.

———. "Topographic, Archeological and Historical Considerations Relevant to Melville's Flight to Taipi." Paper delivered at the Kendall Institute, New Bedford Whaling Museum, New Bedford, MA, August 19, 2003.

Swift, Jonathan. *Gulliver's Travels.* Ed. Albert J. Rivero. Norton Critical Edition. New York: Norton, 2002. Originally published in 1726.

Tomlinson, H. M. "A Clue to 'Moby Dick.'" Literary Review, *New York Evening Post* (November 5, 1921), 141–42.

Turner, George. *Nineteen Years in Polynesia: Missionary Life, Travels and Researches in the Islands of the Pacific.* London, 1861. Quoted in Niel Gunson, *Messengers of Grace: Evangelical Missionaries in the South Seas 1797–1860.* Oxford: Oxford University Press, 1978.

Twain, Mark. *The Adventures of Huckleberry Finn.* Ed. Thomas Cooley. Norton Critical 3d ed. New York: Norton, 1999. Originally published in 1884.

———. "The 'Jumping Frog': In English. Then in French. Then Clawed Back into a Civilized Language Once More, by Patient, Unremunerated Toil." *Collected Tales, Sketches, Speeches, & Essays: 1852–1890.* Ed. Louis J. Budd. New York: Library of America, 1992. Originally published in 1875.

Vason, George. *An Authentic Narrative of Four Years' Residence at Tongataboo.* London, 1810. Quoted in Niel Gunson, *Messengers of Grace: Evangelical Missionaries in the South Seas 1797–1860.* Oxford: Oxford University Press, 1978.

Vega, Suzanne. "The Ballad of Henry Timrod." *New York Times.* September 17, 2006.

Wallis, Mary. *Life in Feejee: Five Years among the Cannibals: A Woman's Account of Voyaging the Fiji Islands aboard the "Zotoff" (1844–49).* With introduction by C. W. Flanders. Santa Barbara, CA: Narrative Press, 2002. Originally published in 1851.

Weaver, Raymond. *Herman Melville: Mariner and Mystic.* New York: George H. Doran, 1921.

Wells, Whitney Hastings. "Moby Dick and Rabelais." *Modern Language Notes* 38 (February 1923), 123.

Weems, Mason Locke. *The Life and Remarkable Actions of George Washington.* Ed. Peter S. Onuf. Amonk, NY: M. E. Sharpe, 1996. Originally published c. 1800.

Williams, Thomas. *The Journal of Thomas Williams, Missionary in Fiji, 1840–1853.* Ed. G. C. Henderson. Sydney. Quoted in Niel Gunson, *Messengers of Grace: Evangelical Missionaries in the South Seas 1797–1860.* Oxford: Oxford University Press, 1978.

Wilson, James. *A Missionary Voyage to the Southern Pacific Ocean Performed in the Years 1796, 1797, 1798, in the Ship* Duff. London: Printed by S. Gosnell for T. Chapman, 1799.

Wise, Henry A. *Los Gringos.* New York, 1849 [1850].

Index

Religio Medici (Browne), 4, 56

religion, 99–100, 107, 112; sermons and, 142, 144, 183, 185, 189. *See also* the bible; missionaries; sermons

Renaissance era, 60

resurrection, 180

"Rethinking Anthrophagy" (Arens), xix, 62, 93

Revel, André, 206n33

reviewers, 3, 159

Revolutionary War, 55

rhetoric, 175

Ringgold, Fayette, 5

rites of passage, 5

ritual, 5, 58–59, 81–83, 112

Robarts, Edward, 21, 122

Robertson-Loran, Laurie, 1, 204n1

Robinson, William, 36

Robinson Crusoe (Defoe), 137, 161

Roderick Random (*The Adventures of Roderick Random*), 137–38

Romans, 59

romanticism, xviii, 84, 139

round robin, 120, 149

Rousseau, Jean Jacques, 78, 142

Rowling, J. K., 164

Royce, James Stephen Hambrook, 107, 126

Rubiés, Joan-Pau, xix

Russia, 84; expedition by, 66–67, 87, 122

Ryland, John, 102

Ryle, Gilbert, 30

Sabbath day, 114–15

The Sacred Wood (Eliot), 23

Sahlins, Marshall, xix, 81–82

sailors, xx, 4, 118, 151, 155, 163, 168–69; cannibal talk and, 88, 138; concision and, 176–78; enchantment and, 201; gothic romanticism and, 139; Ishmael and, 172–73, 175; licentiousness of, 117; methodology and, 196–97; missionaries and, 120, 147, 154; missionary talk and, 99–100, 118–21, 184; myth talk and, 48–52; narrative voice and, 135–36; play talk and, 41–45; *Redburn* and, 162, 164; sailor talk and, 24–28, 30–31, 40–41, 45–48, 53–57, 211n14, 217n10; sermons and, 179, 181, 185, 189–90; social talk and, 35–39; "Stubb's Supper" and, 194; Tommo and, 138, 141;

work talk and, 25–29, 32–35; world view of, 136; written sources and, 148

sail training movement, ix, xiv, 29

Saint Jerome, 86

St. Lawrence (packet ship), 24, 29, 34, 160, 221n23; terminology and, 56

Salem (*Omoo*), 121

"Sally Brown" (chantey), 36

Sal Paradise (*On the Road*), 153

"The Salvation of Seamen Important" (*Boston Recorder* article), 51

Samoa, 106, 112

Samoides, 86

sampling, 196–98

Samuels, Samuel, 54

Sanborn, Geoffrey, xvi, xix–xx, 65, 77–78, 94

sandalwood, 92–93

Sandusky Register (newspaper), 33

Sandwich Islands, 71, 89, 91

Sarah (Biblical character), 172

Satan, 44

savagery, 16, 39, 46, 59, 61, 65, 76, 77–78, 91, 129, 140, 162, 188

Scilly Islands, 43

Scoresby, William, Jr., 12

Scorsese, Martin, 153, 197–98

Scotland, 86

Scott, Walter, 32, 167

Scythians, 59, 64, 86

The Sea Wolf (London), 43

Sealts, Merton M., Jr., xi

Sendak, Maurice, 1

sermons, 109–10, 164, 178, 183–86, 192, 200; inversion of, 141–44; methodology and, 196; *Moby-Dick* and, 189–91; narrative voice and, 175, 179–83; *Omoo* and, 132; "Stubb's Supper" and, 194; translation of, 149; *White-Jacket* and, 169

"The Sermon" (*Moby-Dick*), 179

Sese Islands, 80

Snape, Severus (*Harry Potter* series), 164

Shakespeare, William, 90, 144; *Hamlet*, 168–69; Ishmael's voice and, 174; *King Lear*, 177, 197, 200; *Othello*, 60; *The Tempest*, 26

sharks, 193–94

"The Shark Massacre" (*Moby-Dick*), 91, 193

Shaw, Lemuel, 162

"Shearing Day" (chantey), 38